ABOUT THE AUTHORS

James R. Lewis, Ph.D., is currently a lecturer in religious studies at DePaul University. His academic works have been published by Cambridge University Press, Rutgers University Press, and Oxford University Press. He is also the author of *The Astrology Book* and co-author of *Angels A to Z.* His encyclopedias have been translated into Spanish, Portuguese, Russian, Polish, Chinese, and Japanese. Dr. Lewis's academic and popular books have received awards from the New York Public Library Association, the American Library Association, and *Choice.* He has been interviewed by the *Los Angeles Times, New York Times,* the British Broadcasting Corp., National Public Radio, and "Meet the Press."

Evelyn Oliver, does a transformative type of therapy that is unbelievably effective and powerful in assisting you to create the life of your dreams. Evelyn's energy psychology technique of "Brain Code Exchanging" removes blockages in your business and personal life and replaces them with what you have been trying to achieve despite years of conventional counseling.

During the past 30 years, Evelyn has been interviewed on radio and television, having famous names in Hollywood (as well as infamous criminals) among her clientele. Her telephone consultations have been as far away as Australia, Columbia, England, Russia, and Iraq. Evelyn has co-authored *The Dream Encyclopedia* and *Angels A to Z,* and is the author of *Dream Yourself Awake for Women.*

The DREAM ENCYCLOPEDIA

The
DREAM
ENCYCLOPEDIA

SECOND EDITION

JAMES R. LEWIS AND
EVELYN DOROTHY OLIVER

VISIBLE
INK
PRESS

DETROIT

THE
DREAM
ENCYCLOPEDIA

Visible Ink Press®
43311 Joy Rd., #414
Canton, MI 48187-2075

Visible Ink Press is a registered trademark of Visible Ink Press LLC.

Most Visible Ink Press books are available at special quantity discounts when purchased in bulk by corporations, organizations, or groups. Customized printings, special imprints, messages, and excerpts can be produced to meet your needs. For more information, contact Special Markets Director, Visible Ink Press, www.visibleink.com, or 734-667-3211.

Managing Editor: Kevin S. Hile
Art Director: Jon Wilson
Typesetting: Marco Di Vita
Proofreader: Sharon R. Gunton
ISBN 978-1-57859-216-6

Cover image: clouds © iStockphoto.com/Nick Belton. Back cover: jumping horse © iStockphoto.com/Hedda Gjerpen; moon © NASA.

Library of Congress Cataloging-in-Publication Data

Lewis, James R.
    The dream encyclopedia / by James R. Lewis and Evelyn Dorothy Oliver. — 2nd ed.
        p. cm.
    Includes bibliographical references and index.
    ISBN 978-1-57859-216-6
    1. Dreams—Dictionaries. 2. Dream interpretation—Dictionaries. I. Oliver, Evelyn Dorothy. II. Title.
        BF1091.L53 2009
        154.6'303—dc22
                                                                    2009005132

Printed in the United States of America

10 9 8 7 6 5 4 3 2 1

CONTENTS

CONTENTS

We dedicate this book to our elegant daughter,

Doreen Elyse Berman, and her distinguished husband, Alex Llarena.

Each possesses a brilliance, charm, and entertaining wit,

making them a dream couple that everyone loves and wants to be around.

Acknowledgments

Thanks to the Center for Academic Publishing for permission to reprint material from Evelyn Oliver's *Dream Yourself Awake for Women*.

A sincere thank you goes to Michela Zonta, who researched and wrote some of the historical and many of the world culture entries; and to Nicole Ruskelle who wrote a few of the dictionary entries and who supported this project in other, less tangible ways.

At Visible Ink Press, we are grateful to Roger Jänecke for encouraging us to undertake this second edition, and Kevin Hile who helped bring this project to fruition.

Last but not least, we would like to thank our literary agent, Daniel Bial.

INTRODUCTION

Dreams have long exercised a fascination over the human imagination. We spend approximately one-third of our lives in a state of sleep, much of the night filled with dreams. Peculiarly vivid or disturbing dreams leave behind impressions that are hard to dismiss. But what are dreams? And what significance, if any, do they have for the dreamer?

As early as the fourth century B.C.E., the Chinese philosopher Chuang-tzu raised the following conundrum:

> While men are dreaming, they do not perceive that it is a dream. Some will even have a dream in a dream, and only when they awake they know it was all a dream. And so, when the Great Awakening comes upon us, shall we know this life to be a great dream. Fools believe themselves to be awake now.

> Once upon a time, I, Chuang-tzu, dreamed I was a butterfly, fluttering hither and thither, to all intents and purposes a butterfly. I was conscious only of following my fancies as a butterfly, and was unconscious of my individuality as a butterfly. Suddenly I was awakened, and there I lay myself again. Now I do not know whether I was a man dreaming I was a butterfly, or whether I am a butterfly now dreaming I am a man.

There are various ways of responding to Chuang-tzu's observations. Some traditional cultures may place the realm of dreams on an equal footing with the realm of everyday consciousness, as Chuang-tzu appears to do. This is clearly the case for Australian aborigines who choose in some cases not to distinguish between waking events and dream events. Chuang-tzu's remarks also suggest that perhaps the world as we ordinarily experience it is no more real than a dream. Traditional Eastern philosophies often espouse the assertion that this world is as illusory as a dream.

Dreams often seem to be experiences of a confused parallel world. Reflecting on this experience, we may speculate that during dreams we travel to a real, alternate realm. It has been suggested that one of the principal sources of this idea—a spiritual world distinct from the physical—is dreams. If this hypothesis is true, even partially, then dreams contribute to one of the basic notions of religion.

It has also been hypothesized that dreams may be linked to the idea of a soul distinct from the body. During dreams, we have the experience of traveling to other realms, interacting with people, and doing various things simultaneously while the physical body remains confined to its bed. While the dream realm is shadowy and even surreal, it nevertheless feels like a real place. Because the experience is so real, it is easy to speculate that during dreams the conscious self somehow separates from the body. If we add to this the common experience of meeting departed friends and relatives in dreams, it is no great step to conclude that the same "soul" that separates from the body during dreams also survives the death of the body.

Yet another broad area of agreement among world cultures is that communication between this world and the otherworld—between gods and mortals, or between the living and the dead—is possible. Prophets, as well as the founders of new religious sects, often claim to receive privileged communications from the gods. If dreams constitute experiences with the realm of the spirit, then one possible model for divine-human communication is the dream state.

Dreams and Visions through the Ages: In many cultures, little or no distinction is made between visions and divine message dreams, indicating some intangible quality that waking visions share with dreams. This is especially the case in the Judeo-Christian-Islamic complex of religions. In this family of traditions, religious truth is communicated via direct revelation from God or through one of His messenger angels. When God's message is communicated by an angel in the writings of the Hebrew prophets, it is sometimes difficult to determine whether the message is being delivered in a dream or in a waking vision.

Similarly, no distinction between the sleeping dream and the waking vision was made at the time of Muhammad, who received spiritual instruction in both states. Dreams played an important role in the life of the Prophet, who received his first revelation and became conscious of his vocation in a dream vision. Significantly, his initiation into the mysteries of the cosmos occurred during a great dream known as the Night Journey.

The visionary aspect of dreams prompted the ancients to seek dreams for guidance and even for healing, a practice known as dream incubation. Dream incubation was extremely popular in the ancient world and was a major phenomenon in societies as diverse as ancient Mesopotamia (Iraq), Egypt, Greece, and Rome. The practice of dream incubation in the temples of the ancient world might have developed independently in Mesopotamia and Egypt, or the practice might have emerged in one of these societies and later migrated to the other. The intense focus of Mesopotamians on divination—predicting the future—suggests Mesopotamia as the ultimate source of this practice, indicating that the first systematic use of dream incubation was for the purpose of gaining knowledge of the future.

This contrasts with the Hellenistic period in which the primary purpose of dream incubation was for healing, principally at temples dedicated to the healer-turned-god Aesculapius. The practice continued into the Christian era, with reports of worshippers seeking dream-healing at Catholic pilgrimage sites (particularly at churches built over the remains of Aesculapius's temples) as late as the early twentieth century.

The largest and most complete compilation of dream lore to survive from the ancient world, the *Oneirocritica* ("The Interpretation of Dreams"), was written by a second-century Greek, Artemidorus of Daldis. Artemidorus's overarching concern was with divination. This was the dominant approach to dream interpretation until the advent of modern psychology and psychoanalysis.

Dreams and Nightmares in the Middle Ages: All cultures and all time periods report nightmares. The word "nightmare" derives from the Anglo-Saxon word "mare," meaning demon, which is related to the Sanskrit words "Mara," meaning destroyer, and "mar," meaning to crush. The word "nightmare," therefore, carries with it connotations of being crushed by demonic forces. In this particular type of dream, the dreamer often feels helpless in the face of danger and experiences overwhelming fear and anxiety. Originally, this was thought to be caused by an actual visitation of a *night fiend*.

Given the widespread belief in demons before the contemporary period, it is only natural that the common experience of nightmares would often be explained in terms of the intrusion of demonic forces. This explanation is so widespread, in fact, that it is not unusual to find special prayers and ceremonies intended to protect the sleeper from evil entities. Despite the many revelatory dreams recorded in the Bible, the Christian tradition has generally taken a negative attitude towards dreaming. Some medieval churchmen went so far as to denounce *all* dreams as creations of the Devil. Speculation on the demonic status of nightmares with Christianity goes back to the early Church.

Tertullian was a third century lawyer-turned-priest who was the first significant Christian theologian to write in Latin rather than Greek. Eight chapters of his *A Treatise on the Soul* deal with the closely related phenomena of sleep and dreams. Tertullian felt that the ongoing activity of the mind in dreams while the body was motionless in sleep proved that the soul was independent of the body, and thus immortal. As part of his adherence to the idea of the disjunction between the body and the soul during sleep, he discounted the idea that the condition of the body (e.g., whether one was fasting or had eaten spicy food the preceding day) influenced one's dreams. He was also critical of the idea that the soul left the body and traveled during sleep. Tertullian classified dreams according to their source. While God was responsible for many dreams, so were demons, he believed. With respect to the later, Tertullian asserted confidently that dreamers would not be held responsible for sins committed in their sleep anymore than they would receive crowns in heaven for imaginary acts of martyrdom.

Macrobius was a fourth-century Christian writer whose *Commentary on the Dream of Scipio* became the most influential dream book of medieval Europe. Compared with his contemporaries, Macrobius had a negative and superstitious interpretation of dreams. Clearly indebted to the *Oneirocritica,* the dreambook of the great pagan dream interpreter Artemidorus, Macrobius added material on apparitions and nightmares—topics not explicitly covered by Artemidorus. Macrobius also included a discussion of incubi and succubi, the sexual demons who seduced virtuous men and women in their sleep and who became highly popular creatures in medieval European demonological lore. While these beings are rooted in earlier Jewish folklore, Macrobius appears to have been the person to introduce them into Christianity.

Of particular importance for the Middle Ages was St. Jerome's mistranslation of certain key biblical passages that, in the original, read something along the lines of "You shall not practice augury witchcraft." In Jerome's translation, which became authoritative, the same passage reads, "You shall not practice augury nor observe dreams." These explicit condemnations, in combination with the admonitions of writers like Macrobius who warned against the attacks of demons in one's sleep, served effectively to condemn dreams as little more than stages for Satan's minions to tempt the souls of the faithful.

The medieval attitude is expressed in, for example, the sixteenth-century work *De Magia* by Benedict Peterius, a Jesuit priest: "[T]he devil is most always implicated in dreams, filling the minds of men with poisonous superstition and not only uselessly deluding but perniciously deceiving them."

Nowhere is this suspicion of dreams more clearly demonstrated than in the notion of incubi and succubi—demons who, during their "victims'" dreams, took the form of handsome men and seduced women in their sleep, as well as demons who took the form of beautiful women and seduced men in their sleep. These creatures were particularly useful for explaining sexual dreams in a society in which any form of illicit sex was viewed as demonic and sexual desire was regarded as a weak point through which evil forces could subvert even the most upright Christian. This was an especially crucial point for monastics, for whom celibacy was part of their most sacred vows. Given this general perspective, it was almost inevitable that sexual dreams should come to be viewed as the work of the Devil. One can imagine the dismay of clergy, monks, and nuns who awakened with vivid memories of erotic dreams. By attributing such dream images to evil spirits who seduced them in their sleep, they could absolve themselves of responsibility for such dreams.

The Psychological Approach to Dreams: The contemporary approach views dreams as indicating something about our psychological dynamics. This approach results from the work of Sigmund Freud and other practitioners in the tradition of depth psychology. Part of what makes the psychoanalytic approach compelling is that it explains why dreams should be interpreted.

Freud theorized that dreams allow us to satisfy socially unacceptable sexual and aggressive urges during sleep. So that we do not awaken as a result of the strong emotions that would be evoked if we dreamed about the literal fulfillment of such desires, the part of the mind that Freud called the "censor" transforms dream content to disguise its true meaning. This transformation results in dreams that often seem strange and even bizarre.

By way of contrast, Freud's disciple Carl Jung pictured the unconscious self as a complex mix of lower instinctual and higher spiritual impulses. Instead of *concealing,* the purpose of a dream is to *communicate* something to the consciousness. The unconscious, in other words, harbors a kind of intelligence that attempts to guide and otherwise assist the conscious self. The language of the unconscious is, however, indirect and symbolic, and requires interpretation. Jungian dream analysis is thus a method of helping clients to properly interpret the messages coming from the unconscious.

Other schools of depth psychology that are derived from the larger Freudian/Jungian tradition have also approached dreams as documents from the unconscious mind that have been shaped by our psychological state. In each of these schools of thought, dreams are regarded as less-than-clear communications that require some form of interpretation before they reveal their true meanings. This basic interpretative orientation is evident in Gestalt therapy in which clients act out various dream components as a strategy for discovering, or interpreting, the meaning of dreams. Another interpretive strategy in Gestalt therapy calls for the dreamer to set up a dialogue between different components of a dream, and then to analyze the meanings that emerge from the dialogue.

Psychological Approaches to Nightmares: The modern psychiatric phrase used to refer to nightmares is *dream anxiety attack*. In everyday conversation, however, *anxiety dream* is often used. *Anxiety dream* most often refers to a nightmare that leaves you feeling anxious after you awaken. These two terms are sometimes used interchangeably, but they have different connotations. These differences resemble the differences between the psychiatric definitions of "free-floating" anxiety and phobic anxiety. *Anxiety dreams* are akin to free-floating anxieties; a variety of different situations can trigger them. Nightmares, however, more closely resemble phobic anxieties, being specific to one situation. Phobic anxiety is an exaggerated fear of objects, animals, or situations, and they are believed to be manifestations of ancient, instinctive response patterns.

The common characteristic of any anxiety dream, regardless of how it is referred to, is a feeling of fear or anxiety throughout the dream. Often these emotions linger after the dreamer awakens. The occurrence of what has been termed *delayed anxiety* dreams are not as common. A *delayed anxiety* dream is a dream that is pleasant or enjoyable while we sleep, but that causes distress when one remembers it after waking. A common theme in these particular dreams is incest. This does not mean that the dreamer actually has these taboo inclinations, but often points to other, unresolved issues.

Jung's theory of nightmares maintained that they serve as compensation for our conscious attitude, reflecting worries and fears that plague our waking lives. Freud, on the other hand, held a variety of different views on nightmares. Initially, he attributed nightmares to a failure of the "censor" programmed into us by society. He insisted that this accounts for the majority of anxiety dreams. Freud's theory seems to apply better to phenomena like *delayed anxiety* dreams. Freud later put forward the view that even nightmares could be the subconscious's attempt at wish fulfillment. He maintained that humans want to be frightened—a position supported by, for example, our interest in horror movies and roller coasters.

Anxiety is the second stage our bodies go through in a "fight or flight" situation. Vigilance is the state of consciousness that precedes anxiety. Vigilance shifts to anxiety only after a perceived danger or an immediate threat is encountered. If the threat is not controlled, anxiety will shift to fear, then panic, and eventually terror. The body's response to a terrifying situation is to release adrenaline. This hormone brings on the "fight or flight" response. The physical signs of terror are heart palpitations, labored breathing, trembling, sweating, and gastro-intestinal disturbances—all arising directly from adrenaline in the bloodstream. Although this is most often the formula our bodies use when dealing with a stressful situation in the waking world, it also applies to the changes that occur in our physical and psychological being when we experience nightmares.

Modern Dream Theories: Few modern analysts would adhere to the classical psychoanalytic approach. Taking a more practical, less therapeutically oriented approach, they would consider at least some dreams little more than residues of recent experiences. If, for instance, we spent the day driving across the country, it would not be unusual to dream about driving down a highway, and such a dream would not necessarily conceal any deeper significance.

Some of the more unusual items in dream landscapes come from the dreaming mind's tendency to give concrete expression to figures of speech. Thus, if someone has a dream in which his or her employer is swimming in a lake, it may indicate that he or she wants to tell the boss to go "jump in a lake." Other dreams are more complex, requiring a detailed knowledge of the dreamer's life before they can be interpreted.

While the meanings of a few dreams are reasonably straightforward, many others appear disconnected and nonsensical. The surrealistic quality of most dreams—a quality that causes them to be highly resistant to interpretation—has influenced many people to dismiss dreams as altogether meaningless. This evaluation finds scientific expression in the activation-synthesis model of dreaming. First proposed in 1977, the activation-synthesis model postulates that dreams are the result of the forebrain's attempts to understand the random electrical signals that are generated by the hindbrain during sleep.

In normal waking consciousness, the forebrain sorts through various kinds of internal and external sensory input to create a meaningful experience of the world. Faced with a barrage of disconnected, random inputs generated by more primitive areas of the brain during sleep, the higher mental centers attempt to impose order on the incoming messages, creating whatever narrative structure dreams have. The many dreams that are just masses of incoherent images represent incoming groups of signals that the brain was simply not able to synthesize.

For anyone who has been frustrated with attempts to understand dreams, the activation-synthesis theory holds a certain appeal. However, because almost everyone has had at least a few truly insightful dreams, the theory is ultimately unsatisfying. On a more empirical level, it is an incomplete theory because it does not offer an explanation for such phenomena as common dream themes.

Almost everyone seems to have experienced certain types of dreams. These include such common dream scenarios as falling, flying, and finding oneself naked in public. Such shared dreams arise from experiences and anxieties fundamental to the human condition.

Falling is a good example of a shared dream motif. Psychologists speculate that falling dreams are rooted in our early experiences as toddlers taking our first steps. If this hypothesis is correct, then our childhood experience leaves a deep imprint in our brain that is somehow activated in adult life during periods of high anxiety. Some sociobiologists have further speculated that our fear of falling ultimately derives from an inherited instinct or reflex bequeathed by our prehistoric ancestors, who bore the risk of tumbling out of trees during the night.

Sleep Research: It is easy to understand the desire to ground the study of dreams in measurable physiological phenomena. Because dreams are so subjective, they frustrate the methods of objective, empirical science. While there are some important precursors, modem laboratory-oriented dream research did not really get off the ground until the 1953 discovery of rapid eye movement (REM) sleep, and the subsequent linking of REM sleep with dreaming. Although later studies showed that significant dreaming could take place during non-REM sleep, the postulate of a close correlation between dreams and REM sleep guided scientific dream research for over a decade.

Prior to the discovery of this correlation, researchers had outlined four stages of sleep. These stages were measured in terms of the electrical activity of the brain—specifically, in terms of brainwave activity—with the aid of an electroencephalogram (EEG). The levels range from Stage 1, which represents the state we are in just as we enter sleep, to Stage 4, which is deep sleep. Most dreaming occurs during Stage 2, when we are experiencing REM sleep. For a normal young adult, the typical sleep cycle—the cyclic alternation between REM sleep and deeper levels of sleep—lasts about 90 minutes. Healthy adults tend to go through between four and six such cycles every evening, although there is much variation in the cycle with respect to age.

One of the more interesting lines of research to emerge out of modern scientific sleep study is the relatively recent investigation of lucid dreaming. People are lucid dreaming when they are aware that they are in the midst of a dream. The most unusual aspect of this state is that lucid dreamers can consciously alter the content of their dreams. This characteristic has led researchers to explore the possibilities of utilizing lucid dreaming for the treatment of nightmares and for other therapeutic purposes. The first recorded reference to lucid dreaming is in Aristotle's *On Dreams,* in which he says that "often when one is asleep, there is something in consciousness which declares that what then presents itself is but a dream." Other historical figures, such as Saint Augustine and Saint Thomas Aquinas, have mentioned lucid dreaming in their writings, as well.

For the most part, the intangible nature of this unusual state of consciousness discouraged psychologists from giving serious attention to lucid dreaming, until Stephen LaBerge began publishing the results of his remarkable research in the 1980s. LaBerge, who had experienced lucid dreams since childhood, resolved to study the phenomenon scientifically during his psychology graduate program at Stanford University. The difference between LaBerge's work and that of all previous researchers was that he found a way for dreamers to send messages to researchers while experiencing lucid dreams. LaBerge eventually trained dozens of subjects to dream lucidly and communicate with researchers while asleep.

LaBerge was eventually able to train his subjects to perform a variety of tasks in their dreams—from counting to flying—and to signal the experimenter when their tasks were complete. The results of these experiments were reported in LaBerge's popular 1985 book on the subject, *Lucid Dreaming.* The success of this work stimulated the nationwide formation of dream groups. The mass media also became interested in the idea, and the implications of lucid dreaming were discussed in innumerable articles and on countless talk shows.

The Mythological Aspect of Dreaming: Beyond the specific topic of lucid dreaming, the more general subject of interpreting and understanding dreams appears to be enjoying a resurgence of interest. New books on dreams appear monthly—volumes ranging from scientific studies to self-help books. A trip to any substantial local book store finds several shelves devoted to the subject. At least part of the resurgence of interest in dreams is tied to the emergence of mythology as a popular topic.

Myths are traditional stories that often relate fantastic encounters with gods and spiritual powers that occur in a visionary and "dreamlike" manner. The contemporary connection between dreams and myths was established by depth psychology, particularly the school of thought initiated by Carl Jung. Jung found that the dreams of his clients frequently contained images that seemed to reflect symbols that could be found somewhere in the mythological systems of world culture. He theorized that myths were manifestations of the collective unconscious, a part of the mind that acts as a storehouse of myths and symbols, and which he viewed as the ultimate source of every society's mythology. According to Jung, the collective unconscious also shapes some of the images found in dreams.

In recent years, the notion of mythology as a positive factor in human culture has been popularized through the work of Joseph Campbell and other writers whose work flows out of the Jungian perspective. Thanks to their work, mythology, in the sense of "sacred story," is now viewed as something worthwhile and even necessary for human beings. Campbell's restatement of the Jungian view was that dreams are individual myths, and myths are society's dreams. In Campbell's own words from his much-publicized television interview with Bill Moyers:

> Dream is a personal experience of that deep, dark ground that is the society's dream. The myth is the public dream and the dream is the private myth. If your private myth, your dream, happens to coincide with that of society, you are in good accord with your group. If it isn't, you've got an adventure in the dark forest ahead of you. (*The Power of Myth*, p. 40)

Dreams and the New Age: Yet another factor in the resurgence of interest in dreams is the long-range impact of the new age movement. The new age, which represents a popular movement that draws on an older occult/metaphysical subculture, has influenced the larger society to take more seriously topics that were formerly regarded as marginal and unimportant.

The new age movement has tended to latch onto several aspects of the popular interest in dreams. For example, new dream dictionaries, containing interpretations of specific dream images, have been composed to express a new age perspective. Like its approach to and reevaluation of the other occult arts (e.g., astrology and meditation), the new age approach to dreams sees them as tools for transformation and healing, as expressed in the title of Patricia Garfield's popular 1992 book, *The Healing Power of Dreams*.

The new age movement has also embraced lucid dreaming. Beyond the work of Stephen LaBerge, the notion of lucid dreaming is evidenced in the works of Carlos Castaneda, and through various forms of dream yoga from Eastern religions. As with other new age topics, lucid dreaming is also viewed as a potential tool for healing and self-transformation.

The basic philosophical tenet of the new age movement is that the world as we experience it is malleable with respect to human intention; or, as it is more colloquially expressed, you create your own reality. While this precept is of questionable applicability to the world of waking consciousness, it clearly applies to the realm of dreams. In so-called "dream programming" techniques, for example, the dreamer decides what she or he wishes to dream, and then attempts to "convince" the subconscious with a firm resolution to have dreams on a particular topic. For many individuals, this technique is surprisingly effective.

Another way of influencing dreams is to consciously reshape one's dream landscape. Because the dream landscape is a product of the dreamer's mind, it should be possible to simply will the dream to change. Again, this is often surprisingly effective if one has already mastered the technique of lucid dreaming. Some healers and therapists have begun to make therapeutic use of this technique, asking people who are nightmare prone, for instance, to attempt to manipulate their dreams so that they will have happy endings.

What will the future bring? Will we program our dreams as readily as we program our TV sets? While it is difficult to anticipate the future, clearly the last word has not been said on the subject. Until then, the pages that follow will provide the reader with a compendium of humankind's attempts to understand and come to terms with dreams.

The Dream Encyclopedia attempts to encompass all facets of the popular interest in dreams, as well as provide a broad overview of contemporary scholarly studies of dreaming. Of special note is that *The Dream Encyclopedia* highlights notions of dreams in different cultures and in different historical periods. In the following pages, you will find entries on everything from dreams in the Bible to dreams among the Senoi of Malaysia to modern-day sleep research. To provide you with a thorough treatment of a topic, all entries include boldface cross-references to topics detailed elsewhere in *The Dream Encyclopedia*. A bibliography for further information is also provided at the back of this book. A special effort has been made to include up-to-the-minute sources, while never dismissing the core texts in the field.

If you're interested in grappling with the meanings of your dreams, consult this book's dream dictionary, which contains over 1,000 dream symbol explanations. The dictionary makes no pretense of being exhaustive or of offering the final word on the meanings of dreams. The interpretations are meant, rather, to be suggestive rather than definitive.

I wish you happy reading and pleasant dreams!

—Evelyn Dorothy Oliver

SOMETIMES DREAMS
ALTER THE COURSE OF
AN ENTIRE LIFE.

—JUDITH DUERK

ABRAHAM

Like **Jacob** and **Joseph**, the patriarch Abraham, ancestor of the Hebrew nation, was one of the most prolific dreamers in the Hebrew Bible. The first dream reported in Genesis is a dream by Abraham:

> When the sun was setting, a deep sleep overcame Abram.... Then the Lord said to him, "Know for certain that your descendants will be strangers in a country not their own, and they will be enslaved and mistreated four hundred years. But I will punish the nation they serve as slaves, and afterward they will come out with great possessions. You, however, will go to your fathers in peace and be buried at a good old age. In the fourth generation your descendants will come back here, for the sin of the Amorites has not yet reached its full measure." (Gen. 15:12–16)

Prior to this particular occasion, God had appeared several times to Abraham and spoken with him, but this is the only time God ever came to Abraham in a vision.

In the sleeplike condition that overcame his senses, Abraham was awake to spiritual impressions and was in a condition where God alone could be seen and heard—everything else was excluded. In this manner the establishing of the Hebrew covenant, as well as the prophecy for Abraham's descendants for the next several centuries, was deeply impressed upon his consciousness.

ACTIVATION-SYNTHESIS MODEL OF DREAMING

The activation-synthesis model of dreaming was proposed in 1977 by Robert McCarley and J. Allan

An 1870 engraving by Gustave Dore depicts Abraham visited by three angels, one of whom tells him that the city of Sodom will be destroyed. Abraham also dreamed that God foretold that His people would be enslaved.

Hobson of Harvard Medical School. Examining the purely physiological correlates of dreaming, Hobson and McCarley believed they had put forward a hypothesis that refuted the notion that dreams are meaningful, especially as this notion was formulated by **Sigmund Freud** and promulgated in the tradition of dream interpretation he initiated.

During **rapid eye movement (REM) sleep**, the stage of sleep most closely connected with dreaming, a portion of the brain called the pons (located in the primitive hindbrain) generates electrical signals that go to many different brain areas, including those associated with motor activities, sensory activities, and conscious thought. Hobson and McCarley hypothesized that one of the effects of this electrical activity is to send a series of essentially random images, feelings, and so forth to the higher mental centers of the forebrain. This is the "activation" stage of the theory.

In normal waking consciousness, the forebrain sorts through various kinds of internal and external sensory input to create a meaningful experience of the world. Faced with a barrage of disconnected inputs during REM sleep, the higher mental centers attempt to impose order on the incoming messages, creating whatever narrative structure dreams have. This is the "synthesis" stage of the theory. Many dreams are just masses of incoherent images representing incoming groups of signals that the brain was simply not able to synthesize.

For anyone who has been exasperated by the convolutions of Freudian or other schools of dream interpretation, the activation-synthesis theory has a certain iconoclastic appeal because it dismisses dreams as just so much nonsense. However, because almost everyone has had at least a few truly insightful dreams, the theory is ultimately unsatisfying. Also, on a purely physiological level, it is an incomplete theory because it does not offer an explanation for the dreams that occur during non-REM sleep.

ADAPTIVE THEORY

Adaptive theory speculates that species-wide sleep patterns developed as a way of adapting to the environment. Grazing animals, for example, sleep relatively few hours a day in short bursts. According to adaptive theory, this is a response to the necessity of constant alertness for predators. By way of contrast, animals with few natural enemies, such as opossums and gorillas, sleep up to fifteen hours per day. Adaptive theory hypothesizes that the sleep pattern of human beings developed after the species began living in caves, which offered protection from encounters with powerful nighttime predators.

ADLER, ALFRED

Alfred Adler (1870–1937) was an Austrian psychiatrist who developed a personality theory referred to as individual psychology. He was at one time closely associated with **Sigmund Freud**, but broke with Freud to develop his own form of psychotherapy. Adler placed much less emphasis on dreams than other schools of psychiatry, and his attitude toward dreams is somewhat inconsistent. Even though he did not develop a full-blown theory of dreams, his thoughts on this subject had a significant influence on later dream theorizing.

To oversimplify the difference between Freud and Adler, Freud focused on sex and aggression and Adler focused on power and status. Adler viewed much human motivation as originating during the lengthy period of childhood, when we are relatively powerless to control our lives. In response to this feeling of helplessness, the human being, according to Adler, develops a powerful urge to master his or her world. This desire for control and mastery becomes the central drive in human life.

Dreams would clearly have a different significance for Adler than they had for Freud. In Freudian theory, dreams are fundamentally arenas within which inner tensions, many of them safely hidden from view in the unconscious, could be safely discharged. Often these tensions have roots in infantile conflicts, making dreams past-ori-

ented. For Adler, on the other hand, dreams become part of the larger project of the individual to master his or her life. In particular, dreams come about as a result of an effort—whether that effort is effective or not—to anticipate future situations, so as to allow us to imaginatively prepare for them. Although dreams are intended to help the dreamer acquire more control over his or her world, Adler recognized that many dreams are maladaptive, in the sense that, if one were to actually follow their guidance, the practical results would be to detract from, rather than enhance, the goal of mastery over one's environment.

Adler's views provide a radically different perspective on dreams from Freud's. For Freud dreams serve to discharge inner tensions originating in the past and hidden in the unconscious, whereas for Adler the function of dreams is to anticipate the future. Also, one of the results of Adler's portrayal of dreams is to make them more related to the thoughts and motivations of waking consciousness, in marked contrast to Freud's portrayal, which emphasizes the disjunction between the waking and the dreaming state. Adler's ideas, particularly as developed and formulated by later theorists, have influenced many contemporary therapists.

AESCULAPIUS

Aesculapius (or Asclepius) was the most popular healing divinity of the Hellenistic world. He was a mortal son of Apollo, who was slain by Zeus for daring to bring people back from the dead. Taught the healing arts by the centaur Chiron, he was a healer by profession. He gradually evolved into a god, and by the end of the classical period he was one of the most popular deities of the Greek pantheon.

The central *asclepieion* (temple dedicated to Aesculapius) was situated six miles inland from the Greek city of Epidaurus, the birthplace of the legendary healer. This temple was established in the sixth or seventh century B.C.E. and was the focus of Aesculapius worship for over eight hundred years. The cult of Aesculapius was officially transplanted to Rome in 293 B.C.E. when the *asclepieion* at Epidaurus sent a giant snake regarded as a form of Aesculapius himself to Rome in order to halt a disastrous plague. The subsequent waning of the plague was attributed to Aesculapius, and he became a popular god among the Romans. At least two hundred *asclepieions* were know to have existed in the Greco-Roman world.

The principal activity at the asclepieions was the seeking of cures via the technique of **dream incubation**, the practice of seeking dreams for specific purposes—for everything from healing to practical guidance. (Dream incubation was extremely popular in the ancient world and seems to have originated as a method of **divination** in ancient Mesopotamia.) People went to *asclepieions* to "camp out" and sleep with the intention of receiving a healing dream from Aesculapius. Particularly in the earliest centuries of the cult, it was believed that the dream directly cured the pilgrim. However, as the cult evolved, it came to be regarded as acceptable if the dream merely provided information that, if followed, would lead to a cure. Aesculapius himself sometimes appeared in the seeker's dreams, touched the diseased part of the body with his finger, and then disappeared. In other healings, he appeared in the form of a dog or a snake.

The dreamer fasted and engaged in other rituals before lying down to sleep. In cases where the temple was too far away from the person seeking dream guidance, or when the person was too sick to undertake the required fasts, sacrifices, cold baths, or other rituals, a surrogate could go through the rituals for the seeker. Priests assisted pilgrims in performing the proper rituals and were also available to help interpret their dreams.

AGE AND DREAMS

Sleep patterns vary markedly across different age groups, with people sleeping progressively less soundly in later life. Stage 4, or deep sleep, in particular, practically disappears among the elderly. Studies of dreams through the life cycle have shown less dramatic patterns. For instance, in one study that subdivided subjects into four age groups—21–34, 35–49, 50–64, and 65 and over subjects in the 21–34 and 50–64 groups reported having more dreams than the other two groups. Content-wise, the most dramatic finding was a direct correlation between age and frequency of dreams about death and dying. Dream content also changes among the retired (especially the institutionalized) elderly, who often experience dreams about lack of resources. Finally, dreams among those who are dying often include the theme of life after death.

AGUARUNA

The Aguaruna are a people who inhabit Peru's northern region, where they support themselves through horticulture, hunting, and fishing. Although the interest in dreams and visions among this people has been declining in recent years, it still plays an important role in their response to contemporary problems and in day-to-day decision making.

According to the Aguaruna, dreams may reveal emergent possibilities and events that are developing but have not yet occurred or become fully accomplished facts. Dreams are generally regarded as taking place during the wanderings of the soul during sleep, when it encounters other souls and discovers their intentions. However, the recent exposure of the Aguaruna to Christian concepts of the soul has introduced confusion regarding their understanding of dream experiences, in that some Aguaruna now argue that soul loss of any kind can only result in sickness.

In any case, dreams are considered exclusive events experienced only by the dreamer; they cannot be seen by other people. Dreams can be distinguished according to whether they are spontaneous or intentionally sought. The latter are more significant than the former, in that they require more personal sacrifice and offer greater rewards with respect to their manipulative potential. For the Aguaruna dreams represent a potential field for exercising human control because they occur in an arena of direct contact between people and powerful supernatural beings.

The most powerful Aguaruna dreams concern success in hunting and warfare, and they exercise the same control over the world as magic songs (which might be regarded as magic "spells"). A highly esteemed dream experience is the establishment of contact between a man and an ancient warrior soul that enables him to survive an attack. This type of dream usually involves an initial vision of a terrifying entity that the dreamer must confront, followed by the apparition of the ancient warrior, who acknowledges the dreamer and confirms his future victory in battle. Dreams are often used as vehicles for the expression of authority by leaders and people in positions of power, and their complexity generally invites interpretation by people who have accumulated experience and knowledge in this field.

AKASHIC RECORDS

The akashic records is a theosophical concept referring to the archiving of all world events and personal experiences—of all the thoughts and deeds that have ever taken place on Earth. These events are transcribed in the form of complex images composed of pictures, sounds, and other sensory stimuli. These images are indelibly impressed upon the "matter" of the astral plane (called the akasha) and may be "read" only when the reader is in a special altered (some even say mystical) state of consciousness. In such an altered state of mind, one is able to tap the akashic records and receive direct information about past ages. Certain theosophical descriptions of Atlantis, for example, are supposedly received via this technique. Also, some psychics who do past-life readings claim to receive their information from the akashic records.

It is also said that it is possible to tap the akashic records during dreams. Sometimes the information so obtained is remembered consciously upon awakening. More often, nocturnal perusals of the akashic records are not remembered, although the fruits of such "dream research" may be retrieved in moments of intuition in daily life. The information received in precognitive dreams (clairvoyant dreams relating to an event or state not yet experienced) is often said to be ultimately derived from the akashic records.

ALCHEMY

Alchemy is the ancient discipline from which the modern science of chemistry arose. The aspect of this discipline that is best remembered is the quest to discover how to transform ordinary substances into gold. Alchemy came to be related to

The use of symbols in alchemy has some parallels with dream symbols, noted Carl Jung.

Drinking alcohol is not only bad for your health, it also affects your dreams.

dreams through the work of **Carl Jung**, who perceived **archetypal images** in the symbolic language of alchemy.

Jung postulated the existence of an unconscious urge toward psychological growth and health that he termed the individuation process. This process propelled the individual toward psychic integration, bringing progressively more of the contents of the **unconscious** mind into the expanding awareness of the **ego**. Jung believed that the primary goal of alchemy—discovering the series of operations through which gold is produced—could be read symbolically as the individuation process.

Jung noted four stages in the individuation process—stages that could be symbolized in dreams by the numbers one, two, three, and four. Dreams that seemed to stress duality, triplicity, or

quaternity Jung interpreted as referring to these stages. The ancient alchemists associated certain colors with the stages, and Jung sometimes interpreted the predominance of black, white, yellow, and red in a dream as referring to one of the four stages of personal transformation.

ALCOHOL

Alcohol can have a significant impact on sleep and sleeping patterns. Under the influence of alcohol, the quantity of **rapid eye movement (REM) sleep** decreases and Stage 4 sleep increases, creating the impression that one has slept more soundly under the influence of alcohol. Excessive use of alcohol disrupts the natural pattern of sleep, so that chronic alcoholics who have completely abstained for extended periods of time have been shown to exhibit abnormal sleep patterns. It has been speculated that the disruption of sleep patterns—particularly the reduction of REM sleep (often associated with dreaming)—by alcoholism results in irreversible brain damage.

ALIEN ABDUCTION

In recent times, the subject of UFO abductions has gained immense popularity, both with the public and with a small group of scholars and writers who have turned their attention to the UFO phenomenon. The number of people who claim to have been abducted by occupants of UFOs has been rising almost exponentially since the early 1970s, when the subject first gained attention from the media and the ufological community saw marked growth. Accounts of these abductions have a dreamlike quality, and some abductees have dreams that they claim derive from residual memories of their abduction experience.

With the publication in 1987 of Whitley Strieber's *Communion,* interest in abductions and abductees exploded. Strieber's account, written with skill by an accomplished author, presented the bizarre details of UFO abduction in an accessible way, spurring the book to the top of the *New York Times* bestseller list. In the wake of this success, talk shows on radio and television fed the public interest in the abduction phenomenon with a steady diet of reports of individuals who believed that they, too, had been abducted.

Contemporaneous with the rise in popularity of Strieber's book was the work of UFO researchers who were dedicated to examining abductions. Individuals like Budd Hopkins, whose own book *Intruders* (1987) made it to the bestseller list, came to dominate the field of ufol-

Many psychologists and sleep experts have found that those who believe they have been abducted by aliens report their experiences as if they were dreams, often with visions including religious symbols.

ogy. Hopkins and those who share his methodology believe that UFO abductions are a widespread phenomenon and that they are not always remembered by the victims. Hypnosis is considered a powerful and reliable tool for retrieving these memories, which Hopkins and others argue reveal a specific pattern of action on the part of UFO occupants.

In contrast to Strieber, who considers his own experiences to be mainly inexplicable, hypnosis-using researchers tend to have clearly defined theories about the nature and purpose of the abduction phenomenon. These theories have come to dominate the field of ufology. A quick examination of UFO books published in the last ten years reveals that books on abductions have outnumbered books on all other subjects related to UFOs combined by a substantial margin. Popular magazines devoted to UFOs have become almost exclusively concerned with abductions in recent years.

The popularity of abductions has led to a proliferation of first person accounts—both remembered consciously and retrieved through hypnosis—which are accessible to the researcher. These primary sources reveal a wealth of bizarre details that are not wholly amenable to the neat theories of many ufologists. A careful examination of abduction narratives indicates that the patterns alleged to have been discovered by abduction investigators often have religious overtones or similarities with more traditional types of religious experience. In addition, the abduction experience is often given a religious meaning by the percipient, and these interpretations are habitually overlooked or ignored by UFO investigators.

In coming to grips with the claims of abductees and researchers, the practice of hypnosis must first be considered. The use of hypnosis to investigate UFO abductions dates back to one of the earliest instances of the phenomenon, the story of the Betty and Barney Hill abduction in 1963. In the overwhelming majority of cases available for research, the memory of the abduction event was obtained or clarified through hypnosis. Typically, the abductee consciously recalls little or nothing about the experience. Certain telltale signs—unaccounted for spans of time, uneasy feelings associated with UFOs, or the sense of a presence in the bedroom before falling asleep—serve to clue the

vigilant researcher into the possibility that an abduction has occurred. Hypnosis is then generally used to explore the abduction experience.

While the reliance on hypnosis is heavy among abduction researchers, most seem to be aware of the difficulties inherent in the process. Hypnosis apparently allows access to a subconscious level of an individual's psyche, allowing him or her to recall repressed memories of actual events, but also making it possible to derive "memories" of things that have never happened. Hypnotism greatly increases a subject's suggestibility, infusing him or her with a desire to please the questioner, making the subject very susceptible to leading questions. Although they recognize these limitations, researchers, with few exceptions, contend that hypnosis, when used competently, is an accurate tool for uncovering factual details of the abduction event. It would be premature, however, to dismiss the possibility that many, if not all abduction memories are confabulations of the subconscious, guided by the preconceptions of the hypnotist. Noted UFO debunker Philip Klass favors this view, and rather plausibly discounts some better known cases by applying this theory.

The nature of accounts obtained through hypnosis is important for understanding the religious characteristics of the abduction phenomenon. As **Carl Jung** has argued—specifically in relation to UFOs—the subconscious is a storehouse of religious ideas and symbols. Such symbols can become exteriorized through anxiety or stress. Thus, the religious imagery and interpretation brought out by hypnosis could be confabulations of the subject's subconscious that are, perhaps, worked into a UFO narrative in an effort to please the hypnotist. In his research, Jung noted that certain complexes of religious symbols appeared time and time again in widely separated subjects. The prevalence of similar patterns in part gave rise to his theory of a collective unconscious, a pool of ideas and imagery shared by all people. This theory may also help to explain the similar patterns, filled with religious overtones, which abduction researchers claim to find among their subjects.

The applicability of a Jungian form of analysis to UFO abductions is further strengthened by the markedly dreamlike character of the experience. Dreams are the most common arena in which religious symbolism is encountered. One of the signs noted by abduction researchers as indicative of an abduction event is the prevalence of dreams containing UFO- or alien-related imagery.

In many of the cases in which the abduction is at least partially recalled prior to the use of hypnosis, it is recalled as a dream rather than as an objective event. For example, Kathy Davis, the main subject of Budd Hopkins' bestseller *Intruders,* consistently believes that her experiences were a series of dreams about UFO abductions. In his investigation, Hopkins hypnotically examines the alleged abduction events by directing her towards these dreams and asking her to recount their details. Hopkins explains that Davis remembers these events as dreams in order to shield her psyche from the unsettling implications of their reality. Unless one is strongly committed to a theory of extraterrestrial genetic engineers, as is Hopkins, it is difficult to dismiss Kathy Davis's contention that the events were in fact dreams.

ANALYZE THIS

The 1999 movie *Analyze This* is in some ways a caricature of popular interest in dreams and a caricature of Freudian dream analysis. It reflects our fascination with the prospect of quick cures through dream interpretation, and reflects the impact of this notion on filmdom.

Psychiatrist Ben Sobel (Billy Crystal) backs into gangster Paul Vitti's (Robert De Niro's) car. Vitti subsequently dispatches henchmen to bring Sobel to him so he can listen to Vitti's dreams. He has a persistent nightmare in which he sees himself drinking black milk. He also has sudden anxiety attacks that prevent him from appropriately fulfilling his role as a Mafia Don.

Sobel talks with him, befriends him, and eventually even takes a bullet meant for him. He analyzes his dream as guilt over his father's death, and as symbolic of the negative nurturing he received in childhood. Eventually, the Don recovers from his disorder.

Analyze This is based on an earlier movie, *The Dark Past,* in which an escaped convict barges into someone's house during a dinner party. The convict has a persistent nightmare problem that a psychologist at the party analyzes. This convict is so overwhelmed that when the police arrive he cannot pick up his gun, and he gets killed at the end of the film.

ANCESTORS

The notion of one or more "spiritual" realms existing alongside the world of our ordinary, everyday experience is taken for granted in almost every religious tradition. One broad area of agreement is that communication between this world and the **otherworld** is possible. Dreams, which often seem to be experiences of a confused parallel world, are frequently the medium of communication.

One category of inhabitants of the otherworld is the ancestors. Many cultures revere their departed ancestors, so much so in some societies that they are regarded as quasi deities. As beings who now reside with the gods, they are thought to have access to powers and information unavailable to ordinary mortals. Hence, they are invoked to protect and guide the living. Traditional beliefs and rituals associated with the ancestors are sometimes referred to as ancestor worship, although the appropriateness of the term "worship" is debatable. Ancestor worship is especially characteristic of certain African tribes, some strands of **Buddhism**, Shinto (Japan), and Confucianism (China).

Of particular interest are cultures in which the departed relatives are thought to take an active interest in the affairs of the living. In these societies, ancestors may be requested to help the living with a particular problem, much as one would make requests of a parent or grandparent. Deceased ancestors can intercede with divine forces on behalf of descendants and can provide information—often when the descendants are in a dream state—that will help the descendants live a better life.

ANGELS

Angels are spiritual beings that serve as intermediaries between God and humanity. They are common in Western, monotheistic religions where God is conceived of as being so elevated that He does not intervene directly in the world. Angels are often pictured as delivering messages to mortals, or in other ways carrying out God's will. For example, shortly after Joseph was told by Mary that she was pregnant, he had a dream in which the angel Gabriel appeared to him and said, "Joseph son of David, do not be afraid to take Mary home as your wife, because what is conceived in her is from the Holy Spirit. She will give birth to a son, and you are to give him the name Jesus, because he will save

Angels, a common part of religious philosophy and spirituality, are frequent images experienced in dreams.

his people from their sins" (Matt. 1:20–21). This dream convinced Joseph not to break his engagement with Mary. While angels sometimes deliver their messages to recipients in the daytime, they more frequently communicate with human beings through dreams during sleep.

ANGER AND AGGRESSION

While fear is the most commonly expressed emotion in nightmares, anger holds the second place position. These two emotions, combined with anxiety, are twice as likely to occur in a dream than more pleasant feelings. Once other negative emotions are added into this equation—failure, sadness, and aggression—the rate of occurrence rises to around sixty-six percent. It has been suggested that violence or aggression in a dream is a direct result of anger and frustration in our waking lives.

There have been numerous studies on the different factors influencing the frequency of aggression in dreams—factors such as age, gender, birth order, social class, and even geographical location. The most prevalent of these is gender. As a rule, females of all ages remember dreams more often than their male counterparts; their dreams are also longer and more detailed. More friendly interactions occur in female dreams as compared to males. When it comes to aggression in dreams, males report slightly more aggressive encounters, even though they remember a significantly lower number of their dreams than women.

For children, the statistics concerning aggression in dreams are less conclusive on the role of gender. Most studies indicate that for boys and girls between the ages of two and twelve the level of aggressiveness in dreams is about the same. However, at the age of twelve, these levels begin to drop for girls. In males these levels do not drop until their thirties, at the earliest, and on occasion they have been known to remain high until they are in their seventies or eighties.

Gender is not the only factor that has been studied with respect to aggression in dreams. A study was done on a group of working mothers with preschool children and stay-at-home mothers with children of the same age. The working mothers reported more male characters in their dreams, fewer indoor environments, and experiencing more unpleasant feelings such as failure, aggression, and anger. The stay-at-home mothers

had more friendly encounters in their dreams, but they dealt with more misfortune and hostility. It was also discovered that mothers with dual roles—mother and provider—experienced more work-related dreams than working fathers.

Another factor is birth order. Although men typically experience more aggressive dreams, this is not always true if the male is the first born. In this case he would typically see himself in a more positive manner than his younger siblings of the same gender, and therefore has more positive encounters in his dreams. First-born females tend to have more aggressive characters in their dreams. They are also more likely to be more aggressive than other females of the same age group who are not first born.

Yet another factor that affects the aggression in our dreams is geography. In an East Coast survey, forty percent of the total study group reported being the initiator of a violent act in their dreams. The same study was done on the West Coast and in the Midwest. On the West Coast that figure dropped to twenty-two percent, and it dropped to ten percent in the Midwest.

One final factor that has been studied is social class. Members of lower social classes reported more violently aggressive dreams than those in the middle or upper classes. They also experienced more dreams of anger and misfortune. A study found that lower-class high school girls experienced more angry and aggressive dreams than their male or female counterparts, regardless of social class.

ANIMA (AND ANIMUS)

In Jungian psychology, the anima refers to personality traits regarded as feminine that are often repressed into the **unconscious** of males while the animus refers to traits regarded as masculine that are often repressed into the unconscious of females. In **Carl Jung**'s personality theory, the **ego** represents the individual's sense of personal self. The sense of personal identity is purchased, however, at the expense of certain tendencies (for example, socially undesirable traits) that are rejected as "not-self." According to Jung, these rejected traits come together as a kind of unconscious "counter-ego," which he termed the **shadow**. The anima/animus is similar to the shadow, but, because the rejected traits together constitute a socially typical female or male, they are more often than not distinct from the shadow. For example, when the shadow appears in a male's dreams, it is most often represented by a male figure. The anima, in contrast, is most often a female figure.

Although suppressed from conscious awareness, the anima/animus influences our behavior in powerful ways. In most individuals, for example, it is projected onto people of the opposite sex and accounts for the experience of falling in love with someone we hardly know. In Jungian therapy, the anima/animus is viewed as a potential source of characteristics to be integrated into the patient's ego structure. As the unconscious pole of the self, the counter-ego represented by the anima/animus can also be a guide to one's own unconscious realm. It is often experienced as the guiding female or male presence in dreams.

ANIMAL DREAMS

Humans have been dreaming about **animals** for ages. It has been speculated that some of the ancient cave paintings of animals may perhaps be dream images from cave dwellers whose lives were mostly spent chasing, hunting, and taming animals. In ancient **Egypt**, human-figured deities with animal heads suggest dreams images.

A study carried out by Robert L. Van de Castle found a larger number of animal dreams in children than in adults. Dreams of a group of 741 children (383 girls and 358 boys) aged four to sixteen were examined for the presence of animal figures. The frequency for each animal figure at each age level was tabulated for girls and boys. Animal figures were present in 39.4 percent of dreams from the four- and five-year-old children. The percentage steadily dropped for each subsequent age grouping (six- and seven-year-olds, 35.5 percent; eight- and nine-year-olds, 33.6 percent; ten- and eleven-year-olds, 29.8 percent; twelve- and thirteen-year-olds, 21.9 percent; and fourteen-through sixteen-year-olds, 13.7 percent).

Boys had higher animal percentage figures at ages four through six (44 percent, versus 34 percent for girls), while girls had higher animal dreams at ages nine through eleven (36 percent, versus 26 percent for boys). Overall, animal figures appeared in 29 percent of the combined girls' dreams and 29.6 percent of the combined boys' dreams. There were more than three times as many animal figures in the dreams of children as there were in the dreams of adults. The seven most frequent animal figures for children were dogs (30), horses (28), cats (15), snakes (15), bears (14), lions (13), and monsters (e.g., wolfman) (13).

If the frequencies for all animal figures are considered, it is clear that children dream more frequently of large and threatening wild animals, while college students dream more often of pets and domesticated animals. Bears, lions, tigers, gorillas, elephants, bulls, dinosaurs, dragons, and monsters accounted for twenty-seven percent of the animal figures in children's dreams but only seven percent of the animal figures in adult dreams. This collection of wild animals appeared more frequently (forty-four times) in boys' dreams than in girls' dreams (twenty-seven times). Several theorists have suggested that these large, threatening animals may represent parental figures in the dreams of children.

An interesting gender difference was found in the types of animal figures. Women and girls reported significantly more mammals, while men and boys reported significantly more non-mammals. This may indicate females identify at some level with other forms of life that nurse their young with mammary glands, and this identification is reflected in the type of animals that appear in their dreams.

Animals such as cats and dogs apparently have dreams, too, just like people; animals are also a theme in many people's dreams.

ANIMALS

The observation of animal sleep patterns has long been of interest, dating as far back as 44 B.C.E., when the Roman natural philosopher Lucretius described "the twitching movements of dogs sleeping upon the hearth" (Hobson, p. 151—see *Sources*). However, it was during the 1950s that research into the sleep patterns of animals really peaked: first with the discovery by William Dement, that cats exhibit the phase of sleep called **rapid eye movement (REM)**, followed by the experiments of two Frenchmen, neurosurgeon Michel Jouvet and his co-worker, the neurologist Francois Michel. Jouvet and Michel observed that a sleeping cat, devoid of motor output or movement, still exhibits an activated EEG, which means that while an animal is asleep, its mind is awake. Jouvet's discovery led to the general understanding that during REM sleep "the body's muscles are actively inhibited." In essence, "we would act out our dreams were it

not for this inhibitory suppression of motor output" (Hobson, p. 150—see *Sources*). Further, because it has been found humans experience the most active dreaming during REM sleep, this research may indicate that animals do dream, although it is, of course, impossible to say for sure because of the communication barrier.

It has been suggested that when animals dream, they are focused on the types of things they usually do in their waking state. For example, animals that use their noses a lot, such as dogs, have dreams with a significant olfactory component.

There was one behavioral study that showed that monkeys have visual dreams. Some monkeys were taught to respond to visual stimuli by pressing a button. Later, when they were sleeping, they made hand motions as if they were pressing buttons, suggesting that they were seeing something. To add further credence, in a separate study, a gorilla who had been taught sign language put together two signs to form the combined term *sleep pictures*, presumably a reference to the visual components of dreams.

Again, in an experiment on cats, portions of the brainstem responsible for muscle inhibition during REM sleep were damaged. These cats entered REM sleep, and rather than lying quietly with their eyes moving, they stood up, walked around, and chased imaginary creatures, as if they were acting out their dreams without waking up.

Such findings, as well as our everyday observations of household pets that growl and make movements in their sleep, make it almost certain that animals dream in much the same way that we dream. The implications of this conclusion, however, tend to undermine certain dream theories, such as **Sigmund Freud**'s notion that the sole purpose of dreams is to allow us to act out socially unacceptable urges—an idea clearly inapplicable to animals.

ANTHROPOLOGY OF DREAMS

Anthropology has contributed considerably to the cross-cultural understanding of dreams. The earliest anthropological research on dreams, which dates back to the end of the nineteenth century, considered the dream beliefs and practices of other cultures as evidence of their savagery, in contrast to modern Western civilization's relative disinterest in dreams. The only area of investigation where dreams played a significant role was psychoanalysis, and psychoanalysis had a tendency to portray

dreams as primitive and childish, thus reinforcing the dominant negative image of dreams. With the spread of psychoanalytic theories, various anthropologists tried to prove the accuracy of **Sigmund Freud**'s ideas about dreams by analyzing of dream experiences of non-Western people.

Some anthropologists, such as Kilton Stewart, provided romantic idealizations of dream practices in non-Western cultures. According to Stewart, the **Senoi** of Malaysia reportedly lived a trouble-free life based on their reverence for dreams. Stewart, who lived with the Senoi in 1935, wrote that "the absence of violent crime, armed conflict, and mental and physical diseases … can only be explained on the basis of institutions which produce a high state of psychological integration and emotional maturity, along with social skills and attitudes that promote creative rather than destructive interpersonal relations" (Stewart, p. 160—see *Sources*). According to Stewart's study, the collective life of the Senoi centered around a complex dream psychology that served to integrate the community. However, his theory was soon seriously challenged, and anthropological research on dreams lost credibility.

Anthropologists have long been interested in cross-cultural experiences of dreaming and interpretations of dreams, concentrating especially on the latter interest, rather than focusing on the dream as an experience. With the publication of *Dreaming: Anthropological and Psychological Interpretations* (1987), edited by **Barbara Tedlock**, anthropology emerged as a major field of dream research with important insights to contribute to the modern study of dreams.

According to the authors of *Dreaming*, which is a collection of essays based on fieldwork conducted among various peoples of Central and South America, the culture to which the individual belongs largely determines the social context in which the dream is narrated and how it is interpreted. Dreaming experience also reflects important beliefs about reality, death, the soul, and the boundaries between self and others. Thus, to achieve a good understanding of dream experiences of other groups, it is fundamental to fully understand their culture through the study of their language, their social institutions, and their psychological, philosophical, and religious beliefs.

Tedlock's anthropological research indicates that many other cultures draw lines between more and less meaningful dreams. Also, as one might anticipate, in many non-Western cultures dreaming has religious meaning, in that dreams reflect a culture's spiritual beliefs, and may even create new religious imagery that can influence the individual's as well as the whole society's religious orientation.

ARABIA

Dreams have many meanings in Arabic culture. According to some, sleep is a preoccupation of the **soul**, which detaches itself from external things and experiences events taking place in its interior. During sleep the interior self "absorbs" the five senses, which then cease to perceive and turn back to the mind. According to other views, the soul can perceive the form of things by the senses and by thought, independently of their objective reality. Thought does not fall asleep when the faculty of perceiving sleeps, and during the night images continue to exist as if they could be sensed. Their form is outlined in the soul, and they are presented to the mind of the dreamer in the same way as in the waking state.

It is believed that the soul, when it is freed from the physical limits of the body, can float at ease over everything that it desires to possess, whereas in the waking state it cannot. When dreamers awaken, they still preserve the memory of these fantastic pictures. If the dreamer has a blemished soul, the dreamer is continually deluded by dreams, whereas the dreamer is undeceived when the soul is pure.

Traditional Arab belief also holds that dreams are generated by the fundamental humors of the human body, and that individuals dream according to their temperaments. Certain Arabs completely separate the faculty of perception from the visible body and believe that individuals, when asleep, can leave their bodies and contemplate the world with a lucidity proportional to their purity, a notion supported by various verses of the Qur'an.

ARCHETYPES (ARCHETYPAL DREAM IMAGES)

While the notion of archetypes is at least as old as **Plato**, it is most familiar to the modern world through the work of **Carl Jung**, the prominent Swiss psychotherapist. In contrast to his mentor **Sigmund Freud**, Jung divided the **unconscious** mind into two subdivisions, the personal unconscious and the **collective unconscious** (which he also referred to as the objective psyche). The personal unconscious is shaped by our personal experiences, whereas the collective unconscious represents our inheritance of the collective experience of humankind. This storehouse of humanity's experiences exists in the form of archetypes (or prototypes).

The archetypes predispose us to subconsciously organize our personal experiences in certain ways. We are, for instance, predisposed to perceive someone in our early environment as a father because of the father archetype. If a person's biological father is absent during childhood, someone else (e.g., an older brother) is assimilated into this archetype, providing concrete images for the father complex (the reflection of the father archetype in the personal unconscious).

Archetypes are not specific images or symbols. They are more like invisible magnetic fields that cause iron filings to arrange themselves according to certain patterns. For example, Jung postulated the existence of a self archetype, which constitutes the unconscious basis for our ego—our conscious self-image or self-concept. In dreams, this self is represented in a variety of ways, often in the form of a circle or *mandala* (a circular diagram used as an aid to meditation in Hinduism and **Buddhism**). The self can also be represented by surrogate symbols, such as four of almost anything (according to Jung, four is the number of wholeness and hence a symbol of the self), a pattern Jung referred to as a quaternity. These concrete manifestations of elusive archetypes are referred to as archetypal images or, when they appear in dreams, as archetypal dream images.

Jung asserted that much of world mythology and folklore represents manifestations of the collective unconscious. He based this assertion on his discovery that the dreams of his patients frequently contained images with which they were completely unfamiliar, but which seemed to reflect symbols that could be found somewhere in the mythological systems of world culture. Jung further found that if he could discover the specific meaning of such images in their native culture, he could better understand the dreams in which they occurred. The process of seeking such meanings is referred to as amplification.

ARISTOTLE

The first systematic treatises on the nature of the soul and dreams are to be found in the philosophical writings of Aristotle. Aristotle was the third of a succession of great philosophers (the other two being Socrates and **Plato**) who are together considered the fathers of Western thought.

Born in the Ionian city of Stagira in Chalcidice, Aristotle (384–322 B.C.E.) was the son of Nicomachus, the court physician to Amyntas III, king of Macedon. After his father died, he was brought up by the guardian Proxenus, who sent him to Athens. In 367 B.C.E. he entered Plato's Academy, where he remained until Plato's death in 347 B.C.E., and then joined a circle of Platonists living at Assos, in the Troad (an area surrounding the ancient city of Troy), under the protection of the tyrant Hermias of Atarneus.

After three years, Aristotle moved to Mytilene, on the island of Lesbos, and in 342 B.C.E. he accepted an invitation to supervise the education of Alexander III—later known as Alexander the Great—at the Macedonian court at Pella, where he spent three years. After spending the following five years at Stagira, he returned to Athens, where he opened a new school called the Lyceum. When the school was in danger of attack from the anti-Macedonian party at Athens after the death of Alexander the Great in 323 B.C.E., Aristotle took refuge in Chalcis, on the island of Euboea, where he died the following year.

Aristotle's writings can be classified as popular writings, memoranda and collections of material, and scientific and philosophical treatises. Among Aristotle's most important popular writings were his dialogues, which were based on the Platonic model, and what he refers to as "exoteric writings." None of his popular works and not many of his philosophical works—such as *Eudemus, Protrepticus, On Philosophy, On the Good,* and *On the Ideas*—survived except in quotations and references in later works. The memoranda and collections of material contain 158 constitutions of Greek states, a record of dramatic festivals known as the *Didascaliae,* and *Problems* and *History of Animals.* Only a few of these works survive, such as the Constitution of the Athenians.

Among the scientific and philosophical treatises, which constitute the largest surviving segment of Aristotle's writings are the psychological works *De Anima* and *Parva Naturalia.* According to Aristotle the object of psychology is to discover the essence and the attributes of the soul (**psyche**), which to the Greeks referred to the realm of human consciousness and subjectivity.

He developed his doctrine of the soul through three different approaches, characterizing the three periods into which his thought is usually classified. The first approach, which corresponds to the period of his earliest writings (through 347 B.C.E.) in which he was an enthusiastic defender of Platonism was characterized by a Platonic concept of the soul as a separate substance.

Aristotle's second approach, reflecting an increasingly critical attitude toward Platonism and marking the period from 347 to 335 B.C.E., was characterized by his view of the body as the instrument of the soul. This view of the soul and the body can be found both in the biological treatises and throughout the *Parva Naturalia,* in which the soul is given a physical basis and located in the heart, considered the central governing place of the body.

In Aristotle's final period, beginning in 335 B.C.E., during which he embraced the principle of empirical science and rejected all the essential features of Platonic metaphysics, he developed a the-

The Greek philosopher Aristotle was the first person to write in detail about the connection between dreams and the human soul.

ory of the soul as a form of the body, an extension of his earlier theory of the body as the instrument of the soul, which he postulated in *Metaphysics.* In the treatise *De Anima,* the soul and body are treated as constituting a single substance, standing to each other in the relation of form to matter.

In *De Anima,* Aristotle presents a detailed analysis of the faculties of the soul, which, according to him, form a hierarchy, with the highest faculty, intelligence, found only in man, so that living creatures can be classified in a series according to the number of faculties possessed. Each kind of soul presupposes all that come before it in this order, but does not imply those that follow. The minimal soul is the nutritive, existing in all living beings. It is followed by the sensitive soul, existing in all animals and including the perceptions of touch, taste, smell, hearing, and sight. Besides the function of perceiving, the sensitive soul also has the function of feeling pleasure and pain, and therefore of desiring. There are two other faculties, regarded as outgrowths of the sensitive one: imagination and movement, which can be found in most animals but not in all. Finally, there is the highest faculty, reason, peculiar to human beings.

Imagination is considered the repercussion of perception, both in the body and in the soul, and is described as operating only after the sensed object has disappeared. The main functions of imagination are the formation of after-images and the process of memory, which is a function of the faculty by which we perceive time and which is impossible without an image.

Another important function of imagination is dreams, which are the product of imagination during the state of sleep, and a by-product of previous sensations, since the impressions produced by our senses linger after the senses have ceased to be active. This is evident in the sensuous content of dreams whenever senses themselves are inactive. During the state of sleep, characterized by the absence of stimulus from without, the mind is more free to attend to images and, at the same time, more liable to be deceived by them. Aristotle deals with this subject in a systematic way in three treatises on sleep and dreams, *De somno et vigilia, De insomniis,* and *De divinatione per somnum.*

According to Aristotle, sleep and waking, the examination of which is indispensable for the understanding dreams, are two states of the same faculty, whereby waking is the positive and sleep is the negative state. The waking state is determined by activation of the primary or common-sense faculty, the sleeping state by its inactivity. This inactivity of the commonsense faculty can be considered the ultimate cause of dreaming.

The description of sleep as inactivity of the primary or commonsense faculty is presented in *De somno et vigilia,* in which Aristotle considers sleep and waking as affections of soul and body, taken as a whole. Soul is not considered something foreign to the body, and, during the state of sleep, it is considered capable of attaining the supernatural wisdom that is its original heritage. The heart, which is considered the source of functioning of all the bodily parts, is also the origin of sleep and walking, whereas the brain has a secondary function.

In *De insomniis,* Aristotle speaks about the illusion of "sense-perception," which, in sleep, is due to the improper functioning of the senses, freeing the way for the forming of dreams, without correction by judgement or evaluation. Neither actual perceptions nor thoughts can form any part of the process of dreaming. Finally, in *De divinatione per somnum,* Aristotle denies that dreams may have a divine origin, and that they may be interpreted by reliance on supernatural skills. He maintains, rather, that they may be either causes of actions or symptoms of bodily disturbances, and that "divination" through interpretation of dreams is mainly the result of coincidence.

ART AND DREAMS

In most cultures the relationship between art and dreams is straightforward, though often the two are associated in a negative way. **Plato** maintained that they were based on mere appearances and that they lead people away from the pursuit of truth. In a roughly similar manner, **Sigmund Freud** insisted that both poetry and dreaming are nothing more than defensive measures, designed to substitute pleasure for reality.

The surrealist movement, which began in Europe in the 1920s, is a particularly interesting example of the explicit association between art and dreams. This movement's approach paralleled Freud's ideas about the unconscious, and the repression of irrational urges by the conscious mind, which then manifest themselves in dreams. According to André Brenton's *Surrealist Manifesto* (1924), "The absolute rationalism which remains in fashion allows for the consideration of only those facts narrowly relevant to our experience.... Boundaries have been assigned even to experience. It revolves in a cage from which release is becoming increasingly difficult." Surrealism, like other forms of modern art, attempted to challenge those boundaries. The surrealist artist's hope was to discover new possibilities of human perception and creativity.

Surrealist artists were particularly interested in the powerful sense of freedom their dreams provided. The unconscious was considered to be the primary source of inspiration among surrealists. According to some artists, dreams include images or experiences that are fantastic or absurd. Therefore, they are a direct challenge to what we take to be ordinary or normal. An authentic dream atmosphere can be found in the works of Salvador Dali, Vincent Van Gogh, **Francisco Goya**, and Max Ernst, to name just a few. It was said that Dali used to go so far as to purposefully "induce" his own dreams by falling asleep in a chair, chin propped in the cup of his hand. He would jerk awake just as he entered

A necklace in a dream can symbolize wealth, gifts, or feeling the weight of a milestone on one's mind. For more explanations of symbols, refer to the Dream Symbols section at the back of this book.

the dream state and capture the surreal imagery in his own art.

While the surrealist movement may be one of the more obvious examples of the connections between dreams and art, the association does not end there. Numerous artists have accredited their dreams for portions—if not the whole—of their works of art. Due to mainly visual aspect of dreams, the physical arts are what we frequently associate with dream inspiration, but there have also been accounts of auditory inspiration. The composer Giuseppe Tartini was the most widely known example of this; he attributed his popular "Devil's Trill Sonata" to a dream.

Although there have been a few poets and writers who have claimed that their work appeared to them, in printed form, in dreams, it is more common that authors and poets receive their inspiration while in a dreaming state. It has been observed that very rarely do we read or write in our dreams as the two—dreaming and the literary arts—utilize different areas of our brain. If, however, we look beyond the literal and think instead that the events that transpire in our dreams may carry over into our waking lives, it is not so bizarre to imagine that many great literary works were not only inspired by our dreams but also by our nightmares. This serves to highlight the importance of dreams as messengers of our unconscious, making us aware of thoughts or ideas that our conscious mind refuses to recognize and yet are essential in creative expression.

ARTEMIDORUS OF DALDIS

Dreams have fascinated the human mind throughout recorded history. The ancient Greeks were particularly interested in dreams, as the hundreds of dream temples dedicated to Aesculapius—the deified doctor who healed or provided healing advice in dreams—bear witness. It is thus fitting that the largest and most complete compilation of dream lore to survive from the ancient world, the *Oneirocritica* (*The Interpretation of Dreams*), should have been authored by a second-century Greek, Artemidorus of Daldis.

Little is known about Artemidorus beyond the few autobiographical remarks he makes in the *Oneirocritica*. He was a professional diviner and dream interpreter who was actually born in the Greek city of Ephesus (the location of the congregation to whom the biblical Ephesians is addressed), but signed his work Artemidorus of Daldis to honor the small town in which his mother was born. The *Oneirocritica* is a compilation of Greek dream lore up to Artemidorus's time, with the addition of his own observations. The first three subdivisions (or books, as they are customarily called) of this work comprise a structured treatise on dream interpretation. The last two books were addressed to Artemidorus's son, who was aspiring to follow in his father's footsteps.

The Oneirocritica is largely a **dream dictionary**, but also contains some broader advice on how to interpret dreams. Artemidorus interviewed professional dream interpreters and purchased manuscripts from all over the known world to familiarize himself with what was known or believed about dreams up to that point. Unlike modern dream dictionaries, which are almost invariably arranged in a purely alphabetical order, Artemidorus's work classifies the various items that may appear in dreams into certain categories. Thus he discusses, in a very literal "head to toe" manner, dreams related to various body parts. He then moves on to discuss the appearance of gods and deities, also covering types of animals, weather, fire, flying, and many others. For the sake of completeness, he also committed his third section, the last of the books meant for the public, to any dream he could not find a place for in the previous sections.

There were six pieces of information that Artemidorus considered essential to the proper analysis of a person's dreams: whether the events of the dream were natural, lawful, and customary for the dreamer; what was happening at the time of the dream; and the dreamer's name and occupation. It was Artemidorus's belief that the associations evoked by the dream images in the mind of the interpreter were the keys to successful dream analysis. He was also the first to distinguish between dreams that stemmed from everyday life and the present state of the mind and body, the *insomnium*, and dreams that invoked deeper consideration of the dreamer's life at a mystical level, the *somnium*. The second classification of dreams was believed to foretell future events. It is for his innovative thinking and his commendably flexible approach to symbolic interpretation that Artemidorus is recognized as a prominent figure linking ancient beliefs about dream interpretation to the modern world.

Artemidorus's observations reflect an appreciation of symbolism and a grasp of the dreaming mind's implementation of metaphors that make him as a worthy forerunner to such modern dream innovators as **Sigmund Freud** and **Carl Jung**. Freud actually named his major work on dreams, *The Interpretation of Dreams*, as a way of indicating his debt to Artemidorus. As one of the very first individuals to employ an empirical approach to the analysis of dreams, Artemidorus is said to have investigated and analyzed no less then 3,000 dreams for the *Oneirocritica*.

Artemidorus believed that dreams were neither good nor bad. For this reason he did not touch on the specifics of nightmares. It is not the symbolism of a dream that makes it a nightmare. For instance, if a person suffering from arachnophobia dreamed about spiders she or he would more than likely awaken from that dream terrified and call it a nightmare. In contrast, a person not suffering from fear of spiders would probably not have the same reaction. It is because of considerations like these that Artemidorus stressed the importance of knowing the intimate details of the dreamer's life.

Unlike contemporary dream books, which are psychologically oriented, Artemidorus's book focuses on deciphering dreams as omens of the future. or messages from the gods. For example, Artemidorus (p. 125—see *Sources*) writes:

If the statues of the gods move [in a dream], it signifies fears and disturbances for all but those who are imprisoned or who intend to take a trip. It signifies that the former will be released, so that they can move about easily. It moves the latter from their dwelling place and leads them out.

In this passage and innumerable others, it is clear that the intention behind the interpretation is prediction of the future. Despite this overarching concern with omens of the future, Artemidorus's remarks reflect an appreciation of symbolism and a grasp of the dreaming mind's deployment of metaphors that make the *Oneirocritica* valuable reading for any serious student of dreams. Artemidorus's volume and other such works composed in the classical world also had a broad influence on the tradition of Muslim dream interpretation—a tradition which survives to this day in various parts of the Islamic world.

ASHANTI

The Ashanti, also known as the Akans, are a people who live in the central region of Ghana. As with other African societies, for the Ashanti dreams hold the status of superior realities, and, it has been suggested, for some individual Ashantis dreams have as much if not more reality than waking experiences. R.S. Rattray, for example, has reported if a husband learns that another has dreamed of sexual intercourse with his wife, he will sue the dreamer for adultery because their souls are believed to have had sexual intercourse.

In an ethnopsychiatric study of the Ashanti, M.J. Field focuses on the distinction frequently made between "free" or spontaneous dreams and stereotypical dreams that is, those dreams individuals have repeatedly. Field describes how certain common elements of dream narratives indicate what they represent. For instance, in a dream the theme of being chased—whether by a deity, an animal, or even a weapon—indicates an individual who is afraid of retribution for a sin.

ASSOCIATION FOR THE STUDY OF DREAMS

Several organizations and periodicals are devoted to the study of dreams, including the Association for the Study of Dreams (ASD), headquartered in Vienna, Virginia. While open to laypersons, the ASD is perhaps the closest thing to an interdisciplinary professional association focused on the study of dreams. ASD members are sent the ASD newsletter and a journal, *Dreaming*, on a quarterly basis. ASD hosts an annual meeting at which researchers present papers on dreams and workshops are held on various phases of dreamwork. ASD also provides information on such topics as setting up ongoing dream groups.

Some people believe that they are able to leave their bodies, spiritually, through the practice of astral projection.

ASTRAL PROJECTION

Astral projection refers to the supposed ability to travel—to project oneself—out of the body. Astral projection is the older term for what has come to be known as **out-of-body experiences**. This "projection" is conceptualized in terms of the soul or individual human consciousness traveling outside the physical body in a spiritual or astral body. The astral body is said to be an exact replica of the physical body but composed of subtler elements, etheric in nature, more akin to the life force than to matter. It is supposedly capable of detaching from the physical body at will, or under certain special circumstances. It can also spontaneously leave the physical body during sleep, trance or coma, under the influence of anesthetics or other drugs, or as the result of accidents. The astral body is the vehicle of consciousness, said to particularly embody desires and feelings. When it separates from the denser physical body, it takes with it the capacity for feeling. As one might well anticipate, the existence of such a body has not been proven to the satisfaction of mainstream science.

The concept of bilocation, the ability to be in two places at the same time, is associated with the notion of astral projection. Because a person cannot literally be in more than one place at the same time, one possible explanation is that the physical body is in one place while the astral body is in another.

Many everyday experiences of astral projection have been reported. Among the researchers who have studied this phenomenon is the British scientist Robert Crookall, who compared hundreds of cases in which people left the physical body and reentered it after traveling unseen in the astral body. Sylvan Muldoon and Hereward Carrington, in their famous books *The Phenomena of Astral Projection* and *The Projection of the Astral Body*, maintain that there are degrees of projection, ranging from fully conscious projection to unconscious projection, such as occurs during sleep.

Unconscious projection during sleep is often associated with certain types of dreams, such as "psychic" dreams in which one dreams about something happening many miles away and then later discovers that whatever one dreamed about (for instance, a conversation, a disaster) actually occurred. One possible explanation for such dreams is that during sleep the dreamer unconsciously projected his or her astral body, was spiritually present when the event occurred, and remembered the experience later as a dream.

Astral projection has also been used to explain the prevalence of dreams about flying. **Flying** is one of a handful of dream motifs that are so common that almost everybody has had them on more than one occasion. These motifs include such common scenarios as **falling dreams**, dreams of **nakedness** in public, and **unpreparedness dreams**. Such shared dreams tend to arise from experiences and anxieties fundamental to all people. Although flying is one of these shared motifs, it is difficult to clearly identify the common human experience that might account for the prevalence of flying dreams. (Note that flying was a widespread motif even before the advent of air-

planes, being extensively treated in **Artemidorus**'s ancient classic, the *Oneirocritica*.) One explanation sometimes put forward by occult and metaphysical writers is that during sleep everyone at times travels outside the physical body, unencumbered by such physical limitations as gravity. Such out-of-body experiences are then remembered as dreams in which the dreamer floats and flies.

ASTROLOGY

Astrology is the study or science of the stars. Often derided as medieval superstition, it nevertheless continues to fascinate the human mind. In fact, polls indicate that its popularity is growing.

Most people are familiar with only a tiny portion of the vast subject of astrology, namely, the twelve signs of the zodiac as they relate to the personality of individuals and the use of astrology for divinatory purposes. The Zodiac (literally, "circle of animals") is the "belt" constituted by the twelve signs: Aries, Taurus, Gemini, Cancer, Leo, Virgo, Libra, Scorpio, Sagittarius, Capricorn, Aquarius, and Pisces. The notion of the zodiac is very ancient, with roots in the early cited cultures of Mesopotamia.

The connection between astrology and dreams has been tentatively explored by a few astrologers. One would anticipate that natives of various signs would have more dreams related to the central themes of their sun sign (the sign the sun is in when one is born) than natives of other signs. For example, Cancers should have more dreams about eating, Sagittarians more dreams about long-distance journeys, Scorpios more dreams about sex, and so on.

Also, the moon is thought to be associated with the subconscious mind, which, if depth psy-

In astrology the signs of the zodiac are important symbols; the star groupings they represent supposedly have an influence on people's fates and subconsciousnesses.

chologists are correct, is the source of our dreams. Thus, dreamers should have more vivid, or perhaps more psychologically significant, dreams during a full moon. The water signs are related to the astral plane—the level of the cosmos on which it is said that we dream. Hence, dreams should play a larger role in the lives of natives with a predominance of water signs (Cancer, Scorpio, and Pisces) or with key planets located in the three houses corresponding to these signs— the fourth, eighth, and twelfth houses.

AUSTRALIA

The Australian Aborigines are divided into more than five hundred distinct tribal groups that have developed over a span of fifty thousand years.

Although these groups are very different, they have much in common regarding their beliefs about the human race and nature.

The various tribes all believe in the mutual interdependence of humanity and nature, on the need each has for the other, and on the need to bring the latter into the historical and ceremonial life of the former. According to the Aborigines, each individual must do what the great heroes did in the "dream-time," the mythical age of the past which is simultaneously the present. Humanity and nature exist and are as they are because of the personal actions of heroes in the past. A historical continuity with the heroic past is possible through rites of initiation that familiarize people with that past and thus make them vicarious participants in it. During these rights Aborigines reenact the doings of the hero or heroes concerned, and in so doing, act out the myth.

The common term used by Aborigines for the heroic past also means dreaming, and corresponds with a person's totem, which in this case is a myth marking the feats of a particular hero (or heroes). Dreaming is a symbol of the long-past heroic age, as well as the means of access to it. The Aborigines believe that life and death are part of a cycle beginning and ending in dream-time: the cycle is sustained by totems, ancestral sacred spots, and rituals that keep the tribe linked to the ancestors. During the experience of dreaming, the limitations of space and time are nonexistent, and it is believed that dreams reveal events which have happened or are going to happen in the future, through the mythical and practical information given by dead ancestors and heroes.

Past, present, and future coexist, and the eternal dream-time was manifested in the past through the heroes, in the present through the initiated, and, if the links between past and present are not broken, it will continue to be manifested in the future. By reliving the dream-time experiences of their heroes, the Aborigines believe they can be connected to the time of the heroes' creation and the power of their ancestors, who are still present in the world and protect people.

The dreams of Australian Aborigines represent the universe as it seems to them, and they often assert that in sleep they can see distant people, even those who are dead. A strong mutual interaction exists between dreaming and waking in the Aborigines' life, and they frequently fail to distinguish between waking events and dream events. It has been remarked that many of the rituals performed in dreams are applied to activities in later life, and many ceremonies are adopted directly from what is seen in visions or in sleep by special individuals.

Diverse explanations of dreams are given by the different Australian tribes. For instance, the Dieri tribe believe that the spirit of a dead person can visit a sleeper. When this occurs, the dream is reported to the medicine man, who, if he considers it to he a vision, gives special instructions.

The Narrang-ga say that the human spirit can leave the body in sleep and communicate with the spirits of others, or with the spirits of the dead who wander as ghosts in the bush.

The Jupagalk believe that a person in great pain can be helped by the dream visit of some dead friend. According to the Wurunjerri, who have the same belief, the spirit of each person, which they call Murup, can leave the body during sleep, particularly when the sleeper snores. The Murup, however, can also be sent out of the sleeper by means of evil magic. The human spirit is called Yambo by the Kurnai, who likewise believe that it can leave the body during sleep.

The Ngarigo believe that in dreams, which they call gung-ung-mura-nung-ya, they can see ghosts. The Yuin Gommeras believe in the possibility of receiving songs in dreams, as well as information about approaching enemies. They also think that relatives of a dead man can see who killed him in a dream. The same belief is shared by the Wiimbaio, who say that, when they dream such a thing, they have been to some other country, where a person has told them.

BED-WETTING (ENURESIS)

Bed-wetting, which is technically referred to as enuresis, is common in children up to about age three. Although diagnosed as a disorder (*primary enuresis*) after age three, it does not necessarily indicate a serious problem (e.g., at least 15 percent of all children continue bed-wetting up to age five). In some adults bed-wetting is related to physiological disorders or to a congenitally small bladder, but it is more often the result of excessive stress.

Contrary to what one might anticipate, bed-wetting is not associated with dreams. Most typically, episodes of enuresis occur in the first third of the evening, during non-REM (**rapid eye movement**) sleep (a time of low dream activity).

BERGSON, HENRI-LOUIS

Henri Bergson's (1859–1941) study of dreams is generally considered one of the most creative approaches to the topic. The French philosopher of evolution was born in Paris, where he was professor of philosophy at the College de France from 1900 until he retired because of ill health in 1921. He dedicated his life to teaching, lecturing, and writing, and in 1927 received the Nobel Prize in literature.

Bergson, whose thought owed much to the French philosophical tradition, was convinced that doctrines such as materialism and mechanism could not be considered philosophically tenable, and that no universal system was valid. Nevertheless, in his works he posited a general philosophy of duration and movement that, rather than defining everything in terms of being, permanence, and substance, as most earlier philosophers had done, started from the opposite viewpoint, namely, the assumption that the ultimate reality is time itself.

His major works include *Time and Free Will* (1888), *Matter and Memory* (1896), in which memory is regarded as the means through which human existence is made continuous, and *Creative Evolution* (1907). Among Bergson's minor works is his study on dreams, which was first given as a lecture before the Institut Psychologique on March 26, 1901, and later published in the *Revue Scientifique* of June 8, 1901.

Like other philosophers before him, Bergson accepted the somatic stimuli, or "optical," theory of dreams, according to which some of the visual patterns characterizing a dream may be the result of stimulation of the optic nerve. However, Bergson realized that somatic stimuli are only a product of the biology of dreaming, and he argued, like Freud, that further analysis of dreams was necessary and that the mechanism of memory should also be considered.

Bergson's previous studies of duration and movement had provided him with a considerable basis for his theory of dreams, according to which dreams are the direct link between sensation and memory. Bergson maintained that human beings forget nothing, and all past experiences, perceptions, thoughts, and emotions are collected in the memory from earliest childhood. Following the older association theory of perception, he asserted that memory images that rise to the surface correspond to immediate visual or tactile sensations, and to the mood of the dreamer. Thus, the thread of dreams is formed by memories, although the individual often does not recognize them because the memories are very old and are forgotten during the day, they are memories of objects that have been perceived absently during the day, or they are fragments of broken recollections that the memory brings together in an unrecognizable picture.

In the sleep state the mind is "disinterested" and is not forced to concentrate on a particular object or feeling. Also, the same faculties are active as during the day, although they are in a state of relaxation. While dreaming, the individual still perceives, remembers, and reasons, but lacks the effort required by the precision of the adjustment. Thus, for instance, because a sleeping person is unable to exert the effort required for concentration, the sound of a dog barking may be linked to the memory of a noisy meeting. In contrast, a positive effort would be required for this sound to be perceived as the barking of a dog. According to Bergson, the absence of this effort represents the only difference between the dreamer and the individual who is awake.

BERTI

Unlike other African peoples, the Berti, whose original homeland is the Tagabo Hills region in Northern Darfur province of the Republic of the Sudan, consider dreaming a private affair and only rarely discuss their dreams with others. They are not encouraged to dream or to remember their dreams, and a dreamless night is generally considered normal. They treat the dreams they do remember not as individual manifestations of the dreamer's psychology, but rather as cultural representations, in the sense that the meaning of particular dream motifs are recognized and shared by everyone in Berti society.

In Berti thought, the spirit, which all living things possess (although there is no clear agreement as to where it resides in the human body), is believed to be intangible and detachable from the body. At night during sleep, the spirit is thought to leave the body and wander in different places, or back and forth in time. Its expeditions are experienced as dreams.

According to Ladislav Holy in his 1991 study of Berti dream interpretation, the Berti regard certain dream recollections, which are distinguished by the presence of specific images, as accounts of privileged glances by the soul into the future. In Berti society, everyone is supposed to have the ability to interpret the meaning of such figures and accounts, although some are more skilled than others. Special rules are to be followed, although they are not always systematic and recourse to extra dream contexts such as the current status of the dreamer is often necessary. There are no specialized interpreters, although sometimes a kinsman, a close neighbor, or friend is consulted when a dreamer is not sure about the significance of the dream experience.

Interpretation focuses on particular signs that the dreamer considers significant for the meaning of the dream. The signs appearing in dreams have the character of symbols when they are not in direct relation to the things or events they refer to. An example of a symbol is the wind, which in a Berti dream is recognized as a sign of anything undesirable in the future. The art of interpretation among the Berti varies according to how well the interpreter knows the signs and symbols and the significance of the context of the dream.

BIBLE AND DREAMS

In biblical accounts, the divine–human encounter occurs in a variety of ways, including direct apparitions of God as well as visions and intellec-

In the Bible, Jacob experienced his final dream about God and His prophecy while on his way to Egypt (1870 engraving by Gustave Doré).

tual inspirations. Dreams are one of the more common forms of divine communication. From Genesis to Revelation, God communicates with people through this medium.

Unlike other ancient peoples, such as the Egyptians, ancient Hebrews never actively sought to induce dreams through special practices, because they believed such manipulative divination would provide only false dreams. Furthermore, the Israelites differed from most other Near Eastern peoples in attitudes toward dreams in that they did not view them as coming from the realm of the dead. They also had a different approach to dream interpretation based on principles drawn from the

Talmud, which contains the warnings of the prophets against false dreams and false interpreters.

An important difference between the ancient Jewish view of dreams and that of other peoples of the Near East is that the Jews, having become worshipers of one god rather than many special gods, believed that only this god could be the source of the divine revelations that came in their dreams. The Old Testament records only those dreams that helped to consolidate Judaism and confirm the chosen people's messianic vocation and the spiritual hegemony of their god. Most of the dreams chronicled in the Old Testament come at the beginning of vital stages in Israel's history.

For the biblical Jews, dreams had the function of summoning up events from the past and opening channels into the future. There were two types of dream accounts in Israel, auditory message dreams and symbolic dreams, which is the same division found more generally in the ancient Near East. In the Bible, symbolic dreams are reported solely by Gentiles—the pharaoh of the Exodus and Nebuchadnezzar—and, for this reason, symbolic dreams are less official than messenger dreams. According to Jewish belief, to derive their proper meaning, symbolic dreams must be interpreted by Jews.

In the Bible, the dream is a direct revelation from God concerning His involvement in human affairs. Some of those having dreams are prominent biblical characters, whereas others are just ordinary people. In the ancient world it was believed that God was more accessible to ordinary people in dreams than in daytime visions because in the latter a more subtle reality must compete with and overcome the perceptions of the senses. Thus, waking visions were obtained with difficulty, and only by those who were by nature already more spiritual.

The most prolific dreamers in the Hebrew Bible are the patriarchs, especially **Abraham, Jacob**, and **Joseph**. A particular characteristic of Biblical dreams is that different people, all concerned with the realization of a fundamental event, have dreams with parallel or convergent themes. For instance, in Genesis, Joseph, Jacob, Jacob's father, the pharaoh, and the pharaoh's officers all dream about the fulfillment of Joseph's destiny. Not all dreams and visions reported in the Bible originate from God, although almost all of them have a divine source.

There are fewer references to dreams in the New Testament, and there is no record of Jesus's dreams, although the Gospels, Acts, and Revelation continue to present the experience of God-inspired dreams. The New Testament contains such dreams as Joseph's dreams, Peter's trance dream, the dream of the wise men, and the dream of Revelation. Some of the more significant dreams of the New Testament are found in St. Matthew's gospel, which reports the announcement of Christ's conception, an event revealed directly to Joseph while he is awake: "Behold, the angel of the Lord appeared unto him in a dream, saying, Joseph, thou son of David, fear not to take unto thee Mary thy wife: for that which is conceived in her is of the Holy Ghost" (Matt. 1:20). The flight into Egypt is connected to three dreams: the dream of the wise men, who are warned not to return to Herod; the dream in which an angel tells the Holy Family to go into Egypt to escape Herod; and, after Herod's death, the dream in which an angel again appears to Joseph in Egypt, telling him to return to the land of Israel.

One of the most curious dreams in the New Testament is that of the wife of Pontius Pilate, who urges her husband to release Jesus, rather than Barabbas, "for I have suffered many things this day in a dream because of him" (Matt. 27:19). Biblical dreams are almost all fulfilled, but in this case the advice in the dream is not followed, and Jesus is crucified. This event presents a fragment of an older tradition that can be found in the early Coptic church in which both Moses and Jesus were seen as powerful magicians. Thus, in the noncanonical Gospel of Nicodemus, the Jewish priests actually tell Pilate that Jesus is a conjurer, and with respect to Pilate's wife's dream warning, the chief priests reply: "Did we not say unto thee, he is a magician? Behold, he hath caused thy wife to dream."

BIZARRENESS OF DREAMS

"I had the weirdest dream last night" is a familiar comment. The problem with this assertion is that it seems to imply that dreams should somehow *not* be bizarre, but in fact dreams often present us with twisted, surreal landscapes that almost always depart in significant ways from the logic of our everyday world. There are two major explanations for the surrealistic quality of our dreams, one physiological and the other psychological.

In the **activation-synthesis model** of dreaming, which stresses the purely physiological correlates of dreaming, it is asserted that during **rapid eye movement (REM) sleep**, the stage of sleep most closely connected with dreaming, the brain sends essentially random electrical signals to the higher mental centers of the forebrain. The forebrain then sorts through these signals and attempts to create a meaningful experience. The many dreams that are just masses of incoherent images represent incoming groups of signals that the brain was simply not able to synthesize.

The second explanation is **Sigmund Freud**'s psychological view, which theorizes that the pur-

pose of dreams is to allow us to satisfy in fantasies the instinctual urges that society judges unacceptable. So that we do not awaken as a result of the strong emotions that would be evoked if we were to dream about the literal fulfillment of such desires, the part of the mind that Freud called the censor transforms the dream content so as to disguise its true meaning. This transformation results in dreams that often seem bizarre and weird.

BOSS, MEDARD

Medard Boss (1903–1990) was a mid-twentieth-century therapist who took what he referred to as a phenomenological approach to dreams. The term *phenomenology* has more than one meaning, but in this context it refers to an early twentieth-century philosophical movement that attempted to describe the essential structure of an observed phenomenon—as it is, so to speak—without compelling it to fit any existing theory about what the phenomenon should be. As such, phenomenology is more of a method than what we traditionally think of as a philosophy. While subsequent philosophers have realized that the ideal of "presuppositionless" inquiry advocated by phenomenology's founder, Edmund Husserl, is probably impossible, the descriptive method which he formulated has stimulated many fruitful analyses.

For Boss, a phenomenological approach to dreams meant that the therapist analyzed patients' dreams in terms of their given content—without making a distinction between their surface content and some unobserved, deeper content postulated by **Sigmund Freud, Carl Jung**, or someone else. Boss believed that by so analyzing dreams one could discover the issues with which the dreamer was grappling. Once the issues were found and clarified, the patient

Dreams are very important in Buddhism, which views dreams as very often having to do with prophecy or as resulting from the influence of a deity. (Buddhist statues at the Wat Yai Chai-mongkol, Ayutthaya, Thailand.)

would then be in a position to make choices that would improve the situation.

BUDDHISM

Buddhism is one of the great religions of the world, third in size (in terms of number of adherents) after **Christianity** and **Islam**. Originating as a splinter sect from Hinduism (much as Christianity began as an outgrowth of **Judaism**), Buddhism spread throughout Asia, all but disappearing in **India**, the land of its birth. Buddhism shares many of its basic notions, such as the doctrine of reincarnation, with Hinduism.

As in other areas of the world, Asians have speculated extensively about the significance of dreams, often coming to much the same conclusion as other cultures. Certain dreams, for instance, have often been regarded as messages from the gods. In Buddhism, which claims no supreme divinity as such, dreams can nevertheless represent messages from divine agencies.

The earliest Buddhist scriptures, for example, tell the story of how the future Buddha's mother had a dream in which four kings carried her bed to a mountain peak where four queens greeted her with jewels and escorted her to a palace of gold: "A white elephant with six shining ivory tusks appeared and painlessly pierced her side with a thrust of its tusk. She awoke to the song of a blue bird and realized that she had immaculately conceived" (Van de Castle, p. 39—see *Sources*). This dream was interpreted as signifying that she was pregnant with someone who would become either a world ruler or a world teacher.

Where India outstrips other cultural traditions is in the development of the theme of this life or this world as a kind of dream. According to the mainstream of Hindu religious thought—which was adopted wholesale by Buddhism—the individual soul is trapped in the sufferings involved with life in this world. And because of reincarnation, even death does not release one from this world. In most of the religious traditions of southern Asia, including Buddhism, release or liberation from the cycle of death and rebirth is the ultimate goal of the spiritual life. A metaphor often used to describe the insight that leads directly to liberation is awakening from a dream. However, while certain schools of philosophical Hinduism have argued that this world is literally as *insubstantial* as a dream, most schools of Buddhist thought have emphasized that this world is as *unimportant* as a dream.

In the *Questions of King Milinda* (an early Indian Buddhist work), it is said that the persons who dream are (1) those under the influence of a deity, (2) those who dream under the influence of their experiences, and (3) those with prophetic dreams. This relative sophistication did not carry into the Theravadin tradition, in which dreams generally came to be regarded as the resulting from worldly attachments, and thus as distracting. There was, nevertheless, a distinction drawn between two forms of prophetic dreams: auspicious and inauspicious. The former result from the direct influence of a Buddha, and the latter from the unrefined tendencies of human nature. Some of Buddhism's most interesting contributions to dreams and dream lore have been carried out by Tibetan Buddhists (see **Yoga** and **Tibet**).

GO CONFIDENTLY IN THE
DIRECTION OF YOUR
DREAMS. LIVE THE LIFE
YOU'VE IMAGINED.

—HENRY DAVID THOREAU

CAMPBELL, JOSEPH

Joseph Campbell (1904–1987) was a scholar and writer who, shortly before his death, became something of a pop culture phenomenon. Campbell was at the forefront of the group of thinkers through whose work the notion of "myth" was reevaluated by Western society, so that **mythology**, in the sense of "sacred story," is now viewed as something worthwhile, and even necessary for human beings. Campbell's now-classic early work on hero myths, *The Hero with a Thousand Faces*, was consciously appropriated by creative writers, and even by movie producers such as George Lucas, producer of the popular *Star Wars* series.

Campbell worked within the larger tradition of Jungian psychology, a school of thought that examines mythology for the light it throws on psychological processes. **Carl Jung** understood myths as manifestations of the **collective unconscious**, the part of the mind that acts as a storehouse of myths and symbols to which all human beings have access and which is viewed as the ultimate source of every society's mythology. Much of traditional Jungian analysis focuses on the interpretation of dreams. Jung found that the dreams of his patients frequently contained images with which they were completely unfamiliar but which seemed to reflect symbols that could be found somewhere in the mythological systems of world culture. The notion of the collective unconscious was used to explain this phenomenon.

Campbell did not develop a new view of dreams and their relationship to mythology. He is, rather, responsible for popularizing the Jungian view, which can be stated succinctly as "dreams are individual myths and myths are society's dreams." In Campbell's own words:

> Dream is a personal experience of that deep, dark ground that is the society's dream. The myth is the public dream and the dream is the private myth. If your private myth, your dream, happens to coincide with that of society, you are in good accord with your group. If it isn't, you've got an adventure in the dark forest ahead of you. (*The Power of Myth*, p. 40—see *Sources*).

CANCER DREAMS

In general, the dreams of those who are dying often contain imagery that symbolizes the continuation of life after death. This expectation of death as a form of rebirth into another plane of existence is helpful to those who fear dying because it gives them hope that death is more than passing into oblivion. Having any kind of religious faith often contributes to the ease with which a person will accept the impending loss of life. The belief in an afterlife can help to diminish the fear that many feel when examining their own mortality; by lessening the fear it will decrease the frequency of nightmares as one approaches death. For example, a woman who suffered from terminal cancer experienced the recurring dream of a hand beckoning from the far side of a river. Each time she had this dream the river was a little narrower, until at last she could step over it to the other side. This last dream occurred shortly before her death. It seemed that the river in her dreams represented the river of life and that by crossing it in her dream she felt she was ready to cross it in her waking life as well.

Dreams that diagnose cancer, or at least give the dreamer the idea that an examination may be prudent, have frequently been observed. The writer Marc Ian Barasch suffered from recurring nightmares that involved his neck. After a particularly poignant dream, involving an iron pot filled with red-hot coals that were hung from beneath his chin, he decided to seek out medical professionals. Although the initial round of tests detected nothing, the nightmares continued and Barasch insisted they run more tests. Eventually, doctors detected a hard lump in his neck that turned out to be cancerous. He was treated for thyroid cancer in the very early stages and survived; however, the outcome may not have been so fortuitous if his recurrent nightmares had not driven him to insist that they continue to look. By prompting early detection, the nightmares were likely responsible for saving his life.

Nightmares may also contribute to the dropping of habits that are hazardous to one's health. This was the case of William C. Dement, who coined the term **rapid eye movement (REM) sleep**. At one time, Dement had been a heavy smoker. During this period, he dreamed he had inoperable cancer of the lungs. In this dream, he went through the fear of dying. He experienced the sadness he would face with the prospect of not being able to watch his family grow and the grief his family would go though because of their loss. He quit smoking the next day.

CASTANEDA, CARLOS

Carlos Castaneda (1925–1998) is a popular writer trained as an anthropologist. He wrote a series of books recounting his training as a "sorcerer" under Don Juan, a Yaqui Ian **shaman**, in which he presents himself as a skeptical social scientist who gradually enters into Don Juan's world, eventually taking on the goals and values of his Yaqui mentor. In the first few volumes of the best-selling series, Don Juan attempts to shatter Castaneda's conventional worldview through controlled experiences with psychedelic substances. Initially published during the peak of the sixties drug culture, *The Teachings of Don Juan: A Yaqui Way of Knowledge* became an overnight sensation because of the support it seemed to offer for the drug culture's contention that psychedelics opened the mind to new realities. In later volumes, however, the importance of drugs is diminished, relativized as rather crude tools necessary for piercing Castaneda's stubborn grip on ordinary reality.

Critics have dismissed Castaneda's work as pure fiction, exploiting a gullible public's desire for ancient wisdom, myth, and magic in a guise palatable to modern temperaments. Native American critics in particular have harshly attacked Castaneda for exploiting the New Age's interest in romanticized and sensationalized American Indian religious practices. However, whether fictional or not, Castaneda's books have created an appealing world in which an entire generation of readers have vicariously participated.

Beyond psychedelics, Don Juan instructed Castaneda in other techniques for "stopping the world" (interrupting the plausibility structure of ordinary reality). One of these approaches is what is today called **lucid dreaming**, becoming aware that one is dreaming during a dream and exercising control over the dream. As an initial technique for accomplishing this, Castaneda was instructed to try to remember to gaze at the palms of his hands during a dream. More advanced techniques involve what the Western occult tradition would call **astral projection**— separating one's consciousness from the body and gazing back at one's physical form. Don Juan, however, gives a unique interpretive twist to this experience, instructing Castaneda that his double

is dreaming him at the same time he is dreaming his double. Thus, the **out-of-body experience** is placed in the context of the sorcerer's larger worldview, relativizing ordinary reality and emphasizing the individual's ability to exercise control over his or her world.

CENSORSHIP IN DREAMS

The notion that dreams provide an avenue for the expression of normally repressed desires while simultaneously disguising and censoring our real urges was systematically formulated by **Sigmund Freud**, the father of psychoanalysis. In Freud's view, the purpose of dreams is to allow us to satisfy in fantasies the instinctual urges that society judges to be unacceptable in some way, such as the infantile urge to kill a repressive parent. If, however, we were to dream about the actual, overt murder of one of our parents, the emotions evoked by the dream would wake us up. So that our sleep is not continually disturbed by such dreams, the part of the mind that Freud called the censor modifies and disguises the content of our dreams so that such strong emotions are not evoked. Thus, instead of killing a parent, we might dream about our brother (a projection of ourselves) throwing our employer (a parental figure) out of a window. Freud referred to the process of censoring and transforming dream contents into less disturbing images as the **dreamwork** and explicitly identified five processes through which dreams are censored: **displacement, condensation, symbolization, projection,** and **secondary revision**.

CHASE DREAMS

You are walking down a dark street that you realize is unfamiliar to you. Out of the silence you

Chase dreams are often indications of being under stress or of suffering some sort of emotional trauma.

hear steps behind you. As panic sets in, your pace quickens. The footsteps behind you also increase their tempo, keeping up with you. You start to run, your fear giving unusual speed to your gait. Yet the menacing presence begins to gain ground. By now you are at a full-out sprint, only to realize that, whatever or whoever it is, is right behind you, close enough to grab you. The next thing you know, you are in the safety of your bed, a cold sweat covers your body and your breathing is shallow and labored.

Nightmares in which the dreamer is pursued by a menacing figure are one of the most common types of dreams. While they occur most frequently among children, they are also common for adults. This is particularly true after one experiences a traumatic incident or is involved in other kinds of stressful situations, though they are often more poignant when caused by a trauma. Chase dreams are often associated with the contextualization of emotions resulting in unexpected dream imagery. The most common emotions that are capable of invoking these particular "picture metaphors" are fear, vulnerability, and guilt.

CHAUCER, GEOFFREY

The dream vision constituted one of the most popular poetic forms in fourteenth- and fifteenth-century English literature, and its influence is to be found in almost all the poets of the fifteenth century. This specific medieval poetic tradition was primarily a vehicle for courtly love poetry. The elements characteristic of this school of poetry can be found in the thirteenth-century *Roman de lei Rose* by the Italians Guillaume de Lorris and Jean de Meun. It was the most influential model for several court poets, including Geoffrey Chaucer, who also translated it.

Born in London, Geoffrey Chaucer (1342–1400), the greatest literary figure of medieval England, was the son of a prosperous wine merchant. He became a page at an early age at the court of Lionel, earl of Ulster, where the ideals of chivalry were considered very important. He took part in a military campaign in France during the Hundred Years' War. During one of his trips to Italy, he went to Florence, where he first read the works of Boccaccio and Petrarch, whose influence on his poetry was significant. Throughout most of his adult life he occupied various positions as a government official, such as justice of the peace and clerk of the king's works. He died in London and was buried in Westminster Abbey.

The Canterbury Tales and Troilus and Criseyde are Chaucer's major works. The Canterbury Tales (1387) is a collection of stories told by a group of thirty pilgrims traveling from London to the shrine of Saint Thomas Becket. The stories of the pilgrims, who are typical members of late medieval English society, reflect Chaucer's interest in contemporary attitudes toward religion, love, and marriage. In Troilus and Criseyde, which is an adaptation of Boccaccio's Filostrato, Chaucer explores the complexity of a love relationship, weaving a story of fate, fortune, and personal weakness that finally condemns the lovers' search for happiness.

In addition to translating the Roman de la Rose, Chaucer wrote four dream poems: The Book of the Duchess, The House of Fame, The Parliament of Fowls, and the prologue to The Legend of Good Women. The narrative form of the first three of his dream-poems, which are written as dream visions, recounts a speaker's dream. The choice of this narrative form, which connects visionary experience with ordinary reality, was typical of Chaucer's contemporaries, although it was also used in classical and biblical models.

Chaucer was familiar with the Aeneid, the biblical and apocryphal visions, and the works of Dante, among many others. The most important influence, however, was Guillaume de Lorris, who wrote the first portion of the Roman de lei Rose, numerous familiar elements of which can be found in Chaucer's dream-poems: the May morning, the garden, the god of love, the birds, the paintings on walls.

Chaucer's earliest dream-poem, The Book of the Duchess, was inspired by the death of Blanche, first wife of John of Gaunt, in September 1369, and was written shortly after that date. It is apparently a vision of the otherworld, in which the visionary not only visits another place but also learns a truth from an authoritative person whom he meets there. Throughout the poem, the visionary is rescued from a sickness that isolates him from the vitality of nature through his exposure to an old work of art. Then he gains advice through a subsequent dream and is finally led to the creation of a new work of literary art. The idyllic landscape of the dream vision in The Book of the Duchess is treated in a very inventive way, characterized by the lively juxtaposition of vivid and contrasting images.

The date of The House of Fame, Chaucer's second poem, is uncertain, but it was probably written in the middle or late 1370s, remaining unfinished. In this work, the narrator dreams that he is in a temple of Venus in which the walls are decorated with the story of Virgil's Aeneid. When he leaves the temple, he finds himself in a desert from which he is rescued by a golden eagle. After a long discussion with the eagle, he reaches the temple of the goddess Fame, and the House of Tidings, where he sees the "man of great authority." But the poem breaks off here, rendering its interpretation very difficult.

Chaucer's third dream-poem, The Parliament of Fowls, probably dates from 1382. In this book also, the narrator is still awake and reads a book about a dream, which then provides the impetus for his own dream. He dreams that he enters a beautiful walled garden in which he sees a temple full of famous suffering lovers. The goddess Nature is also in the garden, surrounded by many birds looking for their mates. Among them, a female eagle declares that she needs another year to make up her mind about choosing her mate.

The prologue to *The Legend of Good Women* is the last, and perhaps most enigmatic of Chaucer's dream-poems. In the prologue, which offers another example of Chaucer's fascination with the relationship between books, dreams, and actual experiences, the god of love accuses Chaucer of having libeled women in works such as *Troilus and Criseyde*, and he orders him to write a series of legends about women who have suffered for their love.

In other works Chaucer included dreams and their interpretations, as well as several elaborate discussions of the significance of dreams. Besides the skeptical statement about the validity of dreams made by Pandarus and Cassandra's serious interpretation of one of Troilus's dreams in *Troilus and Criseyde*, a considerable discussion about the significance of dreams—Chauntecleer's dream of the fox—can be found in *The Nun's Priest's Tale* in *The Canterbury Tales*.

THE CHILD ARCHETYPE

The Swiss psychotherapist **Carl Jung** asserted that much of world mythology and folklore represented manifestations of what he called the **collective unconscious**. The collective unconscious represents our inheritance of the collective experience of humankind, storing humanity's experiences in the form of archetypes (or prototypes) that unconsciously predispose us to organize our personal experiences in certain ways. Jung further asserted that the archetypes of the collective unconscious shape the content of our dreams, emerging in various forms of **archetypal dream images**.

One of the more familiar archetypes is that of the "divine child," which should not be confused with the so-called inner child, which represents the child personality we sacrificed on the altar of adulthood. The inner child often embodies a playful, creative side of the self that shows up in dreams as a fully formed child who has already acquired the skills of walking, language, and so on. The divine child archetype, by way of contrast, is an embodiment of the transformational power that propels us along the path of personal growth that Jung called the individuation process. It is also a symbol of our total self, as opposed to the limited sense of self that Jung called the ego or the limited personality of our childhood.

CHILDREN'S NIGHTMARES

Children's nightmares have been noted for centuries. A sixteenth-century Belgian doctor, for instance, made a list naming the fifty-two most common diseases affecting the children of that time. Nightmares received a position as number nine on that list. Nightmares occur more commonly among children than they do among adults. Studies have shown that adults who suffer from chronic nightmares often have exhibited these problems since childhood.

Patricia Garfield conducted a study involving 120 children, 109 from America and eleven from India; the majority of these children were between the ages of five and eight. She managed to collect a sample of 247 dreams, which she classified simply as "good dreams" or "bad dreams." Out of this total, 158 (sixty-four percent) she cataloged as "bad dreams." Nightmares with an overarching theme of being chased were reported seventy-seven times. Dreams in which the child senses danger but is never directly threatened accounted for a significantly lower number of the nightmares, with only twenty-eight reported. Finally, in the third place, are nightmares in which the dreamer is injured or killed by accidental means. This category had twenty-six dreams.

There were only eighty-nine dreams with a positive theme reported in this particular study. Thirty dreams were of general good times, playing with friends, and trips and holidays. Fifteen dreams involved the dreamer receiving some sort of gift. These two classifications represented fifty percent of the total good dreams. Garfield reported these findings in her book *Nightmares in Children*. She also took time to offer parents general advice on how to deal with the frequency of nightmares.

David Foulkes conducted a long-term study on children's dreams, as well. Based on his observations, he concluded that the dreams of young children and young adults do not differ greatly from each other. Contrary to Garfield, Foulkes found that the dreams of children were not predominantly disagreeable or terrifying. He reached these observations based on his initial laboratory studies of two groups of fourteen children, but his study came to include approximately forty in total after additional subjects were added to replace those who dropped out. While Foulkes believed that the only reliable representation of dreams comes from laboratory research, his evidence is in disagreement with the general psychiatric opinion.

Studies have discovered several traits common in children's dreams. One of the more remarkable characteristics is that children seem to have significantly more nightmares in which they are the victims of violence. Nightmares in which the dreamer is pursued, whether by monsters, strangers, or wild animals, are the most common type of dreams with negative content. There is also a general lack of pleasant exchanges; this is especially true for boys. Fear and fear-

Children frequently experience nightmares when they sleep. In fact, they tend to experience many more dreams in which they are victims of violence than adults do.

related emotions are twice as frequent in the dreams of young children when compared to the dreams of adults. This may be, in part, because children often feel that they have no control over their waking lives. They are anxious about their ability to control external events, and this feeling is reflected in the content of their dreams.

One of the leading researchers into the phenomena of nightmares is Ernest Hartmann. He developed a theory of "boundaries" regarding the frequency of not only nightmares, but of remembering one's dreams. Hartmann maintains that, generally speaking, the nightmares of children stem from their underlying feelings of vulnerability. As a child grows, he or she may develop a stronger defense to the stresses of waking life. Children in this group have what Hartmann calls, "thick boundaries." They often cease to experience nightmares as they grow up, except for the same sporadic bad dreams that affect the majority of the population. They also have a significantly lower frequency of remembering their dreams. At the other end of the spectrum are children with "thin boundaries." These individuals often retain a sense of the vulnerability they experienced during their childhood; they continue to experience vivid nightmares into adulthood.

A discussion of nightmares in children would be incomplete without mentioning night terrors. While some sleep researchers insist that they are not exactly nightmares because they occur during the fourth stage of sleep and not during the **rapid eye movement (REM)** cycle, the terrifying effect that they have on children is undeniable. The exact cause and source of these experiences is unknown, but studies have shown that, for the most part, the frequency of night terrors decreases as the child ages. In one study of twenty-three children who regularly experienced night terrors, twenty-two had the phenomena stop completely after the removal of their adenoids. The correlation between the two has not been researched fully, but the original study opened the door for further investigation.

CHINA

The mention of dreams in Chinese history dates back over 4,000 years. The ancient Chinese almanac, the *T'ung Shu*, has been in circulation nearly that long. It contains a section on dreams called "Chou Kung's Book of Auspicious and Inauspicious Dreams." This specific section has been dated to around 1020 B.C.E. Chou Kung, who is still associated with dreaming to this day, was the author.

The *T'ung Shu* divides dreams into seven different categories; it discusses the symbolism of these categories independently of one another. In the section regarding the human body, it states, for example, that to dream of one's **teeth** falling out indicates that one's parents are in danger. If one dreams about the rising of the sun or moon, his or her family will be prosperous in the future. These and other dreams of a similar nature are discussed in the section on the heavens and weather. **Animal dreams** are particularly relevant in ancient Chinese culture; dreams in which a parrot is calling to you is prophetic of an upcoming quarrel that has the potential to be quite serious, while dreams of a swallow flying to you indicate the visit of a dear friend from far away.

The *Lie-tseu* employs the Taoist approach to dream interpretation. In order to comprehend this principle fully, it is important to understand Taoist doctrine, which concerns the unity of the universe and the relativity of the material world. Concepts are empty without their contrasting opposite. The *Lie-tseu* divides dreams into several different classifications, such as: ordinary dreams, which are merely random byproducts of the mind without any previous emotion or influence; dreams of terror; dreams of what the dreamer thought of the previous day; dreams of waking, which are the residue of the dreamer's actions throughout the day; and dreams of joy.

The *Lie-tseu* discusses the need for harmony in one's life, and how our dreaming mind compensates for the imbalances in our waking lives. The Taoist concept of yin and yang exemplifies this principle. For instance, if one is hungry in the waking world, he or she may dream of taking or of having abundant food. In the same way, a person who is wealthy in the physical aspects of life may dream of giving to the less fortunate. A dream of crossing water may indicate that the yin is particularly strong in that individual's life, while walking through a great fire of some sort may indicate the yang is of greater strength. The Taoist approach also includes the use of astrological factors for explaining the meaning of specific dream symbols.

Like other traditional societies, many Chinese have believed that many dreams originated from the realm of the dead. They separated the soul into two distinct forms: the *p'o* and the *hun*. The *p'o* is considered to be the "material soul." It is the physical essence that gives life to the body and then ceases to exist after death. Co-existing with the *p'o* is the *hun*; this spiritual soul could depart from the body while the person is asleep yet retain the appearance of the physical body. During its nocturnal journeys the *hun* often visited the land of the dead, where it communed with the ancestors of the dreamer, but it could also communicate with the souls of others who were asleep. These interludes make themselves known to the dreamer in the form of dreams.

The Chinese developed the practice of acupuncture, which gave them a more complete understanding of the energy fields in and around the human body. Because of this knowledge, they considered it dangerous to awaken a sleeping person. When the *hun* is traveling out of the body, the person must wake up according to the soul's timing. If one was awakened abruptly from sleep, the consequences could be dire; should the *hun*

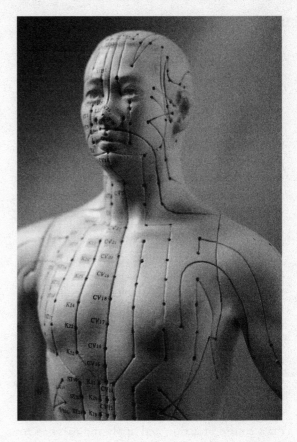

In acupuncture, the energy in one's body can be manipulated by using needles in key parts of the body. This same energy is an important part of dreaming, according to this Chinese philosophy.

be unable to return to the body, the sleeper would be susceptible to chronic health problems or even madness. Alarm clocks and other abrupt means of awakening the body are violent to the soul and thought to result in a variety of negative side effects.

Dream incubation was also a widely observed practice in various temples throughout China; up until around the sixteenth century,

Chinese society expected prominent political figures to seek **dream guidance** periodically to maintain their balance and objectivity. The sequence of preparatory rituals that one went through before receiving a dream usually began with the supplicant burning incense as an offering before an image of a specific god. Prayer or some ceremonial chanting often followed, all of which would invoke the favor of the temple deity. One must note, however, that not all dreams were sought in a temple setting. In the province of Fu-Kien, people called upon their ancestors for dream revelations by sleeping on a grave.

Upon the reception of the requested dream—if indeed the supplicant received one— he or she would seek to establish if a god did, in fact, send the dream. Once the dreamer was able to establish that the dream was divinely inspired, she or he was then free to spend time in careful consideration as to the symbolic meaning or, as often was the case, seek out a professional dream interpreter. Once the true meaning of the dream was deciphered, the dreamer was able to decide on a course of action and apply the message to his or her waking life.

CHRISTIANITY, EARLY

The Christian **Bible** gives dreams, particularly symbolic dreams, a mixed review. While the biblical God does communicate through dreams, they are clearly a less momentous mode of communication, because individuals particularly close to God receive His messages while they are awake. Usually only pagans receive symbolic dreams, which require interpretation.

The early Christians, especially those in the eastern part of the Roman Empire who would eventually constitute the Orthodox church, generally followed in the tradition of taking symbolic dreams (as opposed to visions) less seriously than waking visions. While acknowledging that God could be experienced in dreams, they were also careful to note that dreams are often no more than the eruption of irrational emotions into one's sleeping consciousness. Gregory of Nyssa, for instance, asserted that many dreams reflect the animal side of our nature, the offspring of the passions of anger and desire, a view not far from **Sigmund Freud**'s. He also noted a more mundane class of dreams that arise from traces of memory of our daily routines. Origen, on the other hand, asserted that God sometimes sent messages to the faithful in dreams and noted that many pagans were converted by dreams. Thus, the early Christian view of the significance of dreams can be described as generally balanced.

CHUANG-TZU

The classical Chinese philosophy of Taoism is a way of looking at the world in terms of a unified whole. The separate actions of the parts reflect and correspond to the larger actions of the whole. This union is depicted in the concept of the yin and the yang, the opposed yet inseparable "poles" of everything that is—male and female, positive and negative, up and down.

The dynamic link between opposites, in which yin is continually changing into yang and vice versa, is an appropriate perspective for understanding an oft-repeated story of Chuang-tzu, an ancient Taoist philosopher. It is said that Chuang-tzu once dreamed that he was a butterfly. Upon awakening, he asked himself if he was a man dreaming that he was a butterfly, or a butterfly dreaming that he was a man.

This story has frequently been cited in the context of discussions of the reality of the world as we experience it, as well as in discussions of the felt reality of dreams. With respect to the latter line of thought, it has often been observed that while we are dreaming we rarely question the reality of our dreams, accepting the most absurd situations as fact, until we awaken. And it is usually only from the perspective of waking consciousness that we can judge our dreams to have been bizarre or ridiculous.

As important as this point is, it nevertheless ignores the importance of Taoism as a perspective for understanding Chuang-tzu's statement. While this ancient sage undoubtedly was remarking on the seeming reality of dreams, he was also picturing his waking self as a man and his sleeping self as a butterfly to a dynamic yang-yin relationship. As the seasons cyclically alternate from hot to cold and back again, as night alternates with day, and so on, so do we alternate back and forth between sleeping and waking. This being so, a Taoist might say, Why should we call one real and the other an illusion? Both seem to be necessary to human life, so why depreciate dreams (yin) at the expense of so-called waking consciousness (yang) This seems to be the deeper import of Chuang-tzu's story.

CICERO

The Roman orator and statesman Marcus Tullius Cicero (106–43 B.C.E.) wrote a variety of philosophical works during periods of forced retirement from public life. Most of his philosophical works are dialogues between distinguished Romans and young men just beginning their political careers, preceded by an introduction in defense of philosophical studies.

Among his works on logic are *Academica* (45 B.C.E.), on the dispute between dogmatists and skeptics adhering to the philosophical doctrines of **Plato**'s Academy about the criteria of truth, and *Topica* (44 B.C.E.). *De finibus bonorum et malorum* (45 B.C.E.), *Tusculanae disputationes* (45 B.C.E.), and *De officiis* (44 B.C.E.) are his major ethical writings, whereas *De oratore* (55 B.C.E.) is among his rhetorical works. *De natura deorum, De divinatione,* and *De fato* (45–44 B.C.E.) present Epicurean, Stoic, and Academic arguments and counterarguments about religion and cosmology.

Cicero's *De republica* (51 B.C.E.) contains the famous *Dream of Scipio*, in which dreams are utilized as a convenient mode of exposition. This literary dream portrays the state of virtuous souls after death, which is a more pleasant existence in the region above the moon. It also reveals Scipio's own future, foretells Rome's victory over Carthage, and finally shows Scipio the movements of the heavens and celestial objects, as well as of the earth in its entirety.

Particularly in his essay *De divinntione*, Cicero composed a sophisticated analysis of dreams, and much of what he said anticipated later criticism of all forms of dream interpretation. He criticized the popular conviction that dreams might be prophetic, maintaining that no divine energy inspires dreams and visions. His analysis asked such questions as, Why do the gods not warn us of impending events when we are awake rather than during sleep? How can one distinguish between true and false dreams?

Cicero took little account of cures indicated in dreams; rather, he asserted that human intellect alone has to be considered sufficient to provide for humanity's own future welfare. He also maintained that because there are no objects in nature with which dreams have a necessary con-

Cicero analyzed dreams in his work *De divinntione* in which he asserted his belief that dreams were not prophetic; they were simply the mind thinking about what was happening in the waking life.

nection, and because it is impossible to achieve a sure interpretation of them, dreams should not receive credence, nor be entitled to our respect. Dreams, according to Cicero, are simply the overflow from our waking life.

Although he was highly skeptical about dreams, he was nevertheless very concerned with one of his own dreams, in which he saw Octavius as a man who would rise to supreme power in Rome. In the struggle for power after the death of Julius Caesar, Octavius emerged the victor.

Cicero and his brother Quintus, who had provoked the enmity of Mark Antony, were included in the purge lists and were killed on demand of Antony himself.

CIRCADIAN RHYTHMS

Circadian rhythms are biological cycles that take place every twenty-four hours. Human body temperature, for example, rises and falls in regular twenty-four-hour cycles. Among other behaviors, these cycles make it natural to sleep during the night and to be awake in the daytime. When circumstances such as night-shift work dictate otherwise, the natural sleep cycle—and, as a consequence, the regular dream cycle—is altered. Shift workers often sleep less, for example, as a result of the greater state of physiological arousal that accompanies the circadian rhythm's daylight cycle. Current research indicates that reduction in total sleep time appears to be at the expense of **rapid eye movement (REM) sleep**, the sleep stage during which our most vivid dreaming occurs. Thus, day sleepers tend to have a less active dream life than night sleepers.

CLAIRVOYANCE

Clairvoyance is related to such terms as **ESP** (extrasensory perception), telepathy, and mediumship, and these terms are often used imprecisely and interchangeably. Clairvoyance (literally, "clear seeing") refers to psychic sensitivity, especially in the form of visual information.

One "classic" parapsychology procedure used by J.B. Rhine and other early researchers during the 1950s and 60s was to pair off subjects into senders and receivers, requiring one subject to attempt to send a mental picture to the other. In his experiments Rhine used a limited set of symbols—circles, crosses, squares, and wavy lines—which he placed on cards. Subsequent experimenters used more complex images.

Experimental studies of dream clairvoyance have used this same basic model, but with the receiving subject sleeping during the experiment, the idea being that the image projected by the sender will show up in the receiver's dreams. Even though this basic technique is quite old, going back at least as far as 1819, it was not until the Maimonides Project on Paranormal Dreams in 1962 that the format for dream clairvoyance experimentation was formalized. The Maimonides Project (so called because the dream laboratory housing the project was at Maimonides Hospital in Brooklyn) was initiated by Montague Ullman, who was chairman of the psychiatry department. Two years later he was joined by psychologist Stanley Krippner. Together they published numerous articles and a popular book, *Dream Telepathy* (1973).

While the specifics of different series of Maimonides experiments varied widely, the basic format was to hook up the sleeping receiver to an EEG (electroencephalograph) machine and signal the sender each time the sleeper entered a **rapid eye movement (REM)** period. The sender would then concentrate on mentally sending a picture (which was unknown ahead of time) to the receiver until the REM period concluded. This same basic procedure continued throughout the night, with the image being sent during each REM cycle. In the morning, the receiver was given a choice of eight pictures and asked to rank them in the order of likelihood that they were the image that had been sent during the night.

A series of thirteen major experiments were carried out in the Maimonides Project, nine of

which produced statistically significant results, supporting a parapsychological explanation.

COLLECTIVE UNCONSCIOUS

The collective unconscious, a term coined by the psychologist **Carl Jung**, refers to the storehouse of myths and symbols to which all human beings have access. Jung found that the dreams of his clients frequently contained images with which they were completely unfamiliar but which seemed to reflect symbols that could be found somewhere in the mythological systems of world culture; the notion of the collective unconscious was used to explain this phenomenon.

Jung's unique contribution to modern psychology begins with the observation that the basic structure of many symbols and myths is nearly universal, even between cultures with no historical influence on one another. Most traditional societies, for example, tell hero myths, use circles to represent wholeness, the sky to symbolize transcendence, and so forth. Jung theorized that this universality resulted from unconscious patterns (genetic or quasi-genetic predispositions to utilize certain symbolic and mythical structures) that we inherited from our distant ancestors. The reservoir of these patterns constitutes a collective unconscious, distinct from the individual, personal unconscious that is the focus of Freudian psychoanalysis.

Jung referred to the unconscious, predisposing patterns for particular myths and symbols as **archetypes**; hence, one can talk about the **mandala** (i.e., the circle) **archetype**, the **hero archetype** (the latter made famous by the Jungian thinker **Joseph Campbell**), and so forth. Jung asserted that his notions of the collective unconscious and the archetypes were on par with the theory of instincts (one examines certain kinds of behaviors and theorizes that they are the result of certain biological drives, although it is, of course, impossible to directly observe such drives/instincts).

COMMUNICATIONS WITH GODS

People have attempted to communicate with gods and other spirits throughout history, in all cultures in every area of the world. In ancient times, oracles, seers, shamans, and prophets were the intermediaries between this world and the spirit realm. Ancient Egyptian priests and priestesses, Chinese emperors, Shinto shamans, Greek oracles, as well as the founders of major religions claimed to have communicated with spirits and to have received instructions from them.

Dreams, which often seem to be experiences of a parallel spiritual world, have frequently been the medium of communication. The spirits accomplish dream communication in varied ways, however. Sometimes the spirit itself appears in dreams and instructs the dreamer. On other occasions (e.g., in biblical dreams) an emissary such as an angel is sent bearing a message. Yet other times divinities send symbolic dreams, which must be interpreted.

COMMUNITY DREAMSHARING NETWORK

Several organizations and periodicals cater to both laypersons and professionals. As the name implies, the Community Dreamsharing Network, located in Hicksville, New York, is a networking organization that helps people organize dreamsharing groups and encourages networking among these groups. The organization publishes the quarterly *Dream Switchboard*, which includes networking notices.

The Community Dreamsharing Network researches dreams and sponsors a variety of training sessions, including the training of elementary and high school teachers in utilizing the dreams of their students. The organization also maintains a database of dream-sharing groups.

COMPENSATORY DREAMS

The expression "compensatory dreams" is used to describe several related phenomena. First, it can simply refer to the circumstance that during sleep we continue to process at some level the information that we have taken in during the day. This is one reason our dreams are filled with images from our waking world. Second, it can mean that during sleep dreams provide us with something that is lacking during our waking life. Finally, the expression can refer to dreams that release stress, either stress in our everyday world or stress from repressed unconscious material.

CONDENSATION

The notion that dreams provide an avenue for the expression of normally repressed desires while simultaneously disguising and censoring our real urges was systematically formulated by **Sigmund Freud**, the father of psychoanalysis. In Freud's view, the purpose of dreams is to allow us to satisfy in fantasies the instinctual urges that society judges to be unacceptable in some way, such as the urge to seduce or to kill. If, however, we were to dream about an actual seduction or an actual assault, the emotions evoked by the dream would awaken us. So that our sleep is not continually disturbed by such dreams, the mind modifies and disguises their content so that strong emotions are not evoked. Freud referred to the process of censoring and transforming dream contents into less disturbing images as the **dreamwork**, and explicitly identified five processes through which dreams are censored: **displacement, condensation, symbolization, projection,** and **secondary revision**.

Condensation, as the word implies, is a process that disguises a particular thought, urge, or emotion by contracting it into a brief dream event or image, the deeper meaning of which is not readily evident. Condensation also refers to the tendency of the dreamwork to bring together two or more different experiences or concerns into a single dream narrative or image. In Freud's words,

> From every element in a dream's content associative threads branch out in two or more directions; every situation in a dream seems to be put together out of two or more impressions or experiences.

The overlap of two or more distinct sets of associations in one dream situation effectively disguises the true meaning of the dream.

CONTROL OF NIGHTMARES

Dream analysis is the first and most important step when one seeks to control or treat one's nightmares. Analysis allows for the intrapersonal discovery of the emotions that are the driving force behind the dream. Once the dreamer acknowledges the fears and insecurities from her or his waking life that trigger nightmares, they lose the power they hold in the subconscious and

Nightmares in dreams can be truly frightening and disturbing, but it may be possible to control and limit them through lucid dreaming. (1870 engraving by Gustave Doré).

are no longer a terrifying force. By seeking professional help with the analysis of dreams, the dreamer is able to discuss freely the specifics of the nightmares. The dreamer then becomes able to confront the fearful aspect of the subconscious.

It is the belief of many dream researchers that dream analysis enables the dreamer to more readily attain the state known as **lucid dreaming**. Lucid dreaming takes place when dreamers are aware of the fact that they are dreaming and are then able to control different aspects of their dreams. If a person finds him- or herself lucid in a bad dream, one of the first steps to controlling the nightmare is the rehearsal of pleasant dream imagery. It is possible to do this regardless of what is happening in the nightmare. All that is used in this technique is the imagination to change the dream environment or to alter the experience one is having in a variety of other ways. Once the dreamer is able to call upon pleasant scenes at will, he or she is then able to start actively influencing the content of the nightmares. By taking an active role in the themes of the nightmares, the dreamer is able to manipulate an outcome that is neither fearful nor stressful. When he or she is able to develop a plan of action and then take steps towards its implementation, it greatly enhances one's confidence. Not only is this a very empowering experience, but many people have found it useful in the treatment of some cases of insomnia because it helps one fall asleep and prevents the reoccurrence of the same nightmares in the same night.

Upon awakening from a nightmare, it is often recommended that one record any details that can be remembered into some sort of **dream diary**. It is most effective to write the entry immediately after awakening. It is useful at any time after the dreams have occurred, but the sooner a nightmare is written down the more details are likely to be remembered. The journal is useful as a reference when interpreting the dreams later, but there have been cases of nightmares stopping altogether by the mere act of recording them.

CREATIVE VISUALIZATION

Creative visualization is currently highly popular, even faddish, and is deployed as a technique for accomplishing everything from prosperity to healing to spiritual growth. The basic idea is that visualizing a desired condition sets in motion forces that help to bring it about. The most immediate source for this technique is the New Thought churches—a religious movement composed of such denominational bodies as Unity and Science of Mind, though the utilization of creative visualization and related methods has extended far beyond the bounds of traditional New Thought.

The images that are constructed in the mind during visualization exercises bear more than a little resemblance to the types of images encountered in dreams. It is a natural step from this observed relationship to the use of creative visualization in so-called dream-programming techniques. In these methods, the dreamer decides what he or she wishes to dream and then attempts to "convince" the subconscious to have dreams on a particular topic. Visualization is part of this attempt, which can be surprisingly effective.

Another way of utilizing creative visualization in the context of dreaming is to attempt to reshape one's dream landscape during **lucid dreaming**. In lucid dreams, the dreamer has the unusual experience of being aware of dreaming during the dream. Because the dream landscape is a product of the dreamer's mind, it should be possible to simply "will" the dream to change, just as one does in certain visualization exercises. Again, this is often surprisingly effective if one has already mastered the technique of lucid dreaming. Some healers and therapists have begun to make therapeutic use of this technique, asking people who are nightmare-prone, for instance, to attempt to manipulate their dreams so that they will have happy endings.

CREATIVITY AND DREAMING

The role of dreams in promoting creativity is, like many other issues in this area, unclear. Does paying attention to one's dreams actually stimulate one's creativity, or does dream material simply provide inspiration for creative work? (Most discussions of creativity and dreams focus on the latter assumption.) Is there a meaningful distinction between creativity in dreams and **problem solving in dreams**?

With respect to the last question, consider, for instance, the experience of the nineteenth-century chemist F.A. Kekule, who was attempting to determine the structure of the benzene molecule. Dozing off in front of his fireplace one evening, he dreamed of snakelike benzene molecules dancing in the fire. At one point one of the snakes latched onto its own tail and began spinning. In this surreal **hypnagogic experience** Kekule discovered the key to his problem—that the benzene molecule was arranged in a ring pattern. Here it seems that this scientist's dreamlike experience embodied creative problem solving.

In the more purely artistic realm, artists of all types receive inspiration in dreams. One of the better-known examples is the experience of the eighteenth-century violinist Giuseppe Tartini, who had a dream in which the devil played a tune that so enchanted him that he immediately awoke and attempted to capture as much of it as he could remember. The resulting piece, the *Devil's Trill*, became his most famous composition.

Finally, in traditional societies creative inspiration from dreams cannot be meaningfully separated from spirit guidance through dreams. In a study of the Mistassini Cree, for example, Adrian Tanner remarks that "Power … is sometimes thought to arrive in dreams, in the form of formulae for songs, or shamanistic techniques, or ideas for the decoration of clothing or other objects" (p. 126—see *Sources*). Thus, for the Cree, as for other traditional peoples, religious revelation and artistic inspiration blend together in an indistinguishable whole.

CREE

The Mistassini Cree are a sub-Arctic people living in northern Quebec who attempt to carry on a lifestyle and culture that was traditionally built around hunting and trapping. The Cree have made some partial compromises with Canadian society by spending the summers at government outposts, but in the winters they live much as they did more than three hundred years ago, when Europeans first entered the area.

Particularly during the winter, the Cree are most interested in divinatory dreams as they relate to the hunt. Such divinatory dreams are not straightforward, in the sense that they most often require interpretation. For example, one of the most common rules of interpretation is that meeting a stranger of the opposite sex in a dream indicates a game animal. Events in the dream then serve as metaphors for what will happen during the hunt. For instance, in a study of the Mistassini Cree, Adrian Tanner includes the account of a man who dreamed he met an Eskimo woman who invited him to live with her. The man refused the invitation and later while hunting sighted a caribou, which he shot at but missed, and it got away.

The Cree also regard dreams as sources of creative inspiration and spiritual guidance. Tanner observes, for instance, that "power … is sometimes thought to arrive in dreams, in the form of formulae for songs, or shamanistic techniques, or ideas for the decoration of clothing or other objects" (p. 126—see *Sources*).

Thus, according to Tanner, dreams serve to connect ordinary daily activities with a spirit realm, giving one's life a larger significance in the cosmic view of things.

DREAMS DO NOT VANISH,
SO LONG AS PEOPLE DO
NOT ABANDON THEM.

—PHANTOM F. HARLOCK

DANIEL

Book of Daniel, which consists largely of a series of dreams and visions, may be the most complete treatment of dreams in Hebrew Scriptures (the Old Testament) and is a clear demonstration of the Hebrew regard for dreams. One of the latest books of Hebrew Scripture, it was written in approximately the second century B.C.E., when the Jewish people were struggling against the oppressor Antiochus Epiphanes, who was profaning Judaism. The book is about the young man Daniel, who lived under foreign oppression during the Jewish exile in Babylonia. The historicity of Daniel as a person has been debated. In the Book of Daniel, he is portrayed as an Israelite youth of great ability with a special understanding of visions and dreams.

Chapter 2 reports the story of King Nebuchadnezzar, a man afflicted with insomnia, who during his restless sleep was aware of his disturbing and portentous dreams but was unable to recollect what they were. He consulted a number of Babylonian soothsayers, who, when they were unable to help him, were killed. Daniel alone believed he could solve the king's problem. He sought the mercy of God concerning this mystery, which was revealed to him in a vision during the night.

Daniel confronted the king and told him that his dreams foretold the future. He then proceeded to interpret the king's dream, a dream of an image wrought of many magnificent metals, that was broken and crumbled. Nebuchadnezzar's dream was a portent that the kingdom would one day be divided—the only kingdom that cannot be divided or destroyed is God's.

Daniel interpreted another dream of Nebuchadnezzar's in which Nebuchadnezzar saw a tall tree that grew so high that its top reached to heaven. Then the Lord came to him and told him to hew down the tree and cut off its branches, but to leave the stump in the earth, let it be wet and passed over seven times. Then he was told that God rules the kingdom of men and gives it to whom He wills. The dream, Daniel warned the king, meant that King Nebuchadnezzar had become like the tree, but because he regarded himself as the author of his own power, God would cut him down.

Because Nebuchadnezzar did not heed Daniel's warning. He lost his mind and was brought down by a strange psychosis that lasted seven years, after which he was restored to reason.

DAY RESIDUES IN DREAM CONTENTS

During dreams, we often reencounter elements of experiences from the preceding day (or from the recent past). For the most part, these residual images appear random and devoid of deeper significance. However, **Sigmund Freud** viewed these images from recent waking experience as constituting building blocks out of which the unconscious mind constructs dream fantasies for the purpose of acting out repressed desires. According to Freud and the school of thought he initiated, the dreaming mind usually constructs fantasies in which repressed urges (often aggressive or sexual impulses) are symbolically, rather than literally, acted out. Thus, instead of dreaming about having a forbidden sexual encounter, we might dream about an attractive motorcyclist we happened to notice the day before, and in the dream we might ride a vibrating motorcycle with

our arms around the cyclist—a situation that suggests intercourse, at least symbolically. In this manner, the seemingly insignificant events of the day become vehicles for the expression of repressed desires.

DAYDREAMS

In contrast to sleep research, there has been comparatively little systematic study of what are commonly referred to as daydreams, because "daydreams" can include everything from fairly structured fantasies to the series of disconnected images that emerge during relaxed free association. Clearly, there is a relationship between daydreams and regular dreams, but investigators in this area have hypothesized that somewhat different and perhaps independent cognitive processes are at work.

DEATH DREAMS

Ethnographic reports indicate that association of sleep and dreams with death is widespread in human culture, as is the theme of death in dreams. For instance, the Australian Aborigines beliefs about death, the origin of death, and a person's destiny stem from dreams, whereas for the **Senoi** death dreams can release a positive force within the dreamer. In many different religious traditions, but particularly in the West, dreamers travel out of the body and journey to the underworld, where they receive knowledge or magical power.

Dreams of death often occur as a result of great stress caused by relationships, school, vocational changes, or by the approach of death itself. Such dreams may also be caused by a terminal illness or by the death of a loved one, before or after which a member of the family often receives

Daydreaming and dreams during sleep may be related, but different cognitive processes seem to be at work, too, according to psychologists.

a visitation from the departed. Among the most important traditions in which death dreams are studied is the analytical psychology of **Carl Jung**, according to whom death dreams are to be linked to the universal primordial imagery of personal transformation—when one "dies" to the old self to be reborn as a new self. Jungian psychotherapist **Marie-Louise von Franz** asserts that dreams of dying people can be interpreted as preparation of the consciousness for a deep transformation and for the continuation of life after death.

Studies interpreting and classifying death dreams include those of Edgar Herzog, Hendrika Vande Kemp, and Ann Faraday. In *Psyche and Death*, Herzog attempts to trace the associations between dreams and ancient myths and analyzes five types or sequences of death dreams: repression of death, which refers to the dreamer's refusal to

face the death situation; killing, a ritual in which the killer comes to terms with death; archaic forms of the death-demon, with mythological components; the land of the dead, in which archaic myths are associated with love, procreation, birth, and rebirth; and dreams of death as an expression of the process of development, in which there is an encounter with death that reflects or aids the development or maturation of the dreamer's personality.

In her classification of dreams, Hendrika Van de Kemp delineates the following types of dreams: telepathic, in which the dying person appears in the dreams of friends or relatives; premonitory, in which the dying person appears in the dream with those who are already dead to announce his or her impending death; hypermnesic, in which the dead person conveys information that has been lost to the dreamer's waking memory; predictive, in which the dreamer predicts the time of his or her own death; archetypal, in which death appears in a symbolic form; and revelatory, in which the dead person reappears to convey a religious or philosophical truth that the person had promised to announce to the living.

In *The Dream Game*, Ann Faraday states that death dreams can be considered metaphors, expressing through the death of others that one's feelings for someone, something, or an aspect of oneself is dead; as reminders, when those already dead appear in dreams, of something in need of resolution; or as symbols, when one dreams of death, indicating the need for an old self-image to be transcended.

DEFICIENCY EXPLANATIONS OF DREAMS

Deficiency explanations of dreams stress what the dream state lacks in contrast to the waking state, sometimes even characterizing dreams as superfluous to human functioning. The most extreme example of this view is the **activation-synthesis model of dreaming**, which sees dreams fundamentally as the product of random electrical signals generated by the brain during sleep. **Sigmund Freud** and the theorists in his tradition viewed dreams as important avenues for accessing the unconscious; the psychoanalytic perspective sees dreams as escape valves for infantile desires, allowing us to satisfy in disguised fantasies the instinctual urges that society judges unacceptable. The implication is that dreams are a crutch and would not occur in a society that did not set social standards at odds with instinctual urges. Both these types of explanations tend to characterize the waking state as conscious and rational and the sleeping state as unconscious and irrational, and tend to emphasize the disjunction between them.

Nondeficiency explanations of dreams, by way of contrast, view the dream state as another kind of consciousness, held together by a consciously self-regulating dream **ego**. According to these hypotheses, dreams are seen as "the intelligent result of some dream planning processor, as unconscious information processing, as metaphor, as a visual transduction of cognition, and as the biological basis of poetry and the imagination" (Moffitt et al., p. 202—see *Sources*). These alternative views also note that dreaming is not an entirely unconscious activity (e.g., there is **lucid dreaming**), nor is it invariably irrational. At the same time, the waking state is neither fully rational nor fully conscious.

DÉJÀ VU

Déjà vu is an eerie experience in which there is a feeling that a completely unknown place is familiar, as if one has been there before, or that a new situation has been experienced before. It can characterize events, dreams, thoughts, statements, emotions, meetings, and so on. The expression itself is French for "already seen" and was coined by E. Letter Boirac in 1876. No English expression has quite the same connotations.

Déjà vu is a widespread experience. A poll conducted in 1986 reported that 67 percent of Americans had experienced the phenomenon. Other studies indicate that déjà vu occurs more often to females than males, and more often to younger than older individuals.

There are many theories that attempt to explain déjà vu. In 1884, for instance, it was theorized that one brain hemisphere registered information slightly sooner than the other hemisphere, and that this explained the experience. Other researchers have postulated similar partial delay mechanisms, such as the hypothesis that the subconscious receives information before the conscious mind. These biological explanations have not been demonstrated to actually be a part of the human physiology. A more widely accepted hypothesis, which certainly accounts for at least some such "already seens," is that the new places or experiences that we encounter during déjà vu simply resemble familiar places or experiences.

Another explanation embraces the notion of a **collective unconscious**, through which one is in touch with the universal experience of the human race. From this frame of reference, a déjà vu experience may simply represent a resonance between a current experience and one of the archetypes in the collective unconscious. Of particular significance are explanations that postulate that at least some déjà vu experiences are indistinct memories of past lifetimes.

Yet another explanation is that déjà vu is a form of psychic experience related to certain dream experiences. Thus, the new but seemingly familiar places we encounter may be, for example, places we visited during **out-of-body experiences** while asleep. Dreams may also be precognitive and experienced as déjà vu when what was precognized occurs or is encountered.

DEMOCRITUS

Democritus (c. 460–c. 370 B.C.E.) was one of the earliest Western philosophers, favorably remembered by scientists as the ancient father of atomic theory. Historians often refer to all Greek philosophers who lived prior to Socrates as the pre-Socratics, and Democritus is included in this group. The pre-Socratics, who as a group were active from approximately 600 to 400 B.C.E., attempted to find universal principles to explain the whole of nature.

According to their philosophy, the apparent chaos of the world conceals a permanent and intelligible order, which can be accounted for by universal causes operating within nature itself and discoverable through human reason. They openly disagreed with the content and the method of mythology, maintaining that natural processes were no longer to be at the mercy of gods with human passions and unpredictable intentions. The pre-Socratics were skeptical about dreams, and they usually took a more speculative view of them.

According to Democritus, dreams can be regarded as the emanations from all persons and objects that are able to penetrate the dreamer's body and consciousness. Democritus offered the same explanation for the phenomenon of dreaming animals. Through the pores of the body, the sleeper can perceive a series of images, which may be affected by the person's bodily state and the quality of the air. Also, according to Democritus, images that came through the pores sometime in the past are kept alive in the memory.

Democritus maintained that dream-images seem to be objects of mental apprehension rather than images received in a waking state, and he claimed that they are, to an extent, independent of the senses which are implicitly denounced as the barrier separating individuals from true reality although they are still received in a way very similar to sense-perception. According to Democritus, images of living beings also bring those persons' mental dispositions to the dreamer, that is, their thoughts, reasoning, and impulses.

DEMONS

The belief that malicious entities lie behind natural disasters and other unpleasant aspects of human life is very old and is still prevalent in many traditional societies. Especially before the development of scientific discoveries that proffered more neutral explanations for the irregularities of nature, it was not unreasonable to postulate that such beings were responsible for unexplainable natural disasters and diseases. While scientific explanations have gradually supplanted metaphysical explanations, demons and devils presently survive in the mythology of **Carl Jung**'s collective unconscious and in other schools of the study of the mind that interpret evil forces as projections of human fear and/or as hallucinations.

While often the two words are used interchangeably—devils from Greek *diaballo* (to throw across, i.e., an accuser) and demons from Greek *daimon* (spirit)—their meaning evolved

Demons and devils have become part of our collective unconscious, thus appearing not only in art and literature, but also in our dreams. (Detail of the fourteenth-century Catholic cathedral Duomo di Orvieto, Italy).

through the centuries and within different religious contexts. Devils have always had a negative connotation as evil forces, whereas demons had more individual natures. *Daimones* in ancient Greece were tutelary, semi-divine spirits of either good or bad nature.

In the early days of Judaism, demons did not have a big impact on the religious belief system. During the first Diaspora, when the Jews were in contact with the dualist vision of Zoroastrianism, a more defined role for demons was developed within the tradition, in particular in the *aggadah* that reflected the popular rabbinic beliefs. These mythological figures drew from the indigenous pagan beliefs (such as the *shedim*) and are believed to be either creations of God or offspring of **Lilith**, the first wife of Adam. In the Cabbala during the Middle Ages, the evil forces of the Jewish tradition took definite forms, names, and roles, although they were never really fully accepted into Orthodox Judaism.

The Greek word *daimon* was introduced in the **Roman** and Hellenistic worlds to indicate evil forces, and thus entered early Christian writings with the negative connotation of impure spirits. The Judeo-Christian tradition elaborated upon the concept of the Devil as the fallen angel who tempted Adam and Eve and was forever banished from Paradise. Christian literature also drew upon the belief system of neighboring cultures in the depiction of the Apocalypse, in which demons appear that recall Jewish, Persian, and Mesopotamian myths.

In the transmission of the texts of the Scriptures the devil (in Hellenistic Greek *diabolos*) came to be identified with Satan (a name used in the Hebrew **Bible** to indicate adversary). The belief in evil powers as the source of sicknesses and problems for humans is found in all the early Christian literature, and Christian theology acknowledges evil as necessary for the fulfillment of free will. From very early, Christianity developed the practice of exorcism to expel evil spirits who had taken over control of human individuals. In medieval Europe, the belief in the existence of demons came to be associated with witchcraft and contributed to the development of the practice of exorcism and witch hunting, which faded out only after the introduction of the religious skepticism of the eighteenth-century Enlightenment.

References to demons and their association with nightmares are frequent. Christian theologians often attributed dreams or **nightmares** with any sexual content to the influence of Satan and his demonic minions. **Macrobius** was the first ancient Christian to discuss seductive demons in Christian literature. In his thesis on dreams and nightmares, he included categories of apparitions and nightmares that were not previously cover by **Aristotle**. This included, but was not limited to, references to the nature of **incubi, succubi**, and the demon **Lilith**. The third-century Christian theologian **Tertullian** portrayed them as the most common cause of nightmares in *A Treatise on the Soul*. He assured his readers that any sins committed while dreaming were not the fault of the dream because these types of dreams were merely the attempts of various demons to lead the faithful astray. **St. Thomas Aquinas** also acknowledged the direct or indirect invocations of demons in particular dreams and nightmares.

When considering the emphasis that the western Christian world placed on celibacy it becomes apparent why demons were blamed for **sexual dreams**. It was not common for the clergy of this period to acknowledge their internal demons. Quite often, they just redoubled their efforts on controlling and eliminating external demons.

If one looks farther back, it is possible to find just as many pre-Christian references to demons. In ancient Mesopotamia, demons were included as instigators of nightmares, along with evil spirits and spirits of the dead. A demon that resembled a goat was the cause of erotic dreams. Lilith was associated with sexual dreams that a person experienced while sleeping alone in a house, regardless of gender, because Lilith could change her physical form. Naamah (Lilith's sister) and Igrath were both female demons who were responsible for nocturnal emissions.

DESCARTES, RENÉ

The rationalist philosopher and mathematician René Descartes (1596–1650) was born at La Haye, in Touraine, France. After attending the Jesuit college of La Fleche, he went to Holland in 1618 to serve in the army of Maurice of Nassau, and then traveled in Germany. His first substantial work was the treatise *Regulae ad directionem ingenii*, which was printed in 1701 although it was never completed. It dealt with Descartes's

Philosopher and mathematician René Descartes struggled with the question of whether or not the mind's perception of dreams represented reality. (Library of Congress).

preoccupation with method as the clue to scientific advance.

By 1634 Descartes had completed a scientific work, *Le morrde*, which was suppressed after he heard of the condemnation of Galileo for teaching the Copernican system. In 1637 he published three treatises on physical and mathematical subjects—*Geometry, Dioptric,* and *Meteors*—prefaced by *Discours de la méthode*, which represent a compressed exposition of the foundations of the Cartesian system.

In *Discours de la méthode* Descartes introduced his method of systematic doubt in his attempt to answer the basic question, "What can I know?" which he hoped to answer by critical reflection on his beliefs. His method was to suspend belief in anything in which he could find or imagine the slightest grounds for doubt. He suspended belief in the entire physical universe, including himself; in God; in the past; and even in the truth of mathematical propositions. Among the arguments by which he extended his doubts are the false judgments we commonly make due to illusions of the senses and, in particular, the illusions of dreams, to which he frequently referred.

For Descartes the question of who's dreaming about whom was very difficult to answer, as was the question, How do we know that the perceptions that occur in dreaming are false and those we experience when awake are true, since the former are often as vivid and distinct as the latter? He claimed that dreams are merely the result of activity in the sleeper's organs of sense, and that they respond to the sleeper's desires. And, because we cannot meaningfully distinguish dreaming perceptions from waking perceptions, we cannot regard the information coming to us from our senses as providing a stable foundation for knowledge. Descartes's systematic doubt led him to the only proposition that he could not reasonably doubt, namely, that he the doubter must exist: "I think, therefore I am."

Beyond the abstract use of dream experiences to cast doubt on the veracity of sense experiences, Descartes himself had some important personal dreams. On the night of November 10, 1619, he had a series of dreams that he interpreted as an answer to his desire to find a method that would enable him to pursue truth as a life occupation.

According to his interpretation of the dreams, which he claimed were a divine sign, his destiny was to search for truth by applying the mathematical method—by which he meant analytical geometry, in particular—to all other studies.

He had always been in the habit of recording his dreams in his journal, which he referred to as his *Olympica*. At some point during the seventeenth century, this journal was lost, but the contents are known today because of the efforts of the Abbé Adrien Baillet. He had access to the *Olympica* before it was lost and published a paraphrased version, *La vie de M. Descartes*, in 1691. It is through this record that we know about a dream Descartes experienced, in three parts, on November 10, 1619. The following is an account of the Abbé Baillet's version of the events that unfolded in the first, nightmarish act of the dream, as described in his *La vie de M. Descartes*:

> After he fell asleep he imagined he saw ghosts and was terrified by them. He felt a great weakness on his right side, and, believing he was walking through streets, was forced to lean over to his left side so as to be able to continue his journey.

> Ashamed to be walking in this way, he made an effort to stand up straight, but he was foiled by a violent wind which spun him round three or four times on his left foot.

> With great difficulty he managed to drag himself along, fearful of falling at every step. Then, seeing a college that was open, he entered it hoping to find some respite from his affliction. He tried to reach the college church in order to say his prayers, but on the way he realized that he had passed a man he knew without acknowledging him. He tried to retrace his steps in order to pay his compliments but was again foiled by the wind which blew him back towards the church.

Then, in the middle of the college quadrangle, he saw another person who called him by name and told him that, if he wished to find Monsieur N., he had something for Descartes to give to him. The gift appeared to be a melon that had been brought from some foreign country.

He was surprised to see that people who had gathered round the man in the quadrangle to chat with one another were able to stand firmly upright on their feet, whereas Descartes had still to walk crookedly and unsteadily, even though the wind had abated.

At this point he awoke in pain, fearing some evil spirits were trying to lead him astray. Having fallen asleep on his left side, he now turned over on to his right side. He prayed to God to protect him from all the misfortunes which might threaten him as a punishment for his sins. He recognized that his sins were grievous enough to call down on him the wrath of heaven, although in the eyes of men, he had lead a relatively blameless life. He lay awake about two hours, pondering the problem of good and evil, and then once more fell asleep.

In Descartes's dream, he was forced to lean on his left (corresponding to the unconscious) to continue walking, since his right (corresponding to the conscious) was so weak that it could no longer support him. By giving the left a higher significance than the right, the dream reminded Descartes, who thus far in his life had believed only in reason and rejected both his instinctive and religious life, of the importance and necessity of his irrational side.

In another dream Descartes came across two books with which he was unfamiliar: a dictionary and a poetry anthology entitled *Corpus poetarum* (*The Body [Collection] of Poets*), containing some small portraits engraved in copperplate, which was open at the line *Quod vitae sectabor iter* (What is the path to the way of life?), followed by a fragment presenting the alternative, *Est et non* (To be and not to be). The dictionary represented "all the sciences gathered together," whereas the anthology, full of sentences by poets, recalled the discovery of enthusiasm and imagination. The union of philosophy and wisdom, represented by the two books, constituted the answer for which Descartes was looking and subsequently informed his waking intuition of the unity of all the sciences.

DIET AND DREAMS

A common part of our **folklore** about dreams holds that eating certain types of foods will produce certain types of dreams. It has been said, for example, that eating spicy food before going to bed induces **nightmares**. Although this is unproved, if the spicy food were to induce a case of indigestion, it might disturb sleep, affecting one's dreams.

Historically, overindulgence was associated with nightmares and "false dreams" (in the sense of proffering unreliable omens of the future). Many of the ancient writers claimed that such nightmares were demon-induced and predicted negative incidents in a person's future. **Macrobius** insisted that these nightmares represented the dreamer's present state of mind and did not relate to his or her subconscious or future. He maintained that they were of no use to the great theological issues of the time.

The early Christians believed that fasting would induce true visions. They hoped to please God through humiliation of the human body. This is reflected in both the purposeful fast of the biblical Daniel and the forced fast of Perpetua. Those who inten-

As anyone who has had indigestion can attest, food can interrupt one's sleeping patterns. It can also influence dreams.

tionally fasted for extended periods were hoping to prevent natural dreams in general; this way, they could be sure that any dreams that did occur were sent by God.

Modern research has shown that a sharp decrease in daily calories results in a decreased sexual interest while a person is awake. It also causes fewer nocturnal emissions in men and an overall decrease in the sexual themes of dreams.

The most significant finding on this topic involves the study of individuals suffering from anorexia nervosa. Anorexics sleep relatively little, and fitfully when they do sleep. Naturally, this sleep is light, with proportionally more time spent in **rapid eye movement (REM) sleep** (the stage most associated with dreaming) than is in a normal sleep pattern. When anorexics start to heal (and thus eat more), they sleep more and sleep more deeply.

DISPLACEMENT

Although many aspects of the personality theory formulated by **Sigmund Freud** have been rejected by contemporary analysts, Freud was nevertheless responsible for a significant number of insights into human nature that have been generally accepted. Among these insights are the Freudian "defense mechanisms," one of which is displacement. In displacement we repress a certain urge, which is then redirected to another object or person. A familiar example is the employee who is yelled at by his boss, and who then goes home and yells at his spouse. What he really wants to do is to yell back at his boss, but he redirects the urge and takes out his anger on a safer target. A roughly similar process takes place in dreams.

According to Freud, dreams provide an avenue for the expression of normally repressed desires while simultaneously disguising and censoring our real urges. In this view the purpose of dreams is to allow us to satisfy in fantasies the instinctual urges that society judges to be unacceptable in some way, such as the urge to kill a bullying employer. If, however, we were to dream about the actual, overt murder of our boss, the emotions evoked by he dream would wake us up. So that our sleep is not continually disturbed by such dreams, the mind modifies and disguises the content of our dreams so that strong emotions are not evoked. Thus, instead of dreaming about killing our boss, we

might, for example, dream about our employer's automobile being accidentally crushed by a runaway garbage truck.

DIVINATION

Traditions of dream divination and classification are linked to popular lore and to the attempt to find meaningful patterns in everyday life. The most important tradition of dream divination is found in ancient Mesopotamia, where more interest was shown in divination than in any other known civilization. Only in Mesopotamia did divination occupy a dominant position during the entire span of the civilization, which quite early set down divinatory lore in writing. A number of cuneiform tablets dealing with divination have been found, and some of them make predictions based on the contents of dreams. To properly evaluate the role assigned to the dream in Mesopotamian civilization, it is necessary to place the dream omens in the context of the entire range of the diviner's art.

The Mesopotamian heritage of **oneiromancy** (divination of dreams) was imparted both to the Hellenistic world and to Islamic civilization. Oneiromancy is the oldest form of divination in **Islam**, where the influence of its pre-Islamic past is remarkable. The *Oneirocritica* of the second-century Greek **Artemidorus** represents the basis of a popular tradition of dream classification and interpretation. According to Artemidorus and those who followed him, the analysis of dreams is based on the observation of the commonality of daily experience, rather than on the belief in the existence of a divine spirit.

Dream divination plays a fundamental role in many contemporary traditional cultures. For instance, the power of **Temne** diviners depends upon active accomplishment in dreaming. They derive their abilities from an initiatory dream that they establish a contractual relationship with a patron spirit, whereas most ordinary people are passively acted upon in their dreams by spirits, ancestors, or witches. During divination, diviners do not merely comment on the meaning of a client's dream, but may also ascribe a specific dream to a client who, until then, had been unaware of having dreamed it.

Dream divination can even play a significant political role in a traditional culture, as in societies where succession to leadership or other status is determined by dreams. Dream divination can be used as a way of deciding upon one claim or candidate rather than another, or even of effecting the selection of a successor from among those who had not previously claimed candidate status.

DREAM BODY

Dream body is a designation sometimes given to the astral body, that part of the self that, according to occult lore, travels away from the physical body during **astral projection**. Such projection sometimes occurs during a waking state, but it more frequently takes place during sleep—hence the name dream body.

DREAM CONTROL

Dream control or dream programming refers to the ability to manipulate one's dreams. The control that one is able to exercise during **lucid dreaming** is only one aspect of this ability. Dream control also refers to the technique of requesting one's own subconscious mind just prior to the onset of sleep to accomplish certain tasks during the dream state. A dreamer plagued by **nightmares** might, for instance, make a strong affirma-

tion just before retiring that any unpleasant dream encounters be transformed into positive experiences. If successful, an attack by a wild beast, for example, might be transformed into a romp in the woods with one's pet dog.

DREAM CYCLES

Rapid eye movement (REM) sleep recurs on a regular rhythm of ninety-minute intervals sometimes called dream cycles. The association of this rhythm with dreaming cycles builds upon earlier research that seemed to correlate REM sleep with dream periods. Subsequent research has indicated, however, that significant dreaming takes place during non-REM sleep, which has called earlier notions of "dream cycles" into question.

DREAM DIARIES

As research on **sleep learning** and on so-called **nondreamers** has demonstrated, the memory-processing mechanisms of the brain appear to be switched off (or at least to be "off-line") during sleep. These findings explain why dreams are often so difficult to remember. Even people who remember their dreams every night only remember the last several dreams they had immediately before awakening. Dreams from the early and middle periods of sleep are permanently forgotten.

A widely utilized method for holding on to dream memories is a dream diary, in which individuals record as many dreams as they can remember immediately upon awakening. Controlled studies have empirically verified the common observation among people who keep dream diaries that this recording must be done immediately, before other thoughts, such as considerations about the upcoming day, are allowed to

Writing down one's dreams into a dream diary immediately after waking will help you remember valuable information that can be analyzed later.

intrude. In one experiment, for example, participants were instructed to call up for local weather information immediately upon awakening and write down a couple of items from the forecast before recording their dreams. Subjects who completed this task were able to recall far fewer dreams than participants who went immediately to the task of writing down dreams without first telephoning the weather bureau.

DREAM DICTIONARIES

It is the rare person who has not awakened from a particularly vivid dream with the feeling that

the dream was saying something important, the meaning of which the dreamer could not interpret. This experience is common enough that dream books offering various interpretive perspectives have become popular. When such books are arranged alphabetically to provide meanings for isolated components of dreams, they are referred to as dream dictionaries.

The tradition of dream dictionaries is quite ancient, though ancient and modern interpretations diverge considerably. The thrust of modern dream dictionaries is decidedly psychological. Before the advent of modern psychology and psychoanalysis, the dominant approach to dreams was to view them as omens. A common tool of this approach in the ancient world was the dream dictionary, which contained specific interpretations of various dream elements. While various short lists of dream components and their meanings have survived from ancient Egypt and Mesopotamia, one large second-century Greek dream dictionary, the *Oneirocritica* by **Artemidorus of Daldis**, has come down to us intact. In the *Oneirocritica* ("The Interpretation of Dreams"), the overriding concern is with dreams as omens. Take, for example, Artemidorus's interpretation of lions in dreams:

> Seeing a tame, fawning lion that is approaching harmlessly is auspicious and means benefits to a soldier from his king, to an athlete from his excellent physical condition, to a citizen from a magistrate, and slave from his master. For the animal resembles them in power and strength. But if the lion threatens or is in any way angered it arouses fear and portends sickness. (Artemidorus, pp. 103–104—see *Sources*)

Contemporary dream dictionaries, although they often share similar understandings of particular symbols with ancient dictionaries, are more inclined to give them psychological meanings. Thus, a contemporary interpretation of a lion in a dream might, like Artemidorus's, emphasize the lion's power and strength, but would discuss them in terms of the psychology of the dreamer. Depending on the other elements of the dream, the advice might be, for instance, to strive to develop or to acquire "lion-like" characteristics.

Contemporary dream dictionaries vary in quality. The best provide suggested starting points for interpreting one's own dreams. The worst advance rigid interpretations that make a pretense of having captured once and for all time the definitive meaning of particular dream symbols. Despite the psychological cast of modern dream dictionaries, professional psychotherapists are generally highly critical of them. This is partially because the same symbol can have such a wide variety of meanings, depending on the larger context of the dream, that providing interpretations in a dictionary format is problematic (though the better dictionaries convey this complexity to their users).

DREAM FRAGMENTS

Dream fragments may refer to any of several different types of experiences. They may be parts of dreams that are only partially remembered. Dream fragments may also refer to dreams that appear to be partial and incomplete episodes in some larger narrative. An important subset of the latter are dreams that end just as something important is about to happen.

DREAM GUIDE

A dream guide may be anyone with the expertise to give guidance on the subject of dreams. The term is usually reserved, however, for spirit entities that provide guidance, healing, or teaching during dreams. Although contemporary psychologists, especially those working in the Jungian tradition, may view such guides as symbols for deeper and wiser parts of ourselves that speak to us in dreams, the majority of people who work with dream guides see them as spiritual intelligences that exist independent of the dreamer's psyche.

Dream guides are a subcategory of guardian spirits (which in Western societies are often called guardian angels). The function of these spirits is to watch over and protect individuals. In some cultures, these spirits are believed to be attached to a person from birth; in others, they are acquired later, making themselves known through a vision or a dream. The manner in which these spirits' guidance manifests varies from vague "hunches" and intuitions to visions and dreams. Dreams guides have been especially important among such Native American groups as the **Iroquois.**

DREAM INCUBATION

Dream incubation refers to the practice of seeking dreams for specific purposes—healing, financial guidance, general advice, divination, and so on. Dream incubation was extremely popular in the ancient world, and was a major phenomenon in societies as diverse as ancient Mesopotamia, **Egypt, Greece**, and **Rome**. The theoretical structure underlying this practice in all ancient civilizations has been outlined by Scott Cunningham (p. 19—see *Sources*) as follows:

1. The divinities are concerned about Their worshippers.
2. Dreams can be sent by goddesses and gods.
3. The nearest that a worshipper can be to a deity, while in a corporeal state, is within the confines of Her or His temple.
4. Thus, sleeping within the temple will be the most effective method of producing a divine dream.

The practice of dream incubation in the temples of the ancient world may have developed independently in Mesopotamia and Egypt, or the practice may have emerged in one of these societies and later been transmitted to the other. The seeming obsession of Mesopotamians with divina-

tion suggests Mesopotamia as the ultimate source of this practice, indicating that the first systematic use of dream incubation was for the purpose of gaining knowledge of the future. This contrasts with the Hellenistic period, in which the primary purpose of dream incubation was for healing, principally at temples dedicated to **Aesculapius**. The practice continued into the Christian era, with reports of worshipers seeking healing in dreams at Catholic pilgrimage sites (particularly at churches built over the remains of Aesculapius's temples) as late as the early twentieth century.

The earliest temples to observe this practice were not dedicated solely to the task of guiding worshipers in their dreamwork, but the basic pattern was much the same. People went to temples to "camp out" and sleep with the intention of receiving a dream from the gods that would provide healing or an answer to a vexing question. The dreamer fasted and engaged in other rituals before lying down to sleep. In cases where the temple was too far away from the person seeking dream guidance, or when the person was too sick to undertake the required fasts, baths, or other rituals, another person could act as a surrogate for the seeker. During the period of Babylonian ascendancy in ancient Mesopotamia, the practice was to have a professional dreamer-priest seek the answer to one's question. During other periods when the seeker personally sought dream guidance, priests were often available to help interpret the dreams.

DREAM NETWORK

A number of organizations and periodicals devoted to dreams are available to laypersons and professionals alike. The *Dream Network* is a quarterly journal devoted to exploring the relationship between dreams and myth. Its stated purpose is to "demystify dream work and to integrate dream-sharing into our lives for the enhancement of our culture." The *Dream Network* also provides information on ongoing dream groups.

DREAM SHARING

Dream sharing is a common practice in many cultures, as revealed by a number of anthropological studies. Among the **Hopi**, good dreams are to be held in the heart, whereas bad dreams are considered to contain bad thoughts that must be eliminated by discussing them and working out the problems revealed by the dreams through confession of questionable behavior. The **Quiche**, on the other hand, insist that everyone dreams every night, and daily sharing or reporting of all dreams, whether the dreamer feels they are good or bad, is considered an important practice.

Among the **Rastafarians**, dream experience is among the various subjects of speculation during the communicative event of reasoning, and dream reporting by the elders is used to authenticate their tutorial role. Dream sharing constitutes a fundamental element in the education of children and an important practice in everyday life for the **Senoi**, as they claim that everything in a dream has a purpose beyond one's understanding when asleep.

Dreams play a fundamental role in **Kagwahiv** culture and are to be told at any time; they can be shared in the middle of the night as well as during the day over work. In **Morocco**, in order to acquire a good interpretation of one's dreams, it is very common to share them, to use them in different ways in communication, and to consult an external dream specialist.

Among the **Raramuri** of northern Mexico, dreams are a frequent topic of conversation in the morning within households as well as among members of different households. In addition, since the Raramuri usually sleep for a few hours, wake up, and then sleep again, they frequently analyze dreams during the course of the night. These discussions constitute an important means of transmission of culture and ideology in the absence of more formal institutions.

Among the **Sambia** of Papua New Guinea, dream sharing occurs in a variety of different contexts, both public and private. The principal situation in which dreams are shared is when they are discussed by household members. Dream sharing also occurs frequently at healing ceremonies, initiation rituals, public and secret storytelling sessions, gossip sessions, and during hunting, trading, and gardening trips. It is very common for people living in **Tikopia** to reveal their dreams, although no systematic scheme of telling them exists. Dreams are usually reported in a casual way, at any time of the day.

The **Zuni** of New Mexico share their dreams among members of their matrilocal extended household, as well as among friends. However, not all dream experiences are immediately reported; some are not reported until many years later. Since Zunis are unwilling to give away luck through careless talk or bragging before it can be realized, all good dreams are discussed with others only after the good things foretold have come true. Therefore, accounts of old dreams consist of both bad dreams, including **nightmares**, and good dreams, whereas reports of recent dream experiences always concern bad dreams.

To understand how people experience, share, and interpret their dreams requires a full understanding of their culture. Dream sharing and interpretation often have important effects on other cultural structures. In fact, there is a mutual influence between dreaming and culture.

For centuries, many traditional cultures have believed in sharing their dreams within the family and community. Modern Western cultures have carried on that concept through the idea of group therapy sessions.

Also, it has been asserted that dream sharing presents a number of problems in traditional psychoanalysis, since the manifest content of a dream is insufficient, may be distorted, and must be amplified by free association. Usually the dream as narrated is not meaningful as such, but rather the true message begins with the translation of the manifest dream into its latent meaning, which is removed from the original dream experience.

Dream sharing has recently—within the past couple of decades—gained considerable prestige in contemporary Western societies. Montague

Ullman was a psychoanalytically trained psychologist who founded the Dream Laboratory at the Maimonides Medical Center in New York during the 1960s. He was very concerned with developing ways of making psychiatric services available in communities that did not have easy access to them. In hopes of furthering his work in the realm of community mental health, Ullman moved his practice to Sweden in the 1970s. In both countries, Ullman focused on different aspects of "dream appreciation," but in Sweden he was able to obtain government funding to support his community dream-sharing groups. Ullman believed that sharing dreams and nightmares in a group setting was helpful to the dreamer because it not only provided support, but it was also easier for others to offer different perspectives on the meaning behind the dream symbolism.

Ullman developed a five-step process he found to be effective when sharing dreams in a group setting. The first step must obviously be when the dreamer shares his or her dream, which is followed by group reflection on the dream's content. This includes feelings, images, and metaphors they believe are represented by the dream imagery. During this second step, the dreamer does not comment on the group's opinions. Instead, he or she responds, without further comment from the group, in the third step. The fourth step is when the dialogue between the dreamer and the group actually takes place. Finally, the dreamer is able to reflect, alone, on the meanings discussed by the group. These steps are covered more extensively in the book *Working with Dream* (1979), which Ullman wrote with Nan Zimmerman. Ullman is careful to emphasize that it is only after the five steps of the dream-sharing are completed that the dreamer's job really begins.

One of the other leaders in modern dream-sharing therapy is Jeremy Taylor. He is a Unitarian Universalist minister who held his first formal dream-sharing group during a seminar in which he hoped to raise consciousness on racism. He asked those present at the seminar to discuss any dreams they had of African Americans. The following is an excerpt from his book *DreamWork* (1983):

> The energy for growth and transformation of personality and unconscious attitudes and fears that were released by this work was truly astonishing, even to me. The dream work was effective in bringing deep-seated

unconscious ambivalences to light, and the work was further effective in transforming them, because each of us was forced to "own" both the negative and positive images of black people in our dreams as representations of aspects of our own personalities.

It is Taylor's belief that the invaluable aspect of dreams and sharing them with a group derives from the way the group is able to expose a fuller range of possible meanings and provides the opportunity to explore multiple meanings. He suggests that a group of six to twelve people, with one person serving as the facilitator, yields the most positive results. He also recommends that they meet in a quiet place and have a "touch-in" in which everyone discusses how they are doing, before starting the process of sharing dreams. After the group greets one another, each member proceeds to share one dream. From these the group chooses one they would like to discuss. They are then able to offer comments, ask questions, or suggest meanings that are relevant to that one particular dream; this may take anywhere from fifteen minutes to a few hours, but it is best to discuss more than one dream per meeting.

Taylor's dream groups used the "if it were my dream" method when commenting on the dreams of others. This meant that instead of saying, "You're dream means …" they began their comments with "If it were my dream.…" This reminded the group that the dream ultimately belongs to the dreamer and prevented the group from coming across as confrontational or rude. By considering these factors, Taylor was able to give dreamers more room to reflect on what the dream meant to them, while at the same time taking the suggestions of the group into account. The ultimate goal of Taylor's dream work was to help individuals overcome personal barriers such as race, age, sex, and social class.

DREAMLET

"Dreamlet," coined by the popular author Ann Faraday, is an alternative term for **dream fragment**. Faraday recommends that people working with their dreams keep detailed **dream diaries** in which they record even apparently meaningless fragments. According to Faraday, many of these fragments eventually fit together into a pattern, if faithfully recorded night after night. She also notes that some of these dreamlets are psychic impressions or **precognitive dreams**.

DREAMLIGHT

The phenomenon of **lucid dreaming** occurs when dreamers become aware that they are in the midst of a dream. The most unusual aspect of this state is that lucid dreamers can consciously alter the content of their dreams. **Stephen LaBerge**, a Stanford-trained psychologist, was the first person to scientifically demonstrate the existence of lucid dreams.

Because the dream landscape is a product of the dreamer's mind, it should be possible to simply "will" the dream to change, just as one does in certain visualization exercises. Some therapists have already begun to make therapeutic use of this technique, asking people who are nightmare-prone, for instance, to attempt to manipulate their dreams so that they will have happy endings.

LaBerge recognized the potential usefulness of the lucid dream state early in his research and developed a product that he called DreamLight for helping dreamers to initiate lucid dreaming. Robert Van de Castle, in his important work *Our Dreaming Mind* (pp. 447–48—see *Sources*), describes DreamLight as follows:

It consists of a Lone Ranger-style mask that picks up eye movements with an infrared detection device. When a miniature computer counts eye movements to determine that a **rapid eye movement (REM)** period is probably occurring, flashing red lights are turned on within the mask. Awareness of the flashing red lights then acts as a signal to the dreamer that a REM period is occurring, and the dreamer can use that information to achieve lucidity.

DREAMSTUFF

Dreamstuff, as the name implies, refers to the "material" out of which the world we experience during the dream state is constructed. Although dreamstuff—or such alternative expressions as dream fabric and dream matter—can be used metaphorically, it can also be used in a manner that suggests belief in some actual (though subtle) substance that forms the landscapes we encounter in dreams. The latter idea is especially popular in various occult and metaphysical schools of thought, which postulate a series of "planes" or levels that coexist with the physical plane in what might be called a different dimension. From this perspective, most dreams are said to occur on what is called the astral plane. The astral plane is said to be composed of subtle elements, etheric in nature, more akin to the energies of the life force than to physical matter. This subtle material can be shaped by our imagination and responds to our mind to become the realm we experience during dreams.

DREAMWORK

The dreamwork is **Sigmund Freud**'s expression for the psychological processes that disguise the real meaning of dreams to the dreamer so that sleep is not interrupted by disturbing dream images. The overt, surface content of dreams Freud called the **manifest dream**. The hidden meaning of dreams, which he believed could be uncovered by psychoanalysis, Freud called the **latent dream**.

In Freud's view, the purpose of dreams is to allow us to satisfy in fantasies the instinctual urges that society judges to be unacceptable in some way, such as engaging in sex with a parent (a major theme in Freudian psychology). So that we do not awaken as a result of the strong emotions that would be evoked if we were to dream about the literal fulfillment of such desires, the part of the mind that Freud called the censor transforms the dream content so as to disguise its true meaning. The dreamwork is the censoring process. Freud explicitly identified five processes brought into play during dreamwork: **displacement, condensation, symbolization, projection,** and **secondary revision**.

DRUGS, EFFECT ON DREAMS

While there has been significant research on the relationship between various kinds of drugs and sleep, there have been far fewer studies on the effects of drugs on dreams. Most of the relevant findings concern the impact of drugs on **rapid eye movement (REM) sleep**, the phase of sleep marked by vivid dreaming. Studies of **alcohol** and dreams, for example, indicate the quantity of REM sleep decreases and Stage 4 (deep) sleep increases with excessive alcohol consumption, creating the impression that one has slept more deeply and more soundly under the influence of alcohol.

REM sleep also decreases under the influence of barbiturates, drugs that in the past were

As with alcohol, prescription medications can have a negative effect on sleep patterns, such as REM sleep.

regularly prescribed to help stressed-out patients sleep and relax. As with many other drugs, REM sleep initially decreases under the influence of barbiturates, but later returns to a normal level if the drug is used regularly. Withdrawal is difficult, however, and regular users experience vivid dreams and **nightmares** when they attempt to stop using such drugs. The markedly negative effects of barbiturates have caused them to be replaced by other, less disruptive drugs.

Some over-the-counter allergy medications have been shown to cause dreams and nightmares that are so intense or unusual they are now mentioned as a possible side effect of taking the drugs. Nicotine patches and melatonin, an over the counter sleep aid, are reported to increase the vividness of dreams and nightmares. The nicotine patch, in particular, is said to intensify dreams to the point of distraction; often causing the dreamer to awaken.

The impact of many prescription drugs has also been studied. Drugs that are used for regulating the endocrine system, controlling blood pressure, and the treatment of neurological disorders can wreak havoc on the form, content, and frequency of dreams. "Alpha-one blockers" that are used in the treatment of hypertension are among the drugs recognized for causing nightmares, rather than simply intensifying dreams. This category also includes anti-Parkinson treatments such as L-dopas, bromocriptine, and selegeline, which have been known to cause psychosis. Selective Serotonin Reuptake Inhibitors (SSRI) such as Prozac®, Paxil®, Zoloft®, and Celexa® increase the frequency and intensity of vivid dreams in the non-REM stage of the sleep process. Although the effects of these drugs on dreams are profound, it must be noted that stopping their intake will cause a sudden occurrence of vivid dreams and nightmares that is normally associated with REM rebound and is not recommended without the approval of a doctor.

The influence of illicit drugs on dream content is also a topic of interest. LSD (lysergic acid diethylamide) floods the nervous system with serotonin and results in hallucinations involving all the senses—visual, olfactory, gustatory, and tactile. This phenomenon is quite different from the hallucinations associated with schizophrenia, but in terms of biological responses it is the closest thing to a dream-like experience a person can have without being asleep.

The link between hallucinogenic drugs and dreams has been recognized since the time of the oldest societies. Belladonna was the drug of the ancient oracles of Delphi; it was used to induce trances and dreams. Haoma was used by the early Persians for the same general purpose. The use of drugs is common in almost all ancient societies for the purposes of more easily achieving a dreaming state or a dream-like trance.

ALL MEN WHO HAVE
ACHIEVED GREAT
THINGS HAVE BEEN
GREAT DREAMERS.

—ORISON SWETT MARDEN

ECT (ELECTROCONVULSIVE THERAPY)

Among the many topics explored by sleep scientists is the effect of extreme abuse to the central nervous systems caused by drug overdose, electroshock therapy, and other traumas. Researchers have found that such inquiries significantly increase **rapid eye movement (REM) sleep** (the period of sleep associated with the most vivid dreams) for prolonged periods of time.

It has been theorized that increased REM time is correlated with physiological healing processes, specifically with intensified neuronal protein synthesis. A more psychological explanation might be that survivors of such shocks need more dream time in which to sort out their trauma.

EEG (ELECTROENCEPHALOGRAM)

The human body is an electrochemical organism, although the electrical activities of the body are relatively weak in contrast to electrical appliances. Although weak, the electrical activity of the human body, particularly that of the nerves, can be measured. The brain is especially active in this regard, and electrical variations can be measured by means of electrodes taped to the head and face. The machines used for this purpose produce what is referred to as an electroencephalogram, or EEG. When recorded on a roll of paper, EEGs produce what looks like a wave pattern, hence the expression *brain wave*. Different **stages of sleep** are characterized by different brain wave patterns, and contemporary laboratory sleep research relies heavily on EEG measurements.

A woman undergoes an electroencephalogram (EEG) test.

EGO

In traditional psychology and psychoanalysis, ego refers to one's sense of individual selfhood. This meaning of the term is neutral or even positive and should not be burdened with the negative associations embodied in such expressions as "has a big ego." Particularly important for dream theory, the term ego was used to designate one of the three essential components of **Sigmund Freud**'s theory of the human personality. Freud referred to the ego as the "reality principle," meaning that it is the rational, reasoning part of the psyche that undertakes the task of adjusting our inner urges to the demands and restrictions of the surrounding environment.

The other two aspects of the self in Freud's personality theory are the **superego** and the **id**. The superego represents the internalized mores of society and tells us what is right and wrong. The superego is frequently in conflict with the id, the primitive, animal part of the self expressed in sexual and aggressive drives. The demands of external reality also tend to conflict with certain id drives. Thus, energies of both the ego and the superego tend to repress our sexual and aggressive urges, although we are often largely unconscious of these inner conflicts. When we sleep, however, the ego allows id desires to be expressed in the form of dreams, albeit in an indirect, symbolic manner that does not disturb our sleep. Someone with a strong desire to murder his father may have, for example, a dream about the accidental death (making the killing passive rather than active) of some other authority figure (a father figure).

Another major school of psychological dream interpretation was initiated by Freud's student **Carl Jung**. Jung's analysis of the psyche is related to, yet significantly different from, Freud's. In Jung's personality theory, the ego represents the individual's sense of personal self. This sense of personal identity, however is purchased at the expense of certain tendencies (for instance, socially undesirable traits) that are rejected as "not-self." According to Jung, these rejected traits come together as a kind of unconscious "counter-ego,' which he termed the **shadow**. This shadow self is often experienced in dreams as another person.

EGYPT, ANCIENT

Ancient Egyptian civilization reaches back as far as 4000 B.C.E. It continued basically uninterrupted up to the time of Alexander the Great's conquest in 332 B.C.E. Knowledge of many of the beliefs and much of the culture of ancient Egypt were lost to the world and remained hidden until the nineteenth century brought the first systematic excavations and translation of hieroglyphics. The ancient Egyptians, like the Mesopotamians, viewed dreams as messages from a wide variety of divinities and used them in divination (predicting the future).

From about 3000 B.C.E., Egyptian official religion recognized the pharaoh as the offspring of the sun god, Ra, and thus a god himself. The dreams of the pharaoh were regarded as more significant because the gods were more likely to speak to a fellow divinity. One of the more famous Egyptian dreams was a dream of Thutmose IV, who around 1400 B.C.E. encountered the divinity Hormakhu in his sleep. Hormakhu struck up a deal in which he promised that the kingdom would be united and that Thutmose would be wealthy if he promised to uncover the Sphinx, which at the time was partially buried in sand. Both sides fulfilled their promises, and Thutmose had a stone column erected in front of the Sphinx, on which the story of his dream was recorded.

There were many other gods and goddesses in the Egyptian pantheon whose domains covered everything from natural phenomena like air (the god Shu) to cultural phenomena like writing (the goddess Safekht). The Egyptians even had a god of dreams, Serapis, who had a number of temples devoted to his worship. A particularly significant one, located at Memphis, dates from around 3000 B.C.E. These temples were the homes of professional dream interpreters referred to as "the learned ones of the library of magic."

People also came to these temples to sleep, with the intention of receiving a dream from the gods that would provide an answer to a vexing question—a widespread practice in the ancient world, referred to as **incubation**. As in the later dream temples of **Aesculapius**, the dreamer fasted and engaged in other rituals before lying down to sleep. In cases where the temple was too far away from the person seeking dream guidance, a surrogate could be hired to undergo the rituals.

Among other divinities associated with dreams, the jolly midget god Bes was assigned the job of protecting households from **nightmares**. His likeness was often carved on the headboards and headrests of Egyptian beds. The ancient Egyptians also employed rituals believed to undo misfortunes predicted in inauspicious dreams.

What we know about ancient Egyptian dream lore comes mostly from two collections of dream *omina* (literally, "everything") that have survived to modern day. The earliest of these dates from the twelfth dynasty, which spanned 2050 to 1790 B.C.E., and is known as the Chester Beatty Papyrus III in honor of Chester Beatty, who donated it to the British Museum. The priest who originally compiled this collection of dreams remains unknown. This is because this *omina* is incomplete. We know that it was written by a priest because it was recorded in the cursive style of hieroglyphics that was used exclusively by the priesthood—called *hieratic*. The section we have consists of 143 good dreams, 91 bad dreams, and their interpretations. These are followed by a segment of protection rituals that would guard the dreamer against the evils portrayed in the bad dreams or nightmares.

The second of the dream *omina* has been classified as demotic, which means that it was recorded by public scribes. Unlike the Chester Beatty Papyrus III, which dates from an early period and contains almost purely Egyptian dream lore, the second *omina* dates from the second century C.E. and was influenced by Mesopotamian concepts of astrology and astronomy. When it was originally compiled, the second *omina* consisted of 250 entries, but the passage of time has damaged about 100 of them past the

The winged symbol of the Egyptian god Ra appears in much of the ancient civilization's architecture. Egyptian pharaohs were considered children of Ra, and thus their dreams were seen as being divine.

point of recovery. One of the most unusual qualities of this *omina* is that it contains a section devoted to the dreams of women. Up until this point, women's dreams were largely ignored in Near Eastern cultures.

ELIADE, MIRCEA

Mircea Eliade (1907–1986) was a highly influential twentieth-century historian of religions (an academic discipline also known as comparative religion). His stature in religious studies is comparable to that of **Carl Jung** in psychology. He had a broad influence through his abundant writings and the many students he trained at the University of Chicago. Although many scholars have criticized Eliade, his work remains a standard point of reference in any theoretical discussion of religious phenomena.

According to Eliade, it is the natural tendency of the human mind to make a distinction between the sacred and the profane (the non-sacred or secular). This distinction is drawn both spatially and temporally, so that human societies set aside special sacred places (e.g., temples and churches) as well as sacred times (e.g., religious holidays). The sacred represents a power that is both attractive and repelling—humanity attempts to draw near and "tap" such power, but normally does not wish to be absorbed into the sacred. The sacred is the source of such powers as the power of transformation, rebirth, creativity, and healing. Religious activities such as religious rituals and ceremonies are ways of tapping sacred power.

Eliade mentions dreams in his studies of **initiatory dreams** and **shamanism**. A more creative treatment of dreams is contained in an essay in his *Myths, Dreams, and Mysteries*. In this work, Eliade discusses the religious meaning of ascension, which often symbolizes a breakthrough into another, sacred realm. Transferring this archaic symbolism into contemporary psychology, Eliade observes that dreams during sleep and "waking dreams" (by which he probably means what we today call creative visualization) in which one finds oneself ascending a stairway frequently indicate personal transformation: "In effect, the ascent of a stairway or a mountain in a dream or a waking dream signifies, at the deepest psychic level, an experience of regeneration (the solution of a crisis, psychic re-integration)" (p. 119—see *Sources*). Here as well as in other places in his extensive corpus of writings, Eliade goes beyond the task of describing religious symbols and speculates on their psychological significance. Few contemporary historians of religion have followed Eliade's lead in this regard, largely abandoning the exploration of the territory where dreams and myths intersect to depth psychologists.

EMG (ELECTROMYOGRAM)

The human body is an electrochemical organism, although the electrical activities of the body are relatively weak. Nevertheless, a variety of different human electrical activities can be measured through electrodes taped to the skin or scalp. In sci-

entific sleep and dream research, the most important measurements are **EEGs** (electroencephalograms), which are measurements of brain wave activity, and **EOG**s (electrooculograms), which measure eye movements distinguishing between rapid eye movement **(REM)** and non-REM sleep. A third measurement usually taken along with an EEG and EOG is an EMG (electromyogram), a measure of muscle tone in the neck that is typically made through electrodes attached to the chin. The EMG helps researchers identify periods of head movement that may interfere with EEG and EOG readings, and is also a secondary indicator of REM periods (because muscular activity is at a standstill during REM sleep).

EOG (ELECTROOCULOGRAM)

Modern scientific dream research did not really accelerate until after Eugene Aserinsky and Nathaniel Kleitman's 1953 discovery of **rapid eye movement (REM) sleep** and the subsequent linking of REM sleep with dreaming. Although later studies showed that significant dreaming could take place during non-REM sleep, the postulate that there was a close correlation between dreams and REM sleep guided scientific dream research for over a decade. The measurement of REM is referred to as an electrooculogram or EOG. It is obtained by placing electrodes around the outside of the eyes and recording changes in electrical potential between the back of the eye and the front of the eye.

ESP (EXTRASENSORY PERCEPTION)

ESP, or extrasensory perception, refers to the acquisition of information without the use of any human sense organs. Extrasensory perception is the scientific designation for psychic, intuitive, mediumistic, prophetic, and related phenomena. Related terms are: telepathy, which indicates information originating from the mind of another person; clairvoyance (literally, "clear seeing"), which refers to psychic sensitivity (particularly in the form of visual information); and precognition, which is the perception of information about future events.

Paranormal dreams fall within the range of research on extrasensory perception, although the dividing line between them and normal dreams is often difficult to draw. Various distortions or displacements of details frequently occur. Also, some dreams may involve obscuring personal symbols, causing paranormal information to go unnoticed by an outside researcher or even by the dreamer.

Individuals who experience paranormal dreams usually describe them as being vivid and intense. The paranormal character of telepathic and prophetic dreams is usually quite clear. Sweating and trembling often occur, the dreams produce an impression lasting for days, and they tend to be repeated.

The frequency and thematic content of paranormal dreams can be determined by examining surveys of psychic cases. The largest survey of documented cases—that is, those corroborating the existence of a correspondence between a distant event and the person's report of a psychic experience—is contained in the two-volume work *Phantasms of the Living*, published in 1886 by the Society for Psychical Research. Of the 5,000 individuals who were asked about possible psychic experiences, 702 reported evidence of telepathy. Most of these cases occurred while the participants were awake.

In the book *On Prophetic Dreams: An Experiment with Time* (1927), J.W. Dune claimed that precognitive dreams are to be expected as much as dreams of past events. By putting his own dreams down immediately on awakening and by keeping a record of them, he found that a considerable part of them anticipated future experiences. The results of his study were corroborated by fellow experimenters. The largest survey of undocumented cases is the collection of about 3,290 cases analyzed at the Parapsychology Laboratory at Duke University by L.E. Rhine, who reported that 68 percent of the ESP events occurred during dreams.

Lost objects are frequently found in dreams, although in most cases the mystery can be explained by subconscious memory. An example of this type of dream is the dream in which Hercules appeared to Sophocles to indicate where a golden crown would be found.

Traveling-clairvoyance (the supposed paranormal faculty of seeing persons and events that are distant in time and place) in dreams may explain the experience of **déjà vu**, which is often claimed to be a proof of reincarnation. An interesting attempt to explain the experience of déjà vu is a theory of ancestral dreams put forward by Letourneau in the *Bulletins et mémoires dela Societé d'Anthropologie de Paris*. He claimed that certain external or psychic events that have deeply affected a person may result in a molecular reorientation, which may be transmitted to descendants. In this way, ancestral recollections can be produced and revived.

Vivid dreams often seem to stimulate **out-of-body experiences**, during which the gaining of waking consciousness while still in a sleeping state may result in finding oneself conscious in an astral body, which can move independently of the physical body. However, some experimenters have claimed that such out-of-body experiences may be stimulated by deliberately induced images of release just before the dreamer passes into the sleep condition.

EVIL AND DREAMS

The notion of some form of conscious demonic force has been a part of the human imagination since prehistoric times. The belief that malicious entities lie behind natural disasters and other unpleasant aspects of human life is still prevalent in certain traditional societies, especially in such culture areas as Africa and Oceania, in the form of natural elements (typically animals or such phenomena as floods) or as spirits of the ances-

tors. Especially before the development of scientific discoveries that proffered more neutral explanations for the irregularities of nature, demons were believed to be responsible for unexplainable natural disasters and diseases.

Given this widespread belief, it is only natural that the common experience of **nightmares** has often been explained in terms of the intrusion of **demons**. This explanation is so widespread, in fact, that it is not unusual to find special prayers and ceremonies intended to protect the sleeper from evil entities. During the European Middle Ages, when sex was regarded as evil, erotic dreams were viewed as being caused by special demons called **incubi and succubi**. Some medieval churchmen went so far as to denounce all dreams as creations of the Devil.

THE FUTURE BELONGS TO
THOSE WHO BELIEVE IN
THE BEAUTY OF THEIR
DREAMS.

—ELEANOR ROOSEVELT

FALLING DREAMS

Some dream motifs are so common that almost everybody has them on more than one occasion. These motifs include such scenarios as falling dreams, **flying dreams**, dreams of **nakedness** in public, and **unpreparedness dreams**. Such shared dreams arise from experiences and anxieties fundamental to all people.

Falling is one of these shared motifs. Psychologists speculate that fearful falling dreams are rooted in our early experiences as toddlers taking our first steps on two legs. If this hypothesis is correct, then our childhood experiences leave a deep imprint in our brain that is somehow activated in adult life during periods of high anxiety. Some sociobiologists have further speculated that our fear of falling ultimately derives

from the experiences of prehistoric ancestors afraid of tumbling out of trees during the night.

Whatever the origin of falling fears, in dreams the processes of the human mind tend to deploy images that symbolically express our hopes and fears. Falling dreams thus often tend to reflect a sense that one has failed or "fallen down" in life. For example, a woman brought up to believe in a traditional sexual ethic may dream of falling after an erotic encounter because she believes that she has become a "fallen woman." Dreams of falling also occur when one feels completely overwhelmed or out of control, such as periods when one is going through a divorce or the loss of a job.

Falling dreams are not always symbolic. For example, Ann Faraday, author of *The Dream Game*, recounts an instance of noting that the guardrails on the balcony of her new seventh-

Falling dreams are representations of our waking fears.

FINLEY, CAROLINE

Caroline Finley was a medical doctor (decorated for her activities as a surgeon during the First World War) and dream researcher who, contrary to the prevailing Freudianism of her time, emphasized the physiological dimensions of dreaming. In a 1921 paper she reported on the impact of endocrine gland therapy with a middle-aged influenza patient. Given an extract of pituitary gland on a daily basis, after about a week and a half the patient began to have highly pleasant dreams. The same patient was later given an extract of adrenal gland, which within a few days changed the nature of her dreams to tense **nightmares**. Finley concluded that this case study clearly demonstrated the purely physiological origins of many dreams.

FLYING DREAMS

Among the most common of dream motifs that almost everybody has experienced is the flying dream. Other motifs include such common scenarios as **falling dreams**, dreams of **nakedness** in public, and **unpreparedness dreams**. These shared dreams arise from experiences and anxieties fundamental to all people.

In flying dreams, unlike other types of shared dream images, it is difficult to clearly identify the source of the experience. One explanation sometimes put forward by occult/metaphysical writers is that during sleep we sometimes project ourselves (our spiritual selves) outside our physical body and travel through space unencumbered by such physical limitations as gravity. These **out-of-body experiences** are then remembered as dreams.

Whatever the origin of flying images, in dreams the processes of the human mind tend to

story apartment were rickety. At the time, she was so preoccupied with the other aspects of moving that she did not fully register the dangerous condition of the railing. That night she dreamed of falling off the balcony, which caused her to pay attention to the poor state of the guardrails the next day. Faraday also notes that the prevalent idea that people who do not wake up before they hit bottom will die is simply a superstition, unsupported by actual dream experiences.

A final perspective on falling dreams focuses on the "jolt" that wakes us from such dreams. According to some traditions of occult lore, our consciousness wanders away from the physical body during dreams. When something happens that causes us to awaken abruptly, our spiritual self "snaps" back into the body. This "rough landing" results in our being jolted into wakefulness and is registered in our dream consciousness as a fall.

The exhilaration of flying dreams might represent our hopes and joys in waking life.

deploy images that symbolically express our hopes and fears. Flying dreams may thus reflect a sense that one is "flying high" or that one has "risen above" something. Flying also represents freedom and joy. **Sigmund Freud** associated flying with sexual desire, **Alfred Adler** with the will to dominate others, and **Carl Jung** with the desire to break free of restrictions. Contemporary research tends to support Jung's perspective.

FOLKLORE OF DREAMS

Our culture has, like many others, an informal set of beliefs about dreams that can be referred to as dream folklore. Most are empty of empirical content, such as the following common myths:

- *If you dream you are falling and hit the ground before you wake up, you will die.* This is an interesting bit of folklore that many of us have heard—and may even have repeated—since childhood. Dreamers usually wake up right before hitting the ground, and some have even been known to land safely. Ultimately, who has ever actually known somebody who has related such a dream after they passed away?

- *Sleepwalkers should not be awakened.* It is said that awakening sleepwalkers in the act will induce a heart attack or insanity. Both ideas are incorrect. It is also thought that sleepwalkers will do nothing to hurt themselves. This is also incorrect, as sleepwalkers have been known to walk through glass doors and to fall down stairways. It may be *difficult* to awaken sleepwalkers, so a more effective course of action is to guide them back to bed.

- *Some people don't dream.* Research has shown that everybody dreams, though some people don't recall their dreams. (See **nondreamers**.)

- *Some people dream only in black and white.* Everyone dreams in color, although, unless we are specifically paying attention to colors, they may be deemphasized so that we think we dream in black and white.

Some dream folklore can be traced back for generations and tend to cross cultural boundaries. Such beliefs, passed down through time, eventually lose their original meaning and become mere habit. Some familiar dream beliefs are:

- *You will dream of your future mate if you sleep with a piece of wedding cake under your pillow.* This is a romantic bit of folklore that may have evolved from ancient times as wedding cake has featured prominently in nuptial feasts for centuries. It is a symbol of fertility and good luck.

- Placing a knife under the foot of the bed will ward off nightmares. Such a notion could be tied to the original definition of nightmares, which were said to be menacing female spirits who attacked victims in their sleep. Tradition held that witches and evil spirits are easily discouraged by steel; hence, a knife under your bed will protect you from nightmares.

Other dream beliefs actually have some basis in empirical observation. It has been said, for example, that eating spicy food before going to bed induces nightmares. This is untrue, although if the food induces indigestion, it may disturb sleep.

FOUCAULT, MICHEL

The dream philosophy of famous French thinker Michel Foucault (1926–1984) can be found in his essay "Dream, Imagination and Existence," published in 1954 as an introduction to Ludwig Binswanger's essay "Dream and Existence." This essay appeared when Foucault, even though very young, had already engaged in a considerable amount of philosophical study, which included the works of Edmund Husserl, **Sigmund Freud**, Martin Heidegger, Gaston Bachelard, Jean-Paul Sartre, and Ludwig Binswanger. He was also familiar with a wide variety of observations on dreams found in the literature, drama, religion, and philosophies of other times.

In "Dream, Imagination and Existence" he conducts a deep analysis of humanity's place in the world by seeking the fundamental features of human existence, not in perception but in the dream. Foucault thus reversed the common thesis that the dream is merely one variety of imagination and proposed the uncommon thesis that "the dream is not a modality of the imagination,

the dream is the first condition of its possibility." In other words, the dream represents the fundamental condition for the imagination.

For Foucault an adequate theory of the imagination presupposes nothing less than an adequate understanding of the phenomenon of dreaming. Imagining is rooted in the dream, and the very character of existence is to be discerned in the oneiric (dreamlike). For Foucault the dreamworld is animated by the individual's consciousness and, like perceptual experience, aims at a meaningful whole. The dream is a "quasi world," containing neglected information about ourselves. The quasi world of dream, like the perceptual world, is a fundamental mode of our being and, hence, a realm with its own kind of elusive totality and meaningful structure. Its significance and structure cannot be understood by reference only to the past, especially to a past that is externally related to the dream.

According to Foucault the dream is not a degenerated variety of imagining, but is the parent of the imagination, and the origin of the dream is the origination of existence, that is, the origin of the human soul. He asserted that, while one is dreaming, one's consciousness sleeps, but one's existence (human soul) awakens. Also, dreams about death are to be considered the most important dreams available to individuals, because instead of being about life in its various interpretations, they are about the fulfillment of existence, the moment in which life reaches its fulfillment.

FRANKENSTEIN

Mary Shelley received her inspiration for the epic horror story *Frankenstein; or, The Modern Prometheus* while visiting with Lord Byron, the brother of her future husband, Percy Byron Shelley, at his Swiss villa in 1816. At the tender age of eighteen, she experienced an extraordinary nightmare following a "ghost story" session in which she had participated with Shelley, Byron, his mistress, and a local doctor. Byron, inspired by the stories shared in the group, suggested that all present should attempt to write a horror story. Mary Shelley had a nightmare that night that she recalled vividly enough to use as the basis for her novel. The following is part of her account of that nightmare.

> My imagination, unbidden, possessed and guided me, gifting the successive images that arose in my mind with a vividness far beyond the usual bounds of reveries.... I saw the pale student of unhallowed arts kneeling beside the thing he had put together—I saw the hideous phantasm of a man stretched out, and then, on the working of some powerful engine, show signs of life, and stir with an uneasy, half-vital motion.... He would hope that, left to itself, the slight spark of life which he had communicated would fade; that this thing which had received such imperfect animation would subside into dead matter, and that he might sleep in the belief that the silence of the grave would quench forever the transient existence of the hideous corpse which he had looked upon as the cradle of life.... Swift as light and cheering was the idea that broke in upon me. "I have found it! What terrifies me will terrify others; and I need only describe the specter that had haunted my midnight pillow." On the morrow, I announced that I had thought of the story.

Frankenstein was published in 1818. The novel is based, in part, on Luigi Galvani, a scientist who concluded through a series of experiments that electricity was the secret of life. He believed it was actually possible to reanimate a corpse by using an electrical stimulus.

In the story, Shelley tells a tale of scientific terror in which Victor Frankenstein creates a living being out of the parts of decomposing corpses. The Frankenstein monster in the original version of the story was an intelligent being who was not only able to speak but also reason. He possessed sophisticated reading capabilities and knowledge; the objectionable irrationality of his temperament was his one significant negative characteristic. Shelley describes the monster as being a living travesty of death, comprised of the pieces of the recently buried dead.

The monster's struggle with Victor parallels, in some ways, the biblical struggle of the **demons** and God. When, in the end, the monster is triumphant he exhibits feelings of remorse, regret, and self-hatred. His acknowledgement of the emptiness of retribution shows a sense of human compassion that is absent in most villains. In the end, the creature vows to destroy itself, but the story concludes with it disappearing into the snowy darkness.

FREUD, SIGMUND

Sigmund Freud (1856–1939) was the founder of psychoanalysis and one of the great thinkers of this century. As a practicing medical doctor, Freud became interested in the role of the mind in disease. Partially as a result of his work with patients afflicted with hysteria (a psychosomatic illness), as well as his training in hypnosis under the brilliant French neurologist J. Martin Charcot, Freud was led to specialize in psychological disturbances. His early theorizing about the sexual origins of mental illness was scandalous to contemporaneous polite society, and it was many

Honored in this Austrian stamp, Sigmund Freud put forth many innovative theories about the importance of dreams and how they may be analyzed to alleviate mental and emotional distress.

pleasure, people learn how to repress their animal impulses as they grow up in order to get along in society. They never, however, completely conquer their primitive selves. Freud called this animal self, which constitutes the core of the psyche, the **id**. The other aspects of the psyche, the **ego** and the **superego**, are later developments that arise from the need to survive and to adapt to the surrounding social environment. The ego is the rational, reasoning part of the psyche that undertakes the task of adjusting our inner urges to the demands and restrictions of the surrounding environment. The superego represents the internalized mores of society and tells us what is right and wrong.

The superego is frequently in conflict with the id. The demands of external reality (an ego function) also tend to conflict with certain id drives. Thus, in Freud's theory of human nature, the psyche is a kind of battleground in which the various components of the personality are engaged in an ongoing struggle. At the core of conflicts that lead to mental illness is often a denial of urges that people regard as unacceptable and that they do not wish to admit are a part of themselves. One might, for instance, wish to have intercourse with the parent of the opposite sex (termed Oedipus complex; in women, also termed Electra complex). This desire, however, is so beyond the bounds of what our society regards as proper that we repress our awareness of the urge and it remains unconscious. Mental illness comes about when such desires become too strong to deal with through the normal coping process.

Freudian therapy involves discovery of the repressed urges causing dysfunction. Once patients are confronted with their real desires and accept them as part of themselves, a cure is effected because the psyche no longer need go to extraordinary lengths to hide the "terrible truth"

years before he was able to convince his medical colleagues of the truth of his basic discoveries. Although few, if any, current analysts adhere to "orthodox" Freudianism, certain fundamental Freudian notions, such as the idea that we are influenced by unconscious motivations, are widely accepted among psychotherapists.

Freud's theory of human nature (what contemporary psychologists would call Freud's *personality theory*) presents a highly uncomplimentary picture of the human being. Basically selfish animals driven by aggressive urges and the desire for from the conscious mind. Freud initially hoped that hypnosis would be a useful tool for accessing the unconscious, but soon gave that technique up in favor of free association.

He also came to believe that the analysis of dreams was a powerful avenue for uncovering repressed desires, even referring to dreams as "the royal road" to the unconscious. Freud's principal work on this subject, *The Interpretation of Dreams*, was first published in 1900 and went through eight editions in his lifetime. At one point he wrote that *The Interpretation of Dreams* "contains even according to my present day judgment the most valuable of all the discoveries it has been my good fortune to make. Insights such as this fall to one's lot but once in a lifetime." Despite many minor revisions, his basic theory of dreams remained remarkably constant after its initial formulation.

In Freud's view, the purpose of dreams is to allow us to satisfy in fantasies the instinctual urges that society judges unacceptable. So that we do not awaken as a result of the strong emotions that would be evoked if we dreamed about the literal fulfillment of such desires, the part of the mind that Freud called the censor transforms the dream content so as to disguise its true meaning. Freud called the **censorship** process the **dreamwork**. Freud explicitly identified five processes brought into play during dreamwork: **displacement, condensation, symbolization, projection**, and **secondary revision**.

After undergoing one or more of the dreamwork process, the **secondary processes** of the ego reorganize the otherwise bizarre components of a dream so that it has a comprehensible surface meaning, called the **manifest dream**. The process of dream interpretation in psychoanalysis involves "decoding" the manifest dream content to discover the real, hidden meaning of the dream, called the **latent dream**.

DARE TO LIVE THE LIFE
YOU HAVE DREAMED FOR
YOURSELF. GO FORWARD
AND MAKE YOUR
DREAMS COME TRUE.

—RALPH WALDO EMERSON

GARFIELD, PATRICIA

Patricia Garfield (1934–) is a contemporary dream researcher, clinical psychologist, and author of numerous popular books on dreams. She is a graduate of Temple University and has taught at Temple and lectured for the extension program of the University of California. She is perhaps best known for her 1974 book, *Creative Dreaming*, which, among other things, provided an extensive discussion of **lucid dreaming** a decade prior to **Stephen LaBerge**'s experimental reports in the early and middle eighties.

Garfield travels, lectures, and holds seminars widely and was one of the original cofounders of the **Association for the Study of Dreams**. Her other publications include *Pathway to Ecstasy: The Way of the Dream Mandala* (1979), *Your Child's Dreams* (1984), *Women's Bodies, Women's Dreams* (1988), and *The Healing Power of Dreams* (1991).

GILGAMESH

Humanity made the transition from tribal lifestyles to the more complex forms of social organization we call civilization along four great river basins—in **China, India, Egypt**, and the Middle East. The Middle Eastern basin, which runs along the Tigris and Euphrates rivers in what is now modern Iraq, hosted a series of sequentially related civilizations that together are referred to as Mesopotamia. It is the oldest of the four early sites of civilization, predating the high culture of Egypt by thousands of years.

The Mesopotamians wrote on clay tablets, many of which have survived to the present.

This ancient literature contains, among other compositions, *The Epic of Gilgamesh*. Humankind's oldest recorded hero tale (dating from at least 2000 B.C.E.), the epic is built around Gilgamesh's quest for immortality and is full of dream accounts. A legendary king who ruled the city-state of Uruk around 2600 B.C.E., Gilgamesh was said to be the son of the goddess Ninsun and the king Lugalbanda. His divine heritage on his mother's side, however, did not exempt him from mortality.

The first part of the epic relates the events leading up to Gilgamesh's meeting with a man named Enkidu, beginning with Gilgamesh's dream predicting that he would find a friend whom he would "embrace as a wife." Because the dream message was expressed in symbols, Gilgamesh sought out his mother, who interpreted the dream for him. Enkidu, who began life as a naked wild man, is eventually tamed and becomes Gilgamesh's best friend. Together they travel off and slay Humbaba, the giant of the pine forest. On the way to the forest, Gilgamesh has what he feels may be an inauspicious dream, but Enkidu interprets it for him so that it indicates a favorable outcome to their quest.

Gilgamesh triumphs over Humbaba and is so attractive that the goddess of love herself, Ishtar, proposes that she and the young king become lovers. Gilgamesh responds by recounting the bad ends her partners have met and rejects her proposal. Ishtar is so upset that she persuades the Bull of Heaven to come down from the sky and punish Uruk. Gilgamesh and Enkidu, however, make short work of the bull.

Unfortunately, slaying the Bull of Heaven evokes the ire of the gods, who decide that one of the two friends must die as punishment. They choose Enkidu for this unpleasant fate, and he sickens and eventually dies. (Before falling ill, Enkidu has an omen dream in which he learns that he has been chosen to die.) Gilgamesh is distraught by the death of his best friend, but he also begins to consider his own mortality. In Mesopotamian thought, the gods constructed humans out of clay to be their servants on earth. Pragmatists, they did not bother to include an immortal soul as part of the package. What afterlife there was was a pale shadow of earthly life, much like the Jewish Sheol or the early Greek Hades. Before he dies, Enkidu dreams about the other world, and offers the following description: "There is the house whose people sit in darkness: dust is their food and clay their meat. They are clothed like birds with wings for covering, they see no light, they sit in darkness. I entered the house of dust and I saw the kings of the earth, their crowns put away forever...." (Sandars, p. 92—see *Sources*). Like other cultures that buried the dead in the ground, the Mesopotamians conceived of the otherworld as being a dark, dusty, unpleasant underworld.

With this frightful prospect before him, Gilgamesh resolves to set out on a quest for immortality. He has heard that the mortal man Utnapishtim, the Mesopotamian equivalent of the Bible's Noah, was granted immortality by the gods. To discover how Utnapishtim obtained such a favor, Gilgamesh undertakes an arduous journey.

When he finally arrives, Utnapishtim relates how the gods, in a fit of anger, destroyed all of humankind in a great flood. Only the wise divinity Ea had the foresight to warn Utnapishtim, who built a great boat in which he and his family survived. The gods quickly realized the error of their ways, but only after the fact. Human beings "feed" the gods, and, without them, celestial beings will starve. Utnapishtim, however, was

A statue in Zaragoza, Spain, honors painter Francisco Goya. Goya's artwork sometimes portrayed frightening dreams.

able to make the appropriate offerings, and the gods were able to eat. Out of gratitude, they granted immortality to him and his wife.

As for Gilgamesh, Utnapishtim requires that, as a test to determine his worthiness for immortality, he stay awake for a week. Gilgamesh promptly fails the test and, instead, sleeps for a week. Good host that he is, however, Utnapishtim gives Gilgamesh a "consolation prize," namely, a plant with the powers of rejuvenation (the next best thing to immortality). Unfortunately, on the journey back a snake eats the plant, so Gilgamesh arrives home empty-handed.

As reflected in the *Gilgamesh*, dreams were highly regarded in ancient Mesopotamia as omens of the future. Dreams were also valued as a means by which the dreamer could penetrate

other realities, as when Enkidu gets a glance into the afterlife during a dream. And, finally, dreams were utilized in the *Gilgamesh* as a literary device, foreshadowing events that had not yet occurred.

GOLA

According to W.L. D'Azevedo's 1973 study of traditional artists in African societies, a particular relationship exists between craftwork, dreams, and spirit beings among the Gola artists of Liberia, whose inspiration occurs during the dream experience and is supported by a very special relationship with a tutelary spirit. Singers, musicians, woodcarvers, and some weavers are referred to as dreamers. They all have a personal spirit inspirer, to whom their works are attributed and with whom they have a relationship of friendship, which molds their work as well as their personality and their behavior.

GOYA, FRANCISCO

Francisco Goya (1746–1828) began painting decorative tapestries and then moved on to become a professional portrait artist. He lived during a troubled period of European history, surviving Napoleon Bonaparte's devastating invasion of Spain. The symbolic expressionism of his later work would serve as inspiration for later generations of artists. His depictions of **nightmares**, violence, and human suffering are considered forerunners of the Romantics of the following century.

Goya is particularly remembered for the nightmarish works of art he produced during the later half of his life. In the painting *Saturn Devouring a Son*, he shows the god in the midst of an appalling feast. Somehow, Goya manages to convey the deity's amazement with his own participation in this cannibalistic ritual. His work *The Sleep of Reason Produces Monsters* is a tribute to the fears of "Reason" that the freeing of the imagination may result in the free reign of the unmanageable aspects of the human psyche. Goya was also known for his depictions of the inmates of a madhouse in Saragossa, Spain, and witches' sabbaths.

The aspect of Goya's life that allowed him to realistically portray frightening dreams was the nightmarish quality of his own waking world. He had a habit of "pointing" his brush with his mouth. Over the course of his life, he began to exhibit the symptoms of what we now recognize as lead poisoning. The illness progressed to the point where he was constantly battling intermittent paralysis, deafness, and tremors that affected the paint strokes of his work toward the end of his life.

GREECE, ANCIENT

The Greeks were particularly interested in dreams, and the dream lore of ancient Greece is more complex than that of perhaps any major cultural tradition. Many traces of the thinking of **Egypt**, Mesopotamia, and Persia are found in the attitude of the Greeks toward dreams. Some Greek ideas about dreams, such as the belief that dreams are divine and the notion that dreams sometimes mean the opposite of what they say, are similar to ideas in the Near East.

Another common characteristic was the fundamental distinction between "true" and "false" dreams. Within the class of true and significant dreams, several distinctions also exist. For instance, in a classification transmitted by **Artemidorus of Daldis, Macrobius**, and other writers, significant dreams are broken down into symbolic dreams, the meaning of which cannot

be understood without interpretation; the *horama*, or visions, which predict future events; and the *chrematismos*, or oracles, which reveal without symbolism what will or will not happen, or what should or should not be done.

Homer, whose epics present disparate attitudes toward dreams, maintained that "true" dreams come through what the Greeks referred to as the gate of horn, and "false" dreams through the gate of ivory, and the *Odyssey* makes it plain that not all dreams are truthful. In Homer's epics, the dream is always personified as a divine being that is independent of time and space and appears to the dreamer at the head of the bed, eventually disappearing. In ancient Greece, dreams were regarded as messages from the gods, and it was believed that during sleep the soul was freed from the body and was able to perceive and converse with higher beings. The authors of Greek tragedy maintained that dreams of such dignity should be carefully interpreted. Aeschylus, in particular, said that dream interpretation was one of the most important inventions of Prometheus.

The largest and most complete compilation of dream lore to survive from the ancient world, the *Oneirocritica (The Interpretation of Dreams)*, was written by a second-century Greek, Artemidorus of Daldis. Artemidorus was a professional diviner and dream interpreter whose Oneirocritica was a compilation of Greek dream lore up to his time, along with of his own observations. The *Oneirocritica* is largely a **dream dictionary**, with some broader advice on how to interpret dreams. Unlike the focus of modern dream books, which are psychologically oriented, Artemidorus's concerns centered on deciphering dreams as omens of the future.

The Greeks also viewed dreams as a source of healing, as the hundreds of dream temples dedicated to **Aesculapius**—the deified doctor who healed or provided healing and medical advice in dreams—bear witness. Aesculapius eventually became the most popular healing divinity of the Hellenistic world. The principal activity at the *asclepieions* (temples dedicated to Aesculapius) was the seeking of cures via the technique of **dream incubation**, the practice of seeking dreams for specific purposes, for everything from healing to practical guidance. People went to *asclepieions* to "camp out" and sleep with the intention of receiving a healing dream from Aesculapius, who sometimes appeared in the seeker's dreams, touched the diseased part of the body with his finger, and then disappeared.

GREEK DRAMA

In ancient Greece, dreams were regarded as messages from the gods, and it was believed that during sleep the soul was freed from the body and was able to perceive and converse with higher beings. The authors of Greek tragedy maintained that dreams of such dignity should be carefully interpreted. Aeschylus, in particular, said that dream interpretation was one of the most important inventions of Prometheus.

One of the primary functions of dreams in Greek tragedy, where a fundamental element is the conflict between fate and individual free will, is to reveal the logic of destiny. Different types of dreams are employed in tragedy and find their origin in a more or less direct imitation of the dreams used by **Homer**, although there are many differences between the use of the dream device in Homer's epics and its employment in tragedy.

For instance, with respect to the relations of the poet with his audience, in the epic the narrator is omnipresent and omniscient, even aware of every secret thought of Olympus. By contrast, in tragedy the knowledge of the dramatis personae is limited, as is the knowledge of persons in real life. Thus, the objectivity of the dream must usually correspond to the experiences of the person represented by the actor on the stage.

Divination played the principal role in the tragedies and was the main guide of the plot, with the role of the dream generally being secondary. The dream represented one of many motifs. The tragic poets often used dreams to help dramatize their narratives, even when there was no mention of dreams in the original source material. The dream was often unnecessary to the myth, but was considered a powerful artistic medium through which the poets could guarantee considerable literary effects in the plot.

The first dramatist who successfully employed the dream device was probably Aeschylus, who, like Homer, recognized the importance of the psychological aspects of the dream. In his extant plays there are no indications of the growth of the dream from a less to a more artistic device. In *The Persians*—which deals with the conflict between Oriental despotism and Greek freedom, and the victory of the Greeks over Xerxes— Atossa, mother of Xerxes, experiences a troublesome allegorical dream after her son's departure for Greece. This dream, which is considered the most beautiful in Greek literature, has a considerable influence on the plot, finding its model in the dreams of the *Iliad* and the *Odyssey*.

The dream plays a secondary, yet very important role in *Prometheus vinctus* providing the grounds for the meeting of the hero and Io. In *Choephoroi* the dream, which is sent by the soul of the dead, is employed to produce suspense. In contrast, the objectivity of dreams is emphasized in *Eumenides*, in which the ghost of Clytemnestra rebukes the sleeping Furies. Here

The ruins of a Greek theater in Turkey. The Greeks felt that dreams were very important, and they were to be carefully interpreted in many of their plays.

the dream has theatrical effectiveness and assumes considerable importance as a factor in outlining the plot of the tragedy. Some references in Aeschylus to dreams, such as in *Septem, Supplices*, and *Agamemnon*, are unimportant, although they are picturesque and happy.

The dream device was sparingly employed by Sophocles. Two brief references to dreams can be found in *Oedipus Tyrannus* and *Acrisius*. One fully related dream is introduced in the *Electra*.

Clytemnestra's allegorical dream is not very important for the independent action of the play, but is fundamental for the portrayal of character. There is no direct reference to any deity as the sender of the dream, which appears to a woman, following the convention of tragedy.

Following the Aeschylean tradition, Euripides adopted the dream device in *Hecuba*, in which the ghost of Polydorus is portrayed on the stage before the eyes of the audience. The dream has a considerable role in the plot, in which the emotional state of Hecuba under the lash of sorrow and revenge constitutes the main subject. Another important dream is Iphigenia's dream in *Iphigenia in Taurus*, in which the oracle of Apollo at Delphi represents the mainspring of the action, as elsewhere in tragedy. In this play the dream, sent to a woman, and the oracle, sent to a man, represent the two leading forces. The elaborate dream, as well as the device of misinterpretation, which leads to a truly tragic situation, is important to the progression of the plot. Among Euripides's minor references to dreams are those reported in *Rhesus*, in which the plot parallels an incident from the *Iliad*. The dream is added to the tale as an embellishment rather than as a necessary part of the story. Dreams also serve as embellishment in other Euripides plays, such as *Cyclops, Alcestis, Hercules Furens, Alope, Aeolus, Orestes, Helena,* and *Meleager*.

GUILT

Guilt can carry over into sleep and induce anxiety when we experience it in our dreams. Survivor guilt often surfaces in the dreams of military veterans and in civilians who experienced a traumatic accident that they survived while someone close to them did not. They often ask why they made it through and feel guilty because someone else lost his or her life or was seriously injured, even though the dreamer was not responsible. These feelings are carried over into the dream state; often, the dreamer replays the events in his or her mind over and over in vivid detail. Sometimes the subconscious will modify the dream so that the survivor takes the place of the victim, or other, similar, variations occur. Repeating **nightmares** is a major symptom of the anxiety neurosis caused by a deep emotional trauma. The guilt experienced in these dreams is often accompanied by grief and anger.

Sexual feelings—particularly sexual attractions at variance with social norms such as adultery, homosexuality, and incestuous desires—can also cause guilt that leads to anxiety dreams. **Sex** in dreams or nightmares often represents a more complex aspect of our personalities—something more than simply our attitudes and our desires for the act of sex itself. In other words, in these kinds of dreams sexual relations can be symbolic of other issues; they don't always represent a straightforward desire for physical relations.

Guilt can also manifest in dreams when the dreamer is feeling anxious about her or his "**shadow** self." Our shadow is the neglected or repressed part of each of us. It is common to refrain from confronting this aspect of our personality out of fear of what we might discover about ourselves. It can stem from insecurities about how we feel we are viewed by society or how we might or might not fit into what is acceptable or "normal." The guilt associated with this "shadow self" tends to cause an individual to develop a second personality to hide the traits that he or she feels are unacceptable. Some **symbolism** regarding this dual self can be manifested in dreams. These dreams of "false-self" are most common when dealing with repressed personality traits.

A MAN'S DREAMS ARE AN
INDEX TO HIS GREATNESS.

—ZADOK RABINWITZ

HALL, CALVIN

The twentieth-century psychologist Calvin Hall (1909–1985) approached dreams as a cognitive process. After analyzing thousands of dream reports, Hall identified five principal areas of life about which dreams reveal information:

- *Concepts of self.* The kinds and number of roles we play in dreams are strong indicators of our self-concept.

- *Concepts of other people.* The roles other people play in our dreams reflect our feelings about others and how we interact with people.

- *Concepts of the world.* The setting of our dreams indicates how we view the world (e.g., ugly and threatening, beautiful and inviting).

- *Concepts of impulses, prohibitions, and penalties.* The way we behave is governed by our concept of our impulses and the penalties for gratifying them, which is reflected in dream imagery.

- *Concepts of problems and conflicts.* Dreams especially provide insight into our conflicts and how we attempt to resolve them.

Hall considered dreams a more valid source of information about an individual's personality than questionnaires and personality tests because dreams can uncover a level of self (what depth psychologists call the **unconscious**) beyond the perceived self of our everyday, waking consciousness. Hall's approach to dreams was richer and more interesting than can be portrayed in this brief encyclopedia entry, but his research and thinking on dreams can be found in his book *The Meaning of Dreams.*

HALLUCINATIONS AND DREAMS

It is a common experience to feel that a dream landscape is physically "real" and then awaken to discover otherwise. This contrast is most vivid in attack dreams, from which the dreamer awakens to find that the monster (or whatever) is not really assaulting him or her. Such dream images are hallucinations, in the sense of having no corresponding physical reality. Many visual hallucinations also have a familiar, dreamlike quality, frequently resembling the **hypnagogic experiences** (those induced by drowsiness) one has just before falling off to sleep.

There is no clear boundary between dreams and hallucinations. Dreams are, for the most part, creations of the mind that do not depend upon immediate sensory input for their existence. The phenomena we call "hallucinations" are sometimes highly dependent upon sensory input (as in LSD hallucinations), but at other times seem to arise completely separate from sensory data.

HARTMANN, ERNEST

The psychiatrist Ernest Hartmann (1934–) is well known for his research on **nightmares**. His father, Heinz Hartmann, was also a psychiatrist and studied under **Sigmund Freud**. The senior Hartmann is sometimes referred to as "the son of Freud." Ernest Hartmann directs the sleep laboratory at Lemuel Shalluck Hospital in Boston, Massachusetts. He also teaches at Tufts University.

One of the first studies that Hartmann conducted consisted of thirty-eight adults who suffered at least one nightmare a week for six months or longer. Most had been plagued by chronic nightmares since childhood. Each subject went through an extensive interview process in which his or her nightmare history, as well as the general content of the nightmares, was thoroughly documented. Eleven subjects from the original group were observed in sleep laboratories for a period of four nights. Hartmann was not satisfied with the results of this approach because he felt that the synthetic environment of the sleep laboratories affected the subjects and their dreams, which effectively tainted the data.

A second study group was comprised of three subgroups. The first consisted of individuals who suffered from frequent, lifelong nightmares. Members of the second group reported having vivid dreams but no significantly recurring or terrifying nightmares. The third group could not recall their dreams at all. Psychological tests and in-depth interviews were conducted and the content of the subjects' dreams were examined. After the experiment concluded, Hartmann was able to establish that, while the subjects of the nightmare group did not share an inordinate number of traits with the members of the second or third groups, they did greatly resemble the personality profiles of the members of the original study. All of the nightmare sufferers had jobs that involved the arts (such as musicians or painters), or they were teachers, and none of them fit within society's standard gender roles.

Hartmann went on to develop his theories concerning the "boundaries" of the mind, based on the information provided by these two studies. The development of a person's boundaries is intricately related to the development of mental structures and faculties that begins early in a person's life. These faculties distinguish between opposites, such as between self and others, inside and out, and fantasy and reality. Those who suffered from chronic nightmares were categorized as having "thin boundaries," and shared characteristics of unusual openness, vulnerability, and difficulties with certain ego functions. These thin boundaries make individuals more aware of their inner feelings and the feelings of those around them, and make them more inclined to artistic pursuits. It also makes them painfully sensitive, not only to the threats of the outside world, but also to their own wishes and impulses. People with "thick boundaries" have stronger defenses to the outside world and to their own unconscious fears and impulses.

HAUSA

The Hausa are a predominantly Islamic people who inhabit northwestern Nigeria and adjacent areas of the Niger Republic. According to a study by R.A. Shweder and R.A. LeVine on the development of dream concepts among Hausa children, there are stages through which the children proceed in their attempts to understand their dream experiences.

Initially, Hausa children believe the events in their dreams to be real occurrences that are visible to others. They treat dream events as if they were intrasomatic stimuli potentially capable of public perception, if one could look through the eyes of the dreamer or open him as in an operation. Hausa adults find this view of dreams inadequate and tell their children that dreams are a kind of vision that gives them access to an external, objective realm of the soul. Hausa children later change their minds about the reality or the externality of these events and view dreams as either mirages or internal perceptions.

At a subsequent stage, dream events are understood to be events that can be experienced only by few people. Finally, when they are about ten years old, Hausa children come to believe the events in their dreams are unreal appearances, located inside their bodies, to which only they have potential perceptual access.

HAWAII

Dreams played a significant role in the traditional culture of the Hawaiian islands. As in many other traditional societies, dreams were regarded as communications from deities and from departed **ancestors** to ordinary mortals. Dreams were known as *moe 'uhane* ("soul sleep"). While the body slept, the **soul** exited the body through the tear duct in the corner of the eye (the *lau 'uhane*, or "soul pit"). After exiting, the soul traveled through this earthly realm or through spirit realms. Dreams were remembrances of these journeys. Rather than beginning dream accounts with "I had the weirdest dream …," traditional Hawaiians would say, "My spirit saw. …"

It was believed that **nightmares** could be created by spirits who entered the sleeper's body during the night. Traditional Hawaiians also believed that spirits could have sexual relations with sleepers, and were referred to as the dreamer's "husband of the night" or "wife of the night." When spirits delivered negative predictions about the future, they could be prayed to and supplicated for mercy. If the unpleasant future could not be entirely avoided, it was hoped that the relevant divinity would at least lessen the severity of the impending disaster.

A variety of information could be received in dreams. *Kahunas*, traditional Hawaiian **shamans**, sometimes sought a cure for illnesses in dreams. New information acquired in this way became part of the shaman's medicinal system. Similarly, when a family had problems or questions they wished answered, the head of the household would pray that the relevant information be provided during a dream. This information could be anything from guidance about the best place to fish to the appropriate name for a new baby.

As with other groups, many dreams in traditional Hawaiian culture required little or no interpretation. For dreams requiring interpretation, certain individuals recognized as especially gifted dream interpreters were called upon. These individuals were often not part of the regular priesthood. All important dreams, especially those bearing on the larger family, were discussed by the whole household every morning.

HEALING AND DREAMS

Dreams are associated with healing in several ways. The role of dreams in psychological healing and growth is discussed in several different entries in this book, particularly the entry on **psychotherapy** and the entries on particular psychotherapists, such as **Carl Jung** and **Karen Horney**. Dreams can also play a role in healing bodily ailments, as revealed in customs going back at least as far as the practice of **dream incubation** in the ancient world. The practice of going to a dream temple to seek healing reached its peak in the cult of **Aesculapius**, the legendary healer of the classical Greeks. Seekers could be healed directly in their dreams, or they could receive a diagnosis and a prescription for healing.

In contemporary Western culture, the notion of dreams playing a role in physical healing has recently been widely popularized through Patricia Garfield's book *The Healing Power of*

Dreams. In this useful and very readable work. Garfield, a professional psychologist, makes a case for using dreams in all phases of the healing process, from diagnosis to cure. In addition to recounting concrete instances of how dreams reflect one's state of health and stage of healing, she includes a kind of **dream dictionary** at the end of her book that offers guidelines for utilizing dreams in diagnosis.

Garfield also discusses how to "program" dreams (suggesting the direction or content of dreams to oneself before going to sleep) to assist in the healing process, somewhat along the same lines as using **creative visualization** in healing. Of particular interest is her discussion of how the practice of **lucid dreaming**—becoming conscious of one's dream and controlling its contents—can be used in the healing process.

HERACLITUS

Heraclitus (c. 540–c. 480 B.C.E.) was one of the earliest Western philosophers, best known for his assertion that the world is in constant change. Historians often refer to all Greek philosophers who lived prior Socrates as the pre-Socratics, and Heraclitus is included in this group. The pre-Socratics, who as a group were active from approximately 600 to 400 B.C.E., attempted to find universal principles to explain the whole of nature.

According to their philosophy, the apparent chaos of the world conceals a permanent and intelligible order, which can be accounted for by universal causes operating within nature itself and discoverable through human reason. They openly disagreed with the content and the method of mythology, maintaining that natural processes were no longer to be at the mercy of gods with human passions and unpredictable intentions. The pre-Socratics were skeptical about dreams, and they usually took a more speculative view of them.

Heraclitus, for instance, detached the phenomenon of dreaming from the supernatural, declaring it to be a universal human trait and maintaining that each individual retreats into a world of his own during sleep. According to Heraclitus, dreams have no special meaning and can be regarded as the carryover into sleep of the cares and intentions of waking life.

Heraclitus maintained that knowledge achieved during sleep is inferior to waking knowledge, since the world that the dreamer sees is distinguished by an incommunicable privacy and by a surrealistic character. The dreamer is cut off from communication via the senses with the outside world and does not have the power to perceive things in a coherent manner. Thus, the dream world is very different from the waking world, although they resemble each other.

The hero archetype is a universal concept that people experience worldwide. According to Jungian psychology, the hero is a reflection of our desire for achievement and self-understanding.

HERO ARCHETYPE

Most traditional societies hail one or more figures as heroes. The widespread presence of hero figures in world cultures led **Carl Jung** to postulate that the hero is a universal **archetype**. From a Jungian perspective, the sacred stories of traditional cultures embody certain psychological truths or express certain psychological processes. The hero, in this view, reflects every person's quest for achievement and self-understanding. Thus, dreams in which we see ourselves as dashing heroes fighting fantastic battles against monsters may actually represent more mundane struggles in our daily lives.

A very different way of viewing the hero and dreams—from the standpoint of depth psychology is found in **Joseph Campbell**'s *The Hero with a Thousand Faces*, originally published in 1949. Campbell suggests that our nightly plunge into sleep is a kind of hero quest involving being drawn across the threshold of adventure (often involuntarily) into a realm of fantasy and risk. After a struggle, some important resolution occurs—a gift is won, a maiden is married, a challenge is met—and the hero returns to normal, everyday life. It is not difficult to see how journeying into sleep and returning the next day is a kind of mini hero adventure. If, upon reflection, we gain increased knowledge about ourselves from the adventure, then we have even brought back the boon or gift that represents the goal of the hero.

HILLMAN, JAMES

James Hillman (1926–) is a contemporary American depth psychologist who works in the tradition of **Carl Jung**, although some of his rather radical departures from this tradition sets him at odds with other Jungians. Most strands of depth psychology approach dreams as messages from the unconscious mind that have been shaped by our mental state, and which can thus serve as indicators of our psychological problems. In each of these schools of thought, dreams are regarded as vague communications that require some form of interpretation to reveal their true meaning. This basic interpretive orientation is evident in Gestalt therapy.

Hillman vehemently challenges this formulation of the task of dream interpretation. He questions the assumption that dreams must always be dissected and re-patterned to make sense to the rational waking mind, which necessitates extending the domain of daylight consciousness into nighttime consciousness and making the dreaming mind serve the purposes of the waking mind. Why not, Hillman asks, listen to dreams and allow them to transform the waking mind rather than vice versa? Hillman's proposal is less radical than it sounds, however, because of his fundamentally Jungian understanding of dreams, which sees in dreams the symbolic language of mythology and poetry. Thus, Hillman's proposal is more of a protest against the literalizing, objectivist consciousness of the modern world that he views as a deadening influence on the human psyche than it is a serious proposal to reshape our waking consciousness in the image of dreams.

HITLER, ADOLF

While sleeping in a bunker during World War I, Adolf Hitler (1889–1945) had a nightmare in which an avalanche of earth and molten lava buried him alive. Awakened from his sleep by this bad dream, Hitler left the dugout seeking fresh air to clear his head. He proceeded to wander into the open area that was the battlefield; this was extremely dangerous, but Hitler later insisted that he was being led by a will that was not his own. He remained in a semiconscious state until a sudden burst of enemy fire brought him to his senses. Immediately recognizing the danger, he turned around and sought the relative safety of his bunker only to find that there had been a direct hit on the dugout and all of his comrades were dead. Hitler interpreted this event to be an affirmation of his destiny to be a great leader to his people; he attributed his survival to a force that would protect him so he could carry out that role. He felt himself to be invincible.

Modern day analysts who review this dream do not conclude that it was an unequivocal sign of divine election. Some maintain, though, that it could have been prophetic in nature, predicting his destiny when he died in an underground bunker at the end of World War II. The psychoanalyst **Carl Jung** cited it as an example of "synchronicity."

HOBBES, THOMAS

The political philosopher Thomas Hobbes (1588–1679) was born in Malmesbury, Wiltshire, England. At the age of fourteen he was sent to

Magdalen Hall, Oxford, where he took his bachelor's degree. In 1610, after visiting the Continent, where through Kepler and Galileo he discovered the disrepute into which the Aristotelian system was beginning to fall, Hobbes turned to the classics for a better understanding of life and philosophy, and decided to translate *Thucydides* into English. Upon returning from his third journey to the Continent, he published his first philosophical work, *Little Treatise*, an explanation of sensation in terms of the new science of motion.

During his exile in France, Hobbes's *De cive* (1642) was published, as well as his *Minute or First Draught of the Optiques* (1642–1646), and he began working on a trilogy on body, man, and citizen, the first book of which is *De corpore*. In 1650 his *Elements of Law*, which demonstrated the need for undivided sovereignty, was published in two parts: *Human Nature* and *De corpore politico*.

Hobbes's views on man and citizen were to be included in his masterpiece, *Leviathan*, which was published in 1651. In the same year he returned to England, where the second part of his trilogy, *De homine*, was published in 1657. In *Behemoth* (1668) he interpreted the history of the period from 1640 to 1660 in light of his vision of man and society. He died at the age of ninety-one in Hardwick, Derbyshire.

Thomas Hobbes was fascinated by dreams, to which he dedicated a discussion in the first part of *Leviathan*, in a chapter on imagination. He claimed that dreams consist of compounded phantasms of past sensations, and, in an attempt to determine what distinguishes dreams from waking thoughts and to develop a mechanical theory to explain them, he described dreams as the reverse of man's waking imaginations, and as the result of internal motions of one's organs of sense in the absence of external stimulation. He

maintained that dreams are characterized by lack of coherence, since no thought of an end or goal guides them, and by lack of sense of time. He also pointed out that nothing appears surprising or absurd in dreams.

Like many other, more recent philosophers, Hobbes was inclined to a somatic theory of dreams, that is, the belief that physical factors can affect one's dreams (for example, that overeating leads to certain kinds of dreams). He maintained that there is an intimate connection between dreams and bodily states, since the motions pass both from the brain to the inner parts and from the inner parts to the brain. Motions begin at one end during waking and at the other end during sleep, and this tendency to project images produced by bodily states gives rise to belief in apparitions and visions.

HOMER AND DREAMS

Many traces of Egyptian thought, as well as ideas associated with ancient Mesopotamia and Persia, are found in Greek notions about dreams. Some themes in Greek thinking about dreams, such as the belief that dreams are divine and the belief that they may mean the opposite of what they seem to, are similar to ideas in the Near East. It is difficult to determine whether this reflects direct influence or whether it indicates simply parallel development.

The Greeks drew a fundamental distinction between "true" and "false" dreams. Within the class of true and significant dreams, several distinctions can be found. For instance, in a classification transmitted by **Artemidorus, Macrobius,** and other writers, significant true dreams can be broken down into symbolic dreams, the meaning of which cannot be understood without interpretation; the

The ruins of the ancient city of Troy, which was depicted in Homer's epic *Iliad,* are located in modern Turkey. Like other Greek playwrights, Homer used dreams in his works as an important plot development tool.

horama, or visions, which predict future events; and the *chrematismos,* or oracles, which reveal without symbolism what will or will not happen, or what should or should not be done.

Homer, whose epics present disparate attitudes toward dreams, maintained that "true" dreams come through what the Greeks referred to as the gate of horn, and "false" dreams through the gate of ivory, and the *Odyssey* makes it plain that not all dreams are truthful. In Homer's epics, the dream is always of a personified divine being that is independent of time and space and appears to the dreamer at the head of his bed, eventually disappearing. The primary function of dreams in the

Homeric epics, particularly in the *Odyssey,* is to promote the development of the plot. In the *Iliad,* Homer employed this device only once as a means of advancing the plot. However, the free structure of the *Iliad* forced Homer to use other artifices, such as daytime visions, the physical appearance of living deities, and other divine manifestations because the use of dreams was not adequate.

It is different with the *Odyssey,* in which the dream is more frequently used to forward the action of the plot. Yet, the influence of the dream on the story is more subtle. For instance, it considerably affects the plot by encouraging Penelope and providing Nausicaa's nocturnal vision, the influence of which is extended by a long chain of events that form the story. In other cases the dream may simply provide the atmosphere, and prepare the reader for what is to come.

Homer does not use dreams solely to give indications about what is going to happen in the future. Dreams, which are part of divination, are also employed to show what should be done to avoid transgression of the divine will, as in the episode in which Achilles wants to consult an official seer to know the will of the gods. Thus, in the *Odyssey*, in which the plot is staged largely on earth and not on Olympus (as it is in the *Iliad*), Homer uses dreams as the means through which the gods act.

In both the *Iliad* and the *Odyssey*, Homer introduces dreams during a crisis. In the *Iliad* Zeus is generally regarded as the source of the dreams, and the receiver is in each case a male. In the *Odyssey* the goddess Athena is usually responsible for the majority of the dreams, which are always experienced by women.

HOPI

The Hopi, who live in the southwestern desert plateau of the United States, regard dreams as particularly important. Hopi society conveys much of its religious and recreational experience through a rich imagery derived from dramatic rituals that are frequently translated into dreams. These images are consistently presented to individuals throughout their lifetimes.

It is believed the soul of each person, corresponding to the Spirit of the Breath (*hikwsi*), can resist what the Hopi call the Mighty Something (*himu*), which is a composite concept of divinity. When the *hikwsi* resists the *himu*, the Hopi become confused. The Hopi then look for famil-

iar anchors in their inner world, and this is expressed in dreams.

Dreams are viewed as an attempt by the self to make a statement about the individual's present situation, as well as the extent of the person's cultural integration. They are considered a type of thought-action in which *hikwsi* explores both the inner and the outer world through images provided by Hopi religion. Good dreams have to be held in the heart and can be told only after they have been fulfilled, whereas bad dreams—in that they contain bad thoughts—must be eliminated through the practice of reporting and discussing them, and by working out problems in them through confession of questionable behavior.

The Hopi believe that *hikwsi* is not confined within the mortal individual, but can be projected through thought, prayer, and dreams, and can interact with distant people and things. Also, the conceptual universe of the Hopi is not delimited by the notions of time and space, which make dreams an experience apart from reality.

Hopi dreams are characterized by a number of personally invented and culturally defined symbols that are applicable to personal situations at the time of the dream. For instance, when Palulukon, the Water Serpent, appears in a dream, it can represent both a possible punishing and a possible supportive agent, depending on whether the dream is charged with quiet or fear. The state of being at the time of the dream can determine the specific use of cultural or personal symbols, as well as the rules used to deal with and interpret the dream.

HORNEY, KAREN

Karen Horney (1885–1952) was an American psychoanalyst and a leader in the neo-Freudian school of psychoanalysis. She was impressed by the role that culture played in psychological conflicts. This led her to deemphasize the central importance that **Sigmund Freud** had assigned to childhood sexuality in the formation of neurosis. Unlike Freud and like **Alfred Adler**, Horney gave central importance to insecurity and the drive for superiority as motivating factors in human psychodynamics. One of the key tenets of her personality theory was that human beings were motivated to grow, prompted by an overarching desire for self-realization (i.e., for self-understanding).

Dreams, Homey theorized, expressed a level of the human psyche that was closer to the real self. In dreams one is less defensive, and the part of the self that propels one to seek self-realization will sometimes express the truth more clearly in the dream state than in waking consciousness. For example, someone who always displays optimism and has a self-image of being positive and upbeat might have dreams characterized by sadness, indicating, in Horney's theory, the possibility that the person is actually unhappy at a deep level.

HYPNAGOGIC EXPERIENCES

Immediately before dropping off to sleep and immediately after awakening (but prior to full wakefulness) we are in a state of mind in which we are peculiarly susceptible to certain kinds of vivid hallucinations, usually visual or auditory in nature. Many people have had, for example, the experience of imagining that they have risen from bed only to emerge into full awareness and find themselves still prone. Most everyone has also experienced brief visual or auditory illusions when they were fatigued owing to excessive lack of sleep or overexertion. The technical name that British researcher Frederick Myers gave these experiences

is *hypnagogic*, and the state of mind that accompanies them is referred to as a hypnagogic state.

When falling off to sleep, according to Myers, the brain "produces steady alpha rhythms" that induce the sleeper into full relaxation. When the alpha rhythms break up, Stage 1 sleep is fully realized and the sleeper begins to enter the dream state. The initial hypnagogic "visions" include "formless shapes such as waves of pure color" and often include distorted faces and **archetypal** images.

Recent research into hypnagogic states suggests that these visions occur when, due to the "rapid change in consciousness" the mind is struggling to gain control.

HYPNOPOMPIC EXPERIENCES

The term **hypnagogic** is often used to refer both to the experiences we have in the transitional state from waking to sleeping as well as to the experiences that occur as we pass from sleeping to wakefulness. One can distinguish between these two experiences, however, and restrict hypnagogic to the transition from wakefulness to sleep. The complementary term to hypnagogic is hypnopompic, which refers to the semiconscious state we experience preceding waking.

Like the hypnagogic transition, the hypnopompic state is peculiarly susceptible to certain kinds of vivid hallucinations, usually visual or auditory (sometimes more acutely sensory) in nature. Dreamers report to have heard snatches of conversations, glimpsed visitors passing by the bed, or even smelled perfume or oranges. The experience is so real, that when fully awake, it is hard to believe that it was only a dream state.

Hypnosis is used by many therapists to try and reveal the secrets behind people's dreams.

HYPNOSIS

Hypnosis is associated with dreams in several ways. For various reasons, but especially because of the many formal and informal experiments with mind-altering drugs and Eastern meditation techniques in the late-Sixties, a new field of research was articulated within the discipline of psychology that came to be referred to as altered states of consciousness (ASC). This field became a grab bag of every state of mind that could be distinguished from ordinary waking consciousness. Beyond drug-influenced and meditative states, other mental states associated with ASC research were the more traditional areas of dreams and hypnosis. Hypnotic states and dream states were thus viewed as being in some ways comparable.

Another, more traditional way in which dreams and hypnosis are grouped together is in **psychoanalysis**, in which both are regarded as providing the therapist with an avenue into the **unconscious**. **Sigmund Freud**, for instance, experimented with hypnosis in his early work with mentally distressed patients, but soon gave it up in favor of the therapeutic deployment of free association and the analysis of dreams.

Finally, an early technique of dream research was to make a posthypnotic suggestion for a subject to have a certain kind of dream. The German researcher Karl Schroetter, for example, hypnotized his subjects and suggested that they have particular kinds of sexual encounters in their dreams. His research, published in 1911, relied on Freudian ideas about repressed desires to have intercourse with family members, as well as Freud's notions about how the mind censored the **manifest dream** content. Other, later researchers have attempted to utilize the technique of posthypnotic suggestion in dream research, with ambiguous results. Too many factors influence the results to make this approach a fruitful line of research. The only study in which hypnosis has been shown to have an unambiguous impact on dreams was an experiment in which subjects were able to successfully initiate **lucid dreaming** after receiving a post-hypnotic suggestion to do so.

IF YOU CAN DREAM IT,
YOU CAN DO IT.

—WALT DISNEY

IBN AL-'ARABI

The visionary mystic Ibn al-'Arabi, Muhyi ad-Din (1165–1240), born in Murcia, Spain, is considered the greatest Sufi theorist and expounder of metaphysical doctrine. He studied at Seville and Ceuta, and, after visiting Mecca and Baghdad, he settled in Damascus.

Ibn al-'Arabi provided a remarkable theory of imaginative cognition and claimed to have considerable visionary experiences and a remarkably lucid imagination. He stated that "this power of the active imagination developed in me visually in a bodily, objective, extra-mental figure just as the angel Gabriel appeared bodily to the eyes of the Prophet." This apparition left him in an astonished state for many days, to such a degree that he could not even take nourishment. He

continued to contemplate the figure for a long time without tasting a bit of food, experiencing neither hunger nor thirst.

This visionary event was the source of Ibn al-'Arabi's work *The Spiritual Conquests of Mecca*, which was the product of a long spiritual maturation. During a visit to the Black Stone in Mecca, he met the figure that had appeared to him in his vision, which he recognized and described as a young man who was neither living nor dead. He suddenly perceived the temple as a living being and asked his visitor to accept him as his disciple and to teach him all of his secrets. He was so overwhelmed that he lost consciousness.

An explorer of altered states of consciousness, Ibn al-'Arabi also advocated the practice of what we today would call **lucid dreaming**: "A person must control his thoughts in a dream.

The training of this alertness … will produce great benefits for the individual. Everyone should apply himself to the attainment of this ability of such great value" (Ibn al-'Arabi, cited in Van de Castle, p. 441—see *Sources*).

ID

The id refers to one of the three essential components of **Sigmund Freud**'s theory of the human personality. The id represents the primitive, animal aspect of the self that Freud viewed as constituting the core of the psyche. The other aspects of the psyche, the **ego** and the **superego**, are later developments that arise from the need to survive and to adapt to the surrounding social environment. The id, which embodies such drives as sex and aggression, is often at odds with the environment because society requires us to control our sexual and aggressive urges. The need to control and even repress these urges leads to inner conflicts—conflicts of which we are often largely unconscious and which are frequently expressed in our dreams. Repressed sexual and violent urges may lead to sexual and violent dreams.

IGBO

The universe of the Igbo, a southeastern Nigerian people, is conceptualized into three broad categories through certain metaphors and myths: *Elu lgwe*, the sky, which is inhabited by the supreme deity *Chiukwu; Ala Mmuo*, the land where reside numerous spirit beings which are either back from their sojourn on the earth or awaiting their turn to begin a new travel in the world of living men—and where are also found the revered ancestors, and *Ala Mmadu*, land of the living, where spirits are invisible to man.

Considerable and continuous contact exists between humans and spirits. *Chiukwu* keeps in touch with humans and their affairs through the *chi*, the spiritual entity embodied in a person's identity from before birth, which journeys with him or her through life. In Igbo thought each person's life is predestined through the agency of the chi, although this destiny can be modified by the *ikenga*, the personification of each individual's right hand, representing the power to achieve.

A study by Robert LeVine published in 1966 examined achievement motivation among the Igbo. LeVine analyzed private dreams of personal success as a means of identifying underlying cultural values of achievement motivation. In addition to being a consequence of achievement motivation, dreams, omens, and prophecy are seen in Igbo society as the principal demonstration of extra-human powers in the candidacy for religious office. When the Igbo determine succession to religious office, dreams and the use of dream narratives are sometimes thought to be a manifestation both of the agency of the spiritual entity behind the office and of the candidate's chi.

Dreams are perceived as a means for divine messages, and the role of divination in the succession process is regarded as a means of both interpreting and validating the message of a dream. Usually, the messenger who appears in the dream is either the previous tenant of the office or a manifestation of the spirit to the service of whom the office is devoted. In some cases, the first type of messenger appears in an initial dream, and in a following dream the message is strengthened by the appearance of the other type. The chief mode of communication is always through the physical placement, by the messenger, of the symbols of office in the hands of the dreamer, and in many cases this act is reinforced by a voice telling the dreamer that he has been chosen for office.

INCUBI AND SUCCUBI

[M]en may at times be begotten by means of Incubi and Succubi, [and] it is contrary to the words of the saints and even to the tradition of Holy Scripture to maintain the opposite opinion.

—Malleus Maleficarum

The idea of spirit beings or demons who take the form of people in order to have sex with human beings is actually very ancient. In Western demonological lore, speculation on such ideas grew out of two short verses in chapter six of Genesis:

[T]he sons of God saw that the daughters of men were fair; and they took to wife such of them as they chose. (6:2)

The Nephilim were on the earth in those days, and also afterward, when the sons of God came in to the daughters of men, and they bore children to them. These were the mighty men that were of old, the men of renown. (6:4)

In these rather strange verses, the expression "sons of God" was taken to indicate **angels**. And while scripture does not condemn these actions, the traditional interpretation of these passages is that these sons of God are *fallen* angels. This history of interpretation provided biblical legitimization for the notion of incubi and succubi. The idea was supported in the Middle Ages by St. Augustine, who wrote:

It is a widespread opinion, confirmed by direct or indirect testimony of trustworthy persons, that the Sylvans and Fauns, commonly called Incubi, have often tormented

Female demons known as succubi (and their male counterparts, the incubi) are evil spirits that sexually molest human dreamers for nefarious purposes.

women, solicited and obtained intercourse with them.

Such demons most often attack/seduce human beings at night, thus conveniently explaining why monks, nuns, and priests have erotic dreams.

Although sterile themselves, incubi (**demons in male form**) could supposedly impregnate women with seed taken by succubi (demons in female form) from men—a belief that was sometimes used to explain pregnancies resulting from secret affairs. This type of explanation not only absolved women from charges of licentiousness, but, because the sperm was taken from men, it also saved the child from being executed as an offspring of a demon. The authors of the influential *Malleus Maleficarum* ("Witch Hammer," 1486) were seemingly obsessed with explaining this process, and devoted several sections to explaining its mechanism, such as:

> Devils do indeed collect human semen, by means of which they are able to produce bodily effects; but his cannot be done without some local movement, therefore demons can transfer the semen which they have collected and inject it into the bodies of others.

Some demons can collect the semen from living men by assuming the form of succubi, transforming themselves into incubi and then injecting semen into women. In other cases, semen is transferred from succubi to incubi. Heinrich Kramer and James Sprenger, the authors of the *Malleus Maleficarum,* speculated that this division of labor may have arisen from the prior assignment of demons to specific people—apparently the diabolical equivalent of guardian angels:

> Perhaps one devil allotted to a woman, should receive semen from another devil, allotted to a man, that in this way each of them should be commissioned by the prince of devils to work some witchcraft; since to each one is allotted his own angel, even from among the evil ones....

Alternatively, the two inquisitors speculated that this pairing of efforts may arise from the "filthiness of the deed, which one devil would abhor to commit"—implying that certain demons would object to playing both the male role and the female role in the semen transfer process.

Why, however, are demons so intent on promoting human reproduction? Kramer and Sprenger provide a number of different reasons:

> The reason that devils turn themselves into Incubi or Succubi is not for the cause of pleasure, since a spirit has not flesh and blood; but chiefly it is with this intention, that through the vice of luxury they may work a twofold harm against men, that is, in body and in soul, that so men may be more given to all vices. And there is no doubt that they know under which stars the semen is most vigorous, and that men so conceived will be always perverted by witchcraft.

In other words, people who copulate with demons are more inclined to sin, and human beings thus conceived are somehow corrupted by this process so that they readily give themselves up to Satan after they grow up.

There were, however, other medieval traditions that asserted the incubi *could* impregnate mortal women, and that succubi *could* become pregnant by mortal men. It was, for instance, rumored that Merlin the magician was the offspring of such a union. This notion of semi-demonic children was useful for explaining such phenomena as deformed babies. Incubi were sometimes referred to as *demon lovers.* Also, some writers asserted that succubi were the same as the wood nymphs of European folklore.

Mortals who willingly responded to the seductive wiles of these beings risked damnation. A papal bull issued by Pope Innocent in 1484, for instance, asserted: "Many persons of both sexes, forgetful of their own salvation, have abused incubi and succubi." Some of the church fathers, such as St. Anthony, asserted that demons would take the form of seductive naked women who would try to lure him away from his devotions. These experiences were later taken as evidence for the real existence of succubi.

In the seventeenth century Peter Sinistrari suggested that incubi were not demons but rather higher beings, found somewhere in the hierarchy between men and angels, who honored humankind with their attentions. Since exorcism had no effect on these beings, it is one of the characteristics that Sinistrari used to separate them from the evil fiends to which they had been likened up until that time. He merged his views with those of the Church with regard to the sinful nature of relations with these beings by stating that, as long as the mortal involved believes that they lay with a demon, the sin is just as severe as if they actually did. Thus, he was able to suggest that the sin is rooted in the belief of the sinful nature of the act rather than the act itself.

INDIA

India is the birthplace of many world religions, most notably Hinduism, **Buddhism**, Jainism, and Sikhism. Indians have speculated extensively about the significance of dreams, often coming to much the same conclusion as other cultures. For instance, they have a tradition of regarding dreams as messages from the gods. One of the unique aspects of this tradition is a record of these speculations from as early as the Vedic period (three or four thousand years ago, when the **Vedas** were composed). In the Atharva-Veda, for instance, dream elements indicating good or bad omens are discussed. Also discussed in the same text are rites for counteracting bad omens.

Where India outstrips other cultural traditions is in the development of the theme of this life or this world as a kind of dream. According to mainstream Hindu religious thought, the individual soul is trapped in the sufferings involved with life in this world, and, because of reincarnation, even death does not release one from this world. In most of the religious traditions of southern Asia, release or liberation from the cycle of death and rebirth is the ultimate goal of the spiritual life. A metaphor often used to describe the insight that leads directly to liberation is awakening from a dream. Especially in the philosophical tradition of Advaita Vedanta, this metaphor is developed to stress the dreamlike quality—and hence the unreality—of the world as we experience it in our normal state of consciousness. The doctrine of the ultimate unreality of this world is referred to as *maya.*

Regarding the classification of dreams, the simplest division into auspicious and inauspicious dreams seems to be very ancient, in that the key words for good dreams and bad dreams have stayed constant from the earliest lists down to the twelfth-century work by Jagaddeva. In the Hindu view, during sleep a subtle body that is the basis for dream consciousness can detach itself from the physical body and wander. This view is very similar to that of many traditional tribal peoples, who regard dreams as resulting from the experiences of the wandering soul.

In the Atharva-Veda, men are said to have one of three temperaments: bilious, phlegmatic, or sanguine. Dreams of arid land and burning objects are attributed to bilious persons, dreams of nature's splendor and burgeoning life are attributed to the phlegmatic, and dreams of racing clouds and forest creatures running in terror are attributed to sanguine persons. In the *Questions of King Milinda* (an early Indian Buddhist work), it is said that persons who dream are either under the influence of a deity, under the influence of their experiences, or under the influence of prophecy. The basic Jaina classification, by way of contrast, is into seen, unseen, and inscrutably seen (that is, both seen and unseen). According to some Indian medical texts, dreams are merely past experiences just now being apprehended, while others are considered wish fulfillments.

Dreams of wildlife running are actually an indication that the dreamer is a vigorous and confident person.

The classical schools of Indian philosophy offer two different interpretations of dreams. The terminology presentative theory explains dream cognition as perception of the mind itself in retirement when the external sense organs have ceased to function. Representative theory holds that dream consciousness amounts to a false recollection. Both positions view the mind as a sixth sense. The dream is the object of this sense, since the five external sense organs cease to function during sleep and thus cannot contribute to its perception.

INGESSANA

Dreams have an important institutional aspect among the people of the Ingessana Hills in the Republic of the Sudan, who take them with great seriousness. According to the Ingessana, dreams contain certain messages from components of a cosmology in which the sleeper is situated. Certain significant dreams are regarded as consequences of the activities of supernatural beings.

In general, Ingessana consider dreams as occasions on which ordinarily invisible beings, such as ghosts, ancestors, and gods, make demands, issue warnings, and instruct ordinary people. The messages from dreams may state what has to be done and express the intentions of the senders concerning the material well-being of the members of a household, the inhabitants of a territorial area, or the entire population of the hills. Through dreams, these beings usually demand certain rituals that can restore the relationship between them and human beings, and in some cases promote the restoration of the souls of children. "Restoring the souls of children" or "bringing back to the children their souls" constitutes a typical ritual carried out when the parents of a child who has suffered some frightening experience approach the local dream leader (always a woman), and ask her to restore the child.

Differences in the content of recollections of waking experiences and dream experiences can be attributed in part to the different capacities of certain types of dreamers. The images that ordinary people see while dreaming can be easily seen while awake by "doctor-diviners" and by people who are believed to have a "second sight." These people can have dreams that ordinary people cannot experience, and even while awake are able to penetrate consciously beyond the normal spectrum of visibility to see ghosts.

Usually ordinary people consult a doctor-diviner in order to be enlightened about what appears obscure in their dreams. Since he is able to see in waking consciousness what an ordinary individual can see only in dreams, the doctor-diviner is authoritative on what the dream signifies. Also, the dreams of the men who are the hereditary custodians of certain temples are very important and have enormous social implications. The most feared dreams among the Ingessana, but also the most widespread of socially significant dreams, are those involving *nengk*, ghastly creatures that bring illness and death.

INITIATION

Initiation in the most general, anthropological sense refers to a rite in which the initiate undergoes a transformation in religious or social status.

The imparting of specific knowledge to the initiate, whether social or religious, is often a sig-

nificant part of initiation. When initiation involves the acquisition of religious knowledge, such knowledge can be acquired, in whole or in part, through dreams. In Siberia, **shamans**, the religious specialists of traditional (particularly hunter-gatherer) societies, frequently experience initiatory dreams at the beginning of their vocations. These dreams often include the theme of initiatory death, in which the shaman is dismembered and then reconstructed in renewed form.

Within the Islamic Sufi tradition, many Sufi mystics began their spiritual quest as a result of guides who appeared to them in dreams. In the training of healers among the Diegueno Indians the healer-to-be undergoes a series of initiatory dreams, culminating in a dream in which he learns his secret medicine name. Roughly similar patterns of dream initiation are found among aboriginal Australians (e.g., the Arunta) and in a variety of **Native American** societies (e.g., the **Ojibwa, Iroquois**, and **Mohave**).

INTERPRETATION OF DREAMS

Dreams are often profound experiences that stimulate us to wonder about their nature and meaning. It is the rare person who has not awakened from a particularly vivid dream that seemed to portend something important, but the meaning of which the dreamer could not infer. The frustration these kind of experiences can sometimes induce us to dismiss all dreams as meaningless.

It has often been asserted, even in the ancient world, that dreams are meaningless phenomena. As recently as 1977, a serious, scientific attempt to demonstrate this thesis was put forward in the **activation-synthesis model** of dreaming proposed by Robert McCarley and J. Allan Hobson. Hobson and McCarley believe their hypothesis, which stresses the purely physiological correlates of dreaming, refutes the notion that dreams are meaningful.

While such absolute dismissals of dreams have a certain appeal, they are ultimately unsatisfying. Throughout history and across cultures, the dominant tendency has been to attribute significance to at least some dreams. Until the advent of modern psychology and psychoanalysis, dreams were most often viewed as omens. In some societies, certain individuals were recognized as gifted in interpreting dream omens.

A common tool used to decipher dreams in the ancient world was the **dream dictionary**, which contained specific interpretations of various dream elements. In ancient dictionaries, the connection between the dream component and the predicted event was sometimes tenuous. For example, a dream in which the dreamer is sitting on a rooftop might be interpreted as a sign that the person should not go on a long journey in the near future. In most contemporary dream dictionaries, the connections between dream symbols and their interpretations are more obvious.

Although the connection did not originate with **Sigmund Freud**, it was Freud and the people he influenced who established the importance of dreams for understanding the psyche of the dreamer particularly for uncovering the dreamer's psychological problems. In Freud's view, the purpose of dreams is to allow us to satisfy in fantasies the instinctual urges that society judges unacceptable. So that we do not awaken as a result of the strong emotions that would be evoked if we were to dream about the literal fulfillment of such desires, the dreaming mind transforms dream content so as to disguise its

true meaning. Hence, the purpose of Freudian dream interpretation is to penetrate this disguise.

Carl Jung's view is more benign, picturing the unconscious self as a complex mix of lower instinctual and higher spiritual impulses. Instead of *concealing*, the purpose of a dream is to *communicate* something to consciousness. The unconscious, in other words, has a kind of intelligence that attempts to guide and otherwise assist the conscious self. The language of the unconscious, however, is indirect and symbolic and requires interpretation. Jungian dream analysis is thus the task of helping clients to properly interpret the messages coming from the unconscious.

Other schools of depth psychology derived from the larger Freudian/Jungian tradition have also approached dreams as messages from the unconscious mind that have been shaped by our psychological state. In each of these schools of thought, dreams are regarded as less-than-clear communications that require some form of interpretation to reveal their true meanings. This basic interpretive orientation is evident in Gestalt therapy, in which patients act out various dream components as a strategy for discovering (i.e., for interpreting) the meaning of the dream. Another interpretive strategy in Gestalt therapy is for the dreamer to set up a dialogue between different components of the dream and then to analyze the meanings that emerge from the dialogue.

Finally, some depth psychologists have vigorously questioned the task of dream interpretation as formulated by Freud and Jung. Advocates of this position, stated most eloquently by **James Hillman**, question the assumption that dreams must always be dissected and re-patterned to make sense to the rational waking mind, thus extending the domain of daylight consciousness into nighttime consciousness and making the dreaming mind serve the purposes of the waking mind. Why not, Hillman asks, listen to dreams and allow them to transform the waking mind rather than vice versa? Hillman's proposal is less radical than it sounds, because of his fundamentally Jungian understanding of dreams as the symbolic language of mythology and poetry. His proposal is more of a protest against the literalizing, objectivist consciousness of the modern world that he views as a deadening influence on the human psyche than it is a serious proposal to reshape our waking consciousness in the image of dreams.

INUIT (ESKIMO)

In 1976, Joseph Bloom and Richard Gelardin conducted a study of the dreams of the Eskimo (Inuit) people in which a ghost or a spirit appeared. They noted this occurred most often when the dreamer was just falling asleep or just waking up. They were unaware of the widespread occurrence of hallucinating while in a state of semi-arousal and sleep paralysis. They recognized the Inuit experiences as nightmares and linked their sleep paralysis to Arctic hysteria, labeling both as "non-empirical."

Dreams are an integral part of the Inuit shamanic tradition and are closely associated to the initiatory calling; dreams of dismemberment, death, and rebirth are thought to be a calling to the dreamer to become a shaman. In other instances, they are called, in the dream, by an animal spirit who possesses the dreamer. The dreamer then awakens and proceeds to wander naked through the wilderness, grappling with the spirit for control of the body. Eventually, the dreamer will gain control over the spirit—a victory they mark by the making of a drum—and once again return to their people and start the training as a shaman initiate.

IROQUOIS

The Iroquois are an indigenous North American people, currently centered in upstate New York. The theory of the "soul-wish-manifesting" dream, which is basically similar to psychoanalytic theory, is the most important dream theory of traditional Iroquois. They believe that human souls have desires that are inborn and concealed and come from the depths of the soul. The soul makes these natural desires known by means of dreams.

For this reason, most Iroquois are careful to note their dreams and to provide the soul with what it has requested during their sleep. They also recognize that a **manifest dream** might conceal rather than reveal the soul's true wish. Because the individual cannot always properly interpret dreams, the Iroquois usually rely on a dream specialist.

The Iroquois are aware of the power of unconscious desires expressed in symbolic form by dreams and realize that the frustration of these desires can cause mental and physical illness. In Iroquois dream theory, a dream can reveal not only the wishes of the dreamer but also the desires of supernatural beings. The frustration of these desires may be dangerous, in that they can cause the death of the dreamer or bring disaster to the whole society or even cause the end of the world.

According to the accounts of Jesuit missionaries who reported the theory and practice relative to dreams among the seventeenth-century Iroquois, the dream represented the only divinity of the Iroquois. They submitted to it and followed all its orders. They believed themselves absolutely obliged to execute what their dreams dictated at the earliest possible moment. The Jesuits were frustrated by their inability to discourage this faith in dreams. Quaker missionar-

In the Iroquois tradition, the soul communicates to a person through his or her dreams.

ies, who reached the Iroquois 130 years later, observed in them the same respect for dreams.

The Iroquois faith in dreams is still alive in the twentieth century, although it has diminished somewhat in strength. Even today, dreams are allowed to control the choice and occasion of curing ceremonies, membership in the secret medicine societies, the selection of friends, and even the degree of confidence in life. At the New Year's ceremony, Iroquois still ask that their dreams be guessed, and particularly vivid dreams are still brought to specialists for interpretation.

ISLAM

Muslim civilization has shown considerable concern for dreams, which have influenced the spiritual life of Islam from its very beginning. Islam is fundamentally a prophetic religion based on a series of divine revelations given to the prophet **Muhammad** through an **angel** during the latter part of his life, around 610 to 632 C.E., and contained in the Qur'an.

The Islamic creed presupposes a cosmology that includes an invisible world, consisting of heaven and hell, as well as the visible one, populated by humans and other life-forms. According to Islam, a purposeful force created and now governs both worlds, and will ultimately judge them. This force is only knowable through human intermediaries, the prophets.

Muslim prophecy distinguishes the prophets according to degree of visionary perception, from the sights and sounds of a dream to the suprasensible perception in the waking state. According to this classification, which is probably derived from criteria suggested in Hebrew Scriptures (the Old Testament), there is the simple prophet, who sees or hears an angel in a dream. Then there is the envoy—to a more or less numerous group—who sees the angel while awake. Finally, among the envoys there are the six great prophets who were charged to reveal the new law and who received the dictation of the law from an angel while in a waking state. These six prophets are Adam, Noah, **Abraham**, Moses, Jesus, and Muhammad. Muhammad is the Seal of the Prophets, meaning that his revelation closes the cycle of the six periods of prophecy.

No distinction between the dream while asleep and the vision while awake was made at the time of Muhammad, who received spiritual instruction while in both states. Dreams played an important role in the life of Muhammad, who received his first revelation and became conscious of his vocation in a dream. His great dream of initiation into the mysteries of the cosmos, known as the "Night Journey", began when the angel Gabriel appeared to him while he was sleeping between the hills of Safa and Meeva. Riding Elboraq, a half-human silver mare, Muhammad arrived in Jerusalem, the center of the world, where he conversed and prayed with Abraham, Moses, and Jesus. Then he passed through the seven celestial spheres, each infused with its own color, to reach across the ocean of white light and, finally, to approach God. According to some versions of the "Night Journey", Muhammad also descended to the depths of the Earth, thus encompassing all of human experience.

Muhammad experienced other dreams prior to the revelations given to him and recorded in the Qur'an. These dreams appeared in the form of isolated luminous and sonorous impressions that the prophet was unable to translate, and are placed at the beginning of many chapters of the Qur'an as isolated letters.

The Qur'an inherited several dreams from the Old Testament. For instance, although some details are different, the account of **Joseph**'s dream reported in the Bible is very similar to the account in the Qur'an. It is often possible to find in the Qur'an the evidence of revelations announced in dreams, like the revelation to Moses's mother to give her son to the pharaoh's sister to nurse.

In Islam, it is believed that the angel Gabriel brings true dreams, whereas demons bring false ones. The validity of a dream is determined by the time it occurs, and it is believed that early morning dreams are true dreams. True dreams

In the Holy Qur'an, the angel Gabriel appears to Muhammad in a dream and reveals to him the mysteries of the universe.

are generally believed to be those in which God, the prophet Muhammad, angels, or good Muslims appear, whereas dreams in which demons appear cannot be true, nor can those coming from desires and mental preoccupations, nor those resulting from the tricks of magicians.

According to Islam, it is possible for djinn (spirits inhabiting the earth) and Satan to give diabolic inspiration through dreams. Since Islam prohibits all representations of God, an image of the Deity can occur only in a false dream, as well as the image of an angel playing, or of the sky collapsing.

It is said that the ordinary person receives visions of portent only in dreams, whereas the mystic receives them in the waking state also or in an intermediate state between waking and sleep. Also, some particular dreams that occur naturally are believed to be a form of divine grace through which an individual can have a temporary taste of states above the material level.

Since it is difficult to distinguish between true and false dreams, dream interpretation is necessary in Islam, and it is often a very sophisticated process. Muslim dream codes give priority to the dreams of men, and, among women, to the dreams of married women who are considered chaste and dignified.

In late medieval Islam, dream interpretation was an accepted theological discipline. Muslim mystics of that period, who secluded themselves in gloomy cells to receive inspiration, believed there was a world situated between the material world and the world of intellect. This doctrine of a "realm of images" arose from the Muslim mystics' attempts to establish a morphology (structure or form) for their prophetic revelations in order to establish the reality of their spiritual experiences in dreams and visions. According to this doctrine, the world of images can be approached only through a highly trained imagination. Once an individual has reached a sufficient level of spiritual development, and provided the person's soul is pure and strong enough, he or she can visit and explore this world by means of a heightened spiritual understanding.

DREAM AS IF YOU'LL LIVE
FOREVER ... LIVE AS IF
YOU'LL DIE TODAY.

—JAMES DEAN

JACOB

The second and the third dreams reported in Judeo-Christian Scriptures occurred to Isaac's son, the patriarch Jacob, whose name was later changed to Israel. He is considered the father of the chosen people, and his sons represent the heads of the twelve tribes of the children of Israel. At the time of his first dream, Jacob was on his way to Haran to take a wife from among the daughters of his uncle Laban:

> When he had reached a certain place he passed the night there, since the sun had set. Taking one of the stones to be found at that place, he made it his pillow and lay down where he was. He had a dream: a ladder was there, standing on the ground with its top reaching to heaven; and there were angels of God going up it and coming down. And Yahweh was there, stand-

ing over him, saying, "I am Yahweh, the God of Abraham your father, and the God of Isaac. I will give to you and your descendants the land on which you are lying. Your descendants shall be like the specks of dust on the ground; you shall spread to the west and the east, to the north and the south, and all the tribes of the earth shall bless themselves by you and your descendants. Be sure that I am with you; I will keep you safe wherever you go, and bring you back to this land, for I will not desert you before I have done all that I have promised you." Then Jacob awoke from his sleep and said, "Truly, Yahweh is in this place and I never knew it!" (Gen. 28:11–16)

The purpose of this dream was to confirm the Abrahamic covenant directly to Jacob, and to assure Jacob that, although he was in distress, he was yet the object of God's love and care.

God's manifestation completely altered Jacob's view of his own purpose and destiny, and to Jacob this was no mere dream, but a profound spiritual experience. Fourteen years later Jacob was to have another dream, in which he would realize that he was to return to the land of his birth.

After this the Bible records several manifestations of the divine presence to Jacob, like the famous dream at Peniel, in which God appeared to him in the form of an angel and the two of them wrestled until daybreak. Jacob prevailed and would not let the angel go until he had blessed him. The angel blessed him, and also changed his name from Jacob to Israel.

Jacob called the place Peniel, which means "face of God." "For I have seen God face to face, and my life is spared and not snatched away" (Gen. 32:30). Thus, as a consequence of this dream, Jacob received a new identity, a new status, as the one who provided his people with a name—Israel.

Many years afterward Jacob received a final vision, on his way to Egypt, when God appeared to him personally and assured him that it was in the divine will and plan for him to go to this strange land. God would go with him, but since Canaan was the place for fulfillment of the covenant, God declared that Jacob, as well as his descendants, would be brought back there. Then God promised that Jacob's long-lost son Joseph would be the one to close his father's eyes in death.

JERKS DURING SLEEP (MYCLONIC JERK)

Falling dreams typically occur at the beginning of the night, in Stage I sleep. Such dreams are often accompanied by muscle spasms of the arms, legs, or the whole body that seem to happen just as one hits the ground in the dream. These sudden contractions—the technical name is *myclonic jerk*—are common in many mammals. Sleep researchers have paralleled them to the reflexive actions we experience as hiccups. There has been much speculation as to their cause, but the precise explanation remains unknown. One hypothesis is that it is part of an arousal mechanism. The thought is that this allows the sleeper to awaken quickly in response to possible environmental threats. One of the more common occurrences of the myclonic jerk is when dreamers experience falling dreams and their muscles contract just as they hit the ground.

SAINT JEROME

Jerome was a fourth-century Christian best known for his translation of the **Bible** into Latin. His translation, known later as the Vulgate, was the authoritative Catholic version of the Bible for the next 1,500 years. Owing to mistranslations of certain key biblical passage, Jerome helped to propagate a negative attitude toward dreams throughout western Christendom.

As a young man, Jerome had collected an extensive personal library of pagan literary works, which he believed conflicted with his Christian faith. This conflict surfaced in a dream in which, brought before the Throne of Judgment, he was told that he was a follower of Cicero rather than Christ. After being subjected to innumerable lashes, Jerome swore that he would never read such worldly books again. It is said that when he awakened his back bore the marks of the lash. Later Jerome dreamed about his own death, as well as about having the supernatural power to fly (a common dream theme, though Jerome might not have been aware of just how common it was).

It was perhaps these dream experiences that led Saint Jerome to mistranslate the Hebrew word for witchcraft, *anan*, as "observing dreams" (in Latin, *observo somnia*) when commissioned to translate the Bible by Pope Damasus I. Anan appears ten times in the Hebrew Scriptures (the Old Testament), but Jerome translates it as "observing dreams" only three times, in such statements as, "you shall not practice augury nor observe dreams," which more accurately reads, "you shall not practice augury or witchcraft." These simple changes, which made the Bible appear to discourage attending to one's dreams, significantly altered the course of how dreams were viewed for centuries.

JOHNSON, LYNDON B.

Former U.S. president Lyndon B. Johnson (1908–1973) suffered from chronic **nightmares**, a childhood condition he carried into his adult life. As a young child he often dreamed that he was sitting, paralyzed, in a chair as he faced an oncoming cattle stampede. After becoming the vice president in 1961, the setting of his nightmares changed to the Executive Office Building, but the paralysis theme remained the same. He dreamed he was sitting at his desk, just finishing a pile of paperwork. But when he got up to go home he discovered that ankle straps bound him to the heavy chair he was sitting in. Since he was unable to move, he resigned himself to continuing to do more paperwork.

After the 1968 Tet offensive in Vietnam, the content of his nightmares altered yet again, but the paralysis theme remained. He was now lying in a bed in the Red Room; he was unable to move

or even speak, but he was able to observe that he possessed the frail, paralyzed body of Woodrow Wilson. The trauma of these nightmares carried over into his waking life, so much so that Johnson regularly looked at the pictures of Wilson that hung in the White House halls just to assure himself that, while Wilson was dead, he himself remained alive and capable of action.

Johnson found himself in a difficult predicament as the Vietnam conflict continued and casualties mounted. He felt he could not withdraw the troops and maintain his (and America's) honor, but he also knew that the opposition was building throughout the country. If he were to remain in office, support for the social programs he was promoting would be jeopardized because of his stance on Vietnam. Once again, Johnson's nightmares reflected the fears and uncertainties of his waking life. He dreamt that he was being swept down a river, struggling to swim to the shore. When he tried to reach the nearest bank, he discovered that, no matter how hard he swam, it never go any closer. He then tried to swim to the other side, but the results were the same and he found himself swimming in circles, exhausting all his energy. This nightmare embodied the impossible situation that Johnson was in, and he realized the only way to rectify the situation was to remove himself as an active participant. Shortly after having this nightmare, he announced his decision not to seek another term in office.

JOSEPH (HUSBAND OF MARY)

Among the six dreams reported in the New Testament are the dreams that communicated divine knowledge, instruction, and warning to Joseph, the husband of Mary, mother of Jesus. A certain connection can be seen between the original Joseph of Genesis, the dreamer and interpreter of dreams, and the Joseph of the New Testament, who was also the son of a man named Jacob, according to Matthew's genealogy. Shortly after he was told by Mary that she was pregnant and that she had a visit from an angel, Joseph had a significant dream in which an angel of the Lord appeared to him and said,

> Joseph son of David, do not be afraid to take Mary home as your wife, because what is conceived in her is from the Holy Spirit. She will give birth to a son, and you are to give him the name Jesus, because he will save his people from their sins. (Matt. 1:20–21)

According to Jewish law, betrothal was a binding arrangement, and the penalty for fornication during that period was death to each party. But because of this dream, Joseph tolerated the strange pregnancy that had aroused his jealousy and his anxieties. The angel in his dream was clearly Gabriel, who had already appeared to Mary in a waking state. Gabriel was also apparently the messenger who appeared in Joseph's second dream, after the Magi had already been warned in a dream not to go back to Herod and to return to their country by another route:

> When they had gone, an angel of the Lord appeared to Joseph in a dream. "Get up," he said, "take the child and his mother and escape to Egypt. Stay there until I tell you, for Herod is going to search for the child to kill him." (Matt. 2:13)

In this dream Joseph was given a promise of continued care and guidance, and he was ready to obey the instructions imparted by God.

It is in connection with the death of Herod that the third dream was given to Joseph during the sojourn in Egypt:

After Herod died, an angel of the Lord appeared in a dream to Joseph in Egypt and said, "Get up, take the child and his mother and go to the land of Israel, for those who were trying to take the child's life are dead." (Matt. 2:20)

Joseph again was obedient to God's commands, and left Egypt for the land of Israel.

JOSEPH (SON OF JACOB)

The Old Testament reports that Joseph, the son of Jacob, had at least two significant dreams. Joseph was the eleventh son of Jacob and the firstborn of Rachel. The family lived in Canaan, where all of Jacob's sons were shepherds tending their father's flocks.

Joseph was Jacob's favorite son and was given a coat of many colors by his father, which was a mark of honor to be worn only by the heir. Joseph's brothers became very jealous and began to hate him. When, at the age of seventeen, Joseph told his brothers about a dream he had experienced, they hated him even more. This dream was prophetic and foreshadowed Joseph's preeminence among his brothers: "Listen to this dream I had: We were binding sheaves of grain out in the field when suddenly my sheaf rose and stood upright, while your sheaves gathered around mine and bowed down to it" (Gen. 37:6–7).

Then a second dream is reported: "Listen, I had another dream, and this time the sun and moon and eleven stars were bowing down to me" (Gen. 37:9). When Joseph told this dream to his father, Jacob rebuked him and said, "What is this dream you had? Will your mother and I and your brothers actually come and bow down to the ground before you?" But, while Joseph's brothers

In Jewish tradition, many dreams can be interpreted as relating to passages in the Torah.

their ruler, dreamed dreams the same night and asked Joseph to interpret them. He told the cupbearer that, according to his dream, he was going to be restored to his place within three days. He then interpreted the dream of the baker, which showed that within three days the pharaoh would take his office from him, have him hung on a tree, and he would be devoured by the birds.

The pharaoh himself had two dreams, which, according to Joseph's interpretation, foretold seven years of hunger and famine in Egypt. When Joseph recommended a line of action that would save the nation from famine, the pharaoh was so impressed that he made him prime minister of Egypt. Joseph's family eventually came to Egypt to buy grain during the famine. He was then able to establish his family in Egypt, and they honored him according to his dream.

JUDAISM

Judaism has a rich tradition of dream interpretation. The interest of Jews in dreams was particularly stimulated during their captivity in Babylon, where dream **divination** was a widespread practice. The Jews, like other peoples in this region, distinguished between good and evil dreams.

The Babylonian Talmud, the largest collection of Jewish sacred writings, is full of references to dreams, rules for interpreting dreams, and means of avoiding evil dreams. The Berakhot section of the Babylonian Talmud contains a number of rabbinic stories, teachings, and reflections on dream interpretation. One common theme is that dream interpretation represents an important but very difficult and complex matter, since dreams are always enigmatic. Thus, interpreters must be very careful to distinguish meaningful and revelatory dreams from worthless ones ("just

planned to kill him because of their envy, Jacob correctly interpreted the dream, which made a deep impression on him, and he took it as a divine indication of events that would affect his family.

Not only did Joseph have dreams of his own, he was also asked, like Daniel, to interpret dreams of other people, particularly the dreams of non-Hebrews. After Joseph was sold into slavery by his brothers, the Bible reports that the cupbearer and the chief baker of the king of Egypt, who were in prison for having offended as there is no wheat without straw, so there is no dream without worthless things").

Several Jewish prophets gave warnings against false dreams and false interpreters, recognizing that religious heresy might arise from bad interpretation. Rabbinic Judaism laid considerable emphasis on interpretation. According to the rabbis, a dream that is not interpreted is like a letter that is not read, and without conscious elaboration, a dream's meaning is lost. Many dreams are linked to Jewish Scripture, relating words in dreams to important passages from the Torah.

The Jews had become worshipers of the one God rather than of many special gods, and this idea was reflected in their view of dreams. God alone could be the source of the divine revelations that came in dreams. And, since He was the God of the Jews, they believed He usually spoke clearly to them. In some cases, when the wishes of Jehovah are communicated by an angelic messenger, it is hard to distinguish between dreams and waking visions. In other cases, the dreamer hears the voice of God, or may like Solomon in Gideon, see the Lord himself.

Almost all symbolic dreams in the Old Testament are dreamed by Gentiles. Important examples are the enigmatic messages sent to non-Jews, such as Pharaoh and Nebuchadnezzar, that only Jews were able to interpret (in these cases, Joseph and Daniel, respectively). Although the Jews had begun to give special emphasis to dream theory, they continued to classify dreams in much the same way as the peoples in neighboring territories.

JUNG, CARL GUSTAV

Carl Jung (1875–1961), a prominent Swiss psychotherapist, was second only to **Sigmund Freud** in importance and influence in the field of psychoanalysis. His ideas are best known indirectly, through his influence on such popular thinkers as **Joseph Campbell**. The contemporary reevaluation of mythology as an important component of human life is ultimately traceable to the influence of Jung.

Between 1907 and 1913 Jung was a student of Freud's, and for a while he was even regarded as Freud's "heir apparent." They eventually had a falling out, and Jung went his own way. While both studied dreams, Jung advanced an approach that did not depend heavily on sexual problems, in contrast to Freud, who insisted upon the sexual roots of neurosis. After the break with Freud, Jung went through a period of inner disorder and seeking, during which he carried out a journey of exploration into his own unconscious mind. In his interpretation of the spiritual journey of the human being, he also drew upon Eastern philosophies and various occult ideas, such as alchemy. Jung was preoccupied with the supernatural. He had visions during his childhood as well as later in life.

Jung's personality theory, as well as his theory of psychological disorder and therapy, are clearly modeled on Freud's ideas. Both men advocated depth psychologies, (they both viewed the **unconscious** as particularly significant for understanding the human psyche). Both also viewed the therapeutic process as a task of acquiring insight into one's unconscious dynamics. Jung, however, subdivided the depth dimension of the psyche into the personal unconscious and the **collective unconscious**. He also postulated what he termed the individuation process, which is an overriding dynamic that prompts the individual to seek greater self-understanding, self-integration, and self-fulfillment.

Freud viewed the unconscious aspect of the self that expresses itself in dreams as infantile and

Carl Jung and Sigmund Freud pose with colleagues at Clark University in Worcester, Massachusetts. (First row, left to right) Sigmund Freud, G. Stanley Hall, and Carl Jung; (back row) A.A. Brill, Ernest Jones, and Sandor Ferenczi. (Library of Congress).

animalistic, and the overt content of dreams as a disguised acting out of socially unacceptable urges. Jung's view is more benign, picturing the unconscious self as a complex mix of lower instinctual and higher spiritual impulses. Instead of concealing, the purpose of a dream is to communicate something to consciousness. The unconscious, in other words, has a kind of intelligence that attempts to guide and otherwise assist the con-

scious self. Jungian dream analysis, then, becomes a task of helping clients to properly interpret the messages coming from the unconscious.

In contrast to Freud, Jung also put forward a somewhat different set of components for the psyche of the individual. The **ego** represents the individual's sense of personal self—what we might call one's self-image. This sense of personal self, however, is purchased at the expense of certain tendencies (e.g., socially undesirable traits), which are rejected as "not-self." According to Jung, these rejected traits come together as a kind of unconscious "counterego," which he termed the **shadow**.

The **anima** refers to personality traits regarded as feminine that are often repressed into the unconscious in male psyches. The parallel structure in the female psyche is called the **animus**. Although repressed from conscious awareness, the anima/animus influences our behavior in powerful ways. In most individuals, for example, the anima/animus is projected onto people of the opposite sex, and accounts for the experience of falling in love with someone we hardly know.

In Jungian therapy, both the shadow and the anima/animus are viewed as potential sources of characteristics to be integrated into the patient's ego structure. As the unconscious pole of the ego, the counterego represented by the anima/animus can also be a guide to one's own unconscious realm, and is often experienced as a guiding presence of the opposite sex in dreams. The shadow can also appear as a person in dreams, though usually as a person of the same sex. The **persona** refers to the personality that we project to the world (the self we want other people to see). Dream images of the persona can be anything from the clothes we wear to the actions we perform in the dream.

Jung theorized that dreams serve two functions: They compensate for internal imbalances (e.g., an excessively analytical person might have emotionally charged dreams), and they assist in the individuation process (a kind of individuality development process) by providing the dreamer with prospective images of the future. He also distinguished between objective and subjective dreams or objective and subjective levels of dream interpretation. Objective dreams picture the dreamer's daily life—the person's relationship with the external world and the people and events in that world. Subjective dreams, on the other hand, portray the dreamer's inner life, and the significant actors in such dreams are personifications of the dreamer's thoughts and feelings. Finally, Jung believed that, as in a drama, most dream accounts could be broken down into four components: (1) an initial *exposition* of the setting, (2) plot *development*, (3) the *culmination*, and (4) a quiet conclusion or solution, which Jung termed the *lysis*.

An especially important aspect of Jungian dream analysis is what he termed **archetypes**. While the personal unconscious is shaped by our personal experiences, the collective unconscious represents our inheritance of the collective experience of humankind. This storehouse of humanity's collective experiences exists in the form of archetypes, which predispose us to unconsciously organize our personal experiences in certain ways.

Archetypes are not concrete images in the collective unconscious. They are more like invisible magnetic fields that cause iron filings to arrange themselves according to certain patterns. Concrete manifestations of elusive archetypes are referred to as archetypal images or, when they appear in dreams, as archetypal dream images.

Jung discovered that the dreams of his patients frequently contained images with which they were completely unfamiliar, but which seemed to reflect symbols that could be found somewhere in the mythological systems of world culture. He further found that if he could discover the specific meaning of such images in their native culture he could better understand the dreams in which they occurred. The process of seeking such meanings is referred to as amplification and is a standard procedure in Jungian dream interpretation.

LET YOUR DREAM
DEVOUR YOUR LIFE
NOT YOUR LIFE DEVOUR
YOUR DREAM.

—UNKNOWN

K-COMPLEXES AND SPINDLES

One of the components of contemporary scientific sleep research is the classification of **stages of sleep** according to certain physiological indicators, such as brain wave patterns, which are measured with an electroencephalogram, or **EEG**. Someone drifting off to sleep, in what is referred to as Stage 1 sleep, is really in a transitional state between sleeping and wakefulness. It is not until the EEG machine begins recording patterns referred to as transient sleep spindles and K complexes that one has entered the sleeping state proper. These two patterns characterize what is called Stage 2 sleep. Spindles are half-second (or longer) bursts of EEG activity measuring 12 to 14 Hz. K-complexes are half-second (approximately) wave patterns with a "well-delin-

eated negative component immediately followed by positive deflection" (Anch et al., p. 28—see *Sources*). Sleepers are in Stage 2 sleep just before and just after **rapid eye movement (REM) sleep**, which is the stage of sleep during which our most vivid dreams occur.

KAFKA, FRANZ

Franz Kafka (1883–1924) was born in the Old Town area of Prague, Czechoslovakia. He attended German schools and in 1901 entered Prague University, where he earned the doctor of law in July 1906. He worked for an insurance company from 1908 until 1922. In August 1921 he had begun to cough blood but had dismissed the illness as of purely psychic origin. The disease was later diagnosed as pulmonary catarrh (inflammation of a mucous membrane), with a danger of tuberculosis. After living on an estate at Zuru, near Saaz, for some time, he spent the rest of his life in sanatoria, dying in the Kierling Sanatorium, near Vienna. Among his works are the novella *The Metamorphosis*; the short stories "The Judgement" and "A Country Doctor"; and three novels: *The Castle, The Trial,* and *Amerika*.

Kafka had considerable intimacy with the world of dreams for most of his life and experienced mental states in which dreamlike images and fantasies emerged. In many instances these images were recorded in his notebooks, and they appear here and there in his stories, which are written from inner experience with only limited support of psychoanalytic investigation of dreams and dream symbolism.

The dreams recorded by Kafka are notable for their abundance of detail and their visual preciseness. Kafka was aware of the danger related to such intimacy with the dreamworld, namely, the possible loss of connections to the real world and the breaking off of human relations. His work served to connect him with the real world.

For Kafka, as for other authors of this century, the dream constituted the primary means for representing unconscious experience. The mechanical problems of expressing the dreamworld did not exist for Kafka because of his particular prose style, which undergoes no distortions and is perfectly consistent in reporting events, real or delusional. He was able to erase the boundaries between reality and dream, and his transition from one world to another is as imperceptible as the moment between waking and sleeping.

Kafka's "dream technique" is a product of his concept of the dream as a work of art. He explored the aesthetic properties of the dream and the relationship between unconscious mental processes and the form and composition of the dream. His dream technique is characterized by the particular use of metaphor, which in a dream is represented literally. In Kafka's diaries the evolution of a story (i.e., the details of the story) from a metaphor can often be traced.

In *The Metamorphosis*, the protagonist is a noxious bug, as in a symbolic dream. Although the story does not recount the dream of its protagonist, Gregor, who, as the text explains, has just awakened from a troubled dream and is now presumably back in reality, *The Metamorphosis* does evoke the quality of dream experiences as perfectly as any dream memory. The reader is taken vividly into the dreamworld, which, despite being a surreal universe of fantastic shapes, is a world of incredible clarity and intensity.

KAGWAHIV

The Kagwahiv are a Tupi-speaking people living in small settlements in the tropical forests of the Amazon in Brazil. Dreams play a fundamental role in Kagwahiv culture, and, like myths, they are to be told at any time. Thus, they can be shared in the middle of the night as well as during the day over work.

Dreams are sources of information about the nature of the world and spiritual beings, and are believed to foretell future events—literally, metaphorically, or by way of myths, which are condensed formulations of essential human issues. Dream reports usually contain mythic elements, either in their **manifest dream** or their **latent dream** content, as free associations with the dream make clear. **Nightmares**, for example, represent direct perceptions of the presence of a demon.

Dream sharing among the Kagwahiv, which usually includes a discussion about their meaning, follows particular prescriptions. For instance, an inauspicious dream is told by the fire, to cancel out its prediction, whereas an auspicious dream is told away from the fire, so that its favorable prediction is not cancelled.

The Kagwahiv believe that dreams provide a means of communication between supernatural beings and people, especially people with shamanic aspirations, who are said to commune with spirits of the sky and other mystical beings and to exercise at least some of their power through dreams.

KALAPALO

The Kalapalo Indians of central Brazil are a Carib-speaking community of fewer than 200 people. To the Kalapalo, dreaming represents an experience of life that frees the imagination and memory, and dreams must be interpreted with reference to the future of the dreamer.

The interpretation of dreams requires special linguistic resources that might be different from those appropriate for speaking about the ordinary waking life. Dreaming is believed to occur when, during sleep, an individual's "interactive self" awakens and wanders until it achieves an experience. The dream experience begins when the interactive self stops wandering and starts to participate actively in some event.

According to the Kalapalo, the process of remembering is responsible for the experience of particular images, which can be associated with the memory of recent events. Dreaming is claimed to be a means of communication with powerful beings who visit the sleeper and are drawn to the interactive self when it detaches itself from a person's physical body and begins to wander about. The appearance of powerful beings in their dreams allows the Kalapalo to acquire direct knowledge about them and about their properties, which can be subsequently used in waking life (in the event that the vision is not fatal). A person who experiences frequent and successful contacts with a powerful being becomes a **shaman**, after a period of apprenticeship.

Dreaming provides the Kalapalo with useful insights about some problems and about the formation of new roles and relations. Dreams are usually given great importance and are often associated with states of psychological tension and with critical times in people's lives. It is believed that dreaming is a performative event because it causes the future by revealing the dreamer's life as it is contained in his current motivations and fears. Thus, the Kalapalo often believe the dreaming subject is responsible for subsequent events. The interpretation of dreams is considered a metaphorical process of achieving knowledge about the interactive self.

NEVER LAUGH AT
ANYONE'S DREAMS.
PEOPLE WHO DON'T
HAVE DREAMS DON'T
HAVE MUCH.

—UNKNOWN

LABERGE, STEPHEN

Stephen LaBerge (1947–), a Stanford-trained psychologist working in the Stanford University Sleep Clinic, was the first person to scientifically demonstrate the existence of **lucid dreaming**. People are experiencing a lucid dream when they are aware that they are in the midst of a dream. The most unusual aspect of this state is that lucid dreamers can consciously alter the content of their dreams.

LaBerge, who had experienced lucid dreams since childhood, resolved to study the phenomenon scientifically during his psychology graduate program at Stanford. He initially experimented on himself, using sweeping motions of the eyes—controlled by muscles that are not immobilized during the **rapid eye movement (REM)** stage of sleep—to signal non-sleeping observers that he was in a lucid dream state (he later used clenched fists to send messages in Morse code). LaBerge trained others to dream lucidly, and then experimented with dream control—undertaking a task such as flying or changing the dream landscape at will.

The results of these experiments were reported in LaBerge's popular 1985 book on the subject, *Lucid Dreaming*. The success of this work stimulated the nationwide formation of dream groups. The mass media also became interested in the idea, and the implications of lucid dreaming were discussed in innumerable articles and on talk shows.

LABORATORIES, SLEEP

Because dreams are so subjective, they frustrate the methods of objective, empirical science—we have nothing like a "dream microscope" that allows us to observe the dreams unfolding within the sleeper's mental field. Despite some important precursors, modern laboratory-oriented dream research did not really get off the ground until after Eugene Aserinsky and Nathaniel Kleitman's 1953 discovery of rapid eye movement **(REM) sleep** and the subsequent linking of REM sleep with dreaming. Although later studies showed that significant dreaming could take place during non-REM sleep, the postulate that there was a close correlation between dreams and REM sleep guided scientific dream research for over a decade. While sleep labs had existed prior to 1953, the rapid expansion of the field of sleep and dream research in the wake of the discovery of REM sleep stimulated the establishment of more such laboratories as well as the expansion of existing ones.

A typical sleep lab consists of a number of separate rooms where experimental subjects sleep and an instrumentation room where data from various measuring devices are recorded. In most cases, the data being collected are bioelectrical in nature, and a device called a polysomnograph records ongoing variations in the sleeper's bioelectrical state. The two primary measures are **EOG** (electrooculogram, which records eye movements, the primary indicator of REM sleep) and **EEG** (electroencephalogram, which records brain waves, used to determine the sleeper's **stage of sleep**). Depending on the data being gathered, other instruments might include a closed-circuit TV, a tape recorder, devices for measuring respiration, and so on.

Subjects may be paid or may be students earning credit for one of their classes, usually a psychology course. Participants arrive several hours beforehand to fill out forms and to have electrodes or other instruments attached. Often a physical examination is also conducted. Usually the first night of sleep is atypical because one tends not to sleep as well in a new environment. Depending on the nature of the experiment, the data from this first night might be thrown out or ignored.

LATENT DREAM (OR LATENT DREAM CONTENT)

Latent dream is **Sigmund Freud**'s expression for the real meaning of a dream, distinct from its surface structure and content. The contrasting term is **manifest dream**, which refers to the dream as it is dreamed, remembered, and reported, prior to any analysis. The psychoanalytical view is that the true significance of the dream is disguised so that our sleep is not interrupted by disturbing dreams.

LILITH

The ancient texts of the Assyro-Babylonian civilizations make the first recorded reference to the sexual demon Lilith. They describe a being that resembles the Medieval **succubi** and yet possesses characteristics similar to those of modern vampires. Succubi are night **demons** that cause nocturnal emissions in order to feed on the resulting bodily fluids. Lilith also made appearances in Hebrew texts as the princess of the race of succubi. The name "Lilith" may derive from the Hebrew word "lulti," meaning "lasciviousness," and not "lailah," meaning "night." Commentators sometimes saw Lilith in Hebrew scriptures. For example, according to Midrashic literature, the serpent that tempted Eve in the Garden of Eden was, in actuality, the demon Lilith, a minion of Satan, and not Satan himself.

The texts of some rabbinical translators present the first human being as a hermaphrodite, with the female half being Lilith. When God separated them from each other, Lilith fled the garden when she learned that God expected her to "lay under" Adam. It was after this incident that the more accommodating Eve was created from Adam's rib. In modern times there is a Jewish feminist magazine titled Lilith, a choice of name that associates the content of the publication with Lilith's refusal to be subservient to Adam.

The 1940s movie *Nightmare Alley* also borrows from the ancient legends of Lilith, even going so far as to name the female lead character after her. In this movie, she is a demonic "consulting psychologist" who preys upon the minds of her patients. She extracts damning information from their **nightmares** and uses the facts she obtains to blackmail them.

LOGOLI

Among the Logoli of western Kenya there is generally a positive attitude toward dreams and the telling of dreams, with little worry about their status as godly or satanic and little attempt to censure or control them by the leadership. The Logoli view dreams as resulting from the travels and encounters of the consciousness of one individual with those of others and ghosts of the dead during sleep, even when the specifics of these encounters are not remembered.

LUCID DREAMING

People are engaged in lucid dreaming when they are aware that they are in the midst of a dream. The most unusual aspect of these states is that

While in the Bible, the story of the Garden of Eden begins with Adam and Eve, other stories tell of the first woman being Lilith, who refused to subjugage herself to Adam. Lilith later morphed into a demoness, a creature of nightmares.

lucid dreamers can consciously alter the content of their dreams. This characteristic has led researchers to begin to explore the possibilities of utilizing lucid dreaming to treat **nightmares** and for other therapeutic purposes.

The first recorded reference to lucid dreaming is in **Aristotle**'s *On Dreams*, where he says that "often when one is asleep, there is something in consciousness which declares that what then presents itself is but a dream." Other historical figures, such as Saint Augustine and **Saint Thomas Aquinas**, have mentioned lucid dreaming in their writings. *Dreams and How to Guide Them* (1867), by Marquis **Hervey de Saint-Denis**, a professor of Chinese at the College de France, was probably the first extended discussion of this state.

Although Saint-Denis's work was praised by no less a figure than **Sigmund Freud**, other psychologists discounted the very idea of lucid dreaming, attributing the phenomenon to a partial awakening during the dream state.

For the most part, the intangible nature of this unusual state of consciousness discouraged psychologists from giving serious attention to lucid dreaming until after **Stephen LaBerge** began publishing the results of his remarkable research in the 1980s. LaBerge, who had experienced lucid dreams since childhood, resolved to study the phenomenon scientifically during his psychology graduate program at Stanford University. The first problem he encountered was the infrequency of lucid dreams, a problem he dealt with by a kind of auto-suggestion—repeating "Tonight I *will* have a lucid dream" to himself before going to sleep. He eventually developed his own technique, referred to as Mnemonic Induction of Lucid Dreams (MILD), which increased his lucid dream rate to greater than 20 per month.

LaBerge's second problem was to find a way for dreamers to send messages to researchers while experiencing lucid dreams. Using sweeping motions of the eyes—controlled by muscles that are not immobilized during the **rapid eye movement (REM)** stage of sleep—he was eventually successful in controlling his eye movements during sleep. He later devised a more elaborate experiment, clenching his hand muscles in Morse code to deliver a message to non-sleeping observers.

LaBerge continued to expand his experiments, eventually training dozens of subjects to dream lucidly and communicate with researchers while asleep. These subjects were then instructed to perform a variety of tasks in their dreams, from counting to flying, and signal the experimenter when their tasks were complete. The results of

these experiments were reported in LaBerge's popular 1985 book on the subject, *Lucid Dreaming*. The success of this work stimulated the nationwide formation of dream groups. The mass media also became interested in the idea, and the implications of lucid dreaming were discussed in innumerable articles and talk shows.

The findings of lucid dream research are already beginning to be applied to therapy. One sleep therapist, for example, has taught clients experiencing recurrent nightmares to activate a buzzer during bad dreams. The client is subsequently awakened and the dream analyzed. Alternatively, rather than awaken the patient, the therapist responds to the sleeper's buzzer by in turn buzzing the sleeper, which in this case is a prearranged signal for the client to take control of the dream and attempt to transform the nightmare into a more pleasant experience.

Other psychologists, such as **Patricia Garfield**, have suggested utilizing lucid dreams in a manner similar to the way in which **creative visualization** has been employed for healing. Thus, someone suffering from pains in a particular part of the body, for instance, might picture themselves removing "all sort of junk" (to cite a case mentioned by Garfield) from the afflicted area. Garfield (p. 225—see *Sources*) suggests the following steps when experimenting with lucid healing dreams:

Before a lucid healing dream:

1. Select your healing goal and put it into words. *Examples:* "Teach me to reduce or eliminate my pain." "Help me heal." "Show me contentment."
2. Rehearse your healing goal, repeating it before sleep.
3. Visualize your healing goal being fulfilled.

During a lucid healing dream:

1. Become lucid in your dream.
2. Perform your dream healing or allow it to take place.
3. Accept the wisdom of your dream.

LUCIDITY ASSOCIATION

Several organizations and periodicals are devoted to the study of dreams. The Lucidity Association focuses particularly on lucid dreaming. Its annual periodical, *Lucidity* (formerly the *Lucidity Letter*), publishes articles on both clinical research and personal experiences.

LUCIDITY INSTITUTE

Stephen LaBerge, one of the pioneers of **lucid dreaming** research, directs the Lucidity Institute. The institute sponsors a variety of workshops and lectures on topics related to lucid dreaming. It also publishes a newsletter, *Night Light*, and even offers correspondence courses on lucid dreaming.

MACK, JOHN E.

John Mack (1929–2004), author of *Nightmares and Human Conflict*, studied the childlike characteristics of our reactions to threats in our **nightmares**. He recognized the fact that in nightmares we are often assaulted by powerful forces that we are unable to manage successfully. This corresponds to the emotions of helplessness and the lack of ability to affect the world around us that we experience particularly in childhood. The villains of our nightmares are less important than the feelings of terror and vulnerability they evoke:

> Whether the dreamer is threatened by an ancient demon, a vampire, a lobster, a fairy story monster, a robot, or an atomic ray, his experience is, in each instance, like that of a helpless child confronted by powerful forces with which he is unable to deal with effectively.

When comparing the difference in the nature of children's and adults' nightmares, Mack observed:

> Nightmares occur in response to the characteristic danger of situations that human beings confront in the fear of strangers and the dread of abandonment in infancy and the fear of bodily injury in early childhood, and ending with the fears of failure, death and loss of function in adulthood and old age.... Nightmares may become the prototypical expression of the activities that characterize each stage of development.

Adult nightmares are similar to children's in that they engender a sense of vulnerability. The types and sources of anxieties may change, but feelings of helplessness and insecurity affect people of all ages.

MACROBIUS

Ambrosias Theodosius Macrobius was a Christian author of the late fourth century. His work *Commentary on the Dream of Scipio* is one of the most influential dream books of the Latin Middle Ages. There were over thirty-seven editions printed before 1700. When compared to his contemporaries, Macrobius is considered negative and superstitious. His book clearly derived inspiration from the *Oneirocritia*, the great dream book of **Artemidorus**. It covers five different classes of dreams, including material on apparitions and **nightmares** that Artemidorus did not cover explicitly.

Macrobius applied the Platonic hierarchy to his dream classification, the top three classes being the most significant for they had divine purposes of inspiration. Ghostly apparitions (phantasma), enigmatic dreams (somnium), and oracular dreams (oraculum) are at the top of the hierarchy, and are thus the most divine. **Nightmares** (insomnium) and prophetic visions (visio) are the two classes that Macrobius thought to be inconsequential. He determined that prophetic visions that appear in the state between waking and sleeping are of no consequence because they are not actual dreams and therefore cannot be of divine inspiration.

The *Commentary on the Dream of Scipio* covers three different causes of nightmares. These are: troubles of the body, such as hunger or gluttony; troubles of the soul, such as love or loss; and issues relating to one's profession. Macrobius also included information on **incubi**, sexual male demons, and made mention of **succubi**, the female version of the incubi. These were the first references made to these **demons** in the literature of the Christian faith. Although there are many stories about the incubi and succubi in early Jewish folklore, their inclusion by Macrobius played a significant role in the development of the demonic paranoia evident in later centuries.

MANDALA ARCHETYPE

A mandala is a visual diagram on which one focuses during meditation. The term is derived from *manas*, the Sanskrit word for mind, or, more properly, for the "mind-stuff." Mandalas are common aids to meditation practice and are found in both Hinduism and **Buddhism**, particularly in the strands of these two traditions called tantrism (Tantric Hinduism and Tantric Buddhism). Mandalas may contain elaborate pictures of the various worlds theorized by tantrism, or they may be rather stark geometric diagrams.

The psychologist **Carl Jung** adopted the term to refer to one of the categories of symbols—an **archetypal dream image**—that regularly appear in dreams. Jung postulated a drive towards self-realization and self-integration, which he referred to as the individuation process. The goal of this process was represented by the "self" archetype, an archetype characterized by wholeness and completeness. One of the concrete manifestations of this archetype is the circle, and it was the various forms of the circle that Jung referred to as mandalas. According to Jung, mandala symbols emerge in dreams when the individual is seeking harmony and wholeness, which often occurs during periods of crisis and insecurity.

MANIFEST DREAM (OR MANIFEST DREAM CONTENT)

Manifest dream is **Sigmund Freud**'s expression for the dream as it is dreamed, remembered, and reported, prior to any analysis. The psychoanalytical view is that the true significance of the dream is disguised by the manifest dream content. The goal of psychoanalysis with respect to dreams is to uncover their real meaning, expressed in what Freud called the **latent dream**.

MAURY, ALFRED

The French scientist Alfred Maury (1817–1892) published his *Sleep and Dreams* in 1861. Prior to this, he kept a **dream diary**, paying extra attention to the circumstances he believed contributed to their content and intensity. Among the external factors on which he placed great importance, diet and environmental changes were particularly important to him. He also paid extra attention to the **hypnagogic** hallucinations that appeared in the moments before he drifted off to sleep. It was his belief that these provided an "embryogenesis" of his subsequent dream images.

In experiments he conducted later in his career, he served as the primary subject while an assistant introduced various stimuli to his senses after he entered into the **rapid eye movement** state of sleep. These stimuli were both auditory and olfactory. The hope was that he would be able to report the effects of outside stimuli on the content of his dreams. On one occasion, his assistant tickled his lips and the inside of his nostrils with a feather and Maury dreamed that the skin in those places was being ripped from his face by a mass of burning pitch. In a different instance, heated iron was held close to him and Maury reported a dream in which robbers were putting his feet in fire in an effort to get him to reveal the location of money.

The experiments also indicated that scents could factor into dream content. When his assistant held a burning match close to his nose

Maury dreamed that the magazine of his ship blew up; he also dreamed of a perfume shop when exposed to the scent of a bottle of cologne. The results of these tests lend validity to the theory that the environment affects what we experience while in a sleeping state.

MEMORY AND SLEEP

As studies of **sleep learning** as well as studies of so-called **nondreamers** have shown, the memory-recording processes of the brain seem to be switched off during sleep. In so-called nondreamers who, it has been demonstrated, actually do dream—this memory shutdown is simply more complete than it is for the rest of the population. Even people who remember their dreams every night only remember the last several dreams they had immediately before awakening. Dreams from the early and middle periods of sleep are permanently forgotten.

It has been hypothesized that dreams are easily forgotten because they are so incoherent. Another theory is that dreams are quickly forgotten because they contain repressed material that the conscious mind does not wish to remember. However, although these two factors probably do account for some forgetting, they are inadequate for explaining the extensive loss of dream content that occurs every morning upon awakening. The precise process has yet to be discovered, but there is almost certainly some sort of neurochemical mechanism that shuts down memory during sleep.

METAPHOR, DREAMS AS

Whether we view dreams as arenas within which we act out repressed desires, as communications

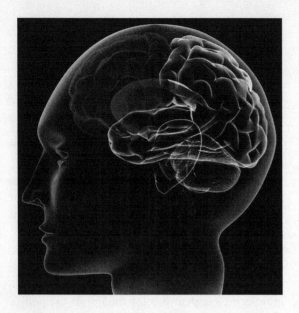

The human brain requires rest (sleep) to remain healthy. Lack of sleep can hamper one's memory, experts have learned.

from the **unconscious** to the conscious, or simply as reflections of our everyday concerns, they are often symbolic and indirect. For whatever reason, the part of the mind that directs our dreams often chooses to embody meaning in dream images by "literalizing" metaphors. For example, a ball in a dream can represent everything from a game or some other form of recreation to childhood itself (depending on what kind of ball is in the dream). However, a ball can also have metaphorical connotations, such as being "tossed around," "the ball's in your court," "having a ball," and "having balls" (having courage). Depending on other elements in the dream landscape, any one of these possible meanings may be indicated by the dream. Many other concrete examples of this literalizing of metaphors can be found in the Symbols section of this encyclopedia.

It is believed that by achieving insight into the metaphors present in **nightmares** it is possible to lessen their occurrence. This is achieved because once the consciousness acknowledges a message from the unconscious mind there is no longer the need to present the unresolved issue in nightmare context. Another approach suggests that by gaining any understanding of what the terrifying imagery represents the dreamer will then be able to confront that aspect of the nightmare and dispel the fear associated with it.

MIDDLE AGES

The **Bible** gives dreams a mixed review. While the biblical God sometimes communicates through dreams, they are clearly a less exalted mode of communication, because individuals particularly close to God receive His messages while they are awake. Furthermore, only pagans receive symbolic dreams, which require interpretation. This mixed heritage is reflected at various stages in Christianity's development.

Of particular importance for the Middle Ages were mistranslations by **Saint Jerome** of certain key biblical passages warning against witchcraft and augury, which he confused with dreams. These explicit warnings, in combination with the admonitions of writers like **Macrobius**, who warned about the possibility of demons in one's sleep, served to effectively condemn dreams as little more than stages for Satan's minions to tempt the souls of the faithful.

The medieval attitude is expressed in, for example, a sixteenth-century work *De magia*, by Benedict Peterius, a Jesuit priest: "The devil is most always implicated in dreams, filling the minds of men with poisonous Superstition and not only uselessly deluding but perniciously deceiving them"

(Van de Castle, p. 83—see *Sources*). Nowhere is this suspicion of dreams more clearly demonstrated than in the notion of **incubi and succubi**, demons who took the form of men and women to seduce mortals in their sleep. These creatures were particularly useful for explaining sexual dreams in a society where any form of illicit sex was viewed as demonic. One can imagine the dismay of celibate clergy, monks, and nuns who awakened with vivid memories of erotic dreams. By attributing such dream images to evil spirits who seduced them in their sleep, they could absolve themselves of responsibility for such dreams.

MOHAVE

The Mohave, a **Native American** tribe of the American Southwest, are said to interpret their culture in terms of dreams, rather than interpret dreams in terms of their culture. For instance, omen dreams, while they may not necessarily reflect what will actually happen, foretell what could happen. While, power dreams of **shamans** and warriors are considered vital for predicting future events.

The Mohave also believe in pathogenic dreams—dreams that cause illness. There are two types of pathogenic dreams in Mohave culture: dreams, during the course of which, the dreamer falls ill because of certain harmful adventures the soul experiences in the dream; and dreams, that are so upsetting the dreamer reacts to them by becoming ill.

For example, a woman becomes severely depressed after dreaming that a dead relative cooked and served her a fish. While eating the fish, the dreamer realizes that the head of the fish is the head of her mother. Dreams such as this, especially about ghosts of relatives, are known to cause actual illness and are particularly dangerous if they involve being fed by, or engaging in coitus with, the ghost of the dead.

MOROCCO

Dreams are valued highly by the Moroccans of northwest Africa. They are most often regarded as indicators of the future, in that they can foretell it or indicate an action that should be taken. Moroccans have a rich, living tradition of dream interpretation, although they have not elaborated a particularly consistent dream theory, nor have they developed complex dream-related rituals. Moroccan dream interpretation and dream classification reflect the various influences of daily experience, folk **Islam**, classical Islam—popular and orthodox beliefs, attitudes, and doctrines. These diverse and sometimes competing elements affect the Moroccan view of dreams—everything from beliefs in the evil eye, to the Islamic ideal of the good man, to *djinn* (the spirits—good and bad—who oversee daily social interactions).

Moroccans, like many other people, believe that dreams result from the wandering of the soul during sleep, whereas daydreams occur when the soul leaves the body but stays close to it. The wandering soul witnesses real events that happen elsewhere in space and time. These dream events are thought to be related to the dreamer's future, most often in a symbolic way. Moroccans classify dreams as being either truthful, divinely inspired dreams, or deceitful dreams coming from the Devil and other sources. Truthful dreams are associated with safety, and deceitful dreams are associated with harm shaped by the evil intentions of spirits and ill-intended people.

In order to achieve a good interpretation of dreams, it is very common to share them, as well

The city of Casablanca in Morocco. The Moroccans, like many other cultures, believe in the precognitive powers of dreams.

as to rely on external dream specialists. In Morocco, not all dreams are trusted, any more than all people are trusted. The only dreams that can be trusted are God-sent, although it is difficult to distinguish them from the Satan-sent. However, Moroccans are not particularly concerned with internal (in the dream itself) criteria by which false dreams can be distinguished from true ones. Rather, they are generally more concerned with the condition of the dreamer himself as a determinant of the truth or falsehood of a dream.

Truthful, God-sent dreams are considered to have a spiritual origin, whereas deceitful dreams are regarded as expressions of psychological realities and everyday experiences. Another type of dream, not to be confused with bad dreams, is **visitation dreams**, which involve the appearance of saints and other spiritual beings. They usually serve to resolve conflicts that may not be clearly articulated by the dreamer by providing a point of primary orientation for the resolution process.

MOVIES, DREAMS IN

The use of dream images in movies is quite prevalent. Through dreams, it is possible to represent a state of mind or a memory via a dream sequence that otherwise would be very difficult to portray. Thus, themes like projection, defense, distortion, symbolism, trauma, obsession, fixation, regression, the Oedipal crisis, persecution delusion, and the inferiority complex have been the subjects of many films. **Freudian** dream work was writ large in society's films.

The films of Fritz Lang and Alfred Hitchcock are filled with remarkable coincidences and are characterized by an order imposed on the world through allegory, fantasy, romance, and dreams. Often an entire Lang movie, such as the *Woman in the Window* (1944) was presented as a dream. In this film, a university criminology professor denies that murder can be accidental and then becomes enmeshed in a set of circumstances that force him to commit one. At the end of the film, the murder is revealed to have occurred in a dream while he dozed in a chair at the faculty club. This movie is particularly involving, so that by the end of it the audience has the illusion of waking from the same dream, after experiencing the same emotions as the main character.

Hitchcock used dream images in various films, such as *Spellbound, Psycho*, and *Marnie*, in which psychiatric explanation reduces the power of dreams to words and formulas. A film like 1960's *Psycho* lures us in with a suggestion of a dream-within-a-dream, with the possible consequence that the dream-within-a-dream is real.

For many people watching a film is like having a dream. The overpowering images on the screen can be frightening and make people feel the same kind of paralysis known in nightmares. Also, films seem real in the way dreams feel real. Their ability to make people believe they are part of the action is, for many, one of film's most important achievements as a form of art.

Movies like *The Deadly Dream* by Alf Kjellin (1971) can raise the fear of never waking up. In this film Lloyd Bridges plays a scientist who has made the discovery that DNA can be changed inside a living person. In his dreams, he is beaten up for discovering this way of manipulating people. When he awakens, he finds the scars from the dream beating to be real. Finally, he is killed in his dreams.

Victor Fleming's **The Wizard of Oz** (1939) and Bob Fosse's *All That Jazz* (1979) can be considered musical movies that explain dreams as the result of physical trauma. In the former, Dorothy, a Kansas farm girl is hurled in her own mind and imagination into a magical world called Oz after a fall during a tornado. The coloring of her imaginative experience during her dream suggests the special reality that she enters during the oneiric experience.

All That Jazz presents the story of director Joe Gideon who suffers from a progressive heart disease. As the film draws to its conclusion, the hero lies in a hospital room and has a dream populated by entertainers and characters from his past, who return to be part of a last tribute to his life.

Characters in films like *The Story of Adele H.* (1975) by François Truffaut, and Robert Redford's *Ordinary People* (1980) are assailed by dreams of traumatic events involving drowning incidents. Fears and uncertainties cause anxiety dreams in such movies as R.W. Fassbinder's *Despair* (1977), and Ingmar Bergman's *Wild Strawberries* (1957). Bergman's movie, in particular, is a tale of one day in the life of an elderly professor of medicine, who is being honored for fifty years of service in his field. Within the framework of the film we find a mingling of dream and reality, of past and present, as well as flashbacks and time shifts that play a curious trick upon the professor, who lives through a dreamlike day while he explores a past that is shot through with painful nostalgia and nightmare.

Similarly, the films of Russian author Andrei Tarkovsky are suffused with a dreamlike quality that resists the audience's need to verify the logic, as well as the credibility, of the events presented on the screen. In fact, the viewer feels that something is wrong with the way things appear on the screen, but is incapable of detecting sufficient proof to discredit presented events on the basis of everyday logic. Especially in *The Mirror* (1975) and *Stalker* (1980), Tarkovsky succeeds in conveying daydreams about the past and the future through pure cinematic means. *The Mirror* is a dream film par excellence, reflecting the author's reminiscences of his own youth, while Stalker is a hallucinatory anticipation of a world that represents the reality of the artist's inner life.

The idea of the transparency of the dreaming and waking states is very popular in Japanese films, such as in Kenji Mizoguchi's *The Stories of the Hazy Moon after the Rain* and *Intendant Sensho*. The best example of the representation of dreams in the Japanese film tradition is Akira Kurosawa's *Dreams* (1990), about the refusal of most Japanese society to take atomic danger seriously. Kurosawa explores the issue with the two episodes that imagine an apocalypse caused by an accident at a nuclear power station. In another episode, famous van Gogh paintings are transformed into dramatic space, and the vivid power of van Gogh's art transports the young Japanese man into the era when it was created. The young man wanders in search of the artist through a full-scale world of his drawings and paintings.

MUHAMMAD

According to tradition, Muhammad, the Prophet of **Islam**, was born in 570 C.E., the same year Mecca was attacked by the army of Abrahah, ruler of Yemen. At the age of forty, during the holy month of Ramadan while he was sleeping in a mountaintop cave between the hills of Safa and Meeva, near Mecca, he received the first revelation of the Qur'an. By that time, he had already experienced visions of isolated luminous and sonorous impressions that he described as "the breaking of the light of dawn." He himself was

never able to translate some of those images, which appear as isolated letters placed at the beginning of several parts of the Qur'an.

In the "Lailatal-Miraj" or ("Night Journey"), the dream in which Muhammad's religious mission as well as portions of the Qur'an were revealed, the angel Gabriel appeared to him, leading Elboraq, a half-human silver mare. Riding Elboraq, and led by Gabriel, Muhammad traveled to Jerusalem in an instant, and there he conversed and prayed with **Abraham**, Moses, and Jesus. Continuing on his journey, he traversed the seven celestial spheres. Each sphere is infused with its own color, the esoteric meanings of which relate to the seven levels of existence: material, vegetable, animal, human, and three more beyond ordinary human nature. Then he reached across the ocean of white light, and, finally, he approached God. According to some versions of the story, Muhammad also descended to the depths of the earth.

Belief in the inspiration given to Muhammad by the angel Gabriel during this dream is a fundamental element of Islam. According to Muhammad, he is the last prophet placed at the end of a long line of precursors, who had been inspired in the same way. Their inspiration, to which Islamic theology gives the name *revelation*, was destined to be made public, and such inspiration ceased after Muhammad's death.

Muhammad showed considerable concern for dreams, and it is said that each morning after prayers he asked his assembled followers what they had dreamed, interpreted the most significant dreams, and reported his own. By doing this, he believed he could glean from the dreams any messages from God.

The principles of dream interpretation that Muhammad used were common to those of

The Dome of the Rock is, according to Islamic tradition, where the Prophet Muhammed was taken to Jerusalem by the angel Gabriel in his "Night Journey" dream.

other Near Eastern religions, and much importance was given to truthful telling of dreams, which was best done immediately on waking, as well as to the quality of the dream interpreter. According to Muhammad, a dream is a conversation between humanity and God.

MYSTICISM

Mysticism has become a highly imprecise term, partially because various popular writers have come to associate it with the occult and anything "mysterious." Originally, mysticism was a purely religious concept, referring to the experience of the direct union of the individual **soul** with the divine. Thus, people like St. John of the Cross, Teresa of Avila, Rumi, and a host of others were mystics in this pure sense. All true mystics would make a sharp distinction between the dream state and the state of divine union. For example, the **Upanishads**, a Hindu scripture that deals with mystical union, distinguishes between our normal waking state, the dream state, dreamless sleep, and the "fourth" state (i.e., the state of union with the godhead). Mystics do, however, often have **visions** and vivid spiritual dreams related to their quest for union with the divine.

Thus, while it is not incorrect to associate dreams with mysticism, the dream state and the mystical state should never be confused.

MYTHOLOGY AND DREAMS

In the disciplines of anthropology and history of religion, mythology refers to the narrative formulation of a traditional society's worldview and values. Myths often relate fantastic encounters with gods and spiritual powers that are visionary and "dreamlike."

The dominant contemporary view of the connection between dreams and myths was advanced by depth psychology, particularly the school of thought initiated by **Carl Jung**. Jungian psychology examines mythology for the light it throws on psychological processes. Jung theorized that myths were manifestations of the **collective unconscious**, a part of the mind that acts as a storehouse of myths and symbols to which all human beings have access, and which Jung viewed as the ultimate source of every society's mythology. Jung found that the dreams of his patients frequently contained images with which they were completely unfamiliar but which seemed to reflect symbols that could be found somewhere in the mythological systems of world culture. The notion of the collective unconscious was used to explain this phenomenon, and Jung called such dreams "grand dreams."

The "mythological motifs" or **archetypes** that manifest in such dreams take the familiar forms of gods, goddesses, heroes, or mythological beasts or dragons. They tend to occur during periods of great transition in a dreamer's life—during puberty, approaching middle or old age, or menopause, or frequently during periods of chaos or distress. In essence, the dreamer is embarking on a quest—seeking a peaceful resolution within her dreamscape amidst the upheaval of her waking life.

NAKEDNESS, DREAMS OF

Dreams of nakedness are among dream motifs so common that almost everybody has had them on more than one occasion. Other motifs include such scenarios as **falling**, and **flying dreams**, and **unpreparedness dreams**. Such shared dreams arise from experiences and anxieties fundamental to all people.

The significance of nakedness motifs varies from society to society, depending on each culture's attitude toward nudity. In Western society, in which public nudity is often forbidden and even illegal, nakedness is a significant and complex symbol with a range of different meanings. Anxiety dreams in which we are naked (or are clothed only in our underwear) seem to be rooted in our early experiences as children, during which disapproving parents taught us that the naked human body is something to be ashamed of, or at least something that should be hidden from public view. If this interpretation is correct, our childhood experiences leave a deep imprint in our minds that is somehow activated in adult life during periods of high tension.

Whatever the origin of nakedness anxieties, in dreams the processes of the human mind tend to deploy images that symbolically express our hopes and fears. On the one hand, dreams of nudity may indicate such positive attributes as honesty and openness (a symbolic connotation found in such common expressions as "the naked truth"). On the other, nudity may indicate fear of exposing oneself, vulnerability, or fear of sexuality. An interpretation of nudity thus depends on the dreamer's feelings, as well as the reactions of the other people in the dream.

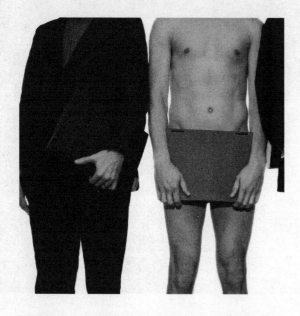

Dreams in which we are naked in public places are, in Western cultures, usually related to unpreparedness dreams involving feelings of anxiety.

The literature on dream **symbolism** indicates many other possible meanings of nakedness. Freud, for example, viewed dreams of nudity as indicating a longing for the relative freedom from care of early childhood. At a more mundane level, a dream of showing up at a bus terminal naked the night before a trip may simply be a subconscious reminder to pack the proper clothing.

NATIVE AMERICANS

The meaning of dreams to Native Americans varies from tribe to tribe. However, dreams are regarded as the most important experiences in the individual's life and as the determining factors in the individual's role in the life of the tribe. All dreams reflect the various supernatural and religious traditions of specific groups and are shaped by each culture's distinctive influence and mythology. Generally, Native Americans regard the individual dream as having significance for the individual, and its influence is judged as good or bad, favorable or unfavorable, pure or impure in part by its content and in part by its effects on the dreamer.

The **Navaho**, the Kwakiutl of the Canadian Pacific Coast, and the Eastern Woodlands tribes usually interpret individual dreams from the point of view of their influence on the life of the individual. If the dream seems to indicate violation of taboos, it leads to purification and other rituals. If it indicates illness, it leads to curing rituals.

In the lower Colorado region, the Yuma see a clear distinction between the power-bestowing dream or dream vision, and the less significant dream of everyday life. Dreams are considered the direct basis of all religion, tradition, and shamanic power and are believed to begin before birth and to be more real than waking. The Yuma believe that whatever is dreamed has happened or is about to happen. The **Mohave**, on the other hand, believe that dreams are the basis of everything in life and that good dreams indicate good luck, whereas bad dreams equal bad luck. Also, they believe that **shamans** ("medicine men") acquire powers by dreaming. According to the Kamia of the Imperial Valley of California and Mexico, dreams are best for young persons, as old people may die during dreams. The Kamia also believe that knowledge of the destiny of human souls can be derived from dreams.

In the Southwest culture area, the Navaho believe that gods, dreams, and sickness are causally related. Dreams represent the cause of illness, and such dreams are referred to interpreters or magicians, who reveal the cause and prescribe the cure. Dreams are viewed as good or

Dreams in Native American cultures are considered very spiritually significant and may help guide the dreamers toward their future purposes in life.

bad according to the aftereffect of the dream. Certain dreams, such as **death dreams**, have standardized interpretations, and it is generally believed that gods and spirits of deceased men and animals can put dreams into the individual's head. The Navaho also believe that good dreams come true only once in a while, whereas bad dreams always come true.

Among the Crow, visions are very important, and success in life is believed to result from the vision. According to the Dakota, dreams are revelations from the spirit world, and prophetic visions are what the person saw and knew in a

former state of existence. Fasting by girls, who then tell their dreams to their parents, is a tradition among the Menomini, central Algonkin, and woodland Pottawatomie. Among the eastern Cree the fasting dream must never be shared lest it give offense to the spirits.

Among the Ottawa and the **Ojibwa**, for whom both pattern dreaming and individual dreaming are regarded as important, dreams are induced by formal parental suggestion to the child vision seeker to keep dreaming until he or she dreams right. Fasting is also important among the Kwakiutl Indians when they seek to gain the help of the spirits. Hunting dreams are regarded as good, and certain dreams are interpreted as indicating the conditions for fishing. The Kwakiutl regard dreams of the dead as bad dreams that will cause an epidemic in which many will die. Persons who have prophetic dreams that are deemed good, however, are considered to be valuable tribe members.

NATURAL DISASTER DREAMS

Some individuals seem to possess the ability to "tune in" to disasters that involve a large number of people. These sort of **precognitive dreams** have been associated with natural disasters that occur all over the world and have probably been experienced for ages. This phenomenon, however, has only been studied for a relatively short period of time.

On October 21, 1966, a massive mudslide engulfed the Welsh mining village of Aberfan. This disaster—spurred on by coal mining activities—killed 144 people, most of whom were schoolchildren. After the incident occurred, a

Many people reportedly experienced dream premonitions of the sinking of the *Titanic* on her maiden voyage.

national paper appealed for information pertaining to any precognitive experiences that people had noticed. The appeal resulted in thirty-five cases being reported, twenty-four of which were told to someone else before the disaster occurred or before the appeal appeared in the paper. Twenty-five of the thirty-five instances specifically involved dreams. The most poignant of these was related by a young girl named Eryl Mai Jones. She tried to share her dreams with her mother on a regular basis, but her mother often dismissed them as pure fantasy. In this instance, she took the time to listen. This is the dream that Eryl described: "We go to school but there is no school there; something black has come down all over it." She then said to her mother, "I'm not afraid to die mommy. I'll be with Peter and Jane." Eryl Jones was among the 118 children buried alive.

Ian Stevenson conducted an investigation into the precognitive dreams surrounding the 1912 sinking of the *Titanic*. He collected information from nineteen people who anticipated the sinking of the great ship, and several of them received their visions in the form of dreams. One

man, who was supposed to be on the ship when it sank, dreamed twice that he saw the ship floating, keel up, with people swimming all around it. These dreams were not enough to make him cancel his voyage, but, as fate would have it, he ended up not taking the trip for other personal reasons.

President Franklin Roosevelt claimed to have experienced this type of precognitive natural disaster dream. On May 25, 1941, he dreamed that the Japanese were bombing New York City while he was safe in his home in Hyde Park. When the dream was analyzed, it was determined that it symbolized that the Japanese were capable of a direct assault on American soil but that the country would be able to withstand the damage.

While many such instances have been reported, they are usually retrospective in nature, opening them to doubt and debate. Premonition dreams can be put into five categories: coincidental, inferential, self-fulfilling, pseudo-anomalous, and anomalous. Coincidental dreams are just that: dreams that just happen to mimic something that occurs in real life. Inferential dreams are those in which the dreamer, given certain knowledge of events and facts, puts this information together correctly in a dream that then reflects real-life results. In self-fulfilling prophecy dreams, a person behaves a certain way *because of* something that he or she has dreamed, thus causing real life to reflect what occurred in the dream. The fourth category is pseudo-anomalous dreams. These are dreams that did not actually occur, but the person reports that they did; in other words, they are simply lies. The fifth category includes dreams that are apparently anomalous, or that are unexplainable in their accuracy, but that actually do seem to predict future disasters.

NAVAHO

Dreams constitute fundamental elements in the everyday life of the Navaho, who generally do not comment publicly on their dreams, which are often regarded as warnings. Dream specialists are usually consulted in order to discover the cause of the dream, what is going to happen, and how to prevent the anticipated event. The diagnostician, often in a trance state, can discover the cause of the dream as well as the dreamer's sickness.

It has been frequently observed that myths play a significant role in the daily lives of the Navaho, and many of them are performed repeatedly in winter. The influence of the mythic narratives on the dreams of the Navaho has often been pointed out. A considerable number of dream interpretations are persistently believed, because later events have corroborated a sufficient percentage of them.

The Navaho, like other people, divide dreams into good and bad, although they are not inclined to arrange gods or other phenomena in categories. They have easily accomplished rituals for dealing with the causes and the results of bad dreams, one of the most common of which is praying at sunrise. Many apparently bad dreams may have an opposite meaning, which is usually revealed by the natural course of events. Among the Navaho, most common unpleasant dreams are minimized or ignored because others have had similar dreams and nothing serious has happened. However, certain particular kinds of dreams are believed to cause sickness and to require diagnosis and treatment. One dream belonging to this category is the **falling dream**.

Another group of dreams may be designated death dreams, of which various interpretations are offered. For instance, if during a ceremony a shaman dreams that his patient is going to die, he must leave and allow another **shaman** to be called. Also, when a Navaho dreams that he is dead, he interprets that as meaning that in his dream he was in the next world with the spirits of the dead. To dream of being there and to come back does not necessarily represent a bad omen: but if the dreamer shakes hands with the dead, it means that he is going to die.

NEAR-DEATH EXPERIENCES AND DREAMS

Near-death experiences (NDEs), sometimes also called "pseudo-death" experiences, are the seemingly supernatural experiences often undergone by individuals who have suffered apparent death and then been restored to life. The systematic scientific study of NDEs is recent, although accounts of NDEs can be found in literature and historical documents dating back hundreds of years. The main impetus for modern studies on NDEs was the 1975 publication of *Life after Life* by psychiatrist Raymond A. Moody. Moody outlined nine stages of the experience, including the tunnel experience, in which the person undergoing an NDE feels as though he or she is being drawn into darkness through a tunnel, or is going up a stairway (or crossing some other threshold). Once the transition has been accomplished, the person meets people who seem to glow with an inner light, as well as friends and relatives who have already died and are there to greet the "deceased."

NDEs are associated with dreams in several ways. For various reasons, but especially because of the many formal and informal experiments with mind-altering drugs and Eastern meditation techniques in the late sixties, a new field of research was articulated within the discipline of psychology that came to be referred to as altered states of consciousness (ASC). This field became a grab bag of every state of mind that could be distinguished from ordinary waking consciousness, including dreams and what at the time were called **out-of-body experiences** (OBEs). NDEs were later classified as a subcategory of OBEs.

Within parapsychology, NDEs became a topic of investigation after Moody had articulated them as a distinct phenomenon. Because parapsychologists also investigate dream states that have a psychic component, it would thus be natural that, within the discipline of parapsychology, NDEs and psychic dreams would be viewed as similar experiences. Certain investigators, such as David Engle in his book *Divine Dreams*, have even attempted to make the case that NDEs and certain types of dreams are basically the same state. The problem with this equation is that survivors of NDEs are usually emphatic that their experiences are far more real than dreams. It has also been discovered that people who have undergone NDEs tend to be transformed by their close encounters with death, an observation that cannot be extended to dreamers. Thus, while there are similarities between the two, they are clearly distinct experiences.

NEW AGE

As a social movement held together by specific ideas, the New Age can be traced to the late 1950s. The following four essential ideas came to distinguish the movement. None are particularly new ideas, their distinctiveness lying in their being brought together in a new gestalt.

- *The self as Divine*. Within the New Age one theological affirmation has found popular support: the identification of the individual as one in essence with the divine. Underlying this notion, which takes a wide variety of forms, is a monistic world in which the only reality is "God," usually thought of in predominantly impersonal terms such as "mind" or "energy."

- *The possibility of personal transformation*. The New Age movement offers the possibility of personal transformation in the immediate future. The transformative process is most clearly seen in the healing process, and transformation often is first encountered as a healing of the individual, either of a chronic physical problem or a significant psychological problem. Healing has become a metaphor for transformation and adoption of a healthy lifestyle, a prominent concern of New Agers.

- *The hope of broad cultural transformation*. The New Age movement offered hope that the world, which many people, especially those on the edges of the dominant culture, experience in negative terms, would be transformed and enter into a golden era. It is, of course, the millennial hope of the coming of a golden age of peace and light that gave the New Age movement its name.

• *The transformation of occult arts and processes.* The New Age movement embraces the familiar occult practices, from astrology and tarot to mediumship and psychic healing. Yet in the New Age movement the significance of these practices has been considerably altered. Astrology and tarot are no longer fortunetelling devices, but tools used for self-transformation.

The New Age movement has tended to latch onto several aspects of the faddish interest in dreams in contemporary culture. For example, new **dream dictionaries,** containing interpretations of specific dream images, have been composed to express a New Age perspective. Betty Bethard's ***The Dream Book: Symbols for Self-Understanding*** (1983), is a useful example. As do the occult arts, the New Age sees dreams as tools for transformation and healing, as discussed in Patricia Garfield's popular book ***The Healing Power of Dreams.***

Some New Agers have also shown interest in **lucid dreaming**, the practice of becoming conscious during one's dreams and learning to control their direction. Of note in this field are the works of **Stephen LaBerge** and **Carlos Castaneda**. Various forms of dream **yoga** from Eastern religions have also influenced New Age thought. As with other kinds of dreamwork, lucid dreaming is viewed as a potential tool for healing and self-transformation.

NEW RELIGIONS (DREAM REVELATIONS)

New religions and sects are constantly coming into being. How, one might ask, does the founder of a new religious movement legitimate his or her new vision? The claim, quite often, is that the founder has received a direct revelation from divinity. The earliest models for this kind of authoritative claim are the various manifestations of Yahweh in the Hebrew Scriptures in which he sets forth the terms of the covenant, most dramatically and elaborately in the revelation to Moses at Mt. Sinai. Some new revelations begin in dreams or in dreamlike trances.

The prophet **Muhammad**, for instance, received the first revelation of the Qur'an during the holy month of Ramadan while he was sleeping in a mountaintop cave. Also significant was the Prophet's "Night Journey," a dream in which he received a revelation of his mission. Many of the new religions to arise among American Indians in response to Euro-American incursions began with revelations in dreamlike trances. For example, Wovoka, the prophet of the Ghost Dance of 1890 (a group dance of a messianic cult believed to promote the return of the dead and the restoration of traditional ways of life), experienced his initial revelation when he fell into a trance and received a revelation in a dream vision.

Because many cultures make little or no distinction between visions and divine message dreams, it is often difficult to determine whether a particular new revelation began in a dream or in a vision during wakefulness. This indicates that there is some intangible quality that waking visions share with dreams.

NIGHT TERRORS

Night terrors are episodes in which people typically awaken with a scream and sit bolt upright in bed as if they had just had a **nightmare**. Unlike in a nightmare, however, the person frequently cannot remember anything except being afraid. Researchers have found that night terrors occur during **non-REM (rapid eye movement) sleep**, which is sleep characterized by little or no dreaming activity. They most often occur in children, but may also affect adults. Although the precise cause is unknown, the incidence of night terrors can be seen in a number of adults who appear to be especially prone to them.

This phenomenon has been extensively studied since the1800s. Even though night terrors more often occur in young children, adults are not immune. There are factors common to adults who suffer from night terrors. It is suggested that stress, lack of sleep, and/or the prolific use of drugs or alcohol are factors. However, nothing has been proven conclusively.

In studies of both children and adults, mild to violent nervous bodily reactions occur before the dreamer awakens from a night terror. Heart and respiratory rates double in seconds, and incidents of muscle twitching, violent physical movements, hitting, yelling, walking out of the bedroom and even the house in an attempt to fight off and escape from attackers have all been documented.

Prior studies of night terrors produced some interesting findings. For instance, in 1899, the *British Medical Journal* published a study of thirty people who suffered from night terrors. Seventeen of the thirty people suffered from the onset of early heart disease. In the 1960s, a group of twenty-three children, all of whom suffered from night terrors, had their adenoids removed. Twenty-two of these children reported an immediate cessation to the terrors. Studies on adults who suffered from night terrors, known to psychologists back in the 1960s as a "disorder of arousal," did not find any correlated personality traits. Per-

sons intimately involved in the personal lives of some of those afflicted with night terrors, however, described them as being "tightly wound" individuals. Current psychology might classify such individuals as having Type A personalities.

NIGHT VISIONS

Night Visions is a quarterly journal that seeks to delve "behind the images of our dreams and to seek that reality which they represent." Different issues focus on different subjects, such as healing and dreams, lucid dreaming, and interpretation of dreams.

NIGHTMARES

Although nightmares were studied long before the era of modern sleep research, much has been learned about them since the discovery of the **rapid eye movement (REM)** cycle—the state of sleep during which the most vivid dreams occur. In the REM cycle, the dreamer is unable to move because all motor control is shut off. Subsequently, the mind may create a horrifying nightmare about the dreamer's being paralyzed and unable to escape.

Researchers disagree about the age at which a child begins to experience nightmares. Some say that children aren't affected by them until about the age of five, while others contend that one-year-olds can have them. Perhaps nightmares begin as soon as a child begins to experience fear and anxiety (e.g., seeing and hearing the child's parents fighting or being injured in some manner). Children have more trouble with their nightmares than adults, largely because they are limited in their ability to articulate what has hor-

Nightmares are the sleeping mind's expression of feelings of vulnerability. More disturbing or frequent nightmares may indicate a more serious problem caused by emotional trauma.

rified them, so they never get to know that the monsters and goblins that chased and almost ate them were not real. Researchers suggest that when children approach the age of six or seven, their ability to communicate and the comfort they receive enable them to accept nightmares as "just a bad dream."

Each and every moment, every experience of a small child's development is internalized. Their feelings of anxiety as they gaze at the faces of unfamiliar people, the threatening images of animals they encounter, as well as the shapes and sounds of their daily exploration of the world often embellish themselves as nightmares during the night.

Adult nightmares are similar to children's in that they engender a sense of vulnerability. The types and sources of anxieties may change, but feelings of helplessness and insecurity affect people of all ages. Psychiatrist John E. Mack explains the difference in the nature of children's and adults' nightmares this way:

> Nightmares occur in response to the characteristic danger situations that human beings

confront in the fear of strangers and the dread of abandonment in infancy and the fear of bodily injury in early childhood, and ending with the fears of failure, death and loss of function in adulthood and old age.... Nightmares may become the prototypic expression of the activities that characterize each stage of development. (p. 331—see *Sources*)

People who suffer from chronic nightmares tend to be extremely sensitive and impressionable individuals.

NONDREAMERS

Some individuals claim that they never (or rarely) have dreams. Sleep researchers have studied this subpopulation and found that so-called non-dreamers simply forget their dreams more quickly than other people. During sleep, the memory-storing part of the brain is apparently "offline," which is why even those of us who remember our dreams frequently have difficulty doing so.

When "nondreamers" are awakened during **rapid eye movement (REM) sleep** under laboratory conditions, they will report having dreamed slightly less than fifty percent of the time. In one study, it was noted that nondreamers tended to report that they were awake and thinking when awakened during REM sleep. However, when the reports of what they were thinking were examined, it was found that their "thoughts" were rather bizarre and dreamlike, indicating that they were actually dreaming, but that they did not label their experiences as "dreams."

HOPE IS A
WAKING DREAM.

—ARISTOTLE

OCCULT

In the same way in which the term **New Age** came to have negative associations after the wave of media attention it received in the late 1980s, the term *occult* acquired negative connotations after a similar wave of media coverage in the 1970s. *Occultism* calls to mind images of robed figures conducting arcane rituals for socially undesirable ends. *Occult* comes from a root word meaning "hidden" and originally referred to a body of esoteric beliefs and practices that were in some sense "hidden" from the average person (e.g., practices and knowledge that remain inaccessible until after an initiation). The term *occult* also refers to practices dealing with energies that are normally imperceptible and thus hidden from the ordinary person (e.g., magical and astrological forces).

Certain aspects of dreams and dream practices have often been associated with occultism. For example, the practice of **astral projection**, during which the spiritual body is "projected" outside the physical body during a trancelike state, has been thought of as a kind of dream experience. There are also certain esoteric practices of **lucid dreaming** in both Western and Eastern occultism. Finally, there are various approaches to the esoteric interpretation of dreams (e.g., certain Sufi practices) that are "occult" in some sense.

OJIBWA

Among the Ojibwa, a group of Algonquin-speaking North American and Canadian Indians numbering about fifty thousand individuals, dreams are viewed as actual experience and constitute important elements of the sociocultural system. In Ojibwa ontology, the focal point is on people, differentiated in two different categories: human beings and personified natural objects—such as the sun, the winds, the thunderbirds—which are thought of as persons and are addressed as such. One of the major sources of information about these other-than-human persons is myths.

It is within the web of social relations with other-than-human persons, as well as humans, that the Ojibwa strive for life in the fullest sense. Social relations with human beings belong to the sphere of waking life, whereas interactions with other-than-human persons occur chiefly during dream experiences. Dream experiences are not confused with waking events, because persons in dreams are not the same kind of persons with whom the individual is most concerned in ordinary waking life.

Ojibwa dream imagery is intimately linked with the motivation of individuals, traditional values, and social behavior. As a matter of fact, interactions with other-than-human persons are sought by individuals in order to achieve a good personal life adjustment. Also, dream experiences are considered fundamental with respect to the social system, because they validate specialized vocations, such as curing.

It is believed that a good life cannot be achieved through relations with other human beings alone, and that the help of powerful other-than-human persons is necessary, especially for men. This help can be obtained primarily through a deep personal face-to-face contact with other-than-human persons in dreams. Help from other-than-human persons implies the fulfillment of particular obligations to them, and these obligations assume a primary moral force in the life of Ojibwa individuals.

ONEIROMANCY

Oneiromancy (from the Greek *oneiros*, "dream," and *mantis*, "diviner") is the technical term for divination by means of dreams. It is related to more familiar words such as chiromancy (literally, "hand divination"; i.e., palmistry) and necromancy (literally, "dead divination"; i.e., mediumship). As noted, the term is Greek, which is fitting in that, perhaps more than any ancient people, the Greeks were fascinated by dreams.

In contrast to modern dream interpretation, which is psychologically oriented, ancient dream interpretation was concerned with discovering clues to the future. Approaching dreams as omens characterized the **interpretation of dreams** in both ancient Egypt and Mesopotamia. While guides to dream divination have been found in the remains of both of these civilizations, a complete **dream dictionary**, the *Oneirocritica* by **Artemidorus of Daldis**, has survived from second century **Greece**. As a concrete example of a dream omen, Artemidorus asserts that dreams about

> Discharging tapeworms through the rectum or the mouth signifies that the dreamer will discover that he is being wronged by members of his household, by those who live with him, and, for the most part, by those who share the same table. He will subsequently drive the wrongdoers away or get rid of them in some other way. (Artemidorus, p. 161— see *Sources*)

How expelling tapeworms could be taken to symbolize expelling someone from one's house is clear enough. This kind of interpretation by symbolic association is characteristic of most forms of **divination**. Contemporary dream interpretation relies on the same sort of symbolic associations, but the goal is to discover clues to the dreamer's mental or emotional state rather than to predict the future.

ONONHAROIA (FEAST OF FOOLS)

The Ononharoia (literally, "turning the brain upside down"), referred to as the Feast of Fools by early missionaries, was an annual dream-sharing festival of the **Iroquois**. According to Jesuit observers, during the Ononharoia, "men and women rushed madly from cabin to cabin, acting out their dreams in charades and demanding the dream be guessed and satisfied" (Wallace, p. 66—see *Sources*). The dreams shared at the festival expressed some desire—not infrequently sexual or aggressive in nature—and were related in the form of a riddle. Often the community supported the dreamers in fulfilling their dream wishes, although violent, aggressive desires against other members of the community were more frequently acted out in pantomime. Twentieth-century writers have observed that traditional Iroquois dream speculation has much in common with the ideas of **Sigmund Freud**, particularly the notion that dreams reveal repressed desires that, if not dealt with in some fashion, poison the psyche of the dreamer. From this perspective, the Ononharoia was an occasion for what could be characterized as community psychotherapy.

OTHERWORLD AND DREAMS

The basic idea of one or more "spiritual" otherworlds existing alongside the world of our ordinary, everyday experience in what we might call a different "dimension" exists in almost every religious and cultural tradition. For many of these traditions, the spiritual realm is more important, and often more real, than the physical realm. Cross-culturally and across many different historical periods, there is widespread agreement on certain important traits of this otherworld.

One broad area of agreement is that communication between the everyday world and this otherworld—between the living and the dead—is possible, although such communication is often not viewed positively. Dreams, which often seem to be experiences of a confused parallel world, are frequently the medium of communication. It has been hypothesized that one of the principal sources of the idea of a spiritual world distinct from the physical is dreams. During dreams, one has the sensation of traveling to other realms, interacting with people, and doing various things. Even though the dream realm is shadowy and even surreal, it nevertheless feels like a real place, apart from the world of everyday experience. Thus, it is not unreasonable to speculate that during dreams we travel to a real alternative world.

OUT-OF-BODY EXPERIENCES

Out-of-body experiences (OBEs) are sensations that one is viewing the world—and especially one's own body—from a position outside the physical body. Persons who have undergone OBEs were usually asleep or under anesthetics at the time, but OBEs can also occur under ordinary, waking circumstances. Some people claim to have experienced OBEs since adolescence or early childhood. The similarity among reports of OBEs—often widely separated by geography and even history—is sometimes proffered as proof of the reality of travel of consciousness out of the body.

People who report out-of-body experiences typically say they were sleeping at the time.

OBEs manifest in a variety of forms. In the most elaborate, people sense their consciousness escaping from their body, which is then perceived as a lifeless object. Usually a mist or ball of light or ethereal body seems to surround the escaping consciousness and to be attached to it by a silvery or white cord. In his highly popular book *Journeys Out of the Body*, Robert Monroe gives instructions on how to produce OBEs. Monroe's work more than any other popularized the expression "out-of-body experience," supplanting the older term

astral projection. Acceptable scientific proof of the ability of human consciousness to leave the physical body has yet to be demonstrated.

OVID

Ovid (43 B.C.E.–17 C.E.) was a postclassical poet of the Roman Empire. He is renowned for his ability to meld the reality of the waking world with dream-like elements in his prose and poetry. Depending on the source, scholars refer to Ovid as being either the last of the poets of the golden age, or the first of the poets of the silver age. He was banished to the city of Tomis in 11 C.E. for unknown reasons.

In a letter written during his exile, he described the agony that refused to leave him, even while asleep, and the suppressed wishes that made themselves known in his **nightmares**. In his great work *Metamorphoses*, he devotes a section to the description of the "Dream of Erysichthon." Erysichthon is cursed, doomed to starve no matter what he eats or how much. In the end, it causes him to devour the entire world, and this is followed by the rendering of his own flesh. Ovid compares Erysichthon to Fames, who is a living corpse surviving on a minimal diet. The incorporation of these nightmarish elements in Ovid's morose poetry exemplifies the irony that characterizes these events.

I DREAM MY
PAINTING AND THEN
PAINT MY DREAM.

—VINCENT VAN GOGH

PASCAL, BLAISE

The French philosopher and theologian Blaise Pascal (1623–1662) was born in Clermont, Auvergne, of a minor noble family. His father, a government official, taught him mathematics, to which Pascal made major contributions throughout his life, working on probability theory, number theory, and geometry. At the age of sixteen, Pascal wrote his first major work, *Essai pour les coniques,* and in 1642 he invented the calculating machine, which was considered one of the first applied achievements of the "new science." He gave up serious concern with mathematics, however after his religious conversion in 1654, when, on the night of November 23, he had a profound experience that led him to dedicate the rest of his life to religious and philosophical interests and activities.

Pascal was deeply involved with the Jansenist movement, which was originated in the seventeenth century by Flemish bishop Cornelius Otto Jansen (1585–1638), who espoused the doctrines of predestination and irresistible grace. Until 1659 Pascal worked on a variety of subjects defending Jansenism, including *Écrits sur la grâce, De l'art de persuader,* and his important work on the philosophy of mathematics, which was probably written around 1657 to 1658 as a preface to a textbook in geometry for the Jansenist school in Port-Royal. This work was left unfinished, like Pascal's *Pensées,* the definitive edition of which was published in France in 1952.

Pensées deals with the problem of knowledge, which is considered a religious one, since the human being can find truth "not only by reason but more so by the heart," and can achieve completely certain knowledge through acceptance of God's revelation. In a chapter dedicated to the weakness of man and to the uncertainty of natural knowledge, Pascal discusses dreams. According to Pascal, if man dreamed the same thing every night, it would probably affect his life as much as the objects that he sees every day,

> but because our dreams are all different, and varied, what we see in them affects us much less than what we see when awake, owing to the continuity of the latter, though that is not so constant and equable as never to change: but it does so less abruptly, except in some remarkable cases, as when traveling, and then we say, "Methinks I am dreaming"; for life is a dream, a little more regular than other dreams. (1985, p. 105—see *Sources*)

Pascal also asserted that, since half of human life is passed in sleep, humanity has no idea of truth, whatever we may suppose, and as we often dream that we dream, it might be that life itself is but a dream from which we awake at death.

SAINT PAUL

After Jesus died, the apostle Paul was to have three visits from him in visions. Paul was born a Roman citizen, the son of wealthy Jewish parents, and his Hebrew name was Saul. He lived in Tarsus, the capital of Cilicia, north of Palestine, and was sent to Jerusalem to be educated by the Rabbi Gamaliel. Paul, who was of the tribe of Benjamin, was a very effective agent in the efforts to suppress Christianity. He went to the high priest in Jerusalem to request a letter addressed to synagogues in Damascus, requiring their cooperation in the persecution of Christians. It was during a trip to Damascus on a mission to suppress Christianity that he had his famous vision:

St. Paul told of many visions he experienced during the night, which some interpreters have considered to mean that he was dreaming. (Statue of St. Paul at St. Peter's Basilica, Vatican City).

> On one of these journeys I was going to Damascus with the authority and commission of the chief priests. About noon, O king, as I was on the road, I saw a light from heaven, brighter than the sun, blazing around me and my companions. We all fell to the ground, and I heard a voice saying to me in Aramaic, Saul, Saul, why do you persecute me? It is hard for you to kick against the gods. (Acts 26:12–14)

When Paul asked, "Who are you?" the voice said that he was Jesus, whom Saul was persecuting. Then the Lord said,

I have appeared to you to appoint you as a servant and as a witness of what you have seen of me and what I will show you. I will rescue you from the Gentiles. I am sending you to them to open their eyes and turn from darkness to light, and from the power of Satan to God, so that they may receive forgiveness of sins and a place among those who are sanctified by faith in me. (Acts 26:16–18)

When Paul got up from the ground, he discovered that he was blind, and he was not able to see for three days. He had previously received a vision of Ananias, a certain devout disciple in Damascus: "In a vision he has seen a man named Ananias come and place his hands on him to restore his sight" (Acts 9:12). After this, God appeared to Ananias and instructed him about his role in fulfilling the vision given to Paul. Ananias went to Paul's house, laid hands on him, and Paul's sight was restored. Then Paul arose, was baptized, and went into the synagogues proclaiming Jesus as the Son of God. Both of these visions were received in the waking state. Other communications that Scripture refers to as visions were received "during the night," which indicates that they were dreams.

Many years passed before Paul had another vision. He was on a missionary journey and during the night had a vision of a man of Macedonia standing and begging him, "Come over to Macedonia and help us" (Acts 16:9). After this dream vision, the apostles concluded that God had called them to preach the gospel in Macedonia.

The next vision occurred to Paul in Corinth, which at that time was the capital of Greece, and where his life happened to be in danger because he was able to convert the chief of the synagogue to Christianity. Here it is again clear that his night visions are dream messages from God:

One night the Lord spoke to Paul in a vision: "Do not be afraid; keep on speaking, do not be silent. For I am with you and no one is going to attack and harm you, because I have many people in this city." (Acts 18:9)

This dream vision encouraged Paul and prevented him from leaving Corinth.

Paul's final dream vision was a message from Jesus in which he encouraged Paul to "take courage! As you have testified about me in Jerusalem, so you must also testify in Rome" (Acts 23:11). This vision assured Paul that he had not yet finished his work, and helped him decide to go to Rome.

PENILE ERECTIONS

Males have the common experience of awakening with an erect penis, an experience that does not always seem to be tied to the erotic content of their dreams. Studies of this phenomenon, referred to in the relevant literature as nocturnal penile tumescence (NPT), have shown that the incidence of NPT is highly correlated with **rapid eye movement (REM) sleep**. REM sleep, in turn, is associated with dreaming. Studies have also shown that a similar (but less noticed) phenomenon occurs in the vagina and associated tissue in females. The precise significance of this correlation between tumescence and REM sleep—which, as noted, does not always seem to be directly tied to sexual content in dreams—has yet to be demonstrated.

PERLS, FRITZ

Gestalt psychology originated from studies of perception. It focuses on the mind's characteristic tendency to organize experience into comprehensible wholes, even when available sensory information is incomplete. In letters of the alphabet with "holes" (missing segments), for example, the perceiving mind tends to supply the missing part, and we cognize the entire letter. In the hands of Fritz Perls (1893–1970), who was originally trained in Freudian psychoanalysis, this understanding of the human mind became the basis for Gestalt therapy. Working with small groups of people at Esalen Institute in California, Perls was a leader of the human potentials movement.

Gestalt therapy seeks to discover our emotional "holes"—the segments of ourselves that have been repressed by the conscious mind—and reintegrate them, the goal being a state of psychological wholeness and unity. Perls believed that dreams embodied rejected parts of ourselves and could thus be used as starting points for discovering what we have rejected:

> The dream … is a message of yourself to yourself … every aspect of it is a part of the dreamer, but a part that to some extent is disowned and projected onto others.… If we want to own these parts of ourselves again we have to use special techniques by which we can re-assimilate those experiences. (Perls, 1970, p. 27—see *Sources*)

At a theoretical level, this basic perspective is not radically different from the ideas of **Sigmund Freud, Carl Jung** and other depth psychologists, for whom the therapeutic process involves finding and recovering aspects of the self that have been repressed into the unconscious.

Where Perls departed most radically from the analytic tradition was in his innovative approach to therapy. In Gestalt therapy, participants describe their dreams in the present tense and then attempt to experience various aspects of the dreams as attributes of themselves; in other words, they *become* the dream by acting out each part. In the case of a woman who dreamed of a spider crawling on her, for instance, the woman would act out the roles of both the spider and herself while the spider was on her and relate how it felt to be each of them in various aspects of the dream. The therapist might then ask the dreamer to set up a dialogue between the different parts of the dream, taking the parts, alternately, of the spider and herself:

> *Liz (as herself in the dream)*: You are important because you keep the insect population down and you are important because you build beautiful webs …. and you're important because you're alive.
>
> *Perls:* Now, change seats again.… I would like you to try and let the spider return the appreciation.
>
> *Liz (as her dream spider):* You're important because you're a human being, and there are fifty zillion of you and so what makes you so important? (Laughter)
>
> *Perls:* Now you notice already the hole in her personality self-appreciation; lack of self-confidence. Other people have feelings of worthiness or something. She's got a hole.…
>
> *Liz:* But it's up to her to fill the hole.
>
> *Perls:* No, it's up to the spider. (Perls, 1969, pp. 84–85—see *Sources*)

In the course of this dialogue, Liz gradually discovers her spider dreams are rooted in feelings of unworthiness that have caused her to reject some of the fun-seeking aspects of herself. Perls refers to these rejected parts as "holes," which Liz can fill only by listening to the spider and realizing that the spider represents a part of her rejected psyche.

PERSONA

The English term *personality* is derived from the Greek word persona, which refers to the masks worn by the actors in ancient **Greek dramas**. In psychology, the persona is the personality that we project to the world (i.e., the self we want other people to see). As a public self, the persona is a means of facilitating social interaction and should not be viewed negatively as a "false" self. One of the most influential formulations of the notion of persona was put forward by the Swiss psychiatrist **Carl Jung**. In Jung's personality theory, the persona is one among several selves: the **ego** represents what we might call the self-image (the self we imagine ourselves to be); the **shadow** (which is a kind of alter-ego) embodies the traits that have been rejected as "not-self"; the **anima** or **animus** is the subconscious counter-self composed of the characteristics our particular culture identifies as belonging to the opposite sex; and the self is an **archetype** from the **collective unconscious** that provides the subconscious pattern for the ego (for the sense of selfhood).

Each of these aspects of the self can appear in dreams in various forms. In the case of the persona, dream images include everything from clothing that we put on or take off in dreams to the roles we assume. In Jungian therapy, the persona is viewed as a means whereby new characteristics can be integrated into the patient's ego structure. In other words, the subject can draw on previously rejected personality traits from the shadow and the anima or animus by acting them out in certain social situations and later identifying with them as part of a new ego concept.

SAINT PETER

One of the most significant visions reported in the **Bible** was experienced by the apostle Peter, whose

A statue of St. Peter at the Seville cathedral in Spain. In the Book of Acts, St. Peter experiences a life-changing dream, after which he accepts that all men are equal in the eyes of God.

Hebrew name was Simon. His dream-trance is connected with a vision given to the God-fearing Roman centurion Cornelius, in which an angel entered Cornelius's house and told him that he was to send a servant to Jaffa to look for Peter and invite him to his house. Cornelius was praying at the time, thus he saw the angel with his physical eyes, not in a dream state. The next day, while the messengers of Cornelius were nearing Jaffa, Peter was praying and fell into a trance:

> He saw heaven opened and something like a large sheet being let down to earth by its four

corners. It contained all kinds of four-footed animals, as well as reptiles of the earth and birds of the air. Then a voice told him, "Get up, Peter. Kill and eat." "Surely not, Lord!" Peter replied. "I have never eaten anything impure or unclean." The voice spoke to him a second time, "Do not call anything impure that God has made clean." This happened three times, and immediately the sheet was taken back to heaven. (Acts 10:11–16)

Peter was wondering about the vision when the men sent by Cornelius found his house. When they were asking for him, the Spirit told him, "Simon, three men are looking for you. So get up and go downstairs. Do not hesitate to go with them, for I have sent them" (Acts 10:19–20).

When he arrived in Caesarea where Cornelius was waiting, the first thing that Peter said was that he knew that no one can be called unclean: "I now realize how true it is that God does not show favoritism but accepts men from every nation who fear him and do what is right" (Acts 10:34–35). Thus, like Paul, Peter is completely turned around by his dream, the contents of which give him a new direction and a new understanding.

PLATO

Plato (c. 429–347 B.C.E.) was born of a family who had long played a considerable part in Athenian politics. He declined to follow the same course, however, because he was disgusted by the corruption of political life in Athens, which was among the causes of the execution in 399 of Socrates, his friend and teacher. The death of Socrates encouraged Plato to protect and preserve his memory by writing dramatic conversations in which Socrates employed the same

In Plato's *Apologia* and *Symposium*, the philosopher viewed dreams as a channel through which the gods communicated to people.

methods of argument that he had used when he was alive.

Plato dedicated the rest of his life to philosophy, convinced that it was the only cure for the ills of society, which would never cease unless philosophers became rulers or rulers became philosophers. He traveled broadly, especially to Sicily, and in Athens founded the Academy, an institution devoted to the study of philosophy.

Although Plato did not discuss dreams at any length, using them rather as a structure for symbolic action and philosophical speculation, various passages of some of his dialogues report his observations about this phenomenon. In his early dialogues, such as *Apologia* and *Symposium*, dreams are regarded as a channel for messages received from the gods and are used as a theological method of acquiring knowledge concerning the gods and their will. An enlightened theology of dreams appears also in the last dialogues, such as *Sophistes*, in which Plato asserts that all four truly existing realities—human and animal, fire and water—possess their specific images, which are created by the gods and are not the product of the realities themselves. Man's image, for example, is his dreaming world. In *Sophistes*, Plato also considers the dream as a philosophical method through which a particular kind of knowledge can be achieved.

A Homeric description of the dream experience prevails in *Crito* and *Phaedo*, both about the last days of Socrates. In each dialogue, Socrates attributes great importance to his dreams by following their suggestions. The first dream pictures the land of the soul's afterlife, whereas in the second dream Socrates speaks of a shift in attention from philosophy to poetry.

Plato gives a definition of the act of dreaming in *Politeia*, asserting that it means "to take the copy not as a copy, but as reality itself." According to Plato, in the actual act of dreaming the dreamer does not have the power to associate the dream experience with waking life, thus establishing his firm belief in the reality of his dreams.

According to Plato's biological theory of dreams, dreams originate in a persistent activity of the respective organs in the belly. The liver, in particular, is described as the biological seat of dreams. Dreaming may be caused either by overgratification or by frustration of those organs in waking life. Plato maintained that when the rule of reason is suspended in sleep, the other two elements of the soul—desire and anger—and all the repressed aspects of personality break through with all their power, and the soul can accept incest, murder, and sacrilege.

Plato delineates a relationship between ethics and dreams by asserting, in *Politeia*, *Theaitetos*, and *Nomoi*, that even the individual whose life is considered decent may be subject to very unethical dreams, and a man's dreams are generally indicative of his ethical attitude or the level of his education. He also maintains that a theological explanation can be given for terror dreams, which may be caused by unethical behavior.

POSSESSION

In ancient times, demonic possession was blamed for everything from bad behavior in young children to **nightmares** to full-blown multiple personality disorders. When a person manifested certain unpleasant personality traits, many ancient societies associated this with possession by devils, **demons**, or spirits. The possessed individual is in a nightmarish threshold state. Traditionally, the appropriate "therapy" was some form of exorcism directed at freeing the individual of the intruding entity.

In later times some believed that real creativity depended on a state of possession or "divine insanity," which gave people access to the subconscious in a liminal state. When a person is able to readily enter a liminal state, he or she potentially has access to the more creative faculties of the brain. Those who can do this at will are usually highly charismatic people with thin barriers between their conscious and **unconscious** minds.

POST-TRAUMATIC STRESS DISORDER

Post-traumatic stress disorder (PTSD) is associated with a set of characteristic symptoms.

Nightmares and flashbacks to the traumatic event or events are probably the most well-known signs of this disorder, but they are not the only ones. Individuals who are suffering from PTSD often display signs of "psychic numbing," a sense of general detachment and reduced responsiveness. They avoid situations or feelings that they associate with the trauma they survived.

Repetitive nightmares depicting the traumatic event as it occurred, with very little variance of the details, is one of the most common symptoms of PTSD. These dreams are usually accompanied by "survivor guilt," in which the dreamer takes the place of those around him or her who did not make it. After a while, the situation becomes chronic, with the dream process becoming stuck when no progress or useful connections can be made between dream content and the healing process. Because of the extremely painful nature of these dreams, any attempt at **psychotherapy** is often resisted. It is more common for survivors to wall off the traumatic event instead of dealing with it. This makes them unlikely to have emotional relationships or deal with any emotions in general; such people develop extremely thick personal boundaries.

PRECOGNITIVE DREAMS

Precognitive dreams are a special case of **ESP**. As the name suggests, in precognitive dreams the dreamer experiences an event, in whole or in part, before it occurs. It has been suggested that at least some experiences of **déjà vu**—the uncanny sense that a completely unknown place is familiar, as if one had been there before, or that a new situation has been experienced before—can be explained by precognitive dreams.

Precognitive dreams are sometimes equated with prophetic dreams and with dream **divination**. There are, however, some significant differences. Prophetic dreams predict the future, but the events predicted relate to important areas of life. As with the Hebrew prophets, there is also some sense that a prophetic dream gives one a chance to actually change the future, as if the dreamed events do not have to happen or can be modified in some way. A precognitive dream, by way of contrast, usually involves rather trivial events over which one does not seem to have much control.

Traditional divinatory dreams, while related to both precognitive and prophetic dreams, tend to be more symbolic in content. One might, for instance, dream about falling off an office building and the next week be fired from one's job. Someone who takes the psychic significance of dreams seriously might say that the falling dream actually predicted the loss of employment. This kind of symbolic interpretation is integral to traditional divination, and sets divinatory dreams apart from most precognitive dreams.

PREGNANCY NIGHTMARES

When one considers the abnormal levels of stress that pregnant women are under, a greater incidence of **nightmares** and anxiety dreams is understandable. When Patricia Maybruck conducted a survey on the dreams of pregnant women, she recorded 1,048 dreams. She found that seventy percent of these dreams were unpleasant, and of these forty percent were full-fledged nightmares. When Maybruck compared the occurrence of nightmares to the duration of labor, she found no direct correlation. However, when she looked at the tendency of some women to confront their fears in the nightmares in an assertive manner, Maybruck found that ninety-four percent of the women who experienced a labor of less than ten hours were assertive in at least one nightmare. On the other hand, of the women who had long labors (over ten hours) seventy percent were victimized in their nightmares.

There are many people who believe in **precognitive** aspects of pregnancy dreams and nightmares. For instance, there are accounts of women who have reportedly dreamed of being pregnant to discover later that they actually are. Most of these reports are retrospective in nature and, while such accounts should not be discounted entirely, they can't be used for scientific or systematic investigation. The same sort of retrospective taint also affects instances in which the diagnostic qualities of pregnancy dreams are examined. Many women have claimed to have had dreams that predicted miscarriages and still births, as well as health problems in their children. These claims, again, are suspect because they were not typically reported until after the foretold event took place.

A common theme in pregnancy dreams is the appearance of architecture as the central subject matter. This seems to be representative of the womb of the pregnant woman. Dreams of small **animals** are the most frequent focus of women's dreams in the first trimester because these animals are like the fetus in many ways. Dreams of being unattractive are the most frequent in the second trimester. The second trimester is also when dreams representing unresolved parenting issues and fears of inadequacy begin to occur.

The appearance of actual babies in dreams does not become a regular occurrence until the woman enters the third trimester. Threatening dreams of robbers, intruders, fires, earthquakes

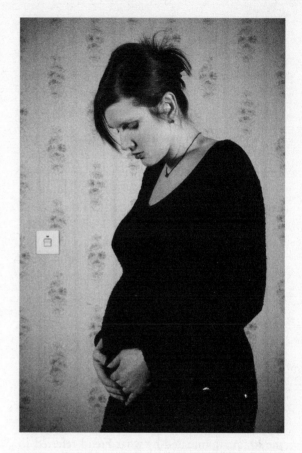

Women often worry about their pregnancies, and such fears can often reestablish themselves in the form of troubling dreams.

and the like also become more frequent in the third trimester. These often reflect the woman's fears concerning complications during labor and the immense task of parenting that follows. Themes of water and waterways, perhaps symbolic of amniotic fluid and birth canals, and themes of growing plants and gardens are common throughout the entire length of the pregnancy.

In general, pregnant women have more dreams that they remember than other populations that have been studied. This is due to the extreme hormonal changes they experience and their irregular sleep patterns. The imagery of these dreams has been described as being abnormally vivid, which reflects the heightened emotional state in which these women are living.

It should also be noted that expectant mothers are not the only ones who experience pregnancy nightmares. Expectant fathers also have them, although they are based entirely on emotional stress. These nightmares often reflect the concerns that face an expectant father, such as, "Will I be displaced in the mother's affections?" or if he will be able to emotionally and financially support his growing family. Not the least of these concerns is the health of both the mother and the child.

PRIMARY PROCESS

Primary process is **Sigmund Freud**'s expression for the psychological mechanism that prompts us to seek immediate fulfillment of our wishes and desires. The primary processes, associated with the **id**, are dominated by what Freud referred to as the *pleasure principle*. The contrasting term is **secondary process**, a mechanism dominated by the *reality principle*. In a normal adult, the secondary processes regulate the primary processes so that one does not immediately act upon every urge that comes to mind. The primary processes are called *primary* because they characterize the psychology of infants, who have no grasp of such secondary process notions as delayed gratification. Freud's understanding of dreams was that they represent fulfillment of desires normally controlled and repressed by our waking consciousness. Dreams are thus the product of primary processes and provide us with direct access to the functioning of the **unconscious** mind.

PROBLEM SOLVING IN DREAMS

Many people have had the experience of being stumped by a particular problem, going to sleep, and waking up with the answer. This common experience may be the source of the familiar expression "I'll sleep on it." Although all such experiences are not always accompanied by dreams that directly provide the sought-after information, at least some are. A well-known example of this kind of problem solving in dreams is the experience of the nineteenth-century chemist F.A. Kekule, who was attempting to determine the structure of the benzene molecule. He had been wrestling with this problem for quite some time when he was dozing off in front of his fireplace, fantasizing that he was seeing snakelike benzene molecules dancing in the fire:

> My mental eye, rendered more acute by repeated visions of this kind, could now distinguish larger structures of manifold conformation; long rows, sometimes more closely fitted together, all twining and twisting in snakelike motion. But look! What was that? One of the snakes had seized hold of its own tail and the form whirled mockingly before my eye. As if by a flash of lightning, I awoke as if struck by lightning; this time again I spent the rest of the night working out the consequences. (Cited in Empson, p. 85—see *Sources*)

Kekule had discovered the key to his problem—that the benzene molecule was arranged in a ring structure—in a **hypnagogic experience** in which a dancing snake grabbed its own tail and spun around in a circle.

A less famous instance of this kind of phenomenon is the case of H.V. Hilprecht, a Pennsylvania University archeologist:

In 1893 [Hilprecht] was given drawings of fragments of agate excavated from the Babylonian temple of Bal at Nippur. He thought they might be finger rings, but wasn't sure. In a dream a tall thin priest informed him that the two pieces came from the same votive cylinder and had been cut in two to make earrings for a statue of the god Ninib. Later in the year he visited the museum in Istanbul where the fragments were kept and demonstrated their exact fit. (Empson, p. 85—see *Sources*)

It is not known exactly what happens during such experiences and during less dramatic incidents in which people fall asleep and awaken with the answer to a problem. Perhaps a different level of the mind—part of the region we designate as the **unconscious**—goes to work on problems with which the conscious mind is wrestling. During a period when the waking brain processes are relaxed, this other level of mind may communicate its conclusions to the consciousness, resulting in the kinds of experiences reported by Kekule and Hilprecht.

PROJECTION

Although many aspects of the personality theory formulated by **Sigmund Freud** have been rejected by contemporary analysts, Freud was nevertheless responsible for a significant number of insights into human nature that have been generally accepted. Among these insights are the Freudian "defense mechanisms," one of which is projection. In projection, a certain urge we are repressing is projected onto another person or group of people. A familiar example is the sexually repressed person who perceives other groups of people (e.g., racial minorities) as being obsessed by sex, whereas in actuality it is the repressed individual who is obsessed by sex. A roughly similar process takes place in dreams.

According to Freud, dreams provide an avenue for the expression of normally repressed desires while simultaneously disguising and censoring our real urges. In this view, the purpose of dreams is to allow us to satisfy in fantasies the instinctual urges that society judges to be unacceptable, such as the urge to go to bed with every attractive member of the opposite sex. If, however, we were to dream about actually having intercourse, the emotions evoked by the dream would wake us up. So that our sleep is not continually disturbed by such dreams, the mind modifies and disguises the content of our dreams so that strong emotions are not evoked. For example, if a man is attracted to someone who is unavailable for sexual relations, he might dream about taking a train ride through a tunnel while seated next to the woman.

PSYCHOMANTEUM

Psychomanteums were ancient **Greek** oracles of the dead where seekers could consult the spirits of the deceased. After fasting and certain other preparatory rituals, a vision of the departed was evoked by the seeker's staring into a pool or pan of water (a technique similar to the practice of "crystal gazing"). Alternatively, seekers sometimes attempted to contact the dead via dreams, an endeavor clearly related to other types of **dream incubation**, in which dreams were sought for specific purposes—healing, financial guidance, general advice, **divination**, and so forth. Dream incubation was extremely popular in the ancient world and was a major phenomenon in societies as diverse as ancient Mesopotamia, **Egypt**, Greece, and **Rome**. In the Hellenistic period, the

Psychotherapy, as pioneered by Sigmund Freud, is the modern-day, scientific approach to evaluating people's dreams.

principal dream incubation temples were the healing temples of **Aesculapius**. The Hellenistic fascination with dreams made them an obvious medium for attempting to contact the departed.

PSYCHOTHERAPY

Before **Sigmund Freud**'s groundbreaking work in the late nineteenth and early twentieth centuries, mental illness was commonly believed to be primarily a *physiological* problem that, at least theoretically, could be dealt with through a variety of physical treatments (baths, bleedings, diets, and the like). One of the chief contributions of Freud and later psychotherapists—a contribution that is difficult to fully appreciate in a culture that accepts Freud's basic discoveries as "obvious"—is the reconceptualization of mental illness as primarily a *psychological* problem. Shifting the locus of these disorders from the body to the mind, however, also makes the task of properly diagnosing, understanding, and treating mental disturbances more difficult.

Freud theorized that so-called civilized human beings were bedeviled by the conflict between the urges of their infantile, animal selves and the demands of society. Under normal circumstances, we can manage this inner conflict by **repressing** awareness of the socially unacceptable urges into the **unconscious** mind. In this view, mental disturbances occur when one's inner conflicts overwhelm the usual coping mechanisms of the psyche. The great majority of contemporary psychotherapists agree with this basic picture, although they disagree with Freud's assertion that all of these conflicts are ultimately sexual.

Freud also established the importance of dreams for understanding the psyche of the dreamer—particularly for uncovering the dreamer's psychological problems. In Freud's view, the purpose of dreams is to allow us to satisfy in fantasies the instinctual urges that society judges unacceptable. So that we do not awaken as a result of the strong emotions that would be evoked if we were to dream about the literal fulfillment of such desires, the dreaming mind transforms dream content so as to disguise its true meaning. Hence, the purpose of Freudian dream interpretation, which is a significant part of traditional Freudian therapy, is to penetrate this disguise.

Other kinds of psychotherapy derived from the larger tradition of depth psychology have also approached dreams as messages from the unconscious mind that have been shaped by the dreamer's psychological state. In each of these schools of thought, dreams are regarded as less-than-clear communications that require some form of interpretation to reveal their true meaning. This basic interpretive orientation is evident in Jungian therapy, Gestalt therapy, and similar treatments.

QUECHUA

The Quechua are a people living in the southern Peruvian Andes. According to the early accounts of colonial, missionary priests, the Quechua have always been preoccupied with dreams and dream interpretation. Specially designated ritual specialists were considered particularly significant. In the pre-conquest period, indigenous curers attributed their calling to dreams, and dream specialists were employed for prognostication by the state.

Dreams are regarded by contemporary Quechua as premonitory signs about events of the day on which they are dreamed. They are said to be world-creating, in that they literally forecast an event. Generally, under normal circumstances, a person arises from sleep by standing first on the right foot, but when a bad omen appears in a dream, one stands first on the left foot.

In addition, dreams can be treated as a narrative from which particular elements are chosen and interpreted according to a lexicon of dream signs, which supplies a general conventional meaning for each. Selecting readily discernible dream signs and taking individual situational factors into account allows for a more specific interpretation, although the interpretation may have absolutely nothing to do with the **manifest content** of the narrative apart from the interpreted signs.

QUICHE

For the Quiche Maya, a patrilineal and patrilocal people located in twenty-six different communities across Guatemala, ancestors are important beings whose visitation in a dream is most often described as a positive experience, although they may demand appeasement in the form of religious rituals and eventual initiation into a religious organization. Human beings are classified as *winak*, and are distinguished from nonhumans by the feature of articulate speech. In addition, each individual possesses one of twenty faces or destinies (or "life-souls"), depending on the person's day of birth on the Mayan calendar. The life-soul arrives at the moment of birth, is located in the heart, and if it should leave the body for any reason for any length of time, the person will die.

A close connection is believed to exist between dreaming and dying, since, when one dreams, one's face or destiny leaves the body as if one were dead. For the Quiche, it is the free-soul, not the life-soul that wanders, which makes dreaming a less threatening experience. Quiche express little anxiety about dreaming, and in their language the verb for dreaming is transitive, indicating that the dreamer is conscious while dreaming.

According to the principal Quiche theory of dreams, the dreamer's free-soul, after leaving the body and wandering about in the world, meets other people's and animals' free-souls. Additionally, the Quiche claim that the gods or ancestors approach the sleeping dreamer's body and awaken his soul, which is supposed to struggle with the visitors until they give the dreamer a message. The dream experience is usually described as a nightly struggle between the dreamer's free-soul and the free-souls of the deities and ancestors, who have important messages concerning the future of people. The Quiche insist that everyone dreams every night, and daily sharing or reporting of all dreams, whether evaluated by the dreamer as good or bad, is considered an important practice. All dreams are treated as immediately and necessarily open to reporting and interpretation.

IN DREAMS BEGINS
RESPONSIBILITY.

—WILLIAM BUTLER YEATS

RARAMURI

The Raramuri Indians of northern Mexico, known also as the Tarahumara, regard dreams as the activities of a person's principal soul during sleep. Dreams are considered very important because it is through them that people communicate with their deities and receive information about their future.

Dreams are a frequent topic of conversation in the morning within a household as well as among the members of different households. Since the Raramuri usually sleep for a few hours, wake up, and then sleep again, they frequently analyze dreams during the course of the night. These discussions constitute an important means of transmission of culture and ideology in the absence of formal institutions, such as schools.

Each individual develops an interpretive framework by comparing what one is taught with what one dreams.

According to the Raramuri, each individual is composed of one body and many souls, which range in size from large to small and are distributed throughout the body. The largest souls are found in the chest and head. People sleep when their souls sleep and wake up when the souls awaken, and if, while they sleep, their largest souls awaken, they dream.

Dreams are considered activities of a person's principal soul while the person sleeps. This does not mean that the Raramuri do not distinguish between their waking and dreaming lives; rather, they attribute comparable reality to both. The main difference between dreaming and waking events is that during the dream state people's souls act independently of their bodies, but in waking life they are linked to them.

The Raramuri claim that waking life is limited and that the abilities of the souls are far superior when they are independent from the bodies in which they live. Since souls are intrinsically alive and capable of visiting places, many of the beings who appear in dreams live in regions of the world too remote to be reached except by souls. Also, most of these beings are active only at night, when most dreams take place.

Dreaming is considered the main method of communication with beings like God and the Devil, and dreams are crucial to the preservation of the individual's and the community's well-being, as they provide insights into the activities and inclinations of other beings in the universe. The Raramuri tend not to initiate actions on the basis of dreams alone, however, since they distinguish between the whole person and his or her soul.

RASTAFARIANS

In the Rastafarian movement, as in other prophetic and millenarian movements, dream experience represents an important source of religious inspiration. Dreams have played a considerable role in the production of Rastafarian ideology, which is based on potent biblical imagery and on the philosophy of Marcus Garvey, the Jamaican father of Pan-Africanism.

The Rastafarian movement—named after Ras Tafari (better known as Emperor Haile Selassie I of Ethiopia)—is a predominantly black form of social protest that originated in Jamaica in the early 1930s. This movement was a response to racial discrimination and to the manifestations of capitalist-imperialist domination that was the legacy of plantation slavery.

Rastafarian faithful can frequently be identified by their distinctive dreadlocks. Their faith allows the practice of smoking marijuana to encourage dreamlike states that help them connect to their spiritual selves.

A fundamentalist approach to the Bible characterizes Rastafarian religion, which can be regarded as a form of black Zionism, with a strong emphasis on the ideology of Ethiopianism. According to Rasta, black people are to be considered the true Israelites, and have awaited the return of the Messiah, Jah Rastafari—manifested in the person of Emperor Haile Selassie I—to repatriate them to Africa. Africa is viewed in biblical terms as the ancestral Zion, which is opposed to Babylon, the white-ruled world.

The principal form of Rastafarian ritual activity, known as "reasoning," during which elders attempt to formulate truths about a variety of social situations, is generally accompanied by the sacramental smoking of ganja—marijuana—which induces active imagination, allowing the Rastaman to be "far seeing" and to participate in a form of inter-subjective visionary communication. Besides a variety of sacred symbols, central to the speech code used during each performance is the pronoun "I," with its sound symbolism related to "high," "eye," and to the idea of vision. During the communicative event of reasoning, dream experience is among the various subjects of speculation, such as historical and contemporary events and biblical prophecy. In particular, elders can draw upon recent as well as long-past dreams in order to authenticate their tutorial role.

In his 1992 report on visionary communication in the Rastafarian movement, J. Homiak discusses three dialogues that include dream accounts, interpretations, and resultant social actions undertaken by Ras Mobutu, a leader in the Jamaican Rastafarian movement. These dialogues, collected in the context of reasonings, contain a number of powerful rhetorical statements and considerable insights into the sociopolitical realities of colonial exploitation. Ras Mobutu's visions, which illuminate specific points in Rastafarian history, are incorporated into an oral tradition in which understandings are shared by participants and consequently cannot be approached as separate from the social contexts and ritual processes through which the ideology is reproduced.

REALITY AS A DREAM

Although the notion that reality is a dream is found in many cultures, it has different meanings for different groups. In certain traditional cultures, for example, it is not unusual to consider the realm of dreams to be as real as—if not more than—the realm of everyday consciousness. This is clearly the case for the aboriginal culture of **Australia**.

However, the more usual meaning of this notion is that this world is like a dream—unreal and thus ultimately worthless. In modern Western philosophies, equating the reality of the tangible world with the illusion of a dream creates a "metaphysical horror to be refuted at all costs. The curse of pointlessness with no escape. ..." (Hunt, p. 217—see *Sources*). Psychoanalytically, patients who regularly describe their experience of the world as "dreamlike" are regarded as potentially schizophrenic.

By way of contrast, in traditional Eastern philosophies the assertion that this world is illusory—like a dream—is commonplace. **India**, in particular, has a strong tradition of regarding life and this world as a kind of dream. According to the mainstream of Hindu religious thought, the individual soul is trapped in the sufferings involved with life in this world. And, because of reincarnation, even death does not release one from this world. In most of the religious traditions of southern Asia, release or liberation from the cycle of death and rebirth is the ultimate goal of the spiritual life. A metaphor often used to describe the insight that leads directly to liberation is awakening from a dream.

Especially in the philosophical tradition of Advaita Vedanta, this metaphor is developed to stress the dreamlike quality—and hence the unreality—of the world as we experience it in our normal state of consciousness. The doctrine of the ultimate unreality of this world is referred to as *maya*. Mythologically, the notion of *maya* is regularly represented by the image of the Hindu deity Vishnu, asleep on the back of Ananta, his serpent vehicle. Ananta, in turn, lies on the cosmic waters while Vishnu dreams the dream that is this world.

RECURRING DREAMS

Recurring dreams are dreams that are precisely or almost precisely the same every time they occur, or dreams with a similar theme each time they occur. For example, a student might periodically dream about a particular high school teacher with whom he has a specific argument. Precisely the same dream, without variation in detail, may recur approximately once a week, once or twice a month, or once a year. Alternatively, the student might have a series of dreams about having disagreements with authority figures—dreams that differ widely in detail but share the same basic emotional tone.

The meaning of either of these patterns, as one might anticipate, is that the dreamer is grappling with some sort of unresolved issue that keeps presenting itself over and over again during sleep. Precisely what the issue is may not be clear, and simple repetition may not make the issue any clearer. In any event, it is not abnormal or even unusual to experience recurring dreams.

RELIGION AND DREAMS

The relationship between religion and dreams can be examined on several different levels. The attitude of each religious tradition about the sig-

nificance of dreams is dealt with in respective entries on those religions. On a less parochial level, one can ask how the common human experience of dreaming might help shape a religious concept of the world. Specifically, because dreams often seem to be experiences of a confusing parallel world, it is not unreasonable to speculate that during dreams we travel to a real, alternative world. It has also been hypothesized that one of the principal sources of the idea of a spiritual world distinct from the physical is dreams. If this hypothesis is true, then dreams contribute to one of the basic notions of most world faiths.

It has also been postulated that at least one of the sources of the idea of a **soul** distinct from the body is dreams. During dreams, one has the experience of traveling to other realms, interacting with people, and doing various things; simultaneously, the physical body remains confined in bed. While the dream realm is shadowy and surreal, it nevertheless feels like a place apart from the world of everyday experience. Therefore, it is not unreasonable to speculate that during dreams the conscious self somehow separates from the body. If we add to this the common experience of meeting departed friends and relatives in dreams, it is no giant step to conclude that the same "soul" that separates from the body during dreams also survives the death of the body. If this hypothesis is correct, then dreams also contribute to the idea of a soul as it has traditionally been formulated in most world religions.

Yet another broad area of agreement among world religions is that communication between this world and other realms—between the divine and mortals, or between the living and the dead—is possible, although there is disagreement about the details of this interaction. For example, the founders of new sects often claim to receive privileged communications from God. If dreams are taken to be experiences of the realm of the spirit, then one possible mode of divine-human communication is the encounters with others that we have in dreams.

REM (RAPID EYE MOVEMENT) SLEEP

In 1953 sleep researchers Eugene Aserinsky and Nathaniel Kleitman reported observing rapid saccadic (tracking) eye movements in sleeping subjects. These were similar in appearance to the eye movements of waking individuals. Further research found that REM sleep was often associated with reports of dreaming.

The postulate that there was a close correlation between dreams and REM sleep guided scientific dream research for a decade. Later studies, however, showed that significant dreaming could take place during non-REM (NREM) sleep. Subsequent research has shown that—although the older correlation of REM sleep with dreaming does not hold—it is possible to draw a meaningful distinction: namely, that REM dreams tend to be more active, visually rich, and bizarre than NREM dreams.

REPRESSION

Repression can be of a social or political nature— as in the repression of racial minorities. The other meaning of the term is psychological, but is closely related to its political meaning. Just as a society represses or suppresses groups of people who are deemed undesirable in some way, so the psyche represses undesirable thoughts, urges, and so forth. The "ghetto of the mind" into which one's unacceptable desires are driven is the

unconscious. Different schools of depth psychology (psychologies that focus on the unconscious) postulate somewhat different types of repression.

For **Sigmund Freud** what is primarily repressed is unacceptable sexual and aggressive urges. One might, for example, hate one's father and wish to kill him (a common desire among men, according to Freud). But this is so unacceptable that we repress awareness of this death wish. For **Carl Jung** a diversity of material is repressed, including sexual and aggressive urges.

The material repressed into the unconscious mind is widely believed to reemerge in dreams. In Freud's view, the purpose of dreams is to allow us to satisfy in dream fantasies the instinctual urges that we have repressed. One might, for instance, dream of slaying an oppressive ogre (a symbolic replacement for a hated father). In Jung's view, dreams are arenas in which the repressed aspects of the psyche may reemerge to balance out the limited self we experience in our daylight consciousness. For Freud, Jung, and other depth psychologists, part of the task of psychotherapeutic dream interpretation is to use the dream to discover what the client is repressing.

REVELATION, BOOK OF

The most powerful dream vision in the **Bible** appears in the last book, Revelation, which presents itself as the prophetic account of Jesus' return to earth. It is the only book of prophecy in the New Testament. The author of the book purports to be John, son of Zebedee and Salome, the latter one of the women who went to the tomb on Resurrection morning. After his brother James was slain by Herod Agrippa, John left Palestine and traveled to Asia Minor in missionary work. Under the reign of

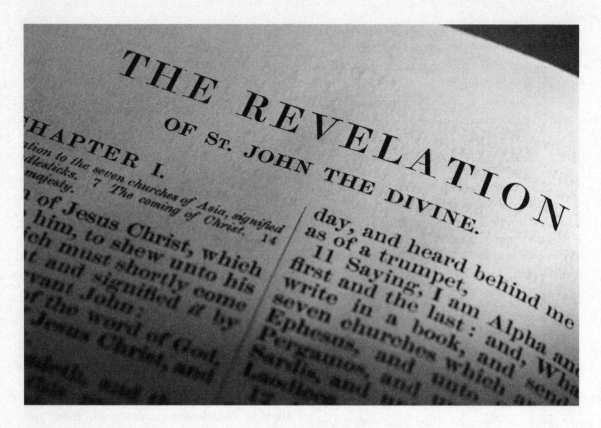

The Book of Revelation was inspired by the dream visions of St. John.

the Roman emperor Domitian, John was banished to the desolate isle of Patmos, off the coast of Turkey in the Aegean Sea. There, according to the text, is where John was given his vision of the future that comprises the Book of Revelation.

The revelation is given to John through signs and symbols contained in a series of **visions**, that an **angel** explains to him. Much of the content of the revelation is apocalyptic in nature, foretelling the terrible events that are to unfold at the end of time. When the first vision begins, John is in a trancelike state. Specifically, the author says that he was "in the Spirit" when he heard a loud voice. While the meaning of this expression is

open to interpretation, it implies that John was in an altered state of consciousness.

In the Judeo-Christian Scriptures, angels regularly relay messages to human beings, both in dreams and while the recipients are awake. Such communications are usually direct and explicit, however, rather than indirect and symbolic, except in certain dream messages.

RIP VAN WINKLE EFFECT

Rip Van Winkle is the legendary character who went to sleep as a youth and awakened as an old man. If he had significant dreams, they are not related in the story. Rather, the interesting phase of the narrative is when Van Winkle walks back to his village and interacts in awkward and entertaining ways with the village residents.

The Rip Van Winkle effect refers to the effects of too much sleep and is, of course, named after the mythical character. Sleep researchers have found that too much sleep is almost as detrimental as too little sleep. In several experiments it has been demonstrated that subjects who sleep even an hour or two longer than normal perform significantly worse on vigilance tasks. Extra sleep also increases the amount of Stage 2 and **rapid eye movement (REM) sleep**, which are the phases marked by the most vivid dreams.

ROME, ANCIENT

The ancient Romans viewed dreams as divine messages and, like many other traditional societies, sought to use them as oracles of the future. The emperors Caligula and Tiberius, for example, both saw their own deaths in dreams. Among native divinities, the agricultural deities Fauna and Faunus were particularly associated with dreams.

While the contrast between ancient Rome and ancient **Greece** can be overstated, it is nevertheless true that the Romans were predominantly practical people, content to borrow heavily from their more cultured neighbors, the Greeks. Following the lead of the Greeks, the Romans established numerous *asclepieions*—temples dedicated to **Aesculapius**, the deified doctor who healed or provided healing and medical advice in dreams. The principal activity at the *asclepieions* was the seeking of cures via the technique of **dream incubation**. People went to asclepieions to bathe, fast, perform rituals, and then sleep with the intention of receiving a healing dream from Aesculapius. The cult of Aesculapius was officially transplanted to Rome in 293 B.C.E., when the central Aesculapius at Epidaurus sent a giant snake—regarded as a form of Aesculapius himself—to Rome to halt a disastrous plague. The subsequent waning of the plague was attributed to Aesculapius, and he became a popular god among the Romans. Other foreign divinities in whose temples dream incubation for the purpose of healing took place included Isis and Serapis.

As one might well anticipate, some Roman thinkers took a less religious perspective on dreams. The naturalistic philosopher Lucretius, for instance, noted that many elements of dreams can be explained as the residues of daily experience: "Generally to whatever pursuit a man is closely tied down and strongly attached, on whatever subject we have much previously dwelt, the mind having been put to more than usual strain in it, during sleep we, for the most part, fancy that we are engaged in the same" (Lucretius, cited in Van de Castle, pp. 65–66—see *Sources*). The Roman orator and thinker Cicero was skeptical about the significance of dreams, reserving particular scorn for professional dream interpreters. At one point he went so far as to remark that if dreams did have any meaning, it was certainly not within the power of most dream interpreters—who were, for the most part, grossly ignorant—to derive such meanings. Citing dreams for which professional interpreters had derived contradictory significance, he dismissed the practice completely: "Let us reject, therefore, this divination of dreams, as well as eleven other kinds. For, to speak truly, that superstition has extended itself through all nations, and has oppressed the intellectual energies of all men, and has betrayed them into endless imbecilities" (Cicero, cited in Van de Castle, p. 66—see *Sources*).

THE BEST WAY TO MAKE
YOUR DREAMS COME
TRUE IS TO WAKE UP.

—PAUL VALÉRY

SAINT-DENYS, HERVEY DE

The Frenchman Hervey de Saint-Denys (1822–1892) was a professor of ethnography, specializing in Chinese and Tartar-Manchu. His book *Les Rêves et les Moyens de les Diriger* was originally published in French in 1867. The English translation, *Dreams and How to Guide Them*, was not published until 1982. Saint-Denys gained recognition as one of the founders of the technique known as **lucid dreaming**.

Saint-Denys first started to record his dreams at the age of thirteen. His **dream diaries** are extensive: twenty-two in total. He reported 1,946 nights in which he recalled his dreams. After the first year he even included pictures of images he remembered from his nocturnal experiences. His first lucid dream is recorded in the 207th entry.

After that, he developed a series of mental exercises to increase his ability to achieve lucidity. Within the first six months of practicing these exercises, he was achieving lucidity two out of five nights, on average, which increased to an average of three out of four nights of lucidity after a year. Since, after only fifteen months, Saint-Denys was achieving lucidity almost every night, he inferred that with his exercises anyone seriously interested could achieve the same results.

By taking this approach to **nightmares**, it is possible to apply one's will to the incoherent qualities of dreams and make them less destructive. The emotional, tumultuous and unpleasant qualities of dreams can be replaced with images that are more enjoyable when the dreamer develops the ability to impose her or his will on the dreaming process. By focusing on the foolishness of the nightmarish aspects of the dream, the dreamer is able to impede the offending aspects of the dream and thus lessen the fear it causes. And when dreamers are able to confront their fears and demonstrate power over nightmares, they decrease and sometimes stop altogether.

SAMBIA

Among the Sambia, a hunting and horticultural people living in the Eastern Highlands Province of Papua New Guinea, dreams bear upon ritual by providing explicit instructions that are followed by initiates in order to head off impending attacks. More generally, many aspects of Sambia social interaction are characterized by a watchfulness and a suspiciousness necessary to anticipate attacks. This type of social paranoia inhibits and frames dream experiences, as well as regulates the sharing of them and their interpretations. Among the most typical dreams, which generally refer to the same images and themes, are the dream experiences of feeling cheated or disgusted, being chased by malevolent people, being threatened with drowning, or seeing a raging fire.

Dreams are regarded as experiences, occurring during sleep, in which the **soul** leaves the body. The soul takes thought with it, leaves the body empty, and visits various places. The dream world exists parallel to this one. Thus, dream reports are viewed as narratives of events. All dream images are supernatural because they occur not to the person but to the soul, for whose actions the person is not responsible.

The principal setting in which dreams are shared is the residence where a person sleeps. Another typical context for dream sharing is a healing ceremony in which **shamans**, who are the mediators between the secular and the spiritual worlds, perform dream rituals. Another context is initiation rituals, where dreams are shared by elders and shamans and where dream interpretations for ritual secrets are taught. Other settings are public or secret storytelling sessions, during gossip and rumor exchanges, and during hunting, trading, or gardening trips.

Dreams are influenced by social status factors such as sex, age, and ritual standing. Thus, men generally share dreams more often than women, and older people report more dreams than younger individuals do, even though children's **nightmares** are regarded as threatening enough to be shared. Dreams are usually shared by the Sambia because they have been part of their basic experience since childhood. However, most dreams are forgotten after awakening, and only significant and troubling dreams are remembered and shared. Accounts of these dreams often become very stylized and stereotyped. If they are shared in public contexts, they may become an important part of public cultural knowledge.

Dream interpretation may reveal bad omens about future events, and sometimes reinterpretations of past dreams make it seem they foretold correctly what happened. The Sambia generally seek dream interpretation when they are beginning new or risky ventures, as well as to relieve the anxiety and troubling feeling associated with some dreams.

SECONDARY PROCESS

Secondary process is **Sigmund Freud**'s expression for the psychological mechanism that regulates our behavior with respect to external reality. The secondary processes, associated with the **ego**, are dominated by what Freud referred to as the *reality principle*. The contrasting term is **primary process**, a mechanism dominated by the *pleasure principle*. In a normal adult, the secondary processes regulate the primary processes so that the person does not immediately act upon every urge that comes to mind. The secondary processes are called *secondary* because they come into being only after infancy, which is dominated by the primary processes.

Freud's understanding of dreams was that they represented fulfillment of desires normally controlled and repressed by secondary processes. However, despite Freud's emphasis on dreams as an arena dominated by primary processes, he noted that secondary processes also play a role in shaping dreams:

> Two fundamentally different kinds of psychical process are concerned in the formation of dreams. One of these produces perfectly rational dream-thoughts, of no less validity than normal thinking; while the other treats these thoughts in a manner which is in the highest degree bewildering and irrational. (Freud, p. 597—see *Sources*)

The secondary processes are responsible for the overtly rational elements in dreams (coming into play at the stage of the **dreamwork** Freud called **secondary revision**), whereas the primary processes are responsible for the seeming irrationality of dreams.

SECONDARY REVISION

Secondary revision is **Sigmund Freud**'s expression for what he regarded as the final stage of dream production. Freud's basic understanding of dreams was that they provide an arena within which our often frustrated desires and urges can

find expression in fantasy. In most dreams, however, the true meaning of the urge being expressed is disguised from our conscious mind so that the emotions associated with a strong desire do not disturb our sleep. Freud referred to the transforming and disguising process as the **dreamwork** and identified five mechanisms by which the unconscious mind accomplishes this transformation: **displacement, condensation, symbolization, projection**, and secondary revision. After undergoing one or more of the other operations, the **secondary processes** of the **ego** reorganize the otherwise bizarre components of a dream so that it has a comprehensible surface meaning—a superficial significance that it would otherwise lack.

SENOI

The remnants of the Senoi, a people that was largely destroyed during World War II by the Japanese forces, live in the mountainous central area of mainland Malaysia. They are part Indonesian and are related to the highlanders of Indochina and Burma. The Senoi have been well known for their **dream control** techniques and their dream theory.

According to the Senoi, the two most important psychic elements—one localized behind the center of the forehead, the other focused in the pupil of the eye—explain dream experiences in that they are able to leave the body when a person is asleep or in a trance. *Ruwaay*, the soul at the center of the forehead, is considered the more important of the two when it comes to dreaming and is sometimes referred to as the dream-soul. The Senoi regard dreams as the experiences these souls have when they encounter other souls that may belong to animals, trees, waterfalls, people, or supernaturals.

In Senoi culture dreams are very important because they can inform people about particular events. For example, it is claimed that they can predict the weather. Also, they are fundamental in communications with the supernatural world, and they play a significant role in healing ceremonies. The Senoi distinguish between insignificant dreams and important dreams, and they often deny that upsetting dreams reflect their own desires. The Senoi are taught how to attain dream lucidity and dream control in order to be able to deal directly at the unconscious level with potential conflicts that might be dangerous in everyday life.

Dream interpretation constitutes a mainstay of the education of children and is common knowledge among Senoi adults. It is a fundamental topic of conversation in everyday life, as the Senoi claim that everything in a dream has a purpose beyond one's understanding when asleep.

Children, whose minds are considered able to adjust inner tension states, are given social recognition for discovering what might be called an "anxiety-motivated psychic reaction to dreams." Anxiety is regarded as an important element in that it blocks the free play of creative activity to which dreams could give rise. Through Senoi interpretation, the dream is given a particular force that is felt by the child as a power that can be controlled and directed. According to Senoi, children should make decisions during the night as well as during the day by assuming a responsible attitude toward all psychic forces and by expressing and thinking upon psychic reactions.

SEX AND DREAMS

Dreams tend to reflect whatever preoccupies us in our waking life, so it is natural that dreams often contain sexual themes. In societies in which sex is viewed as an instinctive part of life, such dreams are usually not regarded as particularly remarkable. The West, however, has been influenced by a dualistic outlook (originally imported into Christianity from Gnosticism) that views matter and spirit as being opposed to each other. Thus sex and sexual desire have often been regarded with suspicion and antagonism.

As Christianity developed, sexual desire came to be seen as a weak point where evil forces could subvert the most upright Christian. This was an especially crucial point for monastics, for whom celibacy was one of their most sacred vows. Given this general perspective, it was almost inevitable that sexual dreams should come to be viewed as the work of the Devil. Medieval folklore went so far as to populate the world of dreams with **incubi and succubi**—demons that, during the dreams of their "victims," took the form of handsome men or beautiful women and seduced the dreamers.

In the early modern world of post-medieval Europe, this kind of folklore tended to be dismissed as superstition, but the old antagonism between the spirit and the flesh continued to shape perceptions of sexuality. In the Victorian era of the late nineteenth century, sexual desire was seen as a force that, if not controlled, could overwhelm rationality and civilization (a creation of the rational mind). It was during this era that **Sigmund Freud** formulated his groundbreaking theory of human nature, which holds that human beings are basically selfish animals driven by aggressive urges and the desire for pleasure. Although people learn how to repress their animal impulses in order to get along in society, they never completely conquer their primitive selves. Mental illness results from a denial of urges that people regard as socially unacceptable and do not

Depending on how one's society regards sexual practices, dreams involving sex tend to reflect the beliefs instilled within us.

admit are a part of themselves. Chief among these urges is the sexual drive, which is often repressed from consciousness so that it remains in the **unconscious**.

Freud came to feel that the analysis of dreams was a key avenue for uncovering repressed desires. In his view the purpose of dreams is to allow us to satisfy in fantasies the instinctual urges that society judges unacceptable. So that we do not awaken as a result of the strong emotions that would be evoked if we were to dream about the literal fulfillment of such desires, the part of the mind that Freud called the *censor* transforms the dream content so as to disguise its true meaning.

The process of dream interpretation in psychoanalysis involves "decoding" the surface content (the **manifest dream**) to discover the real meaning (the **latent dream**)—a meaning that is

often sexual in nature. Given his view of our sexual nature and his belief that our real fantasies are disguised in our dreams, it was natural that Freud would attribute sexual meaning to almost anything that appeared in a dream. Anything long and straight could thus be interpreted to signify a male sexual organ, and almost any open receptacle could represent a female sexual organ. Gushing water in a dream landscape was seen as an orgasm. Even stabbing someone with a knife was interpreted as aggressive sexual activity. While Freud seemed to push his sexual theory of dreams to an absurd extreme, his notions were tremendously influential throughout the greater part of the twentieth century.

One contemporary criticism of Freud's theory is that his notions may have been appropriate for the era in which he lived (an era that thoroughly distrusted the sexual impulse) but are less applicable to the contemporary world—a world in which sexual desire is accepted as a natural and healthy part of the human being. Because sex is now more socially acceptable, fewer sexual conflicts are repressed into the unconscious, and thus fewer dreams have hidden sexual meanings. In this emergent view, even overtly sexual dreams may have other, nonsexual meanings, such as symbolizing the creative impulse.

SHADOW

In psychology, the shadow refers to the personality traits and tendencies that one has rejected in developing one's self-image. One of the most influential formulations of the shadow was put forward by the famous Swiss psychiatrist **Carl Jung**. In Jung's personality theory, the **ego** represents the individual's sense of personal self. This sense of personal identity is purchased at the expense of certain tendencies (e.g., socially unde-sirable traits), however, which are rejected as "not-self." According to Jung, these rejected traits come together as a kind of unconscious "coun-terego" that he termed the shadow.

Although suppressed from conscious aware-ness, the shadow continues to influence our behavior in powerful ways. In particular, we may become unduly anxious or irritated when in an environment or around a person that in some way reminds us of repressed aspects of our self. If a person has rejected his or her own sexual drive, for example, that person may feel irrational fear or anger around an overtly sexual individual. The shadow may appear as a person in one's dreams, usually as an individual of the same sex. In Jun-gian therapy, the shadow is viewed as a potential source of characteristics to be integrated into the subject's ego structure.

SHAKESPEARE, WILLIAM

In the English Renaissance, various playwrights made use of dreams as a favorite channel of com-munication between the human and the divine. Dreams, which were generally regarded in popu-lar belief as the most intelligible form of super-natural warning, represented a useful dramatic device for the Elizabethan playwrights, since they foreshadowed events of plot, provided the audi-ence with needed information, and imparted a vivid atmosphere of mystery to the play. Con-cepts of the dream world were derived from var-ious sources, such as classical Greek and Roman literature and philosophy, the native heritage of English folklore, and the medieval tradition of the dream vision, which culminated in England with the works of **Chaucer**. Among the Eliza-bethans, William Shakespeare (1564–1616)

made selective use of these sources, transforming and refining the material in accordance with his literary purposes.

In dramas the frequent use of dreams has many dramatic purposes. Even in Shakespeare's earliest plays, besides being a form of presentation and a predictive device of plot, dreams are a way of presenting the process of the mind at work in memory, emotion, and imagination. This is the case of the dramatic action of *Richard III*, in which omen, apparitions, narrated dreams, and long soliloquies define the play's world, creating a reality both inside and outside Richard. When Clarence tells Blackenbury the dream foretelling his assassination in the first scene, the images used are some of the **archetypes** usually associated with death, such as crossing the sea, the unsteady deck, stumbling, and drowning.

In the last act of the same tragedy, parallel dreams are experienced by King Richard and his rival, Richmond, who will face each other in their last battle in Bosworth. The personages of these dreams appear among the tents as the ghosts of murdered princes, such as Edward, King Henry's son, Henry VI, Clarence, Rivers, Grey, Vaughan, and Hastings, who try to make Richard yield to remorse, while encouraging his rival to fight and conquer. Thus, in *Richard III* Shakespeare uses the dream also for moral ends, presenting the opposition of good and evil.

The dream is usually the preferred vehicle for premonitions of death, as in *Henry VI*, where the death of the duke of Gloucester is preceded by a dream by the cardinal of Win-chester, and in *Romeo and Juliet*, where Romeo dreams that his lady comes and finds him dead, and Balthazar dreams that his master fights and kills another man. In *Hamlet* and in *Macbeth*, on the other hand, the dream world is closely

The Bard—William Shakespeare—took a lesson from his Greek playwright predecessors and used dreams in his dramas to help advance plot and develop characters.

related to the entire realm of witchcraft, omen, and the supernatural.

In *Julius Caesar* the dream is also vital to the plot and is opportunely inserted into the development of the tragedy, which deals with the conflict between monarchical and democratic parties in the political world of Rome. *Julius Caesar* is full of omens and dreams, such as Calpurnia's dream, the dream of Cinna the poet, and the advice of the augurers, which are misinterpreted, making tragedy inevitable. The dream imagery of this tragedy, in which a primary emphasis is placed on the potential ambiguity of interpretation, also constitutes a means of examining character and consciousness, and, as in *Richard III*, divides men into two categories: those who attempt to control dream and destiny, and those who are controlled by them.

In *A Midsummer Night's Dream*—which deals full force with dreaming—the categories of reality and illusion, sleeping and waking, reason and imagination, are reversed, and the central theme of the dream is presented as truer than reality. Thus, by regarding facts as if they were dreams and dreams as if they were facts, Shakespeare shows how closely dreams skirt the truth, and how fascinating is the attraction of the false.

The subject of *The Winter's Tale* and *The Tempest* is the confrontation that humanity experiences with the irrational and complex role of the dream world in life. The dream world represents the entire world of *The Winter's Tale*, which is fundamentally a play of metamorphosis based on the images of time and change, and on the possibility for things that have already happened to happen again. In *The Tempest*, on the other hand, things happen on an enchanted island which represents the dream world—in order that they need never happen again. The poles of sleeping and waking, and vision and reality are deliberately explored in this play, in which the theme of losing and finding achieves its ultimate expression.

SHAMAN AND SHAMANISM

Shamanism has sometimes been defined as a "technique of ecstasy," a definition alluding to the shaman's ability to enter non-ordinary states of consciousness—including certain dream states—at will. Although the terms *shaman* and *shamanism* have come to be used quite loosely, in the disciplines of anthropology and comparative religion shamanism refers to a fairly specific set of ideas and practices that can be found in many world cultures. Characteristically, the shaman is a healer, a psychopomp (someone who guides the souls of the dead to their home in the afterlife), and more generally a mediator between his or her community and the world of spirits (most often animal spirits and the spirits of the forces of nature).

For smaller-scale societies, especially for hunting and gathering groups, shamans perform all of the functions that doctors, priests, and therapists (and sometimes mystics and artists as well) perform in contemporary Western societies. The religious specialists of traditional American Indian societies that people sometimes refer to as "medicine men" are examples of shamans. True shamans are more characteristic of hunting societies than pastoral or farming societies, although one can often find segments of the shamanic pattern in non-hunting cultures. Shamanism in the strict sense is not found in certain culture areas, such as Africa, although there are religious specialists that fill the same "slot" in traditional African societies.

As a system, shamanism frequently emphasizes contact and communication with spirits in the otherworld, healing practices in which the shamans search for lost souls of the living, and rituals in which shamans guide the spirits of the deceased to the realm of the dead. The word *shaman* comes from the Tungusic term for this religious specialist, *saman*. The term was originally coined by an earlier generation of scholars who were studying societies in Siberia and central Asia and was later extended to similar religious complexes found elsewhere in the world. Depending on how one interprets the archaeological evidence, shamanism is many thousands of years old.

There are a number of different traditional ways in which one can become a shaman. Often the role is simply inherited. At other times, the person to become a shaman is chosen by spiritual forces. This supernatural election frequently involves a serious illness in which the chosen person comes close to death, making this part of the process a kind of initiatory death in which the old person "dies" to his or her former self. The death theme is emphasized in certain traditions (especially in Siberia), in which the chosen individual has a dream of being slain, dismembered, reconstructed, and revived. Sometimes it is during the course of the initiatory sickness that the shaman-to-be learns how to enter non-ordinary realms during dreams and meets the spirits with whom he or she will work as a shamanic. After they heal, shaman novitiates usually complete their training under the guidance of an experienced shaman.

When performing their roles shamans enter an altered state of consciousness in order to contact non-ordinary reality. The ability to enter non-ordinary states is so important to the shamanic vocation that scholars of religion have identified it as *the* defining characteristic of shamanism. These altered states can be brought on by diverse techniques, from drumming and chanting to fasting and sweat baths. Shamans sometimes make use of mind-altering drugs when they are available. Once in an altered frame of mind, shamans can see or sense normally invisible realms and can also serve as mediums. In this non-ordinary state, they can travel to the realm of the gods—usually believed to be in the heavens—and serve as intermediary between their community and divine beings. They can also descend to the underworld.

As masters of altered states of consciousness, shamans can also be masters of the dream state. Thus, in some societies, many of the shamanic tasks are accomplished in dreams. Shamans are also often sought out as interpreters of dreams for the community.

SHAMANIC INITIATORY DREAMS

Shamans are the religious specialists of hunter-gatherer cultures. They are particularly associated with the aboriginal peoples of central Asia and the Americas, and are perhaps most familiar as the "medicine men" of traditional **Native American** cultures.

In almost every society there are diverse methods for becoming a shaman. A shaman is usually recognized as such after having received two kinds of teaching: rote learning of shamanic techniques, names and functions of the spirits, mythology and genealogy of the clan, a secret language, and so on; and ecstatic learning, particularly information received in dreams and trances. These instructions are given by the spirits and by the older master shamans and are equivalent to an initiation. Thus, dreams are a primary means of acquiring the role of a shaman.

Dreams are usually stereotyped in terms of the shaman's traditional culture, and the candidate for following a shamanic vocation generally dreams of spirits and ancestors, or hears their voices. Also, in dreams the candidate is sometimes given initiatory regulations and learns which objects will be needed to perform cures. During a shamanic dream initiation, the candidate usually experiences suffering, death, and resurrection, including a symbolic cutting up of the body, such as dismemberment or disembowelment by the ancestral or evil spirits. Sometimes initiatory dreams begin even in childhood. Usually, the premonitory dreams of future shamans are trailed by mortal illnesses if they are not rightly followed.

A shaman lady from Mongolia, like shamans of many other aboriginal and indigenous cultures, is highly respected by her people for her ability to interpret dreams.

Among the Maidu of the Northeast one becomes a shaman by dreaming of spirits. Although shamanism is hereditary, the candidate does not receive the final qualification until after seeing the spirits, which are inherited from generation to generation, in a dream. Initiatory dreams of some future shamans include a mystical journey to the "center of the world," to the seat of the "universal lord" and the "cosmic tree," from the branches of which the shaman makes the shell of his drum.

The souls of the dead are regarded as a source of shamanic powers among tribes of the Northwest—the Paviotso, the Shoshone, the Seed

Eaters, the Lillooet, and the Thompson Indians. In northern California this method of bestowing shamanic powers is widespread. The Yurok shamans dream of a dead man, usually a shaman. Among the Sinkyone the power is sometimes received in dreams in which the candidate's dead relatives appear; the Wintu also become shamans after such dreams, especially if they dream of their own dead children. In the Shasta tribe the first indication of shamanic power follows dreams of a dead mother, father, or ancestor.

Among the **Mohave** and the Yuma of southern California, power comes from the mythical beings who transmitted it to shamans at the beginning of the world. Transmission takes place in dreams and includes an initiatory scenario. In their dreams the Yuma shamans witness the beginning of the world and experience mythical times. Among the Maricopa initiatory dreams follow a traditional schema: a spirit takes the future shaman's soul and leads it from mountain to mountain, each time revealing songs and cures. Among the Walapai a journey under the guidance of spirits is an essential characteristic of shamanic dreams.

SLEEP, DEATH, AND DREAMS

A natural association between sleep and death has often been noted in different cultures and time periods. Some contemporary metaphorical expressions even convey a sense of this ancient association, as when a sleeping person is described as being "dead to the world," or when a deceased individual is referred to as having gone to his or her "eternal rest."

Beyond external appearances, the inner experience of dreaming is often that of entering another world. In this other, seemingly more spiritual world, one may sometimes meet deceased individuals and may even receive specific information from departed friends and relatives. In such dreams (as well as in **out-of-body experiences**) one may have the subjective sense that the soul can be at least partially separated from the physical body, thus constituting yet another way in which sleep is similar to death.

SLEEP DEPRIVATION

Even though sleep researchers have studied the effects of sleep deprivation for decades, they have discovered little not evident from ordinary, everyday observation: sleep deprived individuals become tired, irritable, and less effective. Empirical tests conducted to discover if sleep is really necessary have shown that laboratory animals deprived of sleep for extended periods of time sicken and die. Human beings have resisted sleep for upward of 11 days under controlled conditions, but, naturally, no experimenter has compelled human subjects to endure sleep deprivation to the point of death. In the course of extended sleep deprivation, subjects tend periodically to experience delusional episodes that are probably forms of **hypnagogic experience**. Whether these episodes (or, for that matter, certain other forms of delusional hallucinations) are "waking dreams" is an open question.

SLEEP DEPTH

A person sleeping heavily is sometimes said to be in a "deep sleep." In experimental approaches to the study of sleep, sleep "depth" has been gauged in terms of how much of a given stimulus (how loud a sound or how bright a light) it takes to awaken a sleeping subject. Empirical sleep research

Without sufficient sleep, overly tired people can experience waking dreams.

has found that we usually sleep deeper early in the evening and lighter toward morning, although this pattern is superimposed upon another pattern in which the depth of sleep varies across ninety-minute cycles. In a typical ninety-minute cycle, a sleeper goes through at least four identifiable **stages of sleep**, which repeat throughout the evening. Sleep is deepest in Stage 4, the stage during which we have the fewest dreams.

SLEEP LEARNING

The idea that we might be able to take in information and learn during sleep is intriguing. At one time, it was believed that playing a foreign-language teaching record during sleep would help in to learning the language. However, although research has shown that the brain is still operating while a person sleeps (e.g., a sleeping mother is so sensitive to her baby that the slightest irregular sound from her offspring will awaken her), the memory-storing part of the brain is apparently "offline" (which may explain why dreams are so easily forgotten). One thing that has been experimentally demonstrated with respect to sleep learning is that during sleep we can become progressively acclimated to things like loud noises and bright lights so that we are less easily awakened.

Another, quite different approach to the general notion of sleep learning is research that indicates that during sleep the brain consolidates and restructures memories in ways that are important for learning new information. Thus, for example, in mice learning to navigate a maze, the brain seems to replay the maze experience over and over during sleep. This seems to "solidify" the memory and, some researchers speculate, "essentialize" the learning in a way that aides learning subsequent, similar tasks.

SLEEP PARALYSIS (SLEEP IMMOBILITY)

Most people have had the experience of not being able to move in a dream. Being unable to run away from some kind of danger—or trying to run and being able to move only very slowly—is particularly common because at some level we know that we are paralyzed when we dream. During the **rapid eye movement (REM)** stage of sleep, when our most active dreams occur, a relay station at the top of the spinal column disconnects the motor cortex from the rest of the body, with the exception of the lungs and the eyes. This is why the neck muscles lose their tone during this stage, which is one of the defining characteristics of REM sleep.

Clearly this is a biological mechanism for preventing us from awakening otherwise we might thrash about during dreams. This disconnection of the motor impulses is the reason **sleepwalking** occurs only during non-REM sleep. It is also a factor in the sleep disorder referred to as sleep paralysis (which is distinct from normal REM sleep immobility), in which the sleeper is completely paralyzed immediately before entering (and sometimes immediately after leaving) sleep.

SLEEP TALKING (SOMNILOQUY)

Somniloquy is the phenomenon of sleep talking—speaking out loud while asleep. It is not an abnormal phenomenon, in that the majority of people have spoken in their sleep, but individuals under stress and some neurotics experience somniloquy with above average frequency. Unlike somnambulism (**sleepwalking**), which occurs only during the deepest levels of sleep (Stage 4), sleep talking occurs with apparent equal frequency during both **rapid eye movement (REM)** and non-REM sleep. People awakened while in deep, non-REM sleep are unable to recall dreams that might conceivably be connected with their talking episode, or with any part of the actual somniloquy. This pattern changes during lighter sleep; when subjects in REM stages are awakened during or after a somniloquy, they are often able to connect dream segments with their sleep talking.

People sometimes fear revealing their deepest secrets via sleep talking. In *The Adventures of Tom Sawyer* (pp. 64–65—see *Sources*), for example, Tom secretly witnesses a murder:

> Tom's fearful secret and gnawing conscience disturbed his sleep for as much as a week after this; and at breakfast one morning, Sid said:
>
> "Tom, you pitch around and talk in your sleep so much that you keep me awake about half the time."
>
> Tom blanched and dropped his eyes.
>
> "It's a bad sign," said Aunt Polly gravely. "What you got on your mind, Tom?"
>
> "Nothing. Nothing't I know of." But the boy's hand shook so that he spilled his coffee.
>
> "And you do talk such stuff," Sid said. "Last night you said, 'It's blood, it's blood, that's what it is!' You said that over and over. And you said, 'Don't torment me so—I'll tell.' Tell what?"

Sleep talking can vary from single-word utterances to extended, comprehensible discourses. One of the more unusual examples of a sleeping monologue (spoken by a sleeper who is a professional writer of lyrics), which has appeared in several psychological publications, is the following:

> Attention! Attention! Let me stand on that table, they can't hear me. Attention! Now this is a scavenger hunt. You all got your slips.
>
> First one there: a yellow robin's egg! Second one: a wolf's dream! Third: a Welsh shoelace! Fourth: a dirty napkin used by Garbo! Fifth: a tree trunk! Sixth: Valentino's automobile hubcap! Seventh: one of the swans in *Swan Lake!* Eighth: a Chattanooga choo-choo! Ninth: a bell from the "Bell Song" in *Lakme!* Tenth: Myrna Loy! Eleventh: the Hudson River! Twelfth: a teller from the San Fran-

cisco Bank of America! Thirteenth: a witch's tail! Fourteenth: David Susskind's mother! Fifteenth: nobody and his sister: That's it! That's it! Now everybody disperse, disperse. Meet back here—three-quarters of an hour, three quarters of an hour. (Cited in Empson, pp. 132–33—see *Sources*)

SLEEPWALKING (SOMNAMBULISM)

Somnambulism—from the Latin *somnus* (sleep) and *ambulus* (walking)—involves involuntary motor acts—particularly walking—during sleep. Research indicates that sleepwalking is a normal phenomenon, although it may be more prevalent among these under a lot of stress. Somnambulism occurs most often in pubescence (ages ten to fourteen years), and there is also a genetic component (some families exhibit a greater tendency to sleepwalk than others). There appears to be a relationship between somnambulistic and hypnotic states.

A typical sleepwalking episode is rather short, rarely exceeding thirty minutes. Although seemingly oblivious to external reality, sleepwalkers typically manage to avoid running into objects. They usually make their way back to bed successfully, but sometimes they lie down on the floor or a couch at the conclusion of an active episode.

Contrary to what one might expect, somnambulistic behavior occurs only during the deepest levels of sleep (Stage 4), rather than during the most active dreaming periods. People awakened in the midst of or at the conclusion of a sleepwalking episode are dazed and confused. They are unable to recall dreams that might conceivably be connected with the walking episode, or any part of the actual somnambulistic experience.

SOMATIC PHENOMENA

Somatic phenomena are the physical sensations the body experiences while dreaming. When our bodies experience the discomfort or annoyance of pain and pressure, such as discomfort from an uncomfortable position our limbs are in while we sleep, this sensory input can be translated into our dreams.

Our mind uses the dream to convey the uncomfortable state of our bodies. Because the mind does not view reality in dreams in the same way it does when we are awake, these messages often come to us in a symbolic way. Herbert Silberer, a German psychologist, recorded a dream he experienced when he was sick with a high fever and laryngitis, which made it very painful for him to swallow. He reported drinking a bottle of water in his dream, only to find that another had taken its place as soon as he finished the one before it. This represents the saliva he had to swallow continuously, even though it pained him to do so. In a different study, blood-pressure cuffs were put around the ankles of subjects and slowly inflated while they slept. Each person reported a different variation on the theme of being tied down, whether by snakes, ropes, or other items of that sort.

SOUL AND DREAMS

The idea of an inner soul distinct from the outer body is both ancient and widespread. Many different religious traditions embrace the notion that the inner self exists independently of the outer self, even surviving the death of the physical body. Among English-speakers, this inner self is usually referred to as the soul. Although sometimes conceptualized as part of a spiritual whole, the soul is usually conceived of as immaterial and separate from the body. Throughout human history the idea of the soul has appeared in many different forms.

It has been hypothesized that dreams are one of the sources of the idea of a soul distinct from the body. During dreams, one has the experience of traveling to other realms, interacting with people, and doing various things—even as the physical body remains in bed. Although the dream realm is shadowy and surreal, it nevertheless feels like a real place, apart from the world of everyday experience. Thus, it is not unreasonable to speculate that during dreams the conscious self somehow separates from the body and travels to an alternate world.

STAGES OF SLEEP

One of the components of contemporary scientific sleep research is the classification of sleep stages according to certain physiological indicators. Most commonly, the two measurements used to classify sleep are brain wave patterns (measured with an electroencephalogram, or **EEG**) and eye movements which, during sleep, periodically exhibit rapid activity, referred to as rapid eye movement (**REM**).

Just before a subject falls off to sleep, an EEG machine will record a characteristic brain wave pattern referred to as alpha waves, which has a frequency of eight to thirteen hertz (cycles per second). As we pass into sleep, the EEG shows a relatively low voltage and mixed frequency of two to seven hertz. This transitional state is referred to as Stage 1 sleep. Stage 2 sleep is characterized by EEG patterns referred to as transient sleep **K-complexes and spindles**. Stages 3 and 4 are characterized by delta waves (having amplitudes of more

than seventy-five microvolts for at least half a second). In Stage 3, the EEG consists of 20 percent to 50 percent delta waves; in Stage 4, the EEG consists of more than 50 percent delta waves.

In the normal sleep cycle of a young adult, the sleeper initially progresses from Stage 1 (lasting half a minute to 10 minutes) to Stage 2 (20 to 45 minutes) to Stages 3 and 4 (these together are referred to as deep sleep and may last anywhere from a few minutes to an hour). The sleeper eventually returns to Stage 2 sleep, and then enters a REM state, typically for a few minutes. At this point, the sleeper has completed the first sleep cycle. After the initial REM state, the sleeper goes back to Stage 2 sleep, repeating the entire sequence all over again (with the absence of Stage 1 sleep, which is more of a transitional state than an actual sleep stage). In each succeeding cycle, the duration of REM sleep (in which most dreaming occurs) becomes longer and longer, until by morning REM periods can last as long as an hour.

The length of a sleep cycle also varies according to brain size. (For instance, the length of a sleep cycle for a cat is 30 minutes.) Typically, in an adult man, a sleep cycle lasts about 90 minutes, and healthy adults tend to go through between four and six such cycles every evening. There is much variation in the cycle with respect to age, and one's sleep tends to become progressively lighter and more broken up with age.

STEVENSON, ROBERT LOUIS

The author Robert Louis Stevenson (1850–1894) suffered from recurrent **nightmares** throughout his life. Beginning in his early childhood, serious nightmares plagued him incessantly up through adulthood. He remained an uneasy sleeper until his untimely death from a brain hemorrhage.

The Strange Case of Dr. Jekyll and Mr. Hyde is one of Stevenson's most famous nightmare-based novels. It describes the story of a man suffering from a chemically induced, dual-personality disorder. Stevenson claimed that the inspiration for the plotline originated in a dream. The author was hard pressed for money, and for two days he brainstormed ideas for a book. He briefly considered the idea of a "double being" as the central character for a novel, but he discarded the concept. He then had a dream of Dr. Jekyll ingesting a powder before the astonished eyes of his pursuers and turning into Hyde. Stevenson claimed that this was only the first in a series of sequential dreams he experienced that went into his story.

Stevenson felt the impact of his dreams on his writing so clearly that he eventually wrote a book devoted to this theme: *Across the Plains*. He made many references to the "nocturnal theater" in his head and attributed the "little people" who ran it as being more responsible for his stories than he was.

The more I think of it, the more I am moved to press upon the world my question: Who are the Little People? They are near connections of the dreamer's beyond doubt.... They have plainly learned like him to build the scheme of a considerable story in progressive order; only I think they have more talent; and one thing is beyond doubt, they can tell him a story piece by piece, like a serial and keep him all the while in ignorance of where they aim. Who are they, then? And who is the dreamer?

STRESS, ANXIETY, AND DREAMS

The closely related emotions of anxiety and fear are common themes of many dreams—such as in

Author Robert Louis Stevenson once said that the inspiration for *The Strange Case of Dr. Jekyll and Mr. Hyde* came to him in a dream. (Library of Congress).

dreams of **falling, nakedness**, being **chased**—and fear dominates the dream landscape in **nightmares**. Anxiety-filled dreams can emerge as a result of inner conflicts, particularly **repressed** conflicts that we attempt to hide from ourselves. **Sigmund Freud** and other therapists in the tradition of depth psychology have explored these dynamics at length, especially those conflicts rooted in childhood experiences.

The content of our dream life is, however, also shaped by external factors that intrude upon our consciousness entirely independently of repressed childhood conflicts. Thus stress in our environment, such as stress resulting from interactions at home or at our place of employment, may be the proximate cause of anxiety-filled dreams. However, while the distinction between inner and outer causes of dreams is clear, anxiety dreams often partake of both realms. In other words, stress on the job may, for example, bring up self-confidence issues from adolescence, or contemporary conflicts at home may resonate with certain childhood conflicts. Thus many anxiety-filled dreams will simultaneously express contemporaneous stress from the environment as well as conflicts from one's past.

STRUCTURALISM

Structuralism is a school of thought initiated in the early twentieth century by the great linguist Ferdinand de Saussure (1875–1913). The structuralist method was applied to the field of anthropology by Claude Levi-Strauss (1908–), who is recognized as the greatest exponent of structuralism. The basic tenet of the structuralist school is that the human mind organizes its apprehension of the world into dyadic structures, so that any given word or concept "makes sense" only in terms of its contrast with its opposite. In other words, *up* has meaning only in contrast with *down, dark* in contrast with *light*, and so on. Another structuralist assertion is that we perceive the world through our language, and hence we cannot separate the contents of our mind into words and wordless concepts. Many of the insights of structuralism have been carried over into post-structuralism/post-modernism. This latter movement is particularly sensitive to the manner in which linguistic metaphors structure our thought.

While structuralism is not often associated with dream analysis, it is easy to see how struc-

turalism explains certain characteristics of dream experience. Dream landscapes often, for example, go through complete transformations, frequently changing into their diametric opposites. Such transformations are easy to understand in terms of the natural link that structuralism postulates between opposites. Dreams often represent certain feelings or situations through literalized metaphors (e.g., one might dream that one's employer is one's Siamese twin, attached at the spine—a concrete symbol of the emotional experience of the boss constantly being "on one's back"). This is a perfect example of the characteristic of language to constantly rely upon metaphors to convey messages.

SUBCONSCIOUS

The term subconscious is confusing because it is used inconsistently. In some discussions this word is used interchangeably with the **unconscious**. The unconscious is that part of the psyche that is normally beyond the reach of consciousness—although psychoanalysis and certain other forms of **psychotherapy** can reputedly access certain parts of the unconscious through such techniques as dream interpretation. In other discussions, the term is used to represent what **Sigmund Freud** termed the *preconscious*, namely, those contents of the mind which, while not within the immediate spotlight of awareness, can be quickly accessed simply by turning one's attention to them. We are normally unaware of, for example, such background noises as the sound of the wind in the trees or the soft hum of a heating and cooling system. However, it would not be difficult to bring these sounds to our consciousness if we so wished.

SUPEREGO

The superego is to one of the three essential components of **Sigmund Freud**'s theory of the human personality. The superego represents the internalized mores of society and tells us what is right and wrong. Because our parents are our primary source of socialization, it might be said that the superego is the internalized voice of our parents. According to Freud, the superego is frequently in conflict with the **id**, which represents such primitive, animal drives as sex and aggression. The need to control these urges leads to inner conflicts—conflicts of which we are often largely unconscious and which are frequently expressed in our dreams. Repressed sexual and violent urges may, for example, lead to sexual and violent dreams. In Freud's view, the superego's drive to repress the id extends even into our dreams, so that socially unacceptable urges are expressed indirectly in dream symbols. A person may, for example, have a dream in which a sudden downpour drenches someone who is the object of sexual desire.

SYMBOLISM OF DREAMS

While the meaning of some dreams seems fairly straightforward, as in the case of dreams that recount our daily activities and experiences, other dreams are confusing and appear meaningless. If we hypothesize that all—or even many—are ultimately meaningful, then it is clear that we need some method of translating or interpreting them.

Dreams seem illogical and bizarre because they do not follow what, in waking life, is rational language. One characteristic of dreams is that they frequently seem to speak in a language of symbols and images. This appears to arise from the brain's subdivision into linear-linguistic (left) and associative-imagistic (right) hemispheres. While most of the daylight thinking and communication takes place in terms of the left hemisphere modes, during sleep both hemispheres are active, resulting in dreams that are a mixture of these two thinking styles. When the right hemisphere is active, it will express itself in terms of symbols and images. Thus, if we are passing through a period of time when we feel that we are "damming up" our feelings, we might have a dream about a dam overflowing and breaking open—a concrete symbol of what we are experiencing.

Psychotherapists have approached dreams as communications that reveal something about the contents of the unconscious mind. **Sigmund Freud** described a linking device in dreams called *similarity*, wherein a person, place, or thing resembles or invokes something in the dreamer's waking life. Often these associations are ambiguous. Frequently, they are repressed, buried, or forgotten, making it all the more confusing to decipher upon waking. Freud also viewed dreams as the arena in which we act out socially unacceptable urges, particularly sexual and aggressive urges. Thus, a dream in which a crane is lowered into a well might be interpreted as a sexual act, with the crane symbolizing the male and the well representing the female.

Other depth psychologists, such as **Carl Jung**, broke out of Freud's seeming obsession with sex to view dreams as containing symbols, which are representations of a larger complex of motivations. For example, circles were symbols of the deep self and symbolized, particularly in dreams, the quest for growth and self-integration.

Contemporary dream researchers have found that individuals develop specific dream patterns; that dreamers consistently use and reuse the same symbols within their individual dream landscapes. This manifestation is called *internal consistency*. Dream researchers **Calvin Hall** and Vernon Nordby have identified the most common form of this pattern as *relative consistency*. Each individual will dream of the same objects—dogs, windows, horses—more or less frequently, depending upon her individual landscape. Whether one dreamer often dreams of dogs, while another will frequently dream of, say, riding a horse, these patterns will remain consistent over time.

SYMBOLIZATION

The notion that dreams provide an avenue for the expression of normally repressed desires while simultaneously disguising and censoring our real urges was systematically formulated by **Sigmund Freud**, the father of psychoanalysis. In Freud's view, the purpose of dreams is to allow us to satisfy in fantasies the instinctual urges that society judges to be unacceptable, such as the urge to seduce or kill someone. If, however, we were to dream about an actual seduction or an actual assault, the emotions evoked by the dream would awaken us. So that our sleep is not continually disturbed by such dreams, the mind modifies and disguises their content so that strong emotions are not evoked. Freud referred to the process of censoring and transforming dream contents into less disturbing images as the **dreamwork** and explicitly identified five processes through which dreams are censored: **displacement, condensation**, symbolization, **projection**, and **secondary revision**.

In symbolization, as the name suggests, the repressed urge is acted out in a symbolic manner. During the late-nineteenth and early twentieth centuries in which Freud lived, overt expressions of sexuality were generally frowned upon in polite society. Hence many of Freud's patients suffered from repressed sexual desires, and he was able to study many dreams in which these forbidden urges were covertly expressed. Freud found that almost anything long and protruding could represent a male organ, and anything concave and receptive could represent the female. Thus, a dream in which a male was pouring champagne out of a bottle into a glass held by a female might symbolize sexual intercourse. Even something more subdued, such as inserting a key into a keyhole, might have the same meaning, depending on the dreamer and on the other elements of the dream. Other kinds of repressed desires, particularly aggressive urges, can be expressed indirectly in dreams through the mechanism of symbolization.

SYNESIUS OF CYRENE

Synesius of Cyrene was a fifth-century Greek convert to Christianity who eventually became a bishop of the Church. He wrote a relatively short work, *On Dreams*, that was perhaps the best book of its kind to be written by one of the church fathers. Synesius had a high opinion of dreams, reputedly even receiving editorial assistance during sleep.

Synesius believed that dreams were capable of lifting the human spirit to the higher spheres, there to acquire a deeper understanding of cosmic mysteries as well as spiritual upliftment. Synesius even encouraged using dreams for **divination**, although he warned against relying on **dream dictionaries** because each human being is unique. Finally, well in advance of his time, Synesius recommended keeping a **dream diary**, which he referred to as a "night book."

DREAMS ARE THE
TOUCHSTONES OF
OUR CHARACTER.

—HENRY DAVID THOREAU

TEDLOCK, BARBARA

Barbara Tedlock (1942–), an anthropologist and
the editor of a groundbreaking anthology on the
anthropology of dreams (*Dreaming: Anthropological and Psychological Interpretations,* 1987) is a
key figure in anthropological dream research.
Anthropologists have long been interested in
cross-cultural experiences of dreaming and, especially, dream interpretation.

In her survey, which examines the history of
Western views of dreaming, Tedlock asserts that
Westerners have tended to draw a sharp distinction
between dreaming and objective reality. Simultaneously, there is a long tradition in the West of naive
veneration of dreams. *Dreaming* combines anthropologically informed psychoanalytic and psychodynamic approaches to dreaming with sociolinguistic and interpretive approaches to the study of
the meaning of dreams. The book expands the
concept of dreams including cross-cultural expressions and focuses on the activities of dreaming and
dream communication in various cultures.

Each essay is based on material gathered by
the authors while conducting fieldwork in various cultures, including those of the **Sambia** of
Papua New Guinea, the **Rastafarians** of Jamaica,
and the Andeans and Amazonians of South
America. The semiotic analysis of Andean
dreams, for instance, treats dreaming and dream
interpretation as a cultural organized system of
signs, whereas the essay on Rastafarian visions
seeks to identify symbols of political and ideological resistance. Systems of dream classification
from ancient Mesopotamia, second-century
Greece, and modern Morocco are also analyzed.

A chapter by Tedlock compares the dream theories of dreaming and **dreamsharing** among the **Zuni** and the **Quiche**.

Among other works by Tedlock are various anthropological articles on the **Zuni** and Maya and on religious change in Highland Guatemala, as well as the book *Time and the Highland Maya* (1982).

TEETH AND DENTISTRY DREAMS

Dreams about teeth are more frequently experienced by women than men. Loosing a tooth is said to represent the process of giving birth—in which a small object is removed from the body—resulting in pain and bleeding. A widespread theme in world **folklore** is that for every child a woman bears she will loose a tooth. **Sigmund Freud** presented a more masculine interpretation, suggesting that the pulling of a tooth is symbolic of adolescent masturbation.

In some cultures, the loss of a tooth in a dream is sometimes interpreted to represent the **unconscious** desire of the dreamer for the death of a relative (e.g., the loss of the central teeth represents the desired death of a parent and the teeth further back in the mouth correspond to more distant relatives). An ancient **Egyptian** interpretation, dating from around 2000 B.C.E., suggests that the loss of a tooth means that the dreamer will die as a direct result of the actions of his or her relatives. Other theories propose that dreams of tooth loss represent the desire to become toothless—a kind of helplessness that causes the dreamer to require care. They may also indicate the desire of the dreamer to no longer have sex as an issue in his or her life. Alternatively these

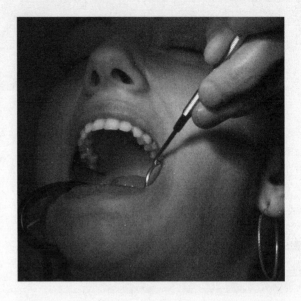

Dreams of losing teeth or having teeth extracted can signify many things, including fears of helplessness or aging or of some sort of loss in one's life.

dreams may signify a fear of aging, which relates to the fact that we often loose our teeth as we age.

Research was conducted regarding people who experienced chronic teeth dreams and the personality traits they exhibit as compared to the individuals who frequently had dreams of flight. While the "flyers" were calm, confident, and generally optimistic people, those who dreamed about teeth were more anxious, apt to bouts of self-criticism, and more likely to feel helpless in situations with which they were unfamiliar. The reason for these personality differences is unknown and open to speculation.

TEMNE

The Temne, a people inhabiting Sierra Leone and the Guinea Coast of West Africa, are characterized by a high degree of cultural diversity arising from invading, migrant, and neighboring peoples, which has resulted in considerable heterogeneity in different areas of Temneland and in a cultural overlap with other ethnic identities. The only two features not shared with other peoples are the highly elaborate nature of Temne cosmological ideas and the large repertoire of techniques used by Temne diviners.

In the Temne cosmological vision, four worlds are distinguished: the visible world inhabited by human beings, the world inhabited by the spirits, the world inhabited by the ancestors, and the world inhabited by witches. The last three worlds are regarded as towns that surround ordinary people, although they are invisible. Only certain people, possessing two ordinary eyes and two invisible eyes, can penetrate the darkness of the invisible worlds. Among these people are the diviners, who are present in every village, where they use more than thirty different divinatory techniques to mediate between the inhabitants of the four cosmos.

An alternative means of mediation is through dreams, by which knowledge is transmitted from the ancestors and from the other invisible worlds to ordinary people. For the Temne, dreams represent a crucial source of knowledge and are as important as waking perceptions, although they are distinguished from them. Among this people, the vision and the knowledge of diviners are attributed to accomplishment in dreaming, through which the diviners become experts on the dreams of their clients, who renounce their interpretation of reality in the face of divinatory authority.

According to Rosalind Shaw's 1992 study of Temne **divination**, the abilities of Temne diviners are revealed in an initiatory dream representing the context in which a contractual relationship with a patron spirit is established. Subsequent encounters with this and other spirits occur in the dream town of Ro-mere, a destination often described as something of an attainment, as dreaming is not considered to be a universal phenomenon. In diviners' dreams, ordinary people are passively acted upon by spirits and ancestors, as their victims or as recipients of their revelations.

TERTULLIAN

Tertullian was a third-century lawyer-turned-priest who was the first significant Christian theologian to write in Latin rather than Greek. Eight chapters of his *A Treatise on the Soul* dealt with the closely related phenomena of sleep and dreams. Tertullian's views on dreams dominated western Christendom.

Tertullian believed that the ongoing activity of the mind in dreams while the body is motionless in sleep proves that the soul is independent of the body and thus immortal. As part of his adherence to the idea of the disjunction of body and soul during sleep, he discounted the idea that the condition of the body (e.g., whether one was fasting or had eaten spicy food that day) influenced one's dreams. At the same time, and somewhat paradoxically, he was critical of the idea that the soul left the body and traveled during sleep.

Tertullian also classified dreams according to their source. While God was responsible for many dreams, so were demons. With respect to the latter, Tertullian asserted confidently that dreamers would not be held responsible for sins committed in their sleep, anymore than they would receive crowns in heaven for imaginary acts of martyrdom. He believed a third source of dreams is climatic and astrological influences, and a fourth the peculiar nature of the dreaming state itself.

THEOSOPHY

Theosophy is a particular synthesis of religious and occult ideas drawn primarily from the philosophical systems of **India**, the ancient Gnostics, and the Neoplatonists. The term also refers to a specific religious movement, the Theosophical Society, which was founded in New York in 1875. As a part of the religious phenomenon known as esotericism, Theosophy offers enlightenment to the individual through knowledge of the world of the divine and its hidden mysteries.

Theosophy postulates a rather complex view of the universe, within which humanity's origins, evolution, and destiny after death are delineated. According to its principles, the visible world arises from an omnipresent and immutable divine "source," an immaterial reality, of which—as in Hindu philosophy—the universe is the manifestation and from within which it is worked and guided. The ultimate goal of human life is, as in southern Asian religions, to free oneself from matter (Theosophists believe in reincarnation) and return to the source, with an increased consciousness.

One of the central teachings of Theosophy is that the cosmos is arranged in a series of distinct vibratory "planes" that coexist with the physical plane (the densest of them all) in what may be called a different "dimension." The soul, which is a spark of the divine source, can operate in the lower planes via a series of vehicles or "bodies," with which it clothes itself. The planes closest to the physical are the etheric plane and the astral plane.

During sleep, according to Theosophy, the soul withdraws to these subtler planes. The level at which the soul stops determines the types of dreams the individual will have. As examples of dreams created or influenced by the physical body, C.W. Leadbeater, in his short work *Dreams*, cites instances in which a sound or other stimulus in the environment is incorporated into a sleeper's dream immediately before the person awakens.

When the soul is operating in the etheric plane, Leadbeater says, we are receptive to the "thought-forms" of other people. By this he means that thoughts radiate out from our minds on the etheric plane, and that these thoughts can be picked up by other minds, usually as an indistinct jumble of images (although, as in **ESP**, a clear idea can sometimes be communicated directly from one mind to another). These cluttered, disconnected, constantly changing thought-forms are often picked up by the mind during sleep, and this accounts for the disconnected nature of much of our dream experience.

According to Leadbeater, when the soul is operating in the astral body, the dreamer may visit distant scenes of surpassing beauty, … meet and exchange ideas with friends, either living or departed, who happen to be equally awake on the astral plane. He may be fortunate enough to encounter those who know far more than he does, and may receive warning or instruction. He may [also] come into contact with non-human entities of various kinds—with nature-spirits, artificial elementals, or even, though very rarely, with Devas (**angels**).… (Leadbeater, pp. 30–31—see *Sources*).

The problem with these experiences, Leadbeater notes, is that the dreamer often does not remember his dreams—not even the more significant ones.

Certain writers in the broader occult-theosophical tradition have asserted that during sleep the soul has the option of advancing itself to the higher planes. For example, the dreamer's soul might attend "classes" in special "classrooms" on the higher planes of existence, though most of us forget what we have learned upon awakening.

ST. THOMAS AQUINAS

Thomas Aquinas was born in Rocca Secca, in the kingdom of Naples, in either 1225 or 1227 (the date is uncertain). He was the son of Landulph, count of Aquino, and Theodora, the countess of Teano. Before his birth, his mother sought out a local hermit to divine her child's future. The hermit told her that he would be a great man who would be devoted to the church, and that the impact of his words would last throughout all time. At the age of five, Thomas received his first tutelage by the Benedictine monks of Monte Cassino. While a student there he was diligent in his studies, devoted in his prayer, and inquisitive as to the nature of God, often asking, "What is God?"

The monks were extremely impressed by the level of dedication they found in the five-year-old child. He stayed with them in Monte Cassino until 1236. It was then that one of the brothers wrote to Thomas's mother and informed her that his brilliance would fade into obscurity if the boy was not pushed to achieve beyond the level of education the monastery could provide him. Shortly thereafter, Thomas enrolled in the University of Naples, where he studied until sometime in the early thirteenth century. When he joined the Order of St Dominica, his family was shocked that someone of noble birth would choose the life of a pauper.

St. Thomas Aquinas gained the discipline to remain chaste after experiencing a dream in which angels bound him in a fiery cord.

Out of fear that his family would come to take him away, the Dominicans decided to send Thomas to Paris. On his way to Paris, however, Thomas was accosted by his brothers at his mother's bequest and held captive for approximately two years in the fortress of Giovanni at Rocca Secca. During his imprisonment, his family tried desperately to talk him out of his chosen vocation. His brothers went so far as to send a beautiful woman to his room to seduce him and break his oath of celibacy. He chased the girl from his room with a poker retrieved from the fire.

That night **angels** appeared to him in a nightmarish dream—angels who wrapped him up in a cord of fire so terribly painful that he awakened with a cry. The cord was a girdle of eternal chastity; he never again suffered from the desires of the flesh and lived the remainder of his life in celibacy. The duration of his imprisonment he then spent in study, just as he would have if he had actually been in Paris. Eventually, his mother granted him freedom, and Thomas finally was able to return to the Dominicans. They were relieved to discover that he was as educated in theology and the scriptures as he would have been if he had not been sidetracked, perhaps more so.

At some point during the years 1244 and 1245, he became a student of Albertus Magnus, a renowned professor of the order. They traveled together to Cologne, where Magnus was to teach at the university. Magnus initially thought that Thomas was slow, due in part to the boy's overwhelming modesty and humility. But after reading Thomas's brilliant defense of a particularly difficult thesis, Magnus had cause to reevaluate his opinions. Then, in 1250, Thomas Aquinas achieved a place among the priesthood.

After spending years with Magnus in Cologne, Thomas traveled to Paris to attend the university and earn his doctorate of theology. A bitter dispute at the university delayed this significantly. It was at the university that Thomas wrote *The Majesty of Christ*, said to be inspired by a suggestion received in a dream in which a heavenly visitor instructed him.

In 1256, he finally received his doctorate. Nine years passed before the Pope chose to honor Thomas Aquinas with the position of Archbishop of Naples. If he had received the position earlier, he probably would never have had the chance to write his chief work, *Summa theologica*. He also collaborated on the *Studia generalia* of the Dominican Order, a system of studies and a handbook of piousness, before he died on March 7, 1274, at Fossa Nuova. On July 18, 1323, Pope John XXII canonized Thomas Aquinas.

Although he lived for less than fifty years, St. Thomas Aquinas signed his name to more than sixty-six religious masterpieces. Each embodied remarkable insight and piety. The *Summa theologica* was his magnum opus. St. Thomas claimed to have been advised on the content of certain passages from a dialogue he had with the apostles **Peter** and **Paul** while dreaming. Regardless of the very non-Aristotelian dreams that plagued his life, St. Thomas attempted to rewrite all of the Christian theology in the language of **Aristotle** and categorized it accordingly. It was his an attempt to diminish the value the common people put in their dreams.

St. Thomas concluded that **divination** through dreams was lawful as long as one was positive that the dream stemmed from divine design and the dreaming state used to achieve said dream lacked artificial influences. He also acknowledged the demonic influence in the common occurrence of prophetic dreams and **nightmares**.

TIBET

In Tibet it is believed that various deities and demons produce dreams. Various **Buddhist** *tantras* (texts dealing with techniques and rituals, including meditative and sexual practices) agree auspicious dreams that come true indicate the approach

Buddhist monks in Tibet are taught from a young age the importance of dreams and the stages of sleep.

of a tutelary (guardian) deity and success in the meditative process, whereas bad dreams indicate that both the deity and success are far away.

Among auspicious dreams, sunrise and the scattering of darkness indicates happiness with oneself and one's country. Dreams of hearing tales of praise while surrounded by a group of servants bode well for moving upward in society. Among bad dreams, a house that caves in or is ruined by fire reveals fears for occupants of the house.

Buddhist tantras assert that a subtle energy passing up and down the central channel of the body generates the four states common to the **Upanishadic** tradition of waking, dream, deep sleep, and "the state beyond the first three." The production of an artificial dream state, often called "purifying or exerting the dream," is very common in the Buddhist tantras. Tantric manip-

ulations of the dream state aim to mix the states of dream, deep sleep, and waking to attain the fourth state. These techniques are practiced especially by Tibetan lamas.

Lucid dreaming, which is the awareness of dreaming while in the dream state, is discussed in a number of ancient Tibetan Buddhist texts, and its teaching is one of the six **yogas** attributed to the Indian tantric Buddhist teacher Naropa. The teacher Marpa introduced the six yogas, including lucid dreaming, to Tibet in the eleventh century.

The six yogas of Naropa are (1) heat yoga, the creation of bodily heat through yogic practices; (2) the illusory body, in which yogic postures and visualizations show that all phenomena are like dreams and are void; (3) lucid dreaming; (4) the clear light, in which some practices are initiated during wakefulness or while dreaming to achieve the experience of clear light; (5) the death state; and (6) the consciousness transference, in which instructions are given to transfer one's consciousness to divine realms or into a living or dead body.

Tibetan lamas do not consider lucid dreaming itself to be a form of meditation, but rather a means of accessing the dream state to learn the doctrine of illusion, to create buddhas to listen to, or to practice meditation in the dream. The ultimate aim of meditation is to achieve nirvana, the transcendence of one's awareness of individuality and liberation from repeated rebirths (reincarnation).

TIKOPIA

The people who live on the Polynesian island of Tikopia, which is located to the southeast of the Solomon Islands, regard their dreams as significant indicators of supernatural influences. Considerable attention is paid to dreams, and it is believed that an accurate interpretation of them can throw light on the events of normal waking life. It is very common to share one's dreams with others, although there is no ritualized context in which to tell them. Dreams are usually reported in a casual way, at any time of the day. Some dreams are not given particular significance, however, and many of them are not reported in public at all.

According to the Tikopia explanation of dreams, which rests on a more general theory of a mobile **soul**, every person embodies an intangible entity (which may be designated the spirit, or life, principle) capable of leaving the body during sleep and wandering abroad, transmitting its experiences to its mortal owner upon its return. The mobility of the spirit explains dreams of visits to distant places. The spirit can also journey to the heavens and have contact with persons long dead.

Many dream experiences stem from the intrusion of spiritual beings who have never belonged to humankind, but who counterfeit familiar forms in order to deceive the dreamer. To this kind of spirit is attributed dreams of physical oppression, such as **nightmares**. The experiences of people in dreams are considered proof of the existence of spirits, and much of the information about supernatural beings is derived from dreams in which they appear. Violent dreams with an unpleasant aftereffect are very common among the Tikopia, although the significance given to such dreams varies, and they may even be entirely neglected.

Some dreams are regarded as being of more importance than others, especially those concerned with fishing (a major economic sphere) and with birth, sickness, and death. These are aspects of human life peculiarly liable to chance,

and some degree of advance assurance about them (provided by dreams) is usually welcomed. In Tikopia the value and the meaning of a dream tends to be a function of the immediate practical situation of the dreamer and his family, to whom it is generally told. The dream is discussed in this context, and its relevance determined.

TIRIKI

Among the Tiriki, a Luyia people of western Kenya, "dream prophets" are specialists for whom dreaming is regarded as a positive event, whereas for ordinary people dreams are undesirable and to be avoided. The gift of dream prophecy is not inherited or confined to any particular lineages or clans, but elders have always maintained control over its exercise. Tiriki dreams are often viewed as rendezvous with the spirits of dead relatives or friends, perhaps portending one's own death.

THE TRICKSTER ARCHETYPE

The Swiss psychotherapist **Carl Jung** asserted that much of world **mythology** and **folklore** represent manifestations of what he called the **collective unconscious**. The collective unconscious represents our inheritance of the collective experience of humankind, storing humanity's experiences in the form of archetypes (or *prototypes*) that unconsciously predispose us to organize our personal experiences in certain ways. Jung further asserted that the archetypes of the collective unconscious shape the content of our dreams, emerging in various forms of **archetypal dream images**.

Jung's theories arose from his observations that the dreams of his patients frequently con-

A home in Las Cruces, New Mexico, displays a design of Kokopelli, a trickster from Native American mythology. Trickster archetypes are seen in cultures around the world.

tained images with which they were completely unfamiliar but which seemed to reflect symbols that could be found somewhere in the mythological systems of world culture. Jung further found that if he could discover the specific meaning of such images in their native culture that he could then better understand the dreams in which they occurred.

One widespread figure in world mythology is the trickster, a powerful spirit or divinity who, as the name implies, delights in all sorts of pranks and jokes. Although the trickster is not actually an evil spirit, the impact of the trickster's activity is often unpleasant. In dreams the trickster archetype may emerge as a clown or other figure who mocks our pretensions or throws light on the ways in which we delude ourselves. The same archetype may manifest in less desirable ways, spoiling our dream pleasures and throwing things into a state of anarchy. Because tricksters are shapeshifters, they are also symbols of transformation.

TSUNAMI (TIDAL WAVE) DREAMS

Although not very many people have experienced a tidal wave in their waking lives, it is a very common theme in **nightmares**. These dreams usually occur after an individual suffers from a traumatic experience. Survivors of fires, for instance, often report dreams of fire and dreams of being consumed by tidal waves (tsunamis). While these two incidents may seem to be completely different, they actually share common characteristics. When a person dies in a fire it is very rarely from their burns. Most often they die from smoke inhalation. The physical sensations of carbon monoxide poisoning are similar to those of a person who is drowning because it is the lack of oxygen that leads to death. Nightmares about tidal waves can also symbolize feelings of losing control or of being overwhelmed. These kinds of feelings are shared

Dreams of tsunamis are one type of disastrous image we may experience that indicates some sort of traumatic event in our lives, or perhaps a sense of losing control of our lives.

by all people, regardless of the traumatic experiences they may or may not have suffered.

TUKOLOR

Dreams are central to most aspects of cultural and social life of the Tukolor of Senegal, for whom dream experiences are often associated with supernatural or spiritual entities. A common belief among the Tukolor is that the **soul**, which is thought to leave the body during sleep and wander across the earth, is responsible for dreams. At night, the soul is believed to experience another reality in dreams, although this is not always the case, as many dreams are dismissed as meaningless. Additionally, the use of dreams is institutionalized in the roles of formal dream interpreters. Certain learned Muslim clerics and other diviners usually induce, evoke, and interpret dreams through specific techniques and procedures. Dream interpretation manuals are common throughout much of North and West Africa and the Middle East.

Dreams generally have two purposes. First, they are used in consultations with clients inquiring after particular advice in certain matters. Second, they are used in combination with prayer and contemplation as a means of acquiring religious knowledge. According to Roy M. Dilley's research on dreams among the Tukolor, dreams have a particular significance in the activities of Tukolor weavers, whose craft is said to have its origin in the spirit world, where an ancestor transmitted it to a man during the time of myth.

The spirit world continues to be a source of inspiration and knowledge for weavers through the mediation of dreaming. Weavers are believed to hold a magical power of transformation that is transmitted by an external source of creativity. The stock of knowledge that weavers possess is rarely divulged, and weavers' dreams, besides being a source of innovation and inspiration, are a means of resolving the paradox of an ideal equality between weavers in Tukolor social ideology and the reality of individual differences. In addition, inspirational dreams constitute part of the basis of a hierarchical differentiation between, on the one hand, craftsmen and musicians, who derive their black lore from the jinn of the forest, and, on the other, marabout clerics—the custodians of **Islam**—whose white lore is provided by Allah and his **angels**.

UNDERSTANDING OUR
DREAMS IS A MATTER
OF LEARNING TO UNDER-
STAND OUR HEART'S
LANGUAGE.
—ANN FARADAY, *THE DREAM GAME*

UNCONSCIOUS

The unconscious is that part of the psyche that is normally beyond the reach of consciousness. The basic notion of an unconscious, as well as the idea that our behavior is influenced by unconscious motivations, is very old. However, it was **Sigmund Freud** who first put forward a general theory of the unconscious and its interaction with the conscious mind. Freud's concept of the relationship between the conscious and the unconscious has been compared to that of an "iceberg"—meaning that only a relatively tiny part (the conscious) is usually visible, while ninety percent (the unconscious) is below the surface.

Freud formulated his view partially as a result of his training in hypnosis under the French neurologist J. Martin Charcot. Freud witnessed numerous demonstrations of what today we would call posthypnotic suggestion. Charcot hypnotized subjects and requested that they perform certain tasks following their emergence from hypnotic trance. The subjects carried out the tasks, but were unable to recall why they did so. These demonstrations in combination with his clinical experiences suggested to Freud that a large part of what we do is based on unconscious motivations.

Freud's view of human nature is that we are fundamentally selfish animals driven by aggressive urges and the desire for pleasure. People learn, however, how to repress their cruder impulses into the unconscious region of the mind as they grow up. At the core of conflicts that lead to mental illness is often a denial of urges that people regard as unacceptable and do not wish to admit are a part of themselves. Mental illness occurs when such urges become too strong to deal with through the normal coping process. Freudian therapy involves discovery of the repressed urges causing the dysfunction. Freud analyzed dreams to gain insights into his patients' repressed desires, and referred to dreams as "the royal road" to the unconscious.

In Freud's view, the purpose of dreams is to allow us to satisfy in fantasies the instinctual urges that we have repressed into the unconscious. So that we do not awaken as a result of the strong emotions that would be evoked if we were to dream about the literal fulfillment of such desires, the part of the mind that Freud called the *censor* transforms the dream content so as to disguise its true meaning. The process of psychoanalytic dream interpretation involves a "decoding" of the censored surface dream in order to discover its real meaning.

Carl Jung divided the unconscious mind into two subdivisions, the personal unconscious and the **collective unconscious**. While the personal unconscious is shaped by our personal experiences, the collective unconscious represents our inheritance of the collective experience of humankind. This storehouse of humanity's experiences exists in the form of **archetypes**, which sometimes determine specific dream images. Both Freudian and Jungian psychology are sometimes referred to as depth psychologies, meaning that they focus on the processes of the unconscious mind.

THE UNDERWORLD

For depth psychology (the psychotherapeutic tradition of **Sigmund Freud, Carl Jung**, and related thinkers), the underworld is a rich symbol of the **unconscious** realm that we enter every night in our dreams. The notion of a world located beneath the surface of the earth where the **souls** of the dead and certain types of spirits exist is a widespread theme in ancient and modern world religions. The basic idea of an underground realm of the dead probably derives from the custom of burying corpses beneath the earth. Although less-than-inviting realms, the underworlds of the ancient Mediterranean peoples from which Western culture derives (e.g., Hebrews, **Greeks, Romans**, Mesopotamians) were not the realms of torture and punishment that the underworld became in Christianity and related traditions. A less widespread but nevertheless common subtheme in world religions is that this underworld dimension can be reached through a tunnel or opening that leads underground. Many myths relate the stories of heroes who enter the underworld to rescue a beloved one, to gain the gift of immortality, or to accomplish some other heroic task.

In the contemporary world, the underworld has come to be viewed psychologically rather than literally, as a symbol for the unconscious. This is particularly the case among thinkers of the Jungian tradition. It is easy to see how the story of a hero entering and reemerging from the underworld might be viewed as a symbol for our nightly journey through the world of sleep and dreams. Furthermore, ethnographic reports indicate that association of sleep and dreams with death is widespread in human culture. In many different religious traditions, but particularly in the West, the heroic journey to the underworld realm of the dead is not infrequently pictured as taking place in a dream state.

The personal unconscious is, in a sense, the burial ground of one's past. However, far from

Typical unpreparedness dreams involve either taking a test or having to give a speech, neither of which one is ready to do. These are common anxiety dreams.

being dead, this past continues to influence us—to "haunt" us, so to speak—in some subtle and some not-so-subtle ways. As we wrestle with our psychological patterns, especially under the stimulus of the therapeutic process, we attempt to "resurrect" our buried past and subject it to closer scrutiny. In fact, a large part of the therapeutic process in depth psychology is conceptualized as making the unconscious conscious—entering the underworld and, like the hero of traditional mythologies, bringing some long—buried part of the self back to the realm of light.

UNPREPAREDNESS DREAMS

Some dream motifs are so common that almost everybody has had them on more than one occasion. These motifs include such common scenarios as **falling** and **flying dreams**, dreams of **nakedness** in public, and unpreparedness dreams. Such shared dreams arise from experiences and anxieties fundamental to all people.

Unpreparedness is one of these shared motifs, although the precise way in which it manifests varies from society to society. In Western society, this motif often emerges in dreams in which we find ourselves taking an examination for which we are completely unprepared. For example, college students often have anxiety dreams around the end of the term if they have not studied adequately for their examinations. The unpreparedness motif can also emerge in other ways, such as when we dream about standing before a crowd on stage or at a public forum and realizing that we either have forgotten what we were supposed to say or were never prepared to say anything in the first place.

Although some unpreparedness dreams give direct expression to anxieties about test-taking or public speaking, the human mind may also deploy test-taking or public speaking images in dreams that symbolically express our hopes and fears. In our everyday language, for instance, we use the expression "passing the test" to refer to anyone or anything that is satisfactory or that fulfills certain requirements. Thus, a dream about being unprepared to take a test or to give a speech might reflect anxieties about everything from how we will do on an upcoming job interview to whether or not we will succeed in a new marriage. The core anxiety concerns doubts about our adequacy.

UPANISHADS (OR UPANISHADIC HINDUISM)

Around 1000 to 1500 B.C.E., a group of aggressive pastoral peoples from central Asia invaded **India** through the northern mountain passes, conquered the aboriginal peoples, and destroyed whatever records might have remained from the original civilization. These peoples, who called themselves Aryans ("nobles"), originated from around the Caspian Sea. The worldview of the Aryan invaders of India was preserved in the **Vedas**. The religious vision set forth in the Vedas, unlike that of classical Hinduism, focused very much on this world. The gods were ritually invoked to improve one's situation in this life, so priests became something approaching magicians.

Around 800 B.C.E. and afterward, Vedic Hinduism, with its heavy dependence on ritualistically knowledgeable priests, was challenged by a more individualistic form of spiritual expression that rejected many of the basic views and values of Vedism. This emergent view was expressed in a set of religious texts collectively referred to as the *Upanishads*. The *Upanishads* postulated an eternal, changeless core of the self that was referred to as the *Atman*. This soul or deep self was viewed as being identical to the unchanging godhead, referred to as *Brahma* (the unitary ground of being that transcends particular gods and goddesses). Untouched by the variations of time and circumstance, the Atman was nevertheless entrapped in this world, the constantly changing world of our everyday experiences. This unstable, fluctuating world is contrasted with the spiritual realm of the Atman/Brahma, which is stable and unchanging. Because of reincarnation, even death does not release the Atman from this world.

In the southern Asian religious tradition, release or liberation from the endless chain of deaths and rebirths represents the supreme goal of human striving. Reflecting the diversity of Hinduism, liberation can be attained in a variety of different ways, from the proper performance of certain rituals to highly disciplined forms of **yoga**. In the *Upanishads*, it is proper knowledge, in the sense of insight into the nature of reality, that enables the aspiring seeker to achieve liberation from the wheel of rebirth. Certain of the *Upanishads* analyze the self in terms of the waking state, dreaming, and dreamless sleep. The

Atman represents a fourth aspect of the self, beyond the facets of the self accessed by these three states of consciousness.

The *Upanishads* also discuss dreaming as a kind of halfway house between this world and the next, as cited by Wendy Doniger O'Flaherty in her *Dreams, Illusions, and Other Realities* (p. 16—see *Sources*):

> A man has two conditions: in this world and in the world beyond. But there is also a twilight juncture: the condition of sleep. In this twilight juncture one sees both of the other conditions, this world and the other world.... When someone falls asleep, he takes the stuff of the entire world, and he himself takes it apart, and he himself builds it up, and by his own bright light he dreams.... There are no chariots there, no harnessings, no roads; but he emits chariots, harnessings, and roads. There are no joys, happinesses, or delights there; but he emits joys, happiness, and delights. There are no ponds, lotus pools, and flowing streams, but he emits ponds, lotus pools, and flowing streams. For he is the Maker.

In this passage one can also perceive the kernel of an idea that would become prominent in later Hinduism, namely, the notion that the world we experience in our waking state is ultimately unreal and, like our dreamworld, simply a projection of consciousness.

VEDAS

One of the traditional criteria for being considered an orthodox Hindu is that one must acknowledge the authority of the four Vedas. These ancient religious texts (three thousand to four thousand years old, although Hindus regard them as being much older) often express ideas and values at odds with later Hinduism, much as the first five books of the Old Testament express a religious ideology at variance from that of current Christianity. Because of the authority and sacredness of the Vedas, many subsequent religious movements claimed to be Vedic, and certain texts of later Hinduism—texts closer to the worldview of contemporaneous Hindus—were referred to as Vedas. The strand of Indian spirituality represented by the Hare Krishna movement, for example, refers to certain Puranic texts— which are sacred texts dated later than the Vedas—as Vedas.

Among the original four Vedas, the Artharva Veda contains a fair amount of material on dreams. Various dream omens are discussed (e.g., riding on an elephant in a dream is considered auspicious, whereas riding on a donkey is inauspicious). The effects of inauspicious dreams can be counteracted by certain purificatory rites. The Artharva Veda also contains the unique assertion that the impact from an omen dream will take place sooner or later depending on whether it occurred at the beginning of the evening (later) or just prior to awakening (sooner).

VISION QUESTS

A vision quest is the active seeking of a vision or other sign from spiritual forces. Vision quests are especially associated with the aboriginal cultures of the Americas and are frequently tied to **initiation** rites and to **shamanism**. The most widespread initiatory ritual is the puberty rite, in which the individual becomes an adult member of the community.

Vision quests are regularly preceded by fasts, purifying sweats, and other ritual preparations, which are believed to open the mind to visions. The distinction between a vision and a dream is often difficult to draw (see **visions and dreams**). One thing is clear: Some aspect of visions make them similar, in some way, to dreams.

For example, in the puberty rite vision quest of the Lakota shaman Lame Deer, Lame Deer's own vision begins during a moment of full wakefulness. Thinking back to his experience, however, he recalls that he worried. "What if I failed, if I had no vision? Or if I dreamed of the Thunder Beings… ?" (p. 13—see *Sources*). He was worried that he might have a vision of beings who, as his guardian spirits, would direct him to undertake a vocation as a sacred clown. However, rather than using the term vision, he refers to this alternative possibility as "dreamed," a change that indicates he regarded visions and dreams as being on par with each other.

VISIONS AND DREAMS

In many cultures, little or no distinction is made between visions and divine message dreams, indicating that they share some intangible quality. This is especially the case in the Judeo-Christian-Islamic family of traditions, in which religious truth is communicated through direct revelations from God or one of His messenger **angels**. When God's message is communicated by an angel in the writings of the Hebrew prophets, it is sometimes difficult to determine whether the message is being delivered in a dream or in a waking vision. When communicated to the Jews, these messages are always clear and direct, whereas those to Gentiles are always symbolic dreams that only Hebrews can interpret.

The distinction between dreams and visions is similarly blurred at certain points in the New Testament, although there is an interesting contrast between them in the Gospels regarding the delivery of the news of Jesus' birth to Mary and Joseph. The angel Gabriel appears directly to Mary in a waking vision, whereas he delivers the same message to Joseph in a dream. The implication here seems to be that Mary is in a more elevated spiritual state than her husband. Dream revelations, in other words, are less venerated than visions. A comparable hierarchy of revelations is evident in **Islam**.

Muslim prophetism distinguishes the prophets according to the degree of visionary perception, from the sights and sounds of a dream to the suprasensible perception in the waking state. According to this classification, which is probably derived from criteria suggested in Hebrew Scriptures, there is the simple prophet, who sees or hears an angel in a dream. Then there is the envoy to a group, who sees the angel while awake. Finally, among the envoys there are the six great prophets, including **Muhammad**, who were charged to reveal the new law, which was dictated to them by the angel while they were awake.

No distinction between dreams and visions was made at the time of Muhammad, who received spiritual instruction in both states. Dreams played an important role in the life of the Prophet, who received his first revelation and became conscious of his vocation in a dream. His initiation into the mysteries of the cosmos occurred during a great dream known as the "Night Journey".

VISITATION DREAMS

Visitation dreams are normally dreams in which the dreamer is visited by a spiritual entity, particularly the spirit of a departed human being. Communication with the so-called dead during the waking state has been accomplished, it is claimed, through especially sensitive human beings, usually referred to as mediums. The reliability of mediumistic communication is said to depend upon the medium's sensitivity to normally unperceived entities. This mediumship can take the form of heightened sensory sensitivity such as clairvoyant (psychic sight) or clairaudient (psychic hearing) messages, as well as telepathic messages and symbolic visions.

Spiritualists theorize that the world of the spirit coexists with this world, separated by a differing "rate of vibration." During mediumship, in this view, the spirits lower their rate of vibration while the medium raises his or her vibratory rate, creating a point of contact between the two realms across which communication may occur. The same basic understanding is applied to dream visitations.

During sleep, our center of consciousness shifts from its usual preoccupation with physical concerns and withdraws into itself, so to speak. From a spiritualist point of view, this can be understood as the mind extracting itself from the dense vibrations of the physical body, and drawing closer to the **soul**. Thus, the sleeping state resembles the mediumistic state, making it easier for disembodied spirits to communicate with dreaming subjects.

VON FRANZ, MARIE-LOUISE

Marie-Louise von Franz (1915–1998) was a student of **Carl Jung**, the great Swiss psychotherapist. Not long before he passed away, Jung was asked if he believed in life after death. Asserting that he did, Jung proffered as evidence the fact that the dreams of individuals approaching death seem to disregard their own approaching mortality, as if it was a relatively insignificant transition.

Von Franz expands upon this point in *On Dreams and Death*, which was translated and published in English in 1987. She argues that dreams about a continuity beyond death cannot simply be wish-fulfillment, partially because dreamers on the edge of death dream about the death of the body in quite stark and realistic terms. If dreams were playing into the dreamer's need to deny death, then such scenes would be conspicuously absent from dreams. Of particular interest is her observation that the dreams of the dying often contain symbols of transformation, particularly death/rebirth motifs that make death appear as a kind of initiation.

VOODOO AND DREAMS

Voodoo is a Caribbean religion derived from African polytheism and Catholic Christianity. Originally a slave religion, it is especially associated with the island of Haiti, although identifiably voodoo forms of spiritual expression are also present in Jamaica and Santo Domingo. Voodoo is a derivative of the Nigerian word *vódu*, meaning tutelary deity or **demon**. Partially because of sensationalistic portrayals in the entertainment media, *voodoo* has come to have negative connotations.

Voodoo postulates a complex and extensive pantheon of divinities, referred to as *loas* or *mys-*

In voodoo, a religion practiced in the Caribbean, it is believed that the "small soul" leaves the body during dreams.

tères. A supreme being who created the world is acknowledged, although he is too distant from the world to be worshiped. Voodoo focuses instead on the more immediate divinities, serving the loas in return for favors. In line with African tradition, ancestors are revered.

The human being is pictured as being composed of several ingredients. Among these, the *gros bon ange* ("big good **angel**") and *ti bon ange* ("little good angel") constitute one's soul. The *ti bon ange* is one's individual soul or essence. This "small soul" journeys out of the body when one dreams, as well as when the body is being possessed by the loa. As in most traditional cultures, it is believed that the soul literally leaves the body during sleep and experiences a different world in dreams. This traveling is also viewed as potentially dangerous, because when the *ti bon ange* is away from the body, it is particularly vulnerable to attack by hostile forces.

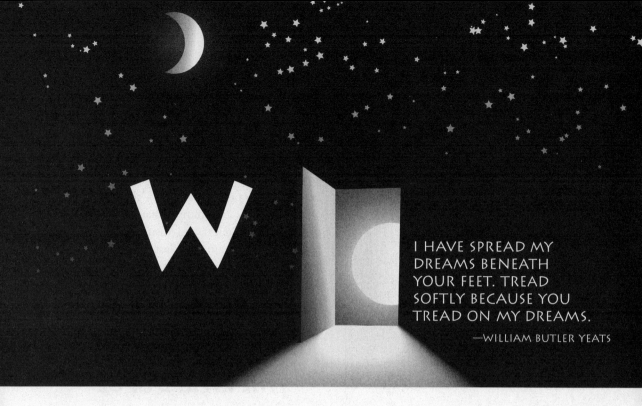

I HAVE SPREAD MY
DREAMS BENEATH
YOUR FEET. TREAD
SOFTLY BECAUSE YOU
TREAD ON MY DREAMS.

—WILLIAM BUTLER YEATS

WATER DREAMS

Water is so common in dreams, and the forms of its appearance are so diverse, that it is nearly impossible to touch on all its symbolism here. It is more feasible to discuss briefly the common associations water has in dreams and the theories behind them.

When a person dreams that he or she is emerging from a body of water (a river, lake, ocean, or even a swimming pool) it can symbolize birth. This may be the birth of a child or of an idea that the dreamer has been working on. Bathing in a dream has a few different meanings, depending on the state of the water in which one bathes. Clean water indicates good health, while dirty water foretells sickness. It is a widespread belief that when people dream about water flooding their homes they are actually receiving a prophetic dream of their own death.

When a person dreams about a large body of water, it is most commonly thought to represent that individual's **unconscious** mind. While these dreams are sometimes **nightmares** that indicate some sort of struggle within one's unconscious, they can also be very pleasant dreams. One of the most important aspects of personal dream analysis is observing the emotions associated with the dream. If the dreamer is relaxed and calm, it is doubtful that the unconscious is trying to send him or her messages of inner-turmoil. Alternatively, if the dreamer is about struggling, panicking, or even drowning, it is probably time for him or her to reflect on the aspects of a life in which he or she feels out of control.

Dreams of dirty water may signal that the unconscious mind is telling us we are in ill health.

THE WISE OLD WOMAN (OR MAN) ARCHETYPE

The great Swiss psychotherapist **Carl Jung** postulated a **collective unconscious**, which represents our inheritance of the collective experience of humankind. This storehouse of humanity's experiences exists in the form of **archetypes** (or prototypes) that unconsciously predispose us to organize our personal experiences in certain ways. We are predisposed, for instance, to perceive someone in our early environment as a mother because of the mother archetype; if our biological mother is absent during our early years, someone else (e.g., an older sister) is assimilated into this archetype, providing concrete images for our notion of mother. Jung further asserted that the archetypes of the collective unconscious shape the content of our dreams, emerging in the form of diverse **archetypal dream images**.

The wise old woman or man archetype is what Jung referred to as one's *mana* personality, representing a primordial energy that could assist one in growth and transformation or, alternatively, in destruction and disintegration. In its most positive dream manifestations, this archetype appears as an authoritative guide who leads one in the quest for growth, spiritual knowledge, or self-actualization. Almost any authority figure—a minister, teacher, doctor, parent—can embody this archetype.

THE WIZARD OF OZ

One of the more familiar classic movies, *The Wizard of Oz* contains substantial dream content. In the movie, the distinction between the dream and waking world is made by the transition to Technicolor. Not only is the whole of this movie set in the dream world, there is also the "dream within a dream" phenomena that takes place when everyone but the Tin Man falls asleep in the poppy field just outside the Emerald City. The association between poppies and dreams dates back to antiquity. The **Greek** god of sleep was said to live with his sons in a cave surrounded by poppy flowers. Hypnos (Somnus in Latin) lends his name to the botanical term for the opium poppy, *papaverum somniferum*. Morpheus was the deity of dreams, and one of Hypnos's sons is also linked to the poppy plant. Morphine, the painkiller that bears Morpheus's name, derives from the opium poppy. After the brief slumber in the poppy field, Dorothy and her companions are primed to enter the Emerald City, a utopian society extravagant in its dreamlike qualities.

It is interesting to note the way that many influential dream theories are incorporated, in an artistic or theatrical sense, into the storyline of this movie. **Sigmund Freud**'s theories of **dreamwork**, the process by which the familiar is converted to the unfamiliar and the unacceptable to the acceptable, are visually evident in this film through the use of the same actors playing two roles, one corresponding to the waking reality and one to the dream world. The transformation of characters corresponds with the description of the transformation of the residue from the preceding day in **manifest dream** content. The universal archetypes advocated by **Carl Jung** also play a role in the story. The good witch, Belinda, represents the embodiment of the "good mother" **archetype**. She is the guardian of the munchkins, who can be viewed as paralleling the children appearing in common dreams. At the other end of the spectrum is the wicked witch, who is obviously representative of the "bad mother" archetype.

HOPE IS THE DREAM OF
THE WAKING MAN.

—FRENCH PROVERB

YANSI

The Yansi belong to the great Central Bantu culture area extending across central Africa from west to east; they inhabit the lower Kwilu and Inzia rivers in Bandundu Province in the Republic of Zaire. Yansi society is characterized by a system of stratification, a system of kinship and marriage, and a priesthood, which holds the spiritual power called *lebui*. Also, in Yansi society there is a particular concern with boundaries and relations between the living and the dead, elders, medicine custodians, and ordinary people.

Dreams play a fundamental role in the life of the Yansi and are as important as waking experiences. Dreams are usually sought in order to obtain commentaries upon current circumstances. For instance, they are carefully examined when someone is ill, as well as before going on a hunt, in order to assess the chances of success. Dreams are regarded as an extraordinary phenomenon, and diverse attitudes are taken toward them by the Yansi, from admiration to fear.

Dreaming is integral to the Yansi witchcraft-sorcery-medicine complex. Among Yansi clan-elders and medicine-owners, who are wise dream interpreters and accurate oracular dreamers, the elaborate distinction made between different kinds and qualities of dreams can be seen as part of a discourse of conceptual authority. According to Mubuy Mubay Mpier's 1992 study on the semantics of Yansi dreams, the Yansi discriminate between recollected dreams that involve reality and those considered mere fantasy.

Dreams that are later concretely realized are generally considered true dreams. Typically, persons who dream true dreams are fetish- or medicine-owners. These people are often feared by Yansi because they can recount dreams that predict misfortune, tragedy, and anxiety. They can dream solutions to difficult problems, however, and foretell good fortune. Also, those dreams in which ordinary people receive information about their state of health and their problems are considered true dreams.

Dreams by infants as well as dreams whose content is removed from everyday life are a matter of indifference to the Yansi, and usually no importance is attributed to the accounts of mentally handicapped persons, although they also dream and can recount their dreams. Recalled dreams are often considered by Yansi elders as the desires or the apprehensions of waking life. In Yansi society, dreams are not considered a source of information about the psychodynamics of an individual; rather, they are taken into account in giving meaning to the actions and interactions of self and others. Dreams are the evidence of extra-human forces in relationship with human beings and are a means of acquiring knowledge about them. The best time to interpret a dream is usually thought to be the instant following its appearance.

YOGA

The two largest religions to originate in southern Asia (the geographical and cultural area that consists of contemporary India, Tibet, Pakistan, and Bangladesh) are Hinduism and **Buddhism**. Both of these complex religious traditions have been shaped by schools of philosophy that regard the world as we experience it as being in some sense "dreamlike," illusory or unreal. In terms of this metaphor, it is the goal of the religious life to "wake up" from the illusion of this world.

The Buddhist exercise practice of yoga has a number of benefits, including helping one learn how to control his or her dreams.

The method by which the "awakening" is accomplished is often conceptualized as some form of yoga. In the West, the widespread popularity of hatha yoga has led the term *yoga* to be associated with an exotic set of physical exercises. However, in its original southern Asian setting, yoga encompasses a complex variety of practices, all of which aim to release the individual aspirant from the cycle of reincarnation.

Despite Hinduism's traditional discourse about "awakening from the dream," a form of yoga directed specifically at controlling the dream state does not seem to have developed until it emerged in Tibetan Buddhism (although it may have had a predecessor in Tantric Hinduism). According to tradition, the teacher Marpa introduced six yogas, including the teaching on dreams, in Tibet in the eleventh century.

The dream yoga of Tibet involves what has come to be called **lucid dreaming** in the West—a state in which the dreamer is aware that he or she is dreaming. The lucid dream state is not itself a form of meditation. Rather, the yoga of the dream state is practiced while one is in a lucid dream. During sleep, the yogi (one who practices yoga) exercises control over the landscape of his or her dream, learning that the dream world is transitory, malleable, and a function of consciousness. If the yogi has properly digested the teaching that this world and the dreamworld are both creations of the mind, the yogi's dream experience helps him or her realize the illusory nature of this world. Learning to control the dream state also prepares the yogi to determine where his or her consciousness goes after death, a major goal of many schools of Tibetan Buddhism.

YORUBA

The Yoruba, considered the most urbane group in Nigeria, with the longest history of Westernization, Christianity, and education, live in southwestern Nigeria and the adjacent sections of Dahomey. They include the patrician families of Lagos and have an ancient tradition of kingship. Yoruba paganism is characterized by a variety of theological elements, such as a supreme being, subordinate deities, ancestors, sacred kings, all sorts of local spirits, and an elaborate system of divination.

According to Yoruba thought, the human being possesses multiple souls, each representing a significant dimension of social experience. Among these is the life-breath, given by Olorun at birth, containing one's personal vitality and strength. The life-breath is nourished by food and may be trapped by witches when it leaves the body in sleep during dreams, causing death.

Peter McKenzie's study of dreams and visions among the Yoruba in the middle of the nineteenth century reports the accounts of dreams told by the Yoruba to the catechists of Christian missions. These dreams can be classified according to four significant themes. First of all is the traditional Yoruba use of dreams in dealing with the contingencies attributed to the gods. The second of them concerns dreams associated with crises of religious identity. Third is a series of explicit accounts of conversion in which dreams are featured. The fourth theme deals with visions of sick and dying early Christian converts.

According to McKenzie's study, traditional Yoruba recollections of dreams contain the themes of neglect of social obligations, estrangement from the gods, and the threatening isolation of sickness, captivity, or a journey. Dreams are used by the Yoruba to achieve both social and personal integration. They can also be adapted to the needs of deep religious change, generally experienced as a crisis of identity or as spiritual conversion.

A SKILLFUL MAN READS
HIS DREAMS FOR SELF-
KNOWLEDGE, YET NOT
THE DETAILS BUT THE
QUALITY.

—RALPH WALDO EMERSON

ZEZURU

The social world of Zezuru, the Shona-speaking peoples who live in the Harare region of Zimbabwe, is divided into various categories. *Mwari*, or God, heads the whole world, that is then divided up into two elements: *Shona*, consisting of the various clans which are linked to the hero spirits and are further divided into lineages, linked to the ancestors; and *non-Shona*, made up of the observable world and of the *shave* spirits (spirits that are not concerned with morality as such but are generally responsible for inoffensive individual differences between people).

In Zezuru society, it is believed that at death a man's personality becomes a spirit that plays a fundamental part in the social affairs of living men. The *makombwe*, or heroes, who are believed to have lived on earth north of the Zambezi River before the founding of Zezuru society, have special powers of healing, prophecy, and rain-making, whereas the *vadzimu*, or ancestor spirits, are more directly concerned with the day-to-day affairs of their descendants. The heroes and the ancestors represent the bastions of morality, whereas the *shave* spirits, which are believed to originate from outside Zezuru society, are responsible for individual talents and for individual differences between people. Healers generally maintain that they derive their powers from their association with a *shave* spirit.

Like the Zulu, the Zezuru believe that dreams mediate between the spirits and the living and make connections between the present and the past. The spirits are believed to use the dreams of the healers to achieve their purposes.

Through dreams they can call, inform, guide, permit, correct, and shape healers, as well as reach the community and direct the actions of its members. The spirits of witches or lost souls can use dreams for nefarious ends: they can cause harm, demand retribution, or scare the dreamer.

In Zezuru society, dreams are claimed to offer protection to the healers by foretelling major incidents and allowing them to prepare for them. Additionally, as Pamela Reynolds's research shows, dreams can also be used to constitute the self, by mediating between the child and society and the supernatural, and can be considered a means of both individuation and socialization.

Children's dreams are sometimes interpreted by adults as direct messages from the spirits, though at other times they are dismissed as meaningless. Sometimes they provoke anxiety in adults, and may even result in punishment. Families seek interpretation of children's dreams usually because they coincide with events or signs such as incidents of illness or misfortune.

Children, who usually know the interpretation that is given to their dreams, choose what to do with it. Thus, they can repress or recall some or all of their dreams, and they can match their behavior to the interpretation or reject the interpretation. In addition, children can use dreams as part of the conversation between themselves and healers, who are most often grandparents, and dreams may eventually become accepted as part of an initiation of the child into the role of healer. Reynolds was struck by the quality of the relationships between healers and children, which, besides the help and companionship that is often observed between the old and young among the Zezuru, offers a forum for the transmission of knowledge and for the exploration of the self, which is conducted in part through the use of dreams.

ZULU

Dreams play an important role for the Zulu, a Nguni people who have lived in southern Africa since the third century C.E. Clan, lineage, and one's age-set determine the basic bonds of Zulu society. All individuals belong to a particular lineage, consisting of the descendants of a common ancestor who founded their line. In addition, within each lineage various subdivisions trace their ancestry to a common grandfather. Above the lineage is the clan, consisting of numerous lineages linked together by a common founder after whom the clan was named. Each person belongs to an age-set including everyone within a three-year span.

The Zulu traditionally live in huts, in the back of which is generally situated a small area reserved for the ancestors, who are believed to dwell in the village. The ancestors are often consulted, and at times are believed to visit the living through dreams, which are interpreted by the diviners, or in the form of snakes. More rarely they return in the form of their ghost, when the appropriate rituals have not been observed after a death.

Zulu dreams, which can greatly influence the life of the individual, are the principal channel of communication with the ancestors, who play a fundamental role in Zulu society. In particular, they are believed to offer protection to members of their lineage, by whom they must be appeased and respected. Through dreams, the ancestral spirits can express both approval and disapproval of the actions—past, present, and future—of their descendants. Also, dreams are of diagnostic and prognostic significance in the tribal medical system, especially when psychogenic disorders occur.

Many dreams are believed to be prophetic and to indicate a course of action to be followed

heard. For example, in Zulu thinking a pain in the shoulders after dreaming represents a sign of spirit activity.

An analysis of Zulu dream contents by the psychiatrist S.G. Lee emphasizes the small number of major categories into which Zulu dreams can be classified. In this study, Zulu dreams also seem to be stereotyped in terms of central imagery.

Lee also compares the dreams of men and women, which appear to be circumscribed and influenced by the social pressures and sanctions of the culture. The dreams of women, in particular, seem to be largely circumscribed by prohibitions from the indigenous system of social sanctions of the last century, and generally their dreams appear to be appropriate to their age, status, and role. Additionally, according to Lee there is little symbolism in dreams connected to important events of personal life, and local interpretations of symbols coincide with orthodox psychoanalytical interpretations.

A Zulu woman performs a traditional dance. In Zulu culture, dreams are a way in which people may learn to communicate with their ancestors.

by the dreamer. For example, as Lucien Levy-Bruhl suggests, a Zulu will treat a friend as an enemy because of a dream in which the latter intended to hurt him. The omen of the dream may be either similar or opposite to its apparent content, presenting a pattern typical of the interpretation of dreams in Western countries, where dream reversal is often suspected.

Dreams possess the status of superior realities and are generally seen to have an active power. Their reality is not limited to what is seen and

ZUNI

With few exceptions, the Zuni of New Mexico do not speak the names of dead persons. Furthermore, they describe visitations of these persons in night dreams as horrible experiences that require a cure through the performance of specified religious rituals, including, in some cases, initiation into either the tribal organization known as the Kachina Society or else into a medicine society.

The living human is referred to as the *shi'-nanne* ("flesh") and the soul or psyche is the *pinanne* ("wind" or "air"). Although the latter is located in the heart and is thus a body-soul, it can leave the body under certain circumstances, such as during trance, curing, singing, and dreaming. It is believed to arrive at birth and to depart at death, although after death it remains closely connected to the earth, toward which it acts as a strong moral agent. According to Zuni, during the dream experience a part of the dreamer's self wanders outside the body and has experiences in remote places, or in past or future times.

One theory concerning which part of the self is involved in dreaming postulates that one's mind or emotions leave the body and wander outside into the night world. Another theory postulates that one's breath—*pinanne*—wanders out into the world. The Zuni verb for dreaming is intransitive, indicating that the Zuni are passive within the dreaming process itself. All dreams are classi-

fied as either good or bad depending on the emotional reactions that they originate. Within the bad, or nightmare, category there is a subcategory of violent dreams, in which the dreamer can perform no voluntary movements.

The Zuni share their dreaming experiences among members of their matrilocal extended household, as well as among friends. However, not all dream experiences are immediately reported, and some of them are reported many years later. Accounts of old dreams consist of both bad dreams, including **nightmares**, and good dreams, whereas reports of recent dream experiences always concern bad dreams. According to Zuni, bad dreams, in which dead people usually appear, should be reported because they must not be allowed to become realized or completed.

INTRODUCTION TO DREAM SYMBOLS

One can walk into any bookstore, even the truncated variety found in shopping malls, and find any number of dream dictionaries—books that claim to interpret dreams according to the particular components of one's dream landscape. The tradition of dream dictionaries is quite old, though ancient and modern interpretations diverge considerably, with the thrust of modern dream dictionaries decidedly psychological. Before the advent of modern psychology and psychoanalysis, the dominant approach to dreams was to view them as bearing omens which augured future events.

Modern dream dictionaries vary considerably in quality. The best provide suggestive starting points for interpreting one's own dreams. The worst advance rigid interpretations that make a pretense of having captured once and for all time the definitive meaning of particular dream symbols.

While the meaning of some dreams may seem fairly straightforward, as in the case of dreams that are residues of our daily activities and experiences, other dreams are very disjointed and are frequently dismissed as meaningless. Because dreams often speak in a language of symbols and images, some of the more unusual items in dream landscapes come from the dreaming mind's tendency to give concrete expression to figures of speech. Thus, if someone has a dream that she shows up at work and the office building or factory looks like a beehive, it may indicate that one feels one is "busy as a bee"; alternatively, it may reflect the feeling that one is just a "drone."

Other dreams are more complex, and require a detailed knowledge of the dreamer's life before they can be interpreted. This is especially the case when the dream component is something as concrete as a beehive or a bee. One needs to ask oneself if the particular dream element flows directly out of personal associations, as in the case of someone who has worked with bees, or someone who has traumatic memories from having been attacked by bees. In such cases, the meaning of bees in a dream is likely to be purely personal.

The following dream dictionary makes no pretense of being exhaustive, or of offering the final word on the meanings of dreams. The interpretations are meant to be suggestive rather than definitive—they show how one goes about exploring the range of possible valences of a symbol, rather than offering the final word on their meaning. As with all such symbols, the feeling, tone, and other settings of the dream indicate whether any of the proffered interpretations are appropriate. Where the interpretations are clearly inapplicable, the reader should not feel bound to accept them.

—Evelyn Dorothy Oliver

DREAM SYMBOLS

ABANDONMENT

Dreams of being abandoned may simply reflect one's actual situation (e.g., as in the case of someone being divorced) or arise from fears of being deserted or rejected. Similarly, such dreams may occur around the time of the death of a loved one or when some other loss occurs. On a more positive note, abandonment may also symbolize the letting go of old attitudes, letting go of the past. Abandonment is a powerful general metaphor for many kinds of anxieties because it harkens back to the experience of feeling left out or left behind by our parents when we were children. Thus, a wide range of different situations, from simple loneliness to a sense of betrayal, can be represented in abandonment dreams.

ABBEY

Dreaming of a convent or monastery may indicate that the dreamer needs to spend some time alone reflecting, or even needs to seek spiritual nourishment. Alternatively, it may symbolize isolation from the normal flow of life.

ABBOT

Dreaming of the superior of a monastery may relate to authority, either secular or spiritual. It is sometimes a symbol of a spiritual guide.

ABYSS

An abyss is a natural symbol of emptiness and meaninglessness. It can also represent the need to detach oneself from an overwhelming condition or relationship.

ACCIDENT

Accident dreams can represent a variety of different situations, from straightforward fears of being in an actual, physical accident (or memories of such an accident) to a sense that one is headed for a more metaphorical "crack up." We may be so preoccupied with something that we are not paying attention, or so involved in the rat race that we need to slow down. As extensions of ourselves, vehicles often represent the physical body, so an accident dream may indicate a health problem or anxieties about health. If the general tone of the dream is positive (even if violent), accidents may symbolize something or some part of life of which one is letting go.

ACID

Can refer to something eating away at one's insides. Alternatively, maybe an idea, a relationship, or a product is going through the "acid test." Might also allude to an "acid tongue."

ACTOR

In Jungian psychology, the persona—the side of ourselves that we present to the world—is portrayed as an actor. Unless we are somehow involved in actual acting or have unrealized ambitions to act, dreams in which we or others appear as actors tend to refer to the persona. As with other symbols, much depends on the overall tone of the dream. When they are unpleasant, acting dreams frequently refer to situations in which we feel forced to "put on an act" or situations in which we feel ourselves acting out the expectations of others.

ADVERTISEMENT

Seeing or hearing an advertisement in a dream could mean that one's unconscious mind is attempting to communicate with the conscious mind. Alternatively, perhaps one wishes either to attract the attention of others or to communicate something about oneself to others.

AGGRESSION

Aggression in a dream may indicate repressed sexual or ego needs, particularly if the dreamer is the primary aggressor. More generally, aggressive action in a dream often reflects a conflict in one's life.

AIR/ATMOSPHERE

Air was one of the four elements of classical Greek philosophy (the others were earth, fire, and water). As such it is a complex symbol, and interpreting the meaning of air depends heavily on the larger context in the dream. The classical element air symbolizes the intellect, ideas, creativity, communication, travel, and related matters. Thus, the state of the air (e.g., whether clear or foggy) may be a commentary on one's ideas or communications.

AIRPLANE

Airplanes in dreams may carry the same connotations as air (e.g., ideas, intellect) or simply represent flying dreams. Particularly if one is the pilot, an airplane may represent one's body, freedom, the power to "rise above" a situation, soaring to new heights, or even escape from everyday concerns.

AIRPORT

Some new idea or venture may be ready to take off. If planes can't get off the ground, the venture may be grounded for awhile. An airport can also represent a transition in one's life.

AIR RAID

In most cases, the meaning of an air raid is straightforward. It reflects a feeling of being assaulted, of being under attack.

ALCOHOL

The meaning of consuming an alcoholic beverage depends on certain other specific contents of the dream as well as on the individual's associations with alcohol. Negatively, alcohol represents escapism, addiction, and self-destructive tendencies. More positively, alcohol may indicate simple socializing or the release of one's inhibitions. Alcohol has also been utilized as a religious symbol, as in the "new wine" of the Christian tradition, and to indicate certain mystical states in Sufism.

ALIEN

An alien in a dream may indicate that there is difficulty adjusting to new conditions or a new environment. Space aliens may indicate issues about ones boundaries; the dreamer may feel his or her personal life is being invaded.

ALLEY

An alleyway may simply be one form of the symbol of the path, which indicates seeking, transformation, and the transition from one stage of life to another. Alleys have certain other connotations, however, such as that of a shortcut, a sidetrack, or a dead end. Alleys also convey a sense of being narrow and limited, therefore requiring that they be followed closely. In contemporary society, alleyways often have sinister connotations as a location where one might be attacked. As with all dream symbols, the tone and setting of the dream determine which meaning is indicated.

ALTAR

The meaning of an altar depends on certain other specific contents of the dream, as well as on individual associations. Clearly, an altar has a more complex range of meanings for a priest than for someone who has never attended a religious service. When an altar does not relate to worship or to specific associations with one's church, it often connotes sacrifice (e.g., letting go of something, symbolically letting go of parts of oneself), dedication (e.g., entering into a marriage), or new beginnings (renewal).

AMBUSH

An ambush is a surprise attack. Concretely, it may represent some unpleasant surprise or unanticipated turn for the worse in one's life. If one was headed for a clear destination at the time of the ambush, it may represent a sense of being blocked. Ambushes may also be more general symbols of sudden loss and emotional upheaval.

AMPUTATION

Amputation has different connotations depending on the tone of the dream. When amputations do not refer to actual removal of limbs, they refer to the radical removal of something from one's life. Positively, a dream about an amputation may refer to the removal of something that, although formerly quite close to the individual, is no longer necessary or desirable. Negatively, it may mean the abandonment of talents and powers represented by the amputated limb. Sometimes amputation may also represent a situation that one has been ignoring but which has finally reached a crisis point.

ANCHOR

Anchors generally convey positive connotations of security, stability, and a harbor against storms. Large bodies of water frequently symbolize the unconscious (or, sometimes, the emotions), making boats vehicles for negotiating the unconscious. Anchors may thus indicate a stable relationship with the unconscious or shelter against the "storms" of the emotions. Loss of an anchor indicates feeling adrift. Less positively, anchors may symbolize a resistance to change or a clinging to a sense of security. As with all dream symbols, the tone and setting of the dream indicate which interpretation is appropriate.

ANESTHETIC

To dream of being anaesthetized may represent the residue of a memory (e.g., from a medical operation). It could also reflect a desire to be relieved of some painful experience—physical, mental, or emotional.

ANGELS

Angels symbolize purity and goodness. They are also thought of as protectors and guides. Traditionally, they are conceived of as messengers of God to humanity. In psychological terms, one may think of them as messengers from the unconscious or the higher self. If an angel (who in a dream may simply be a figure clothed in white) conveys a message to the dreamer, it is an indication that the message is important and that one should pay careful attention to it.

ANIMALS

The symbolism of animals is highly complex, as different creatures have been used to represent a variety of different notions. A proper interpretation also depends on one's personal associations with animals. Generically, animals symbolize the physical, instinctual, "animal" self, and wild dream beasts that one cannot specifically identify usually represent this aspect of the self (or "beast-like" people in one's environment). One should be careful about this generalization, however, because certain other, more specific animals (e.g., birds) can symbolize precisely the opposite (e.g., the higher self or the soul).

ANTLERS

Because they are particularly characteristic of certain male animals, antlers tend to represent masculinity, masculine sexuality (virility), and male aggression (particularly conflict between males). In a dream, they may represent masculine power and assertiveness or a metaphorical "trophy of the hunt."

ANTS

Ants have a rich symbolic tradition out of proportion to their small size. Positively, they have been used to represent diligence, hard work, and foresight (because they store up food for lean times). Less positively, they have been deployed as a symbol of conformity and mass action. Most contemporary urban dwellers experience ants only as pests that disturb picnics and invade our kitchens, making them creatures that "bug"

human beings. As with all dream symbols, the tone and setting of the dream indicate which interpretation is appropriate.

ANXIETY

Worries, fears, and apprehension that may have been discounted or banished from one's mind often find expression in dreams of anxiety.

APE

As our closest animal relatives, apes can represent the natural, instinctual wisdom that most of us have lost, particularly if the dream animal is a gray-haired ape. We also sometimes associate simians (especially chimpanzees) with humor, and with the "chained up" animal self inside (e.g., King Kong). "Ape" can also mean to mimic.

APPLAUSE

Giving oneself recognition or the desire for recognition.

APPLES

To dream of bountiful apple trees traditionally signifies good fortune and the realization of the fruits of endeavor. Alternatively, rotten apples, or apple cores, may mean that what the dreamer is striving for is not fulfilling, and perhaps, even harmful.

APRON

Aprons were formerly associated with certain masculine occupations such as blacksmithing, but in contemporary society they are almost always associated with the kitchen and the female domestic sphere: mother, home and cooking. Apron strings have the less positive connotations of being "tied" to the home, one's mother, or wife.

ARMOR

Armor, or a shield, in a dream can have the positive meaning of being protected. Negatively, armor can connote psychological armor that prevents individuals from opening up and sharing themselves.

ARMS

Arms are the functional and creative extensions of the body, allowing one to hold and embrace one's desires. If the arms are obstructed in any way, a loss of one's power and ability may be indicated.

ARREST

If one is being arrested in a dream, it could be a reflection of feeling guilty about something one has done or something one would like to do. As a metaphor, it can mean a process that has been cut off prematurely, as in the expression "arrested development."

ARROW

Arrows have a rich and complex set of meanings. A person can be described as "straight as an arrow." Cupid is known for using his bow and arrow to shoot love into a lover's heart. Arrows can represent conflict, war, and aggression. More positively, they are used symbolically in business to point in the direction of company goals. An arrow also has masculine, phallic connotations, so that shooting someone with an arrow in a dream can have sexual overtones. Less obviously, arrows have been associated with inspiration, truth, sudden illumination, and poetry.

ARTIST

Artists are natural symbols of creativity. Dreaming of an artist at work may indicate a repressed desire, and possibly a potential talent, to express oneself in a creative arena.

ASCENT

Dreaming of moving up—in an elevator or by other means—indicates accomplishment and reward for achievements.

ASHES

Ashes are usually associated with dreams of loss or bereavement. The dreamer could be experiencing the physical death of a loved one or the separation of a friend or spouse. It could also be an indication of lost chances or opportunities.

ASS

An animal that signifies hard work and extreme stubbornness, the ass is also associated with stupidity.

ATTACK

If one is being attacked in a dream, it can reflect feelings about something threatening in one's environment. Defensiveness. The same kind of dream can mean feeling threatened by one's own repressed aggressiveness, anger, or sexuality, especially if one is being attacked by an animal. If one is the attacker, it can reflect everything from self-assertiveness to the desire to attack something or someone in one's environment. "Attack" can also be used as a metaphor, as in attacks of hunger, illness, conscience, guilt, etc.

AUDIENCE

If the dreamer is in front of an audience, this could reflect a situation in one's environment in which one feels that one is attracting more attention than usual. It could also represent anxiety about being exposed. If one dreams about being in an audience, one might be witnessing something about oneself or some aspect of one's life.

AUTUMN (FALL)

The autumn season has mixed associations. On the one hand, the fall is traditionally harvest time, indicating a sense that one is finally reaping the benefits of prior efforts. On the other hand, it is associated with a winding down of energies before the barrenness of winter, as in the expression "the autumn of one's life."

AVALANCHE

An avalanche signifies being overwhelmed, especially by emotions that could not be experienced or previously expressed owing to the "frozen" nature of the individual.

AWAKENING

A dream of waking up while still dreaming may indicate awakening to new states of consciousness in ideas and creativity.

AXE/HATCHET

Axes have a complex range of meanings. Their meaning must be determined from the larger context of any particular dream. Axes are symbols of execution (beheading), and can therefore represent anxieties about being punished or killed. We also speak about being "axed" from our position of employment (job anxiety). In ancient times, axes were made from meteorites, and they were associated with the divinities of the sky and the power expressed by rain (fertility), thunder (power), and lightning (illumination). In the hands of the dreamer, axes are thus symbols of personal power; how they are utilized shows how the individual is using or misusing his or her power.

DREAM SYMBOLS

B

BABY

Babies are very complex dream symbols that represent everything from the rebirth of the self, the emergence of new possibilities in your life, or being rendered helpless and vulnerable. Even a new baby in the dreamer's life may be indicated by this dream, but not always. This symbol often shows up when the dreamer is entering a new phase of life, which is like giving birth to oneself. Bad dreams in which a baby is deformed, has injuries, or is stillborn are not uncommon for parents who are anxious about the pregnancy, especially for expectant couples who have never had children before. Even though it feels like a dreadfully horrible nightmare, it's usually nothing to be taken seriously, unless it becomes a nightly event. (Also see Embryo, Miscarriage, Pregnant).

BACHELOR

Bachelors can represent being alone; the feeling of loneliness. Could indicate a desire for freedom, particularly if the dreamer is married.

BACK

Because of the dreaming mind's tendency to literalize metaphors, the back can signify meanings from familiar sayings. For example, in a dream the back may mean "watch your back" (beware of treachery).

BACKWARD

A dream of moving backward may mean the dreamer feels he or she is losing ground in some endeavor. Retracing one's steps may indicate that information from the past may be needed to bring about an understanding of a current situation, especially one that has gone wrong.

BAG

Bags can carry connotations of secrecy, particularly sexual secrets (bags can symbolize wombs). Placing something in a bag or similar receptacle may represent something unpleasant we wish to avoid, so a bag dream could indicate the repression of awareness. Bags can also hold gifts and nourishment (grocery bags), and represent our hopes, wishes and plans. The key to determining which of these meanings apply is the emotional tenor of the dream. (See also Basket, Sack).

BAIT

As a lure, bait is usually associated with fishing, although in a dream fishing can symbolize anything from fishing for a deal to fishing for a compliment.

BAKER/BAKING

Baking can represent something on which one is working, perhaps even psychological reflection (working on oneself). It also might refer to the connotations of expressions like "half-baked" or "If I knew you were coming I would have baked a cake."

BALL

Balls can indicate everything from a game or some other form of relaxation to memories from our childhood. Balls can also have metaphorical connotations, such as being "tossed around," "the ball's in your court," "having a ball" (having a good time) and "having balls" (courage). Any of these may be helpful in determining the meaning of this dream. A deeper, more universal symbolism is that circles and balls represent completeness and wholeness.

BALLOON

Balloons are often used to celebrate someone or something. In dreams they sometimes also represent the freeing and releasing of feelings or creative ideas, while the strings keep them from flying away. A deflated balloon may indicate disappointment.

BANANA

The banana has been seen as a sexual symbol, as in the jest, "Is that a banana in your pocket or are you just glad to see me?" But since the banana is the staple food for monkeys, the dreamer may need to get serious about some situation in which they are "monkeying around."

BAND

Dreaming of participating in a band indicates a committed team player. A band can be a complex dream symbol, depending upon the dreamer's past associations.

BANDAGE

The sense of being hurt, either physically or emotionally. It can also represent the sense of healing.

BANK

A bank in a dream may signify something that needs safekeeping. Further, it indicates solidity, stability, and security. Note whether the dreamer feels overdrawn or secure to indicate whether he or she is maintaining a balance in business or personal life.

BAPTISM

To be baptized in a dream may signal that the dreamer is undergoing spiritual renewal in waking life. Perhaps the dreamer has been going through great change and upheaval and has come through it a new person.

BAR/ROD

The male member. Power. Rigidity. What we do with a bar in a dream can indicate how we are expressing our power. Also note "bar" in the sense of blocking the way, or a barrier, as in the expression "color bar."

BAR/SALOON

Bars can have a range of meanings, depending on our personal associations. They could indicate good times and congeniality, or escapism and loneliness.

BARRIER

A barrier may signify that the dreamer is experiencing some obstacle in an arena of his or her life.

BASEMENT/CELLAR

Unless one's dream flows directly out of associations with an actual basement, the connotations of an underground room are obvious enough, which is that a basement represents the unconsciousness. (Freudians view basements as symbols of sexual energy.) Being afraid of going into a basement in a dream, for example, often symbolizes fear of the unknown or fear of repressed aspects of oneself. And being locked in the basement can indicate feeling immobilized by the power of the unconscious.

BASKET

For traditional psychiatrists, baskets, like almost any receptacle into which something can be put, can represent the female principle. Baskets have more general connotations with harvests, babies, baked goods, and so forth, any of which could be indicated, depending on what the dreamer sees in the basket during her or his dream. An empty basket, on the other hand, can symbolize a feeling of emptiness or a sense of lack. (See also Bag).

BAT (ANIMAL)

Bats symbolize the powers of the unknown or of the unconscious. Negatively, they can represent fear, the threatening power of the unknown, and, traditionally, death. Positively, as creatures who are quite at home in the dark, bats can also indicate the skill and knowledge to face the unknown and/or the unconsciousness.

BAT (BASEBALL, CRICKET AND OTHER SPORTS)

Unless one's dream flows directly out of associations with actual games and bats—either in childhood or in the present—the usual connotations of a stick with which one hits things is that of violence and aggression, though it can sometimes represent authority. Traditional psychiatrists also view anything long and straight—especially something like a bat—as a symbol of the male principle.

BATH

To determine the meaning of bathing in a dream, one might first ask what the individual associates with bathing. For some people it is simply cleaning, so a dream of bathing indicates the cleansing, or need for cleansing, of some area of life. For other people, a bathtub represents the supreme arena of relaxation, during which she or he is free from the demands of work and from the rest of the family. Baths can also represent baptisms, an initiation ritual in which the old person is cleansed or purified to make way for the rebirth of the individual undergoing the baptism. Finally, water represents the unconscious, so bathing can mean immersion in the unconsciousness.

BAY

A body of water often represents the unconscious, so the shoreline of a bay indicates the threshold between conscious and unconscious. As an open semi-circle, a bay can also represent female sexuality. Additionally, it might refer to idioms such as to "keep one at bay." (See also Beach).

BEACH

Similar to the meaning of bay, the threshold between the conscious and unconscious mind. To most people, beaches also represent recreation and relaxation. Where we go to absorb the light from the sun. (See also Bay, Sand).

BEANS

Beans often have individual meanings that depend on the dreamer's personal associations with this particular legume. Beans may, for instance, be tied to memories of being nurtured by one's mother as a child. From the perspective of traditional psychiatry, beans can symbolize the phallus and fertility. In folklore, there is the story about a magic bean ("Jack and the Beanstalk") in which a bean plant provided access to a different realm and, ultimately, to wealth. In the ancient world, such as in classical Greece, beans were a sacred food, associated with the underworld, the dead, transmigration, and immortality.

BEAR

As large, powerful creatures, bears are natural symbols for strength and power. As potentially fierce animals, they can also represent the untamed, animal side of the self. Paradoxically, bears are also regarded as soft, cuddly creatures, and thus can symbolize the softer side of human nature. (See also Teddy Bear.)

BEAVER

Beavers have many different symbolic possibilities. In particular, our culture tends to associate beavers with industriousness, as in the expression "busy as a beaver." In slang usage, this animal also has sexual connotations. Finally, beavers build dams which, because emotions are often symbolized by water, can indicate building emotional barriers.

BED/BEDROOM

Beds and bedrooms have a range of different meanings, from rest and sleep to sex and marriage. In dreams of marriage or romance, the state of a bed, whether neat or disordered, can be interpreted as a symbolic comment on the state of a relationship. Also, something underneath a bed may show that something about a relationship is not out in the open. (See also Mattress).

BEES

Bees have a rich symbolic tradition out of proportion to their small size. Positively, they have been used to represent diligence, hard work, and organization. Less positively, they have been deployed as a symbol of conformity and mass action. Bees or honey in dreams sometimes carry connotations found in common metaphors, such as "busy as a bee," "flitting from flower to flower," a "drone," and "you can catch more flies with honey than with vinegar." Some people fear bees because of their sting. As with all dream symbols, the tone and setting of the dream indicate which interpretation is appropriate.

BEGGAR

There are some obvious associations with a beggar, such as feeling needy or feeling one has to beg for what one wants. Perhaps a feeling of failure (one is "reduced to begging"). Finally, it may represent inner needs or desires one does not feed, and which have thus reduced the person to the status of beggar.

BEHEADING

A dream of being beheaded may indicate traumatic memories about bad judgments and wrong decisions made by the dreamer. The head symbolizes the intellect, so beheading can also represent alienation from feelings or from one's own body. (See also Decapitation, Guillotine).

BELL

Something calling for attention. Perhaps a warning bell or an alarm. Bells are also sounded at beginnings and endings. In Western culture, bells are associated with weddings (wedding bells) and freedom (the liberty bell). Also, bellwethers influence or presage the future.

BIBLE

The meaning of a Bible in a dream often depends on one's religious upbringing. Can indicate insight (revealed knowledge), "good news," tradition, or even intolerance ("Bible thumpers"). The Bible is often used metaphorically to describe authoritative publications in other realms, as in the "bible of marketing" or the "back packer's bible."

BICYCLE

Getting somewhere through personal effort. Depending on one's childhood experiences, bicycles can also represent the freedom of youth. There is also an idiomatic expression, "like a fish needs a bicycle," which refers to something one does not need.

BIRDS

Birds are complex symbols with many possible meanings. As creatures that fly aloft with no attachment to the ground, they can represent freedom, either physical or psychological. Because they navigate in an unseen—and thus seemingly spiritual—medium, birds can have a variety of different religious meanings, as messengers of the divine (e.g., the Holy Spirit), as symbols of the soul, as heralds of spiritual aspiration (the desire to "soar aloft"), and so on. Blackbirds were traditionally thought of as omens of death, although they can also represent the shadow side of the self. Various other meanings are associated with particular kinds of birds (e.g., vultures). Also, birds in dreams sometimes allude to such metaphors as "bird-brained."

BIRTH

Dreams of oneself or others giving birth most obviously relate to actual physical birth. Pregnant women and the husbands of pregnant women often dream about strange or difficult births (e.g., giving birth to puppies). This merely reflects anxiety about the birth process and should not be taken as indicating a difficult birth

or a deformed child. Birth can also symbolize the beginning of a new idea or project. It also often represents the beginning of a new stage of life, in which one feels "reborn" in some sense.

BITE

If one is being bitten in a dream, it can reflect feelings about something threatening in one's environment, or feeling threatened by one's own repressed anger or sexuality. If the dreamer is doing the biting, it can reflect everything from self-assertiveness to the desire to attack something or someone in one's environment. Biting finds expression in an usually large range of idioms that might find expression in dreams: "bite the bullet," "their bark is worse than their bite," "bite off more than you can chew," "bite the dust," "bite the hand that feeds you," "bite their head off," and "they won't bite." (See also Dentures, Teeth).

BLINDNESS/BLINDFOLD

Dreams about being blind or dreams in which someone else is blind only rarely indicate the state of physical blindness. As a dream symbol, blindness represents lack of awareness, either being truly unaware of something important that is occurring in one's life or "turning a blind eye" to something about which one does not wish to know. Also, because our culture associates blindfolds with firing squads, blindfolds may indicate the sense of carrying out an execution, or of being executed.

BLOCKAGE

A blockage of any kind signifies repressed expression and depleted energy flow. The dreamer should identify where the blockage is, such as at the throat where one cannot express or voice opinions.

BLOOD

Blood has a rich and complex symbology and can represent any number of different kinds of human experiences. Because of certain familiar experiences and metaphors, many of these do not require explanation (e.g., menstrual blood may symbolize fertility; one can be "bled dry"; one may have "blood on one's hands"). Blood often represents vitality and the life force. Images of confused, bloody violence often occur in the dreams of people undergoing some sort of emotional upheaval.

BOAR

The wild boar is an aggressive and potentially dangerous animal. As a cliché, the boar is used to depreciate the personality of some people; e.g., the statement, "they are such a boar." Perhaps the dreamer is bored by a person or a situation (or have they become the boar?)

BOAT

See Ship.

BODY

Dreams that somehow emphasize the physical body may represent something about one's state of health. Because our personal identities are so tied up with the body, the body can also appear as a more general symbol of the self (e.g., a naked body may indicate that we feel exposed). Dead bodies are an entirely different matter. (See also Death).

BOMB

A bomb is quite an attention-getter if it goes off in a dream. Perhaps a situation is becoming too explosive and the dreamer needs to tread carefully to avoid "land mines." Alternatively, perhaps the dreamer is so tightly wound because of some situation that he or she feels ready to explode.

BONE

Bones can obviously represent death, either literal or metaphorical. They can also symbolize a state of reduction or deprivation (as in being "stripped to the bare bones" and being left with a "skeleton crew"). Less ominously, bones may simply refer to the structure of something.

BOOK

Books often symbolize knowledge and wisdom. Dusty old books may represent neglected or forgotten knowledge, or an earlier "chapter" of one's life. Opening or closing a book may symbolize opening or closing a stage in one's life. Other meanings embodied in familiar expressions may be evoked in dreams, such as the connotations of "bookworm" and "book learning" (abstract knowledge without the benefit of practical experience available from the "book of life"). To someone reared in a traditional Christian home, "the Book" represents the Bible and God's commandments.

BOSS

Dreaming of one's boss may indicate over involvement with work. Alternatively, it may represent a parental figure—the father if the boss is a man, and the mother if the boss is a woman.

BOTTLE

A bottle of wine can mean celebration, the good life. Or, more negatively, "hitting the bottle" or to be "on the bottle." A baby bottle can be associated with infantile desires or, more positively, nurturance. We also talk about how one "bottles up" emotions, or how "the genie is out of the bottle."

BOTTLENECK

A bottleneck may mean the dreamer is squeezing through a tight situation.

BOX

Boxes have a complex range of meanings, so deciphering the meaning of a box that appears in a dream is often difficult. For Freud, boxes represented the womb or the vagina. Much depends on one's circumstances and on the particular disposition of the box in a dream. During a move, boxes in a dream might simply reflect the moving experience. Certain common metaphors, such as "feeling boxed in," can be expressed by boxes in dreams. Boxes may contain danger (as in "Pandora's box") or gifts (a "gift box").

BREAD

Break often represents our source of nourishment. Less obviously, it is often used to refer to financial "nourishment," as in one's "bread and butter." Similarly, the expression that one "cannot live by bread alone" indicates that one needs more than simple, physical nourishment.

BREAK

Something physically broken in a dream can refer to non-physical breaks, such as a broken promise, spirit, dream, heart, hope, and the like. But we also have more positive associations with the word, as in "break with the past," "lucky break," "break a habit," "break new ground," "breakthrough," etc., any of which might be symbolized by a physical break.

BREASTS

In a dream, women's breasts may simply indicate sex and sexual desire. Breasts may also symbolize nurturing, whether physical or emotional, as well as the mother principle. Further, naked breasts may represent a feeling of exposure.

BREATH/BREATHING

Many people have problems breathing during sleep, even if they do not have full-blown apnea, and this can be reflected in one's dream life. If not an apnea symptom, holding one's breath in a dream represent an expression of will, or repressing one's anxieties or emotions. Breathing is also central to an unusually large number of idioms: "a breath of fresh air," "a waste of breath," "take your breath away," "catch your breath," "out of breath," and the like, any one of which could find expression in one's dreams.

BRIDE/BRIDEGROOM

In Jungian psychology, dream images of a bride or bridegroom may embody the anima (in males) or the animus (in females). Traditionally, brides symbolize purity and innocence. Beyond the obvious meanings of a spouse or spouse-to-be, a bride or a bridegroom can also represent someone else with whom we are in a partnership (e.g., a business partner). (See also Marriage.)

BRIDGE

Bridges often indicate literal travel. They also frequently represent life transitions. Because bodies of water symbolize the subconscious as well as the emotions, a bridge may indicate a structure that keeps one from falling into one's subconscious or into one's emotions (as in "bridge over troubled water"). Bridges are also links between two otherwise separated shores. Any one of these connotations might be indicated, and thus bridge images must be interpreted in the larger context of the dream.

BROKEN/BREAK-IN

The state of brokenness can be used to symbolize everything from poverty ("broke") to forcible entry (a "break-in") to fundamental damage ("broken down") to emotional abandonment (as in having one's heart "broken"). Breaking may also have positive connotations, as when one breaks open the seal on a letter or the packaging of a gift or a new purchase. Any one of these connotations might be indicated, and thus brokenness must be interpreted in the larger context of the dream.

BROTHER

A dream about one's brother or any other close family member is difficult to interpret because of the extensive shared history. One's real-life brother sometimes represents the concept of brotherhood (fellowship, alliance).

BUBBLE

Bubbles can represent anything from a womb (especially if one dreams of emerging from a bubble), to merriment (a glass of "bubbly") to disenchantment (bursting one's bubble). Any one of these connotations might be indicated, so bubble images must be interpreted in the larger context of the dream.

BUDDHA

In Western culture Buddha is thought of as a benevolent sage. Unless the dreamer has other, more specific associations, a dream about a Buddha may be a sign that the dreamer desires the blessings of wisdom, insight, or compassion.

BUILDING

In contemporary society, we live much of our lives in one sort of building or another. Thus, buildings in a dream may simply be stages for other kinds of dream scenarios (i.e., they do not necessarily have a symbolic meaning in and of themselves). Particular kinds of buildings may also symbolize the institution or business they

house (e.g., a school building may symbolize public education). Buildings, especially houses, may also represent the self, particularly the physical body. In many-storied buildings, movement between floors sometimes symbolizes rising or falling in status or awareness.

BULL

The bull is a rich dream symbol. Perhaps the dreamer is being too bullheaded about some issue and needs to seek compromise. The bull can also symbolize a large, powerful, and somewhat clumsy person ("a bull in a china shop"), as well as a person optimistic (bullish) about the future course of events, as in business.

BULLET

Can be a symbol of violence, or of an attack. In traditional psychoanalysis, a bullet can be a sexual symbol (penis, impregnation). We also sometimes talk about "biting the bullet" and "sweating bullets."

BURGLAR

Dreaming about burglars can represent anxiety about someone taking something away. Less obviously, a dream burglar can be a neglected part of ourselves. (See also Robbery, Stealing, Thieves/Theft).

BURIAL

A dream about attending someone's burial service may symbolize bidding farewell to old conditions and relationships in the dreamer's life. (See also Coffin, Crypt, Dead/Death, Grave, Hearse).

BUS

Because of our early experiences with school buses, as well as the widespread availability of buses as public transportation, buses can have a wide variety of individual associations. Also, buses may simply be stages for other kinds of dream scenarios (i.e., they do not necessarily have a symbolic meaning). In and of themselves, and especially in contrast to more individualized means of transportation such as automobiles, buses may represent collective action, or even going along with the crowd.

BUTTERFLY

Butterflies sometimes carry the same range of meanings as birds. However, because of the metamorphosis of caterpillars into butterflies, butterflies are potent symbols of transformation. They also represent beauty and pollination.

BUTTONS

Buttons as fasteners (as opposed to campaign buttons) are closely related to the symbolism of clothing. Clothing frequently represents the outer self or persona. Thus, tight buttons (tight clothing) may indicate the feeling of being bound by our social roles, and the act of unbuttoning the opening of the self to others (or, in some instances, sexual opening).

DREAM SYMBOLS

CABBAGE

The state of this vegetable in the dream determines whether it is a good or bad portent. If rotting and with a bad odor, it may represent old, stagnating conditions in the dreamer's environment or emotional state. Fresh cabbage is considered to be a cleanser and healing agent for sickness and depression.

CAFETERIA

Food in varieties and in abundance such as in a cafeteria or an "all one can eat" environment may suggest ideas that need to be digested. The statement "food for thought" may be a meaningful way of understanding this dream. Too much may mean one is fed up with a condition or relationship. If fear surrounds the selection of food, the dream may be indicating the basic fight or flight response to something threatening to eat you, or that a lot has been "eating at" the dreamer lately.

CAGE

A cage may indicate the dreamer feels cooped up. Being in the cage may signify the need to escape from a confining situation or relationship.

CAKES

Cakes often signify a time to rejoice at one's accomplishments or to celebrate new relation-

ships or work efforts that have been successful and have sometimes gone unnoticed by the dreamer, family, friends, or colleagues.

CALENDAR

Dreaming about a calendar can be the subconscious's attempt to remind one of an important appointment or event. Alternatively, it could be about the passing of time.

CANAL

As a waterway that must be constructed (in contrast to a stream or a river), dreaming about a canal might be about channeling or directing our feelings. It could also be emblematic of our goals.

CANCER

To dream about cancer does not necessarily mean that the dreamer either has or will contract this disease. Often dreaming of cancer indicates a condition in the dreamer's life that is hopeless and has been consuming physical or emotional resources for too long.

CANDLES

Because of their association with light in the darkness, candles can indicate something of spiritual significance—protection from the unseen, and guidance through the unknown (the light in the window to welcome you safely home). Many candles together unify a purpose or a cause (e.g., a mass, a march, a wake, a celebration). Extinguishing candles portends the passing of a problem, or perhaps a wish to cease overindulgence from "burning one's candle at both ends."

CANE

Male sexuality. Could also indicate weakness or, alternatively, something that supports us. "Caning" is also a form of punishment.

CANNIBALISM

Cannibalism often represents an insatiable lust to own and possess the life force of the victim(s). Being the victim of cannibalism denotes that the dreamer may feel "eaten alive" by work, a relationship, or a condition in his or her life. Like incest and murder, cannibalism represents the worst form of something forbidden.

CAP

A hat, a cover over an oil well, a snow-capped mountain, a nightcap for sleeping, or a nightcap before bed may all indicate sense of completion of some issue, job well done, or a mission accomplished.

CAPTAIN

Captains in dreams often represent authority and decision makers. If one dreams about being a captain, one typically feels in charge (as in the "captain of our ship").

CAR

A boxcar on a train, a car in an amusement park ride, a lift car on a ski tram, or an elevator car may symbolize the self, and many car dreams denote self-control issues. Taking charge of one's life would be indicated if one were "in the driver's seat."

Allowing one's life to be driven by others might be indicated by a "backseat driver" or by "taking the backseat." The dreamer may be being driven to new heights before he or she is ready. Or perhaps the dreamer is finally lifting himself or herself out of a rut. The emotional feeling about the car determines the meaning. (See also Vehicles.)

CARDS

Playing cards in a dream can be about recreation or, alternatively, about gambling with our destiny. Cards in a dream can also reflect the meaning of many idioms: "a card up one's sleeve," "the cards are stacked against you," "to hold all the cards," "trump card," "house of cards," etc.

CARPET

A carpet decorates but can also hide, as in the expression "to sweep under the carpet," so a carpet in a dream can indicate something that is hidden. Carpets also have a positive, welcoming meaning, as in the expression "to roll out the red carpet."

CARRIAGE

As a vehicle drawn by an animal, a carriage dream can indicate how we are dealing with our biological drives. Are we in control, or are we having a difficult time controlling the horses?

CARROT

The carrot is a symbol of good health for the eyes, particularly if the dreamer eats the carrot. It is a prolific symbol because of the association of rabbits with carrots. It may also symbolize a lure, as in the expression, "dangle a carrot," depending on how the carrot is experienced.

CARRY

If one is being carried in a dream, it can indicate nurturance or a sense of dependence. Alternatively, perhaps we are simply being "carried away" by some enthusiasm. If we are carrying something, it can represent an emotion, as in the expression "carrying a grudge." We also talk about "carrying the day," "carrying the ball," or "carrying a torch" for someone.

CASTLE

As a house of royalty, a castle may show reward or honor bestowed to the dreamer in the form of recognition and praise for outstanding achievements. Alternatively, a castle may carry the same connotations as a fort, in which one defends oneself or walls oneself off from others.

CASTRATION

Castration can symbolize repulsion to, or inadequacy of, sexual expression and fear of losing oneself in the sexual act. It sometimes indicates deep guilt, and sometimes fear of either growing up or growing old. Castration also symbolizes feelings of emasculation and impotence.

CAT

Cats symbolize independence and power. They also represent the animal self. Cats are symbols of the feminine, prosperity, sexuality, and power. In dreams cats often represent some of their more common attributes or associations, such as "sleek," "cunning," "cat burglar." The witch with her black cat commonly denotes evil and bad luck. "Catty" describes a person who makes mean or malicious remarks. Both positive and negative connotations surround the mystique of the cat. As with all dream symbols, the tone and setting of the dream indicate which meaning is appropriate.

CAVE

Caves often represent a place to hide or seek refuge. Coming out of a cave may mean the emergence of the self. A cave may also symbolize the womb, childbearing, new life, contemplation, or creativity. (See also Hole, Pit).

CELLAR

A lower level of a building is a natural symbol of the subconscious mind. Going down into the cellar may signify descending into one's stored (and perhaps repressed) past.

CEMETERY

Finding oneself in a cemetery in a dream may indicate sadness or unresolved grief. Alternatively, it may simply represent one's "dead" past.

CEREMONY

Ceremonies can be simple celebrations, but often they mark an important transition in life, such as a graduation ceremony or a marriage ceremony. In the dream, ceremonies can represent that one has acquired new skills or moved into a new phase of one's life.

CHAINS

"The chains that bind" may portend a happy union or marriage or be the missing link to the solution of a problem or situation. A succession of events can be linked together in a chain reaction. Ideas and opinions can be bound up in old ways of doing things. The dreamer may be needing to break free of the chains that bind or to link up with new ideas, people, or situations. (See also Rope).

CHAIR

A chair may symbolize sitting down to take time out to contemplate a situation before proceeding. If the dreamer is providing the chair, it's time to sit for a while with oneself to contemplate new directions. If the chair is being offered, the dreamer should be open for taking advice. If, however, the dreamer finds himself or herself on the "hot seat," then caution should prevail.

CHASE

Being chased in a dream suggests running from a situation that the dreamer finds threatening or frightening. If the dreamer is the pursuer, he or she may be chasing after a difficult goal.

CHASM

Uncertainty. The unknown. Wondering how we will get from here to there. If a deep, dark chasm, it may represent the unconscious mind or feelings about death.

CHEMIST

A chemist in a dream can represent a doctor or a therapist. It could represent research one needs to undertake. One's inner wisdom. Alternatively, a form of negative knowledge, as in the stereotype of the evil scientist.

CHERRY

Cherries can have a wide range of meanings in our society. Traditionally, because of the story of George Washington chopping down the cherry tree, this fruit is associated with truthfulness. As in song, life may be a bowl of cherries, signifying sweetness and good fortune. Also, vehicles in particular are described in terms of fruit: one in good condition is called a "cherry"; a bad one, a "lemon."

CHILDREN

Dreaming of children may symbolize the inner emotional needs of the dreamer. Returning to a less complicated state and way of life may be indicated. Dreaming of children frequently symbolizes a longing for the past, for another chance to satisfy repressed desires and unfulfilled hopes.

Therapists engaged in trauma work have reported that parents who grieve the loss of a child will dream of that child until they have accepted their loss.

CHIMNEY

Chimneys are often associated with cultural implications of Santa Claus arriving to reward those who have been good with gifts. They also symbolize the warmth and cheer of family as in the traditional "home-sweet-home" scene on the front of greeting cards, gifts of candies, and food and homemade items of every description featuring the smoking brick chimney.

CHOCOLATE

For most people chocolate is considered an indulgence. Chocolate in a dream may therefore symbolize that the dreamer feels the need to be rewarded and deserves special treatment. Alternatively, perhaps the dreamer has been indulging in too many excesses and needs to practice some restraint.

CHOKE

If not a direct reflection of something happening to one's body during sleep, a dream about choking can indicate indecision or conflict. Choking is also related to emotion, as when one is "choked up" from fear. Alternatively, to "choke off" is to stop something.

CHURCH

A dream of a church often represents something sacred to the dreamer or symbolizes that the dreamer's prayers, or prayers by others are being answered. It may also represent a deep inner need for spiritual nourishment or atonement.

CIGAR/CIGARETTE

A psychoanalytic symbol for the male organ, though when Freud was once asked about his cigar, he famously responded that "sometimes a cigar is just a cigar." Smokers tend to associate anxiety and/or relaxation with cigarettes.

CIRCLE

A circle encompasses many meanings in numerous areas: the wholeness of numbers in mathematics, the spiritual oneness depicted by the circle and the mandala, protection from evil by the ritual drawing of a circle, bringing attention to something by circling it. It may also express frustrations, as when one doodles in circles or goes around in circles. Socially, it may represent being "in" the right circle of friends. The love relationship is sometimes symbolized by the wearing of a ring, around the finger, the neck, or in the nose. In Jungian psychology the circle is a symbol of the self archetype. (See also Zero.)

CITY

The meaning of a dream about a city very much depends on one's perspective and personal associations. In earlier cultural times the city was the place of action and excitement, with very positive connotations, the place to market wares and to buy food, goods, and services. Entertainment and songs glorified particular cities (e.g., New York, Chicago, San Francisco, London, and Paris). More recently, the city has become associated with crime, gangs, drug wars, and police brutality.

CLASS

A dream of a school group in which one is a participant or the teacher may symbolize learning life's lessons or being the authority in matters of life. In certain esoteric traditions, dreaming of being in a classroom is interpreted as meaning that the soul attends classes on the "inner planes" during sleep. Such a dream may also relate to one's social, political, or economic status, or even to one's uniqueness (e.g., "in a class of her own"). Divisions, often prejudicial, of race, color, or creed may also be indicated by such a dream (e.g., class consciousness, most significantly as practiced in India). (See also School, Seminar).

CLIFF

Sometimes, standing on the edge of a cliff can represent that one has a broad view of something, or we might feel as if we are living on the edge. More often, it represents things like anxiety, fear of failure and the unknown, and taking a risk. We can also feel threatened, as when we are pushed to the edge.

CLIMBING

Climbing up a rope, a ladder, or the side of something often reveals a struggle to overcome obstacles or having just recently overcome them. Mountains may also be a form of obstacle (e.g., "a mountain of work," making a "mountain out of a molehill.") Climbing also indicates rising with respect to social, economic, or artistic pursuits and intellectual and spiritual growth.

CLOAK

All forms of cover-up are denoted by this word, including the mysterious and the macabre depicted in the expression "cloak-and-dagger operation." In a dream, wearing a cloak as a garment might suggest the dreamer needs to feel protected or is trying to cover up something.

CLOCK

Clocks as symbols often reflect the dreamer's anxiety about not being on top of things, and thus behind schedule. A clock may also symbolize the biological clock that ticks away for people who want children, or those who feel that time is running out for them.

CLOSE

Closing a door can mean closing a chapter of one's life. We can also close our hearts to someone or close our eyes to something.

CLOSET

A closet may represent a place to store or hide people or things. Movies and other narratives often show people hiding in a closet. People with an unsavory past are said to have "skeletons in the closet." In more modern times, the closet has also come to signify the unveiling of previously hidden aspects of the self, as in "coming out of the closet."

CLOTHING

Clothing in a dream often depicts the self's persona. Old ragged clothing can mean old ways and ideas need to be, or are about to be, changed. Much changing of clothes or costumes can also suggest the need for change, and trying to fit into a new way of being in the world. Likewise, the wearing of new and beautiful garments often suggests new things in the life of the dreamer, such as social or economic improvement. (See also Costume.)

CLOUDS

If one's viewpoint is clouded over, a dream of this symbol would be appropriate. If the clouds are stormy with lightning bolts, chances are anger is about to storm into the dreamer's life. Such dreams sometimes depict confusion and lack of clarity. Seeing clouds roll across a pleasant blue sky may portend the clearing up of obscure issues.

CLUB

If used as a weapon either by or against the dreamer, feelings of either aggression or submission could be at issue. If the dream is of the other type of club (a social organization), chances are the dreamer is aspiring to acquire social, economic, or cultural identity.

COCK

Cocks as symbols have several different interpretations. One is the consistent daily "alarm clock" that greets the day. Cocks can also signify thankless tasks, overachievement, and aggressive pursuits of power. This may be the wake-up call the dreamer has been needing.

COCKROACHES

These insects are associated with food and also with uncleanliness. Dreaming about them may indicate that the nourishment or "food for thought" or the "soul food" that is being ingested in the dream is contaminated with hidden or undesirable motives. Information or reassessment of immediate issues in the dreamer's life may be indicated.

COCOON

Cocoons represent a place of safety, healing, or transformation. Dreaming of a cocoon may be a response to a sense of feeling overburdened with life issues and the consequent longing for relief. Such a dream may indicate a place where the consciousness can restore and re-create new paths of expression, or perhaps the birth of a new aspect of the self.

COFFEE

For regular coffee drinkers, this could simply be a reflection of one's everyday life experience in one's dreams. A social ritual; friendship. Alternatively, it might mean something we thirst for. A common idiom is to "wake up and smell the coffee," meaning to give something more attention.

COFFIN

A coffin may represent physical confinement or a restricting of the freedom to express oneself physically. There may be a dead or decaying situation in the dreamer's life. As with the cocoon, a dream of being in a coffin may have a restorative meaning of rebirth. (See also Burial, Crypt, Dead/Death, Grave, Hearse).

COLLAR

Collars represent confinement and restraint (e.g., to "collar" someone). They also indicate completing or finishing something, as in putting the collar on a garment. Collars often are an indication of control (e.g., prisoners) or a token of subservience (e.g., slaves). This kind of dream may well describe a frustrated work situation or a confining relationship.

COLORS

Many colors in a dream may depict energy, as colors are vibrations of light. A single color seen in a dream can be interpreted only in the context of the dreamers relationship with that color. For example, the color red may be experienced as love, romance, and sex. For someone else, or in another dream, the color red may denote blood, death, and destruction. Black may mean evil, witches, and black cats, or sophistication and elegance.

COLUMN

Columns symbolize strength and work, as they usually hold something up. They also represent organization (e.g., columns of numbers to classify groups of entries in accounting, columns of

soldiers). A dream about columns may indicate the dreamer is trying to hold up under burdens or to support others.

COMB

In a dream, the use of a comb could represent tidying up something such as a presentation. It can also represent careful examination, as when we go over something with a "fine tooth comb."

COMPASS

Guidance. Finding one's way out of situation in which one feels lost. We also talk about our "moral compass," which guides us in making ethical choices.

COMPOSER

Many famous musicians received inspiration from their dreams. To dream of being a composer may be a symbol for creating or directing in one or more arenas of life.

COMPUTER

For someone who works in front of a computer every day, this could simply be a reflection of daily life in a dream. A computer can also indicate research, analysis, or communication, depending on how one uses a computer. We sometimes say that something doesn't "compute" as a way of saying we don't understand, so a broken computer in a dream could represent confusion.

CONTAMINATION

The meaning of a dream of contamination often depends on the occupation of the dreamer. A sanitary engineer might be fed up with the garbage he deals with on a daily basis. Another dreamer might be experiencing an internal contamination from conflicts in the person's value system (e.g., the dreamer might be stealing supplies from the workplace while at the same time receiving bonuses for being an exceptional employee).

COOK/COOKING

This could be little more than a reflection of a daily activity in our dream life. Preparation. Creation, as in the expression "to cook something up." We also use "cook" in idioms like one's "goose is cooked" and to "cook the books."

CORD

Sometimes restriction, but, alternatively, the bonds we have with others. The umbilical cord indicates dependency, and in those kinds of situations we talk about "cutting the cord."

CORN

Throughout history corn has been celebrated, symbolized, sanctified, ceremonialized, ritualized and even used to describe substandard humor ("corny"). Corn dreams may thus indicate anything from nourishment to the kind of humor the dreamer may be inflicting upon others. Corn may also represent abundance, growth, or fertility.

CORPSE

In dreams, corpses are not usually symbols of death. Rather, a corpse is a part of us or a part of our life that has died, for good or for bad. Alternatively, it can sometimes represent the feeling that our life is dead.

CORRESPONDENCE

To receive much correspondence in a dream may represent an overdue letter or communication that one is expecting. To be writing in a dream may indicate that the dreamer needs to send a letter to someone.

CORRIDOR

Symbol of transition; going from one situation to something different. Alternatively, a corridor can represent a route to one's unconscious mind. In psychoanalysis, a womb symbol. (See also Hallway).

COSTUME

In a dream, a costume can indicate things that may be obscured about the dreamer's or another's identity, owing to conscious or subconscious disguises. (See also Clothing.)

COUCH

A couch may represent getting needed rest, healing therapy, or the therapist's couch. It may also symbolize a romantic encounter or "first love" experience on the living room couch.

COUNTRYSIDE

A sense of the natural, as in feeling natural. Non-rural people associate the countryside with relaxation.

COURT (OF LAW)

Courts stand for a place of authority, presumed justice, and order, or the facade of these characteristics. The dreamer may be struggling with issues of fear and guilt, and this kind of dream may be the person's conscience trying to communicate. Courts also reflect issues of judging or feeling judged. (See also Judge/Judgment).

COW

The appearance of a cow in a dream may indicate passive, docile, or fertile aspects. It may also indicate nourishment and fulfillment if the cows are waiting to be milked. To dream of contentedly grazing cows usually signifies prosperity and happiness.

CRAB

A symbol of both the sea and the sky, the crab can stand for physical nourishment from the ocean and intellectual nourishment from the interpretation of the horoscope. Claws are tenacious and clinging, which can indicate something about the relationships the dreamer is in, especially with the opposite sex.

CRACK

Can represent a flaw or weakness. A crack in a dream could be drawing on the meaning of an idiom, such as "papering over the cracks," "cracking up," or "falling through the cracks."

CROSS

To a religious Christian, a cross carries a clear theological meaning. To someone raised in Christianity but not a practicing Christian, a cross in a dream can represent some aspect of their childhood. We also talk about an unpleasant responsibility, as in a "cross we have to bear."

CROSSROAD

As a symbol, it should be reasonably obvious that a crossroad in a dream represents a decision, a direction we must take.

CROWD

Dreaming about being in a crowd can mean many different things. We may have had anxieties about being in crowds as a child, so crowds could simply represent anxiety. We can feel good about being part of the crowd, or unhappy about being part of the herd; we may feel "lost in the crowd" and want to "stand out from the crowd." If people are looking at the dreamer, one could be anxious about public opinion.

CROWN

Success, as in "crowned with success" or one's "crowning achievement." Leadership. The "jewel in the crown" is what is most valuable.

CRUCIFIXION

Beyond the obvious religious connotations, a dream crucifixion can represent an excruciatingly painful situation. Feelings of guilt or, alternatively, feelings of being a scapegoat. Crucifixion can also be an initiatory symbol, representing the "death" that takes place before rebirth.

CRYPT

In a dream a crypt or a catacomb can represent the womb. Alternatively, a space beneath the ground often represents the unconscious mind. (See also Burial, Coffin, Dead/Death, Grave, Hearse).

CRYSTAL

A crystal can represent something beautiful or even spiritual. Alternatively, it can mean something that has "crystallized," either in the sense of manifesting or in the sense of becoming rigid. We are also familiar with "crystal" balls that are used to divine the future.

CUP

In psychoanalysis, a cup is a symbol of the female and female sexuality. Alternatively, an empty cup can represent receptiveness.

CURTAINS

To draw the curtains or experience being behind curtains suggests that the dreamer is trying to hide something from themselves or from others. Alternatively, dream curtains might allude to such common expressions as "it's curtains."

DREAM SYMBOLS

DAGGER

A dagger is usually taken to be a symbol of strong male power. Alternatively, it may be a symbol of treachery (in fiction, people are frequently stabbed in the back with daggers). Daggers sometimes also indicate hostility ("daggers in men's smiles").

DAISY

Daisies can represent beauty, purity, and innocence. Their color also links them to the sun, and thus to enlightenment and illumination.

DAM

A dam may signify repressed emotional energy. The dreamer may feel like crying, but instead is holding back the tears.

DANCE

Dancing is a rich symbol, capable of many different interpretations. Depending on the type of movement in which we engage, dancing may be associated with romance and sex, with the experience of freedom from constraints, with participating in life or in social activities (the dance of life), with frivolity, with gracefulness, or with group cooperation.

DANGER

Any kind of danger signal in a dream may be warning the dreamer to be more cautious in some aspect of life. Other components of the dream should help indicate where the dreamer should exercise more caution.

DARKNESS

Like many other common elements of our everyday experience, darkness can represent a wide range of things. As the polar opposite of light, darkness may represent evil, death, fear of the unknown, or feeling lost. Darkness or a dark region in a dream is often symbolic of the unconscious, the womb, or unseen possibilities. As with all dream symbols, the tone and setting of the dream indicate which interpretation is appropriate.

DAWN

As a symbol, the dawn can have most of the meanings generally associated with light (e.g., enlightenment, vitality). More particularly, the dawn is the emergence of a new stage of life, a new understanding, or a new start, and the emergence from darkness.

DAY/DAYLIGHT

Daytime as opposed to nighttime represents the conscious mind as opposed to the unconscious. Seeing what we are doing. Can refer to one's mood: a sunny day is bright and cheerful whereas an overcast day is different. The word "day" plays a role in many idioms, from "bad hair day" to "make my day."

DEAD/DEATH

Dreams about the dead or about death are not usually omens of literal death, although they may indicate anxiety about death. Violent death may represent anger and aggression, although much depends on the more general tone or "atmosphere" of the dream. When the dreamer dies but is not particularly unhappy or distraught in the dream, death often symbolizes the letting go (or "death") of an old part of the self or the destruction of a prior stage of life. This kind of dream death is, in other words, a symbol of self-transformation. A lifeless corpse, on the other hand, may represent a feeling of devitalization—a kind of death in life that comes from adhering to a lifeless routine. (See also Burial, Coffin, Crypt, Grave, Hearse).

DEAD END

In a dream, a dead end usually represents the obvious, namely the sense of one's efforts coming to naught, or pursuing a line of research and reaching a "dead end."

DECAPITATION

Dreams of being beheaded are not usually omens of death or even of punishment, although they may indicate anxiety about punishment. Because of the complexity of symbolism associated with the head, decapitation can have a wide variety of different meanings, from losing touch with one's emotions (a split between the mind and the body) to losing control (as in the expression "losing one's head"). As with all dream symbols, the feeling, tone, and setting of the dream indicate which interpretation is appropriate. (See also Beheading, Guillotine).

DECAY

Decay may symbolize the degradation of a situation. More positively, it represents the death of an old situation before rebirth into a new state. Other associations come from such common idioms as "rotten apple." (See also Maggots).

DEEP

Any sense of depth, particularly going down, in a dream usually represents the unconscious mind. This can be accompanied by feelings of discovery or dread. "Deep" is also found in a number of interesting idioms, such as at the "deep end" or in "deep water." One can be deeply hurt or deeply troubled.

DEER

The deer, as one of the most widely hunted species in North America, is naturally associated with hunting. It also symbolizes grace and gentleness ("gentle as a deer"). In folklore deer are messengers of fairies, which may give them a symbolic role in dreams as messengers of the unconscious.

DEFECATE

The act of defecating in a dream can indicate that one has unloaded something one has been carrying around. Alternatively, natural self-expression. We can also feel "defecated on." From a psychoanalytic point of view, toilet training is a major step in one's development, so defecating has multiple interpretations.

DEMOLITION

A sense of major changes in one's life, for better or for worse. A breakdown of old ways of doing things. Alternatively, a sense of being scattered and chaotic.

DEMON/DEVIL

Dreams of demons are not always dreams of evil, or even symbols of torment. Devils can, for example, represent intelligence, cunning ("devilishly clever!"), and even sexuality ("You devil, you"). These traditional representatives of the dark side often symbolize the unconscious, especially one's shadow self.

DENTIST

Owning to childhood associations, dentists in dreams often symbolize anxiety and fear of pain. They represent the principle of inflicting pain "for your own good." The primary activity of dentistry is drilling and removing decayed matter, and replacing it with new dental material an activity that, in a dream, may be a metaphor for other situations in one's life.

DENTURES

You may be needing to "get your teeth into" something, or be "biting your way through" a situation. If you are being bitten, perhaps there is a struggle for control within yourself or within your relationships, personal or business. Losing your teeth relates to feeling that you have lost your personal power and your sense of control in your life. (See also Bite, Teeth).

DEPARTURE

Breaking away from a situation or relationship, a way of doing things. Seeking independence by "leaving home."

DESCENT

A dream of descending in an elevator—or by any other means—may indicate a decline in energy or status. Alternatively, it may symbolize descent into the unconscious in a journey of self-discovery.

DESERT

Deserts may be fairly straightforward symbols for a sense of barrenness, poverty, lack, exhaustion, loneliness, or even death. On the other hand, as the unsettled "wilderness," deserts often represent the unconscious, particularly the shadow self. Deserts have a wider range of meanings for someone from the desert Southwest than for someone from the East Coast. As with all dream symbols, the atmosphere and setting of the dream indicate which meaning is appropriate. (See also Sand).

DESK

If we work at a desk daily, dreaming about a desk can just be a reflection of our daily lives in the dream state. Otherwise, desks can represent work or established authority.

DESSERT

Our society is obsessed with food, especially with tasty, fattening food, making something as seemingly simple as dessert a rich source of symbolic associations. Desserts can represent enjoying the good things of life, indulgence, overindulgence, celebration, reward, and temptation. Because they are served at the end of the meal, they often indicate the final stage or the completion of a project.

DESTINATION

Traveling toward a destination or arriving at a destination in a dream is often a fairly straightforward representation of the achievement of our desires and ambitions.

DETOUR

The meaning of a detour in a dream is fairly straightforward. It indicates either that we have encountered an obstacle in some area of life or that we have decided not to confront something directly, and must therefore try to find a way around.

DEVOUR

Being eaten in a dream can reflect our feelings of being "eaten up" by someone or by the demands of our lives. If we are the devourer, then it can indicate that we are hungering for something, or that we are possessive. Being swallowed whole by a large creature is a widespread shamanic motif for personal transformation (e.g., Jonah and the whale). (See also Eating, Hunger).

DICE

Dice fall under the meaning of the broader category of gambling because they are symbols of chance and even of fate (e.g., "the roll of the dice").

DIGGING

Digging in a dream may indicate a struggle to unearth one's reputation or integrity, a search for something lost or buried, or an effort to bury some unpleasant aspect of the past. Any downward movement can also symbolize digging into the unconscious in an effort to understand oneself. (See also Shovel).

DINOSAUR

In a dream, any creature can symbolize the animal self. As a long-extinct creature, a dinosaur can represent the sense that, at some level, we are the products of a very ancient process.

DIRT/DIRTY

Dirt is associated with farming, and therefore with fertility and growth. Something underneath the ground symbolizes the unconscious. Because of the social importance of cleanliness, "dirtiness" has acquired many different connotations, from

guilt, to unworthiness ("dirty white trash"), to sexuality ("dirty minds").

DISCOVERY

Discovery has a negative meaning, as in finding out about something that has been concealed, and a positive meaning, as when one makes a new discovery. Dream discoveries in the first sense may simply indicate anxiety, rather than something actually being hidden. Dream discoveries in the second sense may show the dreamer is entering into a new phase of life or a new phase of personal development, such as recovery from a major upheaval.

DISMEMBERMENT

Dismemberment is a very ancient and widespread motif in initiation, especially in shamanistic initiation, in which one is taken apart and put back together in a renewed, improved form. If the experience does not feel unpleasant during a dream, dismemberment may well indicate the closing of one phase of life and rebirth into a new phase. If accompanied by strong emotions of fear and anxiety, dismemberment may simply reflect a feeling of "coming apart."

DIVING

From a Freudian standpoint, diving into water may represent sexual intercourse. Also, bodies of water appearing in dreams often symbolize the unconscious, so diving may indicate jumping into and exploring the unconscious. More mundanely, diving in a dream may simply reflect a task from waking life into which we are "diving."

DOCTOR

Doctors symbolize healing or the desire for healing, either physically or psychologically. They also represent authority, even the higher self. To someone attuned to alternative medicine, a traditional doctor may also represent mainstream orthodoxy as opposed to natural healing.

DOG

Dogs participate in the larger meaning of beasts or creatures, all of which can refer to our natural selves, in either the positive or negative sense of "animal." Dogs, however, as some of the first domesticated animals, can refer to a wide variety of symbolic meanings, from going along with the "pack," to hunting (dogs "sniff out" the quarry), to loyalty ("man's best friend"), to abuse ("treated like a dog"), to exhaustion ("dog-tired"), to tenacity ("doggedness"). Also, as animals who guard the underworld, they can be messengers of the unconscious. As with all dream symbols, the tone and setting of the dream indicate which meaning is appropriate.

DOLL

Dolls in dreams may indicate children, childhood, or childlikeness. Depending on the dream, they sometimes embody either the persona or the shadow self. Dolls also indicate fashion (as in manikins), beauty (a "doll"), manipulation (as in puppets), and revenge ("voodoo dolls").

DOLPHIN (PORPOISE)

Large bodies of water often symbolize the unconscious, so any sea creature can represent a message from the unconscious or diving into the unconscious. As seagoing mammals, dolphins can symbolize the connection or interaction between our conscious (air) and unconscious (water) selves, or between thoughts (air) and emotions (water). They also represent guides to the unconscious. Because of our society's general knowledge about dolphin behavior, they also symbolize rescuers.

DOOR/DOORWAY

Doors may have a variety of different meanings—meanings that can usually be ascertained depending on how the door is disposed in a dream. An open door indicates a new opportunity; stepping through a doorway means appropriating a new opportunity, or entering into a new phase of life; a choice of many doorways shows a juncture at which a choice must be made; and a locked door indicates something repressed or hidden. A closed door may represent something hidden, or it may symbolize an opportunity that is closed to us. (See also Gate.)

DOVE

Doves participate in the larger meaning of birds, but they also have more particular meanings. These meanings range from peace, to the Holy Spirit, to love (especially if two doves appear in the dream).

DRAGON

Dragons can have the same meaning as snakes and other serpents. Dragons symbolize very different things in the Western and Eastern traditions. In the West, heroic knights slay evil dragons that guard treasure or helpless damsels, which may symbolize the struggle between the noble and the ignoble elements of the self. In China, dragons are wise spiritual beings associated with the sky and air (Chinese dragons have wings), which indicates a very different set of connotations.

DRAWERS

Drawers may convey a sense of being hidden or of putting something away. They also represent one's inner state, so a disorderly drawer may indicate internal chaos, and an orderly drawer, psychological order.

DRINKING

Because water is a symbol of the unconscious, drinking water may indicate being nourished by the unconscious. Drinking alcohol may mean that one is seeking either pleasure or escape. Alcoholic ecstasy is also sometimes used to symbolize divine ecstasy, so that drinking in a dream may show a "thirst" for spiritual experiences.

DRIVE

The sense of guiding, of being in control, of being at the helm. Vehicles such as cars often represent the physical body, so what happens to us in driving dreams can indicate something about the body. "Drive" is also a component of many idioms, from "driving a hard bargain" to "driving someone over the edge."

DROWNING

Large bodies of water often symbolize the unconscious, so drowning may indicate being overwhelmed by unconscious, repressed issues. This need not being entirely negative; being forced to face issues one has been avoiding can have a positive outcome. Water also symbolizes the emotions, and dreams about drowning sometimes occur during periods of crisis (e.g., loss of a loved one) when one feels overwhelmed by emotions. Finally, drowning sometimes is initiatory symbolism, indicating that the dreamer is entering a new stage of development and "dying" to the old self.

DRUM

A drum can represent everything from primitive urges, to dance, to the rhythms of life, to entrepreneurialism ("drumming up business"), to ejection (being "drummed out of town"). As with all dream symbols, the tone and setting of the dream indicate which meaning is appropriate.

DRUNK

Being drunk, as opposed to simply be intoxicated, can represent loss of control and abandonment to irrational forces. Drunkenness can also symbolize exhaustion, as in the expression "punch drunk."

DUCK

Ducks fall under the larger meaning of birds, especially if one dreams of them flying through the air. Ducks are also marine creatures, however, and submerge in water, the realm of the emotions and the unconscious. Thus, a diving duck indicates probing the emotions or the unconscious mind. Bringing something up from the depths may represent the surfacing of unconscious material.

DUTY

To feel bound by duty in a dream may be a reflection of the dreamer's past experiences in the military. If, however, the dreamer is overly concerned with duty in their dreams, perhaps compulsive behavior or control issues are posing problems.

DWARF

Dwarfs are small people, traditionally regarded as possessing magical qualities or powers of divination. This may thus be a highly fortuitous dream symbol. Alternatively, dwarfs can be negative symbols, representing some part of the dreamer's psyche that is stunted or repressed.

DYNAMITE

Dynamite or any other explosive device is a natural symbol for anger, aggression, or other "explosive" emotions. In a dream, dynamite that has not exploded may indicate a person or a situation that is about to blow up. Dynamite is also related to firecrackers, which have connotations of celebration.

DREAM SYMBOLS

EAGLE

Eagles fall under the larger meaning of birds, especially as spiritual symbols. Eagles are also associated with the sun, and thus have solar symbolism. A common mythological motif is an eagle in combat with an earthbound animal, which symbolizes the spirit or the mind (the eagle) struggling with more mundane needs or desires. Eagles are also traditionally associated with nobility (especially with kings) and authority, which in dreams can be a symbol for the father or for the animus. Other traits commonly associated with eagles include pride, fierceness, and courage.

EAR

Ears naturally symbolize "giving ear" to something, whether it be advice, the promptings of one's conscience, or divine inspiration. Ears are also often associated with women and sex.

EARTH

The earth can represent solidity, stability, practicality, fertility and a sense of being "grounded" or "having both feet on the ground." It symbolizes the physical body and the physical world, as opposed to the world of ideas or the world of the spirit. The area beneath the surface of the earth represents the unconscious. The entire earth seen as a globe can indicate wholeness, the mother principle ("mother earth"), and "global consciousness."

EARTHQUAKE

Dreams about natural disasters often occur during life crises—during major "shake-ups." The earth represents the material basis of life, so an earthquake can be an especially appropriate symbol of financial upheaval. Dreams about earthquakes may also occur during life-threatening illnesses or in the recovery period following life-threatening accidents.

EAST

The east, as the direction from which the sun and other celestial bodies rise, naturally symbolizes new beginnings and rebirths. Dreams about the East (in the sense of the Orient) have other associations, sometimes of a spiritual nature. For someone living in the Midwest or California, "back East" would mean the eastern United States.

EATING

Eating sometimes symbolizes partaking of nonphysical forms of nourishment. It may also represent enjoyment or indulgence. Because the English language uses certain eating metaphors, eating in dreams sometimes indicates anxiety

("What's eating you?") or being overwhelmed (being "eaten alive"). (See also Devour, Hunger).

ECLIPSE

The sun is often taken to represent the conscious, rational self and the moon, the subconscious, emotional self. Their union in an eclipse may signify a coming together of separate parts of oneself (self-integration). It may also stand for the "eclipsing" of reason or consciousness by emotion or the subconscious (in a solar eclipse), or vice versa (in a lunar eclipse). We sometimes speak of being "eclipsed," and this may also be the meaning of a dream about eclipses.

EEL

Eels embody many of the meanings of snakes or serpents, although their watery habitat links them more explicitly with the powers of the unconscious. As phallic symbols, they indicate unconscious sexual desires. They may also symbolize something in the unconscious of which we are afraid.

EGG

Eggs are universal symbols of wholeness, fertility, new birth, and rebirth (or resurrection; hence, their association with Easter). Broken eggs may present a state of brokenness in one's life or "breaking out of a shell."

EGYPT (ANCIENT)

The meaning of a dream about ancient Egypt partly depends on one's conscious associations. Because of biblical associations, it can symbolize the material as opposed to the spiritual life. Otherwise, Egypt can symbolize ancient wisdom. Additionally, because we usually think of the pyramids as mausoleums, a dream about Egypt can represent the unconscious mind.

ELECTRICAL PLUG

Electricity is associated, naturally enough, with energy and power. Electricity can also be dangerous or "shocking." As a slang, "electric" means superlative.

ELEPHANT

Elephants symbolize mammoth size and memories. In a dream the elephant may symbolize a daunting task or an effort to remember something considered important.

ELEVATOR

Because they travel up and down in space, elevators participate in the larger meaning of height and depth. Thus, an ascending elevator in a dream can mean almost anything from rising in status to rising in awareness, whereas one descending may mean lowered status or submerging into the depths of the unconscious. In and of themselves, elevators are often regarded as threatening, because on elevators we are often forced into close quarters with strangers and because they sometimes plummet down the elevator shaft, killing the passengers.

ELEVENTH HOUR

The eleventh hour is a widespread symbol for indicating that one's time is almost up, referring either to death or to a deadline. Among certain Christian groups, it is a symbol for the short time remaining before Christ's return. Dreaming about a clock face reading eleven o'clock often expresses anxiety about a deadline.

EMBRYO

An embryo can represent the most vulnerable part of ourselves, the "inner child." (Also see Baby, Miscarriage, Pregnant.)

EMPTINESS

An empty container or vessel may indicate a feeling of having nothing to show for all the time and effort invested in something, such as a business venture or a personal relationship.

ENCLOSURE

If we dream about being inside an enclosure, it often represents our psychological defenses, such as our pride or anger. If we feel trapped within the enclosure, it may refer to our life circumstances, such as feeling bound to a particular job, relationship, or location.

END

Can refer to one's goals or simply to the end of some situation, as in such expressions as "the end of the road" and "the light at the end of the tunnel." End is often utilized in idioms, such as "I'm at the end of my rope," "I'm at my wits end," and "at loose ends."

ENGINE

If we do not normally work on or around engines, a dream about an engine can represent our vitality or our drive. The body considered as a machine, particularly the heart.

ENTRANCE/ENTRYWAY

Entrances, as the name suggests, often symbolize entering into a new stage of life. Entryways into one's home indicate entering more deeply into oneself. Entrances into caves, basements, or some other underground chamber may symbolize entering into the unconscious. Blocked or locked entrances may show difficulties or fears associated with entering.

ENVELOPES

Envelopes usually signify anticipation or opportunity within a dream. If envelopes remain unopened, it may indicate that the dreamer has missed an opportunity. If the dreamer is eagerly anticipating an envelope's contents, it may mean that the dreamer will experience a wonderful outcome of an event in waking life.

ERUPTION

An eruption, such as a volcanic eruption, usually indicates the forceful breakthrough of unconscious material—repressed thoughts or urges—into consciousness. More generally, an eruption may indicate an upheaval in one's life.

ESCAPE

The act of escaping in a dream sometimes indicates the need to face an issue or a condition that one is evading. Alternatively, one may need to "escape" something that is about to collapse, such as a burning building.

EVERGREEN (PLANT)

Evergreen plants, such as pine trees, traditionally represent immortality because they do not shed their leaves, even in the dead of winter. They also symbolize hope in the midst of despair for the same reason. Because of their association with Christmas, evergreens also symbolize gift-giving.

EXAMINATION

Dreaming about taking a test could indicate that the dreamer has a fear of failure. Alternatively, such a dream could indicate that a specific issue of great importance to the dreamer reminds them of being in school. "Passing the test" can also be a metaphor for successfully concluding any number of different activities.

EXCREMENT

Excrement is waste, but it is also fertilizer and nourishment for new growth. It has a wide range of associations, partly due to its deployment in many linguistic expressions, any one of which may be the meaning of excrement in a dream. As with all dream symbols, the tone and setting of the dream indicate which meaning is appropriate.

EXPLOSION

An explosion may indicate the forceful breakthrough of unconscious feelings into consciousness, particularly repressed rage. More generally, explosions in dreams often reflect an upheaval in one's life. More positively, explosions may represent the breaking down of barriers.

EYE

Eyes have many associations, and thus constitute a difficult symbol to interpret. Eyes are associated with wisdom, knowledge, enlightenment, perceptiveness, and gods and goddesses. Eyes may also be crossed, blinded, or half-shut. Certain kinds of glances are revelatory ("she looked right through me"); others are dangerous ("if looks could kill," "the evil eye").

EYEGLASSES

If not related to one's eyeglasses in the real world, dream spectacles could indicate that something needs to be examined more clearly or attended to more carefully. Alternatively, looking at the world through "rose colored glasses" would indicate a reality check is in order.

DREAM SYMBOLS

F

FACE

If we see our own face in a dream, it can represent concerns about our self-image and how others see us. The dream also could be drawing on associations with common idioms, such as "to lose face," "face the facts," "face the music," "poker face," and "face value."

FAILURE

Dreaming about failing, in school or in some task, may simply be an expression of anxiety (i.e., it is not a sign predicting that someone will fail). People who regularly dream of failing are often perfectionists.

FAIRGROUND

A dream about being on a fairground often draws on the feelings we had when at fairs as a child. These could be happy, fun feelings, or unpleasant feelings. Otherwise, the dream indicates something about one's life in the public arena, or social connections.

FAIRY

Fairies are associated with childhood fantasies of nymphs and gnomes and magical helpers who come to fix human problems. In dreams fairies can also show unrealistic fantasies or a sense of magic with respect to life.

FALCON

Falcons and hawks have many of the same associations as eagles (e.g., nobility, high aspirations), although the culturally familiar image of a blindfolded falcon resting on a huntsman's glove brings additional connotations—hunting, temporary blindness, capture/control, and so forth—into play.

FALLING

Falling is a universal dream motif. Psychologists speculate that fearful falling dreams are rooted in our early experiences as toddlers learning to walk. Falling dreams often reflect a sense that one has failed or "fallen down" in life. Dreams of falling also occur when one feels completely overwhelmed or out of control, such as during a divorce or the loss of a job.

FAMILY

Because each person's family experiences are so involved and vary so much from individual to individual it is difficult to say anything definitive about families in dreams. If the dream does not seem connected to our actual family, then it could relate to our inner "family," the different aspects of our own psyche.

FAMOUS PEOPLE

The appearance of a specific famous person in our dreams—particularly a person we regularly think about—can simply be a reflection of our waking state. Otherwise, a famous person can represent a higher status to which we aspire, or, alternatively, a parental figure.

FANS

Fans are used to "cool off," a common metaphor for calming down after being in a highly emotional state. Fans can also have the opposite effect, however, by increasing the power of a raging fire (by feeding it with oxygen)—the source of such expressions as "fanning the flames." Old-fashioned folding fans can symbolize both women and the phases of the moon. Finally, electric fans can represent danger because of their blades and their potential for causing electrocution.

FARE

Paying a fare in a dream can reflect the price we have to pay to achieve a certain aim.

FARM/FARMER

Farms and farmers are naturally associated with growth and nourishment. Also, many city dwellers have older relatives who live on a farm, giving farms secondary associations with the past, with childhood, and with earlier stages of society. Other aspects of farm symbology are related to various stages of the agricultural cycle, such as planting and harvest.

FAT

Being fat in a dream is a straightforward symbol of overindulgence, but it can also represent wealth and opulence. The dreaming mind often literalizes common verbal expressions in an effort to convey something to the conscious mind. Thus, an image of a fat person in a dream can indicate anything from a "fat cat," to "fat chance," to "fathead," to "fat city." (See also Obesity).

FATHER

Next to mothers, fathers usually exert the most powerful influence over our psychological makeup. The appearance of the father or a father symbol in a dream is thus extraordinarily difficult to interpret, because the meaning depends so heavily on each individual's experience with his or her own father. At a general level we can say that fathers represent power, authority, caring, the law, responsibility, and tradition. A father, as one of the co-producers of a new life, is also a creator.

FEAR

Fearful dreams are quite common, reflecting either anxiety about concrete problems in the world or anxieties arising from inner tensions. For a deeper understanding, the dreamer should attempt to identify the source of fear in the dream.

FEATHER

Feathers carry all of the connotations of birds. Additionally, because they were traditionally used in pillows and down coats, they can represent softness and warmth. Finally, because of the dreaming mind's tendency to literalize verbal expressions, feathers can symbolize lightness ("light as a feather") and certain associations ("birds of a feather").

FENCE

A fence is a blockage, but it is also protection. Dream fences are sometimes symbolic of certain common verbal expressions, such as feeling "fenced in" and "straddling the fence."

FERRYBOAT

A ferryboat is often a symbol for being transported across the threshold of the unconscious to inner realms of one's psyche. Dreams of ferryboats can also relate to changes in life circumstances.

FIELD

The meaning of a field in a dream depends on the other elements in the dream and the dream's general atmosphere. Thus, a wild field might represent nature and the freedom of running through a field. A cultivated field might represent new growth or a harvest. A barren field can be a powerful symbol of lack as well emotional barrenness. A completely different set of associations comes to mind with respect to playing fields.

FIG

Figs and fig trees are associated with sex and eroticism. This is partially because of our culture's images of Adam and Eve, who are often pictured in fig leaves following their act of sin.

FIGHT

Because life itself is so full of conflicts, dream fights can refer to any number of different struggles in our everyday life. Also, the culture in which we are raised can place so many conflicting demands upon us that we are filled with inner tensions, and these various inner conflicts can all be symbolized in dreams as physical fights. As with all dream symbols, the tone and setting of the dream indicate which meaning is applicable.

FILM

One way of examining parts of ourselves we do not wish to look at is to dream that we are seeing them portrayed in a film. Alternatively, it can mean escaping reality.

FIND

Finding an object in a dream often symbolizes discovering something in our lives—finding our sense of self-identity; finding our place. The dream might also be drawing on the meaning of common idioms, such as to "find out," "find one's bearings," or "fault finding."

FINGER

Fingers and thumbs have a rich symbolic association because of the wide variety of meanings in various hand gestures. Thus, we may do everything from thumb a ride, to point an accusatory finger at someone, to point the way. Fingers have other connotations because of certain symbolic rings (e.g., marriage rings) and certain verbal expressions (e.g., "fingering" a guilty person). In Freudian psychology, fingers can be a phallic symbol. The particulars of the gesture in the dream should indicate the meaning.

FIRE

Fire, like many familiar elements from everyday experience, is a complex symbol. It can symbolize passion, anger, the spirit, cooking, purification, transformation, illumination, and destruction. Our language contains expressions like "being fired," "getting fired up," "getting burned," and "passing the torch." The particular meaning of fire in a dream can be determined from other cues in the dream landscape.

FISH/FISHING

Large bodies of water often symbolize the unconscious, so any sea creature can represent a message from the unconscious or "diving" into the unconscious. Completely at home in the ocean, fish are the best-equipped creatures for exploring its depths, and are thus positive symbols for anyone engaged in therapy or self transformation. The activity of fishing can indicate a quest, particularly for nourishment, and it can indicate an exploration of the unconscious. Fish can also be sexual symbols and, because of their association with Christianity, can be Christ symbols.

FLOATING

Dreams in which one simply floats can indicate freedom, as reflected in the expression "free-floating." Floating through the air can have the same meaning as flying. Large bodies of water are frequently symbols of the unconscious, so floating in calm waters indicates being at peace with the unconscious. A curious aside—pregnant women often have floating dreams.

FLOOD

Because water is a universal symbol for the unconscious, a flood dream can indicate being overwhelmed by unconscious material, such as repressed emotions. It can also represent a feeling of being overwhelmed by circumstances in one's life. Floods are related to initiation, in the sense that they can symbolize the destruction or washing away of the old in preparation for something new. Finally, a flood, as the bursting forth of fluids, can be a sexual symbol.

FLOWER

Flowers are natural symbols of beauty, delicacy, harmlessness, and attraction (e.g., the attraction of bees to nectar). Flowers are also symbols of the deep self. In both southern Asian yoga systems and the Western esoteric tradition, flowers represent the psychic centers referred to as chakras ("wheels"). The expression "spiritual unfoldment" is a flower-related image. Finally, the dreaming mind often literalizes common verbal expressions—such as "wallflower" and "flower power"—in an effort to

convey something to the conscious mind.

FLYING

Flying is a universal dream motif. Flying can reflect a sense that one is "flying high" or that one has "risen above" something. Flying also represents freedom and joy. Sigmund Freud associated flying with sexual desire, Alfred Adler with the will to dominate others, and Carl Jung with the desire to break free of restrictions.

FOG

Fog represents a sense of being lost and confused—not knowing where one is going. Fog can also symbolize the realm of the unconscious, which one may be exploring or attempting to navigate in a dream. Finally, a fog can obscure things, for good or bad.

FOLLOW

To follow something in a dream indicates that we are attracted to something or that we are being influenced by whatever we are following. Being followed in a dream can mean that we are influencing others; negatively, it can represent the feeling that we are being pursued or followed by something out of our past—such as pain or guilt.

FOOD

Food can symbolize the taking in of physical or nonphysical nourishment. Food can also represent enjoyment or indulgence. Finally, the dreaming mind often literalizes common verbal expressions—such as "food for thought" and "let me digest that"—in an effort to convey something to the conscious mind. (See also Groceries).

FOOT

Feet can symbolize everything from sex to humility. They also represent mobility, freedom, and a foundation. Various metaphors may be represented by literal feet in the dream state: "taking a step in the right direction"; "give him the boot"; "foot in the mouth"; "foot in the door"; "kick the bums out."

FOREIGN COUNTRY

Dreaming about being in a foreign country depends on one's associations with that specific country. Otherwise, it can represent feeling that one is in a whole new condition, or that one has a completely new attitude about something.

FOREST

Forests, as a segment of nature not brought fully under the dominion of humankind, are symbols of the unconscious. Thus, traveling into the forest indicates exploration of the unconscious realm. Forests also represent a comforting refuge from the demands of everyday life. (See also Jungle).

FORT

Forts represent safety and protection. Perhaps the dreamer needs a fortress against worldly invasion, or perhaps the dreamer is deliberately erecting barriers against life.

FOUNTAIN

Fountains capture a symbol of emotions and of the unconscious; they combine water with the elements of air and light, symbolizing a highly controlled and intellectualized examination of the self. Fountains are also symbols of nourishment (the fountain of life) and eternal life (the fountain of youth).

FOUR

Four is the number of stability, upon which all is based: the four sides to the square; the four seasons; the four directions; the four elements; and, the four mental functions (thought, feeling, sense, and intuition).

FOX

Foxes are symbols of cunning and craftiness. In older times, they were symbols of the devil. Because of the connotations of such expressions as "fox" and "foxy," this animal has also become associated with seductive female beauty and charms.

FROG

Frogs are associated closely with water, which makes them symbols of the unconscious. Because of the widely known story of the prince who was turned into a frog and then back into a prince, frogs also represent transformation.

FROZEN

Being frozen in a dream has a range of possible meanings, from feeling emotionally or sexually cold to simply feeling that one is unable to do something different from whatever one is doing. We also speak about "frozen assets" and waiting until "hell freezes over."

FRUIT

Fruits are complex symbols, representing everything from transcendence, to the self, to abundance, to spiritual knowledge. (See entries on particular fruits for more information.) The dreaming mind often literalizes common verbal expressions in an effort to convey something to the conscious mind, so fruit dreams can also indicate anything along the lines of "first fruits," "forbidden fruit," "fruitcake," and so on.

FUNERAL

People often dream about watching their own funerals. This usually indicates that part of one's life—or perhaps old ways of seeing things—have died. Alternatively, it can mean that one feels like some aspect of one's life is dead. Someone else's funeral in a dream can represent the unconscious desire to see that particular person dead, or a fear that someone might die.

FURNITURE

A dream that emphasizes furniture can refer to attitudes from the past, particularly if the piece of furniture is a familiar item from one's childhood. Can also represent current attitudes and beliefs. Self-image. Another possibility is the familiar expression about having been around so long that one has become "part of the furniture."

DREAM SYMBOLS

G

GAMES

Games appearing in a dream may show relaxation, play, or competition. Depending on childhood experiences, we also tend to associate games with feelings of competency or inadequacy. Dream games can express such notions as "life is just a game," "they're playing games," "play to win," and so on.

GANG

Dreaming of being a gang member may be an unconscious expression of the need to achieve things through force and intimidation. If threatened by a gang, one may feel that life conditions or the factors associated with a particular issue have "ganged up" on them.

GARAGE

Dreaming about a garage can have variable meanings, depending on how one utilizes her or his garage. Is it a tool shed and hobby room, or just a place to park the car? In general, the garage refers to one's reserves of energy and motivation.

GARBAGE

Garbage in a dream often symbolizes discarding or expelling outworn ideas or eliminating stagnation in one's life. It can also represent disposal of excesses that may have been overwhelming the

dreamer. Smelling garbage may indicate rotting and decaying conditions.

GARDEN

A beautiful garden in glorious bloom is said to represent the psyche and the growth of the soul; the transition from earthly realms to heavenly planes, and peace and harmony. A sparse, weed-infested garden suggests that the spiritual needs of the dreamer should be tended.

GARDENER

The caretaker of a garden could symbolize a spiritual protector, a guardian angel, "spirit guide," or God. If the dreamer is the gardener, then one's own higher self is tending to their needs.

GATE

Gates represent entrances to a new place or new circumstances in life. They also symbolize the "exit" from old, unwanted conditions. (See also Door.)

GATEKEEPER

The gatekeeper allows passage from one form or condition to another. If the dreamer is the gatekeeper, the dream may mean the dreamer should be careful about what he or she allows to pass through or hold on to in his or her life.

GATHERINGS

The nature of a particular gathering suggests the meaning of this symbol (e.g., a happy and sociable assembly or a sad or angry crowd). Groups also suggest the collective opinion of others.

GENITALS

While many common objects can symbolize genitals in dreams, a dream that includes one's genitals is usually referring to the sexual side of life. Exactly what is being said about one's sexuality is a function of what happens in the dream, and whether the dreamer feels pleasure, pain, guilt, or some other emotion. (See also Penis.)

GHOST

Ghosts symbolize the essence of what no longer is obtainable (e.g., people sometimes believe they don't have "a ghost of a chance").

GIANT

Giants can be good and friendly symbols (e.g., "the jolly Green Giant") or a fierce and terrifying one (e.g., the "fee fie foe fum" ogre in the story "Jack and the Bean Stalk"). They also symbolize what is outstandingly large and overwhelming in the dreamer's life, such as a "gigantic" obstacle.

GIFT

Gifts represent rewards for a job well done or for inner spiritual blessing (gifts of the spirit).

GLASS (WINDOW)

Glass (in the sense of glass windows rather than a drinking glass) frequently represents the invisible social or emotional barriers we erect between ourselves and others. A dream in which glass breaks can thus mean a breaking down of barriers. (See also Window).

GLOBE

Having control of one's world can be indicated by a stationary globe. A spinning globe often symbolizes the opposite situation—that one's world is out of control.

GLOVES

Trying to avoid getting one's hands "dirty" or being in a situation so delicate that "kid gloves" are required for handling it suggests a situation where the utmost diplomacy is required. Alternatively, putting gloves on to "duke it out" indicates aggressive behavior is required.

GNOME

Gnomes symbolize the magical world of wishes and make-believe related to one's "inner child," the inner treasures that the dreamer may possess.

GOAT

The sacrificial "scapegoat," the tenacious "old goat," and "getting someone's goat" all indicate the sturdiness of this animal. This symbol is also associated with sexual vitality ("lecherous old goat"), especially when depicted as a satyr, such as the god Pan in pagan mythology.

GOLD

This metal suggests that a bright event in the future may hold one of life's finest rewards. The color gold also represents a high state of illumination.

GOOSE

"The goose that lays the golden eggs" symbolizes opulent fertility and wealth on the physical plane of life. Also, because the dreaming mind tends to literalize linguistic metaphors and idioms, dream geese can imply that one's "goose is cooked."

GRAIN

Grain represents an opulent harvest and is often symbolic of a good life.

GRANDMOTHER

Grandmothers are symbols of wisdom and caretaking. A grandmother in a dream can indicate that important life lessons are assuming a prominent role in the dreamer's life. This symbol can also indicate a regression to childhood needs.

GRAPES

The grape is a symbol of harvest and of sacrifice. Because of popular images in which beautiful damsels hand-feed grapes to reclining revelers, grapes may represent wealth, opulence, or decadence. Christian rituals incorporate grapes to represent the blood of Christ.

GRASS

Flowing green grasses, sweeping meadows, or farms suggest an image of peaceful, pastoral lifestyles. The more common grass of suburban lawns can represent domesticity.

GRAVE

Graves often represent the end of the line, the end or "death" of something, rather than literal death. They also suggest grave issues that require depth of thought and contemplation before making a decision. Because of their underworld connotations, graves can indicate the realm of the unconscious. (See also Burial, Coffin, Crypt, Dead/Death, Hearse).

GREEN

Green is widely considered to be the color of healing and prosperity. Money is green in the United States, and plants and herbs are the life-giving color of green. This symbol can also indicate that a project or idea has been given the "green light" to proceed.

GROCERIES

Groceries in dreams indicate abundance of nourishment for either the body or the soul. They also indicate a "grocery" list depicting the many chores and obligations one is trying to accomplish. (See also Food).

GROUPS

Groups of people, animals, or objects may represent the collective consciousness in the arena of mind and spirit.

GROWTH

A dream in which we witness something growing (e.g., a plant) can represent ways in which we have grown personally, or ways in which our life situation has changed and grown.

GUILLOTINE

Dreaming about having one's head cut off in a guillotine could indicate a loss of one's rational perspective on something. Perhaps the dream is a literalizing of the expression "to lose one's head." (See also Beheading, Decapitation).

GUN

The gun is a symbol of aggression and protection. The dreamer may feel the need for protection from real or perceived danger. The gun can also symbolize aggressive male sexuality.

GURU

A symbol of spiritual authority. Meeting a guru in one's dream can mean encountering one's own inner guidance—a variation on the wise old (wo)man archetype.

GYMNASTICS

Gymnastic displays in dreams symbolize agility and strength to spontaneously leap and twist in and out of circumstances and dilemmas, with artistry, grace, and poise.

GYPSY

Dreaming about gypsies may indicate the desire to roam freely without responsibilities and obligations, or to venture forth to seek one's fortune by chance.

DREAM SYMBOLS

HAIR

Hair has been a sacred and spiritual symbol throughout history. For example, it was the secret of the strength of Sampson in the biblical story. Hair carries an aura of sexual virility, seduction, and health. White hair denotes wisdom and age.

HALF

The notion of half can be expressed in dreams in a number of different ways. A door half open can indicate indecision. If cut in half, one is in conflict with oneself, between one's mind and one's body.

HALLWAY

Hallways often symbolize the unconscious passageways through which people travel to either life or death. They also represent a new level of consciousness or a new experience, as well as a journey into the unknown. (See also Corridor).

HALO

A dream of oneself with a halo may signify that perfection is a goal for the dreamer. Alternatively, it may represent an exaggerated "holier than thou" attitude.

HAMMER

Hammers suggest the power to forge new ways and build new dreams (e.g., as in the popular song "If I Had a Hammer"). A hammer can also indicate destructive force, as in hammering winds or hammering an opponent as well as an attempt to communicate a point, as in hammering away on some subject.

HANDS

Hands symbolize building, healing, and praying. Clasped hands depict unity and completeness or agreement. One can "give a hand" to help and to soothe. Negative connotations of this symbol include a "heavy-handed" manner in relationships and theft or deceit ("caught with his hand in the cookie jar"). Wringing and washing of the hands suggests a worrisome issue that the dreamer needs to work through.

HARBOR

A ship anchored at harbor can symbolize the feeling that something or someone is "all washed up", as well respite from a hard siege. Ships also represent a place of security to hide or to regroup.

HARE

See Rabbit.

HARNESS

A harness is an obvious symbol of restraint and control. Also, could indicate a need to "harness our potential."

HAT

Hats represent concealment (e.g., a magician's hat) and a covering of one's head and mind ("keep this under your hat"). A tipped hat suggests a greeting, and different types of hats symbolize different situations (e.g., a beret suggests the military and a top hat represents magic, a formal occasion, a dance routine).

HAWK

To watch someone "like a hawk" is to suggest that suspicions are aroused and caution is advised. The hawk is also a high-flying regal messenger and symbolizes keen eyesight.

HEAD

The head symbolizes the source of all wisdom. Being made the "head" of an organization, or being sent to the "head of the class" denotes that one has accomplished much.

HEALING

Healing in a dream often reflects a need for physical or emotional healing, the power to put right those things in the dreamer's life that need to be cared for and made well.

HEARSE

Dreaming about a hearse can be a reminder of our mortality. Otherwise, a part of ourselves or a part of our life that has died. (See also Burial, Coffin, Crypt, Dead/Death, Grave).

HEART

The heart is the eternal symbol of love, romance, and the very life force within all of humankind. Getting to the "heart of the matter" suggests that the heart rules the source of truth and love. When one is unfair in a particularly insensitive manner, the person and the act are described as "heartless." Friendship, courage, romantic bonds, and emotional expression are also embodied in this symbol.

HEARTH

The hearth signifies a place to return to home values and nurturing feelings. It is traditionally the center of sacred beginnings and also of sacred rituals. It also represents a chance to begin again.

HEAVEN

Over and above the obvious theological connotations of heaven, dreaming about heaven represent an individual's sense of harmony and joy. Could also represent a retreat from life's difficulties.

HEEL

The heel is often used synonymously for the foot as a symbol, for example, to represent violence or oppression (e.g., under the heel of a dictator). As the part of the body most often in contact with the ground and dirt, it can be a symbol of the base or ignoble, for instance, a low, vile, contemptible, despicable person (a "heel"). The heel is also often represented by the analogous part of a shoe, which is frequently in shabby condition ("down at the heels"), perhaps signifying something in the dreamer's life that needs attention. Finally, the heel can also represent vulnerability, as in an Achilles' heel.

HEIGHT

A dream about high elevation may signify reaching the zenith of one's career or achieving some other high objective. If one fears heights in a dream, then one may be striving for things that seem beyond their reach. Such a dream can also relate to other concepts associated with height, such as being "above it all."

HELL

Hell symbolizes a place of suffering and torment. Someone who dreams of hell may be suffering from a seemingly inescapable situation caused by having given away his or her emotional power to someone else.

HELMET

An instrument of protection, a helmet can mean that either the dreamer is secure physically or the dreamer's thoughts and ideas need to be guarded.

HEN

The hen symbolizes gossip and calamity as well as being annoyingly pecked at by a person or a situation ("henpecked").

HERMAPHRODITE

Dreaming about having characteristics of both sexes can show, on the one hand, a balance between our masculine and feminine character traits. On the other hand, it could reflect confusion about our sexual identity.

HERO/HEROINE

The hero(ine) is a universal archetype, a symbol, among other things, for the self, even our ideal self. Our creativity and our sense of initiative. Dreaming about being rescued by a hero(ine) is more complex. It could represent either the intervention by our own higher self or a feeling of weakness, helplessness, incompetence, and, as a consequence, a need to be rescued.

HIDING

Feeling anxious about our situation, and a desire to escape our situation. Alternatively, feeling anxious about our own unacceptable inner promptings; hiding something is a way of not looking at it.

HIGH

Dreaming about being elevated can reflect, on the one hand, a sense of broad scope, of standing above and observing other things. On the other hand, it can indicate a sense of detachment, of not really being involved. Dreaming about seeing something elevated can indicate being impressed or being challenged.

HILL

To climb and climb is to struggle and not succeed, whereas to reach the top of the hill is to have succeeded.

HIVE

The hive is a symbol of industriousness and teamwork. If stung by a bee or many bees, one needs to either get to work or slack off from overworking (being "busy a bee").

HOLDING

A dreaming emphasizing holding can have a multitude of meanings. We can hold things as an act of protection, ownership, as an act of control ("holding our breath"), intimacy, or responsibility. So one has to determine which meaning of holding is being expressed in the dream.

HOLE

A hole in the ground represents a pitfall if one dreams of falling into a hole or one's life is represented by dark holes. It can also mean that the dreamer is "stuck" in a hole or that something is hidden. (See also Cave, Pit).

HOLIDAY

Dreaming about being on a holiday (vacation) can indicate either a feeling of relaxation or a desire to be in a relaxing situation. Also, it can represent a sense of independence and fulfilling one's own needs.

HOLLOW

Something that is hollow retains the outer form, but is missing the core, the substance. A dream about a hollow object can reflect a feeling that despite the fact that everything is outwardly okay, something essential is missing.

HOLLY

The symbol of Christmas cheer decorating the fireplace hearth, holly represents memories of friends, family, and the nurturing feelings associated with childhood and the holiday season.

HOME

Independence and dependency mark the feelings of going home. Home also represents security issues and childlike desires that need to be fulfilled. (See also Mansion).

HONEY

The sweet taste of honey is like the sweet taste of success. As a symbol, honey also means too much sweetness ("dripping like honey"). A dreamer who experiences this symbol might need to be less vulnerable and more honest in communicating with others.

HOOD

Mystery and death are the associations of a hooded figure. The hood can indicate either the passing away of old obstacles or cowering and hiding from a person or a situation.

HORNS

Horns in a dream sometimes indicate a "wake-up call" and the need to pay attention to the inner voices of one's intuition and spiritual guidance.

Also, because of the dreaming mind's tendency to literalize linguistic metaphors and idioms, dream horns can mean that one is on "the horns of a dilemma."

HORSE

The horse is a powerful animal representing noble and forthright actions. If the dreamer is riding the horse, the dreamer is most probably in control of his or her life. The drives of power and sex can also come into play in this kind of dream.

HORSESHOE

The horseshoe is often a lucky portent of success in the dreamer's endeavors. Myth and folklore associate good fortune and protection with this symbol.

HOSE

A hose is an obvious phallic symbol. Hoses are also used for washing and for watering (i.e., nurturing something that is growing), and a dream about hoses can reflect either meaning. Also note the slang meaning of "hosed"—namely, being cheated.

HOSPITAL

The hospital is a place to heal and get back to health and back into the flow of life. The hospital also suggests the need to pay attention to one's health.

HOT

Passion, warm feelings. If something in a dream is so hot that it burns, it can indicate painful feelings. Also note various idiomatic uses of hot, such as "hot headed," "being in hot water," the "hot seat," and "hot air."

HOTEL

A place of temporary housing, a hotel may indicate the need for a new state of mind or a condition that requires a short move away from home and familiar conditions.

HOURGLASS

An hourglass represents the passing of time and the end of a cycle in one's life or a project.

HOUSE

Because a house is a personal dwelling place, a house under construction shows inner work is being performed on the psyche. The condition of a house—whether it is in disrepair or it is fixed up and newly painted—is also symbolic.

HOUSEWORK

Dreaming about housework can simply be a reflection of our everyday tasks. Otherwise, it can refer to "getting our house together," or cleaning out the things that no longer serve us.

HUNGER

Feeling hungry in a dream may represent a feeling of unfulfillment. The dreamer may be starving for recognition, or hungering to obtain or to achieve something long desired. Alternatively, this dream experience could simply indicate that one is actually hungry and needs to nourish oneself with good food. (See also Devour, Eating).

HUNTING

Hunting for something indicates that one is seeking to fulfill inner desires, whether emotional or physical.

DREAM SYMBOLS

ICE

Ice often symbolizes the dreamer's emotional state. The dreamer may not be conscious of being blocked or frozen emotionally. Falling through the ice suggests the dreamer may be "skating on thin ice" and should alter course to avoid mishap.

ICE CREAM

Ice cream is often associated with childhood. Alternatively, the dreamer may be celebrating a release of cold, repressed emotions that have melted at the heart of some situation.

IDENTIFICATION

The state of one's self-confidence can be symbolized by the form of identification one has in a dream. A lost or stolen wallet, driver's license, or passport may suggest confusion about the dreamer's self-identity or self-confidence.

IGLOO

Dreaming about an igloo might refer to a home life that one feels is "cold," or a parent one feels was aloof. Alternatively, an igloo can be shelter against the threatening cold.

ILLNESS

Dreams of illness may suggest that the dreamer should pay attention to health matters especially to the areas of the body revealed in the dream. (See also Infection, Vaccination).

IMMOBILITY

A dream that one is immobile can symbolize an inner inflexibility, especially with regard to resolving one's problems. It can also mean that the dreamer feels trapped. People afflicted with sleep paralysis sometimes dream they are immobile or unable to run, but such dreams do not necessarily have deeper psychological meanings.

INCEST

The age of the person having a dream about incest must be considered, for obvious reasons. If one has never had this type of dream before, there could be any number of innocuous reasons behind it. What is important to evaluate is how the dreamer's body feels about the dream after awakening. If incest dreams are recurrent—with a strong bodily awareness that corresponds with sexual violation, either as a victim or a predator—please seek professional care immediately. Incest in America is a national epidemic, and paying attention to relevant dreams will help heal this issue.

INDIAN

See Native American.

INDIGESTION

Indigestion in a dream can mean that something does not "sit well," upsetting the dreamer the dreamer, who would like to be rid of the unwanted situation.

INFECTION

A dream about being infected might represent anything from absorbing (being "infected by") the negative attitudes of others to concerns about one's health. Possibly, the dream infection represents negative thoughts or feelings. (See also Illness).

INFIDELITY

Dreams of infidelity often indicate that one needs to confront feelings of guilt about sexual relationships.

INITIATION

A dream about an initiation ceremony can mean that a change is taking place in the dreamer's life. The dreamer may be evolving to a new level spiritually. Such a dream can also indicate that one is moving into a new career or advancing in status in some other area.

INJECTION

In traditional psychoanalysis, a dream about an injection is often viewed as a dream about sexual intercourse. Can also indicate an influence that is forced on us. If we had bad experiences with being inoculated as children, then an injection dream can represent any number of different anxieties and fears.

INSECTS

A dream about insects indicates that something is "bugging" the dreamer, perhaps some person or condition in the person's life.

INTERVIEWS

Facing an interview in a dream carries the same connotations of anxiety as dreams about exam taking. The dreamer may feel that he or she is being judged by others or by herself.

INVALID

A dream about being an invalid may signify the lack of confidence and energy to pursue some issue. Hopelessness may have crippled the dreamer's will to stand up and perform.

INVENTOR

We can dream about an inventor, or about being an inventor, when we are trying to figure out something. Otherwise, an inventor can simply represent our own creativity.

INVISIBLE

Invisibility is a natural symbol of the unconscious mind. Also, something that is forgotten. Hidden influences.

IRON

Iron is associated with strength and willpower (an "iron will"), which may play into the meaning of a dream in which iron is explicitly a part.

ISLAND

To escape to an island in a dream may mean the peace of solitude is needed by the dreamer. A further meaning is that the dreamer is afraid of the surrounding waters of his or her unconscious and wishes to remain isolated from his or her inner feelings.

DREAM SYMBOLS

JACKAL

Jackals are considered negative creatures because they scavenge dead bodies. In Egyptian mythology, the jackal led souls to the land of the dead. As a dream symbol, the jackal can signify transformation. It can also symbolize someone's worst nightmare.

JAGUAR

The jaguar represents speed, agility, and sleek power. It is also associated with mystical powers.

JAIL/JAILOR

Dreaming about being in jail usually reflects a sense of restriction one feels in one's outer life, the limiting of one's creativity. It could also indicate a sense of guilt or self-criticism. Alternatively, the dreamer may need to "put a lock on" certain actions and behavior. Dreaming about being the jailor is similar, though it shifts the focus to our own agency—we are the ones restricting ourselves.

JAWS

Some dream interpreters believe that jaws signify the gates to the underworld. Jaws in a dream can also indicate a bad meal, spiritual indigestion, or a bad mix of food that produces an old-fashioned "nightmare."

JELLYFISH

Jellyfish are creatures of the sea, a frequent symbol of the emotions or of the unconscious mind. Thus, jellyfish in a dream can represent unconscious, painful emotions.

JEWELS/JEWELRY

Jewels in a dream often signify value in the spiritual sense of protection. Magic cures and healing energies are also traditionally attributed to jewels. In addition, they can signify inner wealth. (See also Necklace, Ring).

JOB

Dreaming of being at work while asleep signifies either overwork, overinvolvement in one's job, or a subconscious desire to be more productive in one's professional life.

JOKE

Humor in a dream is a good indication of lightheartedness and release from the tension that may have surrounded some issue. There is, however, also a negative side of humor, such as when someone or something is derided as "a joke."

JOURNEY

See Travel.

JUDGE/JUDGMENT

A judge may represent an authority figure—in real life or in the dreamer's psyche—who constantly condemns or criticizes spontaneous actions that are considered to be unruly and frivolous. A dream in which one feels guilty about committing a wrong may indicate a subconscious need to condemn one's actions—self-judgment. Alternatively, judges may represent justice or good/bad judgment. (See also Court).

JUMPING

To jump or leap over hurdles, even mountains, in a dream may indicate that the dreamer is experiencing great successes in waking life. The greater the leap, the greater the achievement.

JUNGLE

The wild parts of the dreamer's personality that may have been inhibited by social conditioning may express themselves in dreams of the jungle or the wild. (See also Forest).

JUNK

Junk symbolizes things that need to be let go of and discarded. In a dream, junk can also indicate rejected parts of the self that need to be reappropriated.

JURY

Juries represent the part, of the self that weighs the evidence and reaches a verdict. A jury may imply that the dreamer is guilty of self-abnegation and self-abandonment.

DREAM SYMBOLS

KALEIDOSCOPE

The kaleidoscope signifies the fragments that come together to form a whole, perhaps indicating something diverse, such as a situation with varied aspects, or piecing together the parts of a symbolic puzzle.

KEY

Keys can symbolize having a secret. They can also represent "locking away" one's inner feelings. The holder of the key has the power to unlock whatever the dreamer needs.

KICK

Kicking is a rather obvious symbol for aggression and self-assertiveness. Being kicked in a dream can mean feeling abused, getting "kicked in the teeth." The meanings of certain idioms can also find expression in dreams, idioms like "getting your kicks," "kick the bucket," and "kick yourself."

KILL

The act of killing in a dream need not be negative. As we grow and change, it often feels like we are "killing off" old parts of our life. Alternatively, killing in a dream may mean that one has murdered the incentive or enthusiasm for life. (See also Murder).

KING

A king is a power symbol, either for good or for bad. In a dream a king may represent a boss, a father, or the dreamer.

KISS

A kiss in a dream often signifies a romantic interest, as in the kiss that awakens Sleeping Beauty from a deep sleep. At the other extreme, a kiss can signify betrayal, as in the kiss of death with which Judas betrayed Jesus. Whether the dreamer is receiving the kiss or giving the kiss and the kind of feeling evoked by the kiss determine its meaning.

KITCHEN

A kitchen signifies a place of physical or spiritual nourishment. The food being cooked or eaten in the dream may indicate what food the dreamer's body needs.

KNAPSACK

A knapsack in a dream can carry either our difficulties or our personal resources. Perhaps we are carrying burdens from the past, a heavy load that keeps us from fully actualizing ourselves in the present.

KNEEL

Kneeling in a dream can reflect, on the one hand, a sense of humility and cooperation; or, on the other hand, a sense of surrender.

KNIFE

A knife can signify the need to cut to the quick, to lay open one's innermost fears. It may indicate being "stabbed in the back" or being the victim or perpetrator of an act of violence. A knife in a dream is also often seen as a male sexual symbol, and is generally associated with aggression.

KNIGHT

A knight in a dream can mean that the dreamer is looking for a "knight in shining armor" as a mate or a savior. It can also mean that the dreamer possesses the sterling qualities revealed in the dream.

KNITTING

Knitting is an obvious symbol for something we are building, either in our career or in our relationships. Knitting together a relationship, particularly one that needs mending. (See also Sewing).

KNOB

Knobs may symbolize turning issues or conditions around so that the dreamer can get a handle on things again. The knob is also a symbol for a threshold, for passing from one condition to another.

KNOCK

Hearing a knock in a dream is often the subconscious mind's way of getting our attention. You are not noticing something important, or there is something within you that you need to heed. If the dreamer is doing the knocking, it represents a desire to get attention.

KNOT

A knot is an obvious symbol of constraints and restrictions on one's freedom of thought, feelings, or actions, indicating a difficult situation that needs to be untied. Anxieties about getting married ("tying the knot") are sometimes denoted by this dream symbol. More positively, a knot can symbolize control, and having something "all wrapped up." (See also Necktie).

DREAM SYMBOLS

L

LABEL

A dream about labels is often about self-projection, either how we want to be perceived or how we imagine others see us.

LABORATORY

A laboratory symbolizes a place to experiment with one's inner feelings, beliefs, and fears.

LADDERS

A ladder can symbolize an aid in one's climb to new levels of awareness of one's inner world as well as greater understanding of outer conditions. Career and social standing are also symbolized by the ladder ("climbing the social ladder"), as is material prosperity ("the ladder of success").

LAKE

A lake can represent our subconscious or our inner feelings. A dream about a lake might also be alluding to the familiar idiom "go jump in a lake."

LAMB

"As gentle as a lamb" is a common metaphor brought to mind by this symbol. In a dream this symbol can indicate the Lamb of God (Christ), or being sacrificed like a "lamb to the slaughter." The dreamer's relationship with this symbol determines its meaning.

LAME/LIMP

A dream about limping could represent feelings of weakness, inadequacy, or uncertainties about a particular situation. A dream about lameness might also be alluding to the metaphorical use of "lame" as being pathetic or unoriginal.

LANDING

An airplane landing may be a symbol for feelings of completion. The dreamer may have felt out of control with issues that were "up in the air" but are being grounded.

LANE

Dreaming about a lane can have the same meaning as dreaming about a road: namely, the direction of our life or our life path. Whereas a dream about a country lane might be alluding to a "trip down memory lane," a lane on a multi-lane highway could indicate "life in the fast lane."

LANGUAGE (UNFAMILIAR)

Overhearing or being spoken to in an unfamiliar language in a dream can symbolize anything we are having difficulty understanding in other parts of our life. Alternatively, another part of our mind might be trying to communicate something to us that we don't quite understand.

LATE

An experience of being late in a dream often reflects a sense of being too late in some area of our waking lives. Alternatively, perhaps the message of the dream is "better late than never."

LAUGHING/LAUGHTER

Laughing in a dream often has the same meaning as it does in ordinary life: namely, taking something lightly or putting others at ease. Alternatively, a dream laugh can be alluding to one of many idioms, from "have the last laugh" to "laughing all the way to the bank."

LAVA

Dreaming about lava can reflect a number of different conditions, from a fever to overheated sexuality or emotions. Something from our past that erupts to the surface.

LEAD

Associations with lead revolve around heaviness. Lead in a dream may represent a condition that has weighed so heavily upon the consciousness that it feels like lead. Alternatively, lead is related to sluggishness, as in the expression "get the lead out."

LEAF

A green leaf represents new life, whereas a falling leaf can represent something that is falling away. Because Adam and Eve supposedly wore leaves, leaves can symbolize something we try to hide. A dream leaf can also be drawing on the meaning of certain idioms, such as "turn over a new leaf" or "shake like a leaf."

LEAK

If one dreams about something leaking out, then it can represent a feeling of being depleted or wasted energy. Water leaking into a sinking boat is often a straightforward reflection of a "sinking" feeling. Sometimes dreaming about a leak is a simple reflection of our need to wake up and "take a leak."

LEFT BEHIND

See Abandonment.

LEG

To "get a leg up" on issues and conditions may symbolize that the dreamer has regained the confidence to stand up and take control again. Legs also signify movement, especially running.

LENS

Lens symbolize taking a better or a closer look at things. The dreamer may need to concentrate on something or focus on a situation that has been neglected.

LETTER

Dreaming about receiving and reading a letter can indicate either our intuitions or our fantasies about what the sender thinks about us. We send letters in a dream when we want to tell someone something. A dream letter can also be an allusion to certain idioms, from doing something "to the letter" to receiving a rejection "Dear John letter."

LETTUCE

Lettuce is a slang word for money. Depending on the dreamer's association with this symbol, the dream may indicate fruitfulness or financial matters.

LIBRARY

Libraries in a dream suggest the search for knowledge and the hunger for ideas. It may be time for the dreamer to seek out new meanings in life.

LIFT

Being lifted in a dream may indicate that the dreamer is rising above unpleasant conditions or issues. Being lifted can also have the same connotations as ascension and height.

LIGHT

Illumination in a dream can symbolize the shedding of light on a situation or problem, enlightenment of one's consciousness, and lighting the way on a physical or spiritual journey. The extinguishing of light may signify the end of an old situation. Spiritually, this is a very positive symbol.

LIGHTHOUSE

The lighthouse is a symbol of guidance through the dark waters of the unconscious or through tumultuous emotions to a safe harbor.

LIGHTNING

Lightning can symbolize sudden awareness ("like a bolt of lightning") as well as purification and purging through the flash of light.

LILY

The lily is said to be one of the most spiritual of flowers. It possesses a fragrance that stimulates the glands and the chakras (the psychic centers). The fragrance of this flower is said to transform one's mood into a peaceful and blissful state.

LION

The lion symbolizes daring, strength, and ferocity. As king of the jungle, it also symbolizes royalty, leadership, and dominion ("the lion's share"). The specific implication depends on the dreamer's associations with the lion in the dream.

LIPS

Lips in contemporary culture often represent sensuousness, sex, love, and romance. They are also associated with communication, as in the familiar expression "read my lips."

LIQUID

Because of the perceived "fluid" nature of emotions, liquids can symbolize emotions. Additionally, liquids are sexual symbols. Any liquid can also represent alcohol, as in the expression "liquid refreshment."

LITTLE

Dreaming about being little can relate to childhood or to "feeling small." Little also finds a place in numerous idioms, any one of which might indicate the meaning of one's dream: "little by little," a "little horror," "too little too late," "Oak trees grow from little acorns," etc. (See also Shrink, Small).

LIVER

Dreaming about liver can be a dream about one's health: either we need a diet change or perhaps we are hurting our liver with alcohol or prescription drugs. Also note the expression "lily-livered," which refers to cowardice.

LIZARD

Though a dream about any kind of an animal can represent our "animal" nature, lizards are not natural candidates for this role. Perhaps the lizard is a chameleon, which changes its color to conform to the environment. A dream lizard might also be a "lounge lizard."

LOBSTER

A crustacean can symbolize someone with a hard exterior and a soft interior. A lobster is also a creature of the depths, thus representing something from the unconscious mind. Or perhaps dreaming about a lobster is just a dream about an expensive meal.

LOCK

Locks in a dream may represent an inability to get what one wants, or being kept out. Perhaps some ability is locked up inside and needs to be expressed. Locks can also be symbols of security.

LOCKOUT

Losing one's keys and being locked out in a dream can indicate fear of losing your position in life. If another person has locked the dreamer out, then control is an issue to be confronted and dealt with—in the dreamer's career or personal life.

LOSS OF SOMETHING

Losing an object in a dream can be a straightforward representation of something we feel that we have lost in our waking life, such as an opportunity, a relationship, or even a loss of health. (See also Missing).

LOST

Being lost in a dream can reflect feelings of being "lost" and confused in everyday life. Being unclear about which direction to go in life. Also note certain idioms to which the dream may be alluding, such as "making up for lost time," "lost for words," or "lost in the shuffle."

LOUDSPEAKER

A loudspeaker may be the mind's way of trying to get our attention, especially about something that we have forgotten or an action we have delayed.

LOVER

To see a beautiful lover in one's dream is a special gift to one's inner self. It signifies acceptance of self-worth and acknowledgment of one's true inner value.

LUGGAGE

Luggage may indicate the dreamer wants a vacation. Alternatively, it may mean it is time to move on.

DREAM SYMBOLS

MACHINERY

To know the inner workings of something indicates that attention is being paid to the details of self and others. If one dreams of functioning like a piece of machinery, then the person's self-image or a relationship may be in need of repair.

MADONNA

The Madonna is a symbol of blessings, the goddess principle of the mystical mother, the giver of life and beauty.

MAFIA/MOBSTER

If we do not otherwise have associations with the mafia, then a dream about a mobster can represent the part of us that would like to violate the law and take what we want. Alternatively, a dream mobster could be the part of us that would like to exact some vigilante justice.

MAGGOTS

Maggots are associated with death and decay. Maggots in a dream can thus represent anxiety about our own mortality. We also commonly refer to certain despicable people as maggots. (See also Decay).

MAGIC

Magic has both positive and negative connotations. Positively, magic may represent a creative

mind that will "magically" achieve just what the dreamer is hoping for. Alternatively, black magic is a symbol for evil, and for getting what one wishes through underhanded "tricks."

MAGICIAN

Dreaming of a magician doing tricks may indicate that an issue the dreamer is dealing with may be trickier than realized. Magicians can also be symbols of creativity or of evil.

MAGNET

Magnets represent a pulling closer to things that need to be examined or drawn out of the unconscious. They also represent a certain kind of personal power, or personal "magnetism." They sometimes also represent being inexplicably drawn to something, as if by some mysterious magnetic force.

MAKEUP

Makeup in a dream can imply a cover-up to conceal one's inner self, indicating discomfort about revealing oneself to the world. At the opposite extreme, the dreamer may feel that putting on makeup is putting on one's best face, presenting oneself in all one's glory and accomplishments.

MANDALA

A mandala is an intricate design, usually of circular or square patterns, used in meditation to focus the mind: One gazes at and concentrates on the center or on a dot within the center of the design. This meditative concentration brings about a state of mind in which healing, harmony, and order can be restored. In Jungian psychology, mandalas represent the Self. To dream of a mandala may signal that it is time for the dreamer to look inward, or it may be a reflection of the positive changes the dreamer is experiencing in waking life.

MANSION

Our house is often a symbol of our body, so a mansion in a dream can represent a "rich" sense of self or even an exaggerated sense of self. A mansion might also represent our future potential, as something we might eventually grow into. (See also Home).

MANURE

Manure can be seen as something disgusting or, alternatively, as rich fertilizer. Many of our life experiences are like manure: something that is initially unpleasant but which becomes the basis for a later insight or achievement.

MAP

Following a map in a dream signifies the dreamer is being guided and led in a direction that will fulfill the person's needs, as well as provide growth experiences.

MARCHING

Marching in step with a line of soldiers, with a band, or in a political demonstration can indicate participation on a team. Marching alone can signify that the dreamer is "marching to the beat of a different drummer."

MARKET

Dreaming about a market is often a dream about everyday life in the economic realm. The exchanges that take place in relationships sometimes also have a market quality about them. Note that a dream market might be drawing on the meaning of a common idiom, such as "being in the market" for something, "cornering the market," or the metaphorical meaning of a "cattle market."

MARRIAGE

Marriage in a dream symbolizes commitment of oneself to another. It can also represent the inner marriage of formerly disjunctive aspects of oneself. (See also Bride/Bridegroom.)

MARSH

See Swamp.

MASK

Wearing a mask in a dream can suggest presenting a false persona to others to protect against ridicule and shame.

MASOCHISM

Masochism can represent a desire to punish oneself out of guilt for a crime committed. Physical masochism in a dream can also represent psychological masochism.

MATTRESS

Dreaming about a mattress carries with it the same connotations as dreaming about a bed, though a bare mattress is more about resting or sleeping or having sexual relationships somewhere other than one's own bedroom. (See also Bed/Bedroom).

MAZE

Mazes can represent the almost endless task of hide-and-seek with issues that need to be made simpler and faced more directly. They can also signify feeling like a "rat in a maze."

MEASUREMENT

If we dream about something being measured out, it may represent a feeling of waiting, of "How long will this last?" It could also allude to the fact that we are making comparisons in our waking life.

MEAT

Eating meat sometimes indicates that one is getting to the heart of the matter or finally getting down to the "meat of an issue." Meat can also represent a bold and hearty grasp of the dreamer's needs.

MEDICINE

Giving or receiving medicine in a dream is a very powerful experience. It is a cure to problems known and sometimes unknown. This is a very spiritual symbol of "healing guides" attending to the dreamer during sleep.

MEDITATION

If we meditate regularly in our waking life, a dream about meditating can be a simple reflection of our everyday experience. Otherwise, it can be a message from a deeper part of our minds, telling us to slow down or to reflect.

MELTING

Melting ice or snow may suggest a meltdown of frozen emotions that were previously held in check. Molten metal may symbolize a major transformation taking place.

MENDING

Mending signifies that one is fixing one's problems. Repairing clothing or fabric is to knit or heal what has become unraveled.

MERMAID/MERMAN

A mermaid or merman is a double symbol of our instinctual life because (1) a merperson is half animal, and (2) a merperson is at home in the water, a potent symbol of the unconscious. So a dream communication from a mermaid or merman is a message from a deeper part of ourselves.

METAL

Metals are hard but malleable, a potent symbol of strength and character. Metals can also be cold and, because of their association with technology, represent the inhuman side of our society.

METEOR

Ancient peoples believed that witnessing a meteor streaking across the sky or possessing a piece of a meteor meant that the gods had bestowed a gift from the heavens, which is where the custom of wishing upon a falling star derived. Seeing a meteor in a dream may symbolize a strong desire of the dreamer's or suggest that the dreamer is merely engaging in wishful thinking with regard to some aspect of his or her life.

MICROSCOPE

Dreaming about a microscope can be a message that we should look at something more carefully. Alternatively, it can represent the feeling that someone else is examining us in detail.

MILITARY

To see people in military uniforms of specific branches of the armed forces may be identifying with actual life experiences and memories if one has been in the military. Otherwise, the military in a dream may indicate rigid authoritarian and disciplinary methods that are being brought to bear upon the dreamer, or upon others by the dreamer. It may also suggest extreme emotional repression. If the dreamer is in a ship on the high seas, the dream may suggest sailing through emotional issues of divorce or other personal loss, bravely and dutifully.

MILK

Milk is the elixir of life from mother to child. If the dreamer is receiving the milk, it can indicate that a deep inner nourishment is being received. Should the dreamer be giving the milk to one's self or to another, much love and caring is being expressed in the dreamer's life. Also, perhaps a caretaking profession is being sought.

MILL

Something that is being ground to flour or meal can indicate the disintegration of the ego and false beliefs in self. It is the coming to grips with the "nitty gritty" of life, and behaving according to one's true values and beliefs.

MINE

Going into a mine can represent going to the depths of an issue or condition in the dreamer's life. It can also signify the inner terrain of the subconscious from which something valuable is being mined.

MIRROR

The mirror reflects oneself from the inner depths. If the mirror is clear, one is gazing upon one's true self. This may be a shocking or a pleasant experience, depending upon how many shortcomings or false images the dreamer pres-

ents in the real world. A cracked or cloudy mirror reflects the distortions that are projected into the world.

MISCARRIAGE

Expectant parents often have dreams about miscarriages. This is almost always a symbol of their anxiety about the baby rather than a prediction that the baby will be miscarried. Miscarriages are also potent symbols of projects or business deals that have gone wrong. (Also see Baby, Embryo, Pregnant).

MISSING

A missing article, such as a set of keys, denotes a sense of being out of control. A missed plane, bus, train, appointment, or time commitment can symbolize a missed opportunity, and the frustration of being behind and unorganized is also suggested. (See also Loss of Something).

MIST

Mist or fog can symbolize a confused state of mind, as well as the desire to see things more clearly.

MIXING

A dream about mixing may occur during a corporate merger, or during a social, political, or economic integration. The dreamer is putting together diverse situations or people.

MOLE

A blemish on the body suggests that something is marring or interfering with the dreamer's personal esteem or that the dreamer is unable to obtain the desired esteem of others. A mole can also refer to a ground-dwelling rodent. It may represent thoughts arising from the dark depths of one's subconscious mind, unearthing hidden agendas that need to be brought to light.

MONEY

Money in a dream is usually an extension of one's self-worth and self-esteem—a positive sign if abundance and accumulation is experienced; and a negative one if losses occur in the dream, suggesting one's inner resources may be depleted. Investing energy in oneself, one's career, or one's family is sometimes indicated by this symbol.

MONK

Monks are a symbol of spiritual discipline, asceticism, and inner wisdom. The dreamer's own religious beliefs determine the meaning of this dream symbol.

MONKEY

We typically think about monkeys as foolish, humorous and curious. Dream monkeys can represent any of these qualities. The also might be alluding to the meanings of such common idioms as to "monkey around," "monkey business." or to "make a monkey" out of someone.

MONSTER

Dreams of monsters are usually caused by repressed emotions and fears. Some ugly and scary aspect of the dreamer's personality may be reflected in, or confronted during, interaction with the monster.

MOON

The moon reflects our inner emotional feelings and the ways we express those feelings. The ebb and flow of the oceans of the planet with respect to the lunar phases often reflect cyclic increases and decreases of emotional energy states within

human beings. How the moon appears to the dreamer determines the meaning of this symbol.

MORNING

New beginnings, the renewal of one's life, starting over, enlightenment, and the awakening of inner creativity are all associated with the morning. An idea that dawns on you or an answer to a problem or a situation is sometimes the interpretation of a dream about the morning.

MOTH

Moths live in darkness but are attracted by light. An answer to a condition or a problem that the dreamer has been "kept in the dark" about may be revealed and "brought into the light."

MOTHER

The mother bestows life, love, and nurturing. Seeing a child being nursed suggests shelter, comfort, and protection. Seeing one's own mother in the dream reflects guidance and care. Being the mother in a dream denotes taking care of self or of a significant relationship in the dreamer's life. Alternatively, a mother can be a negative symbol if one has unpleasant association's with one's own mother.

MOTORCYCLE

Unless we regularly ride one, motorcycles in dreams often represent youthful energy and/or adolescent rebelliousness. A sense of freedom and/or a sense of danger.

MOUNTAIN

Climbing the mountain and reaching the top denotes achieving one's goals. Descending the mountain is returning after a success or letting go of insurmountable issues. Looking at the mountain may denote evaluating a major decision.

MOUSE

A mouse in a dream can indicate much scurrying, flitting, and running about—like a scared little mouse trying to hide in a hole and not having to confront things that could get one trapped. (See also Rat, Rodent).

MOUTH

A big mouth indicates gossip and the spreading of lies, or perhaps spoken words of goodness and truth. Romantic or sexual urges are associated with this symbol, too.

MOVIE

See Film.

MOVING

As a dream symbol, moving can indicate "moving up" in life or in one's state of consciousness. It can also suggest changes in the dreamer's life, especially if the person is moving into or out of a house.

MUD

Plans or conditions are obscured by the "muddy waters" of emotional indecision. Solutions or new directions may become clear by washing away mud from shoes or a roadway.

MUMMY

A mummy is a preserved dead person, so a dream about a mummy can be referring to something that has died but which we continue to preserve. A mummy is also concealed beneath layers of cloth, so a mummy can represent something we are hiding from ourselves.

MURDER

Murder symbolizes aggression and repressed rage at oneself or others. If the dreamer is murdered, the release of obstacles in one's life or a major transformation may be indicated. (See also Kill/Killing).

MUSEUM

Valuable ideas or inner gifts that need to be dusted off and brought out into the world are suggested by a museum. How the dreamer relates to a museum may reflect the ways in which they relate to their material possessions.

MUSHROOMS

Grown totally in the dark, mushrooms can denote a very challenging situation or relationship, especially if the mushrooms are poisonous. If seen growing wild in the forest's moist earth, then the dreamer's creative ideas may be the solution to the potentially dangerous situation the dreamer is concerned about.

MUSIC

To hear music or to be composing music indicates emotional expression. It can also indicate playing with one's emotions, or playing off of the emotions of another. Celestial music is like food for the soul, and a very special spiritual gift may be given to the dreamer of this symbol.

DREAM SYMBOLS

NAIL

A nail holds or binds objects together that need to be fixed or repaired. To "get nailed" is to get caught at something. Another slang expression, "hit the nail on the head," may indicate that an accurate appraisal may repair a problem or relationship. This symbol may be seen as a fingernail or toenail. If a fingernail is pointing at something, a new direction or viewpoint is being created. If one stubs a toenail, carelessness may have caught up with the person.

NAKED

Being naked in a dream suggests exposure of self to others, being vulnerable to how others see one, feeling ashamed of being found out. If one is naked like a baby, nakedness can also represent the desire for freedom or freedom of expression. Nakedness also suggests being unencumbered and uninhibited.

NAMES

Forgetting one's own name, or the names of others, is common in anxiety dreams. Being overburdened in waking life becomes so overwhelming that the dreamer feels unable to identify with his or her true self and can no longer recognize others.

NARROW

Dreaming about being in a narrow space can simply reflect the feeling that one has restricted options in some situation in one's waking life. Can also represent a "narrow escape," "narrow-mindedness," or "the straight and narrow."

NATIVE AMERICAN

Native Americans have been romanticized to the point where they symbolize certain ideals, from attunement with the natural world to stoicism in the face of the inevitable to spiritual wisdom. Alternatively, they can represent our "savage" desires. Any of these meanings might be expressed by dreams of native tribal people.

NATURE

Nature symbolizes life-giving forces—freedom, restoration, renewal. It suggests that one's basic instincts are experienced and expressed. Peace, calmness, simplicity, and tranquility can be denoted by this symbol.

NAUSEA

Purging and getting rid of a sickening situation or condition in the dreamer's life can be indicated by this dream symbol.

NAVEL

A navel can represent the center, as in the navel (the center) of the universe, or in the sense of personal centering. Dreaming about one's navel can also indicate something about the relationship with one's mother.

NEAR

If something is very close in a dream, this can indicate that the matter being dealt with in the dream is close to consciousness. The dream also might be drawing on a familiar idiom, such as "nearest and dearest" or a "near miss."

NECK

To "protect one's neck" is to not get caught at doing something in secret or to participate in a situation where one's actions could be condemned. Often the phrase "don't stick your neck out" is said as an admonishment. "Necking" describes romantic physical expressions of kissing, hugging, and overt passion arising aroused from the erogenous zones in the neck.

NECKLACE

A dream that focuses on one's necklace can indicate feelings of specialness or wealth, or associations with a person who might have given one the necklace as a gift. Alternatively, it could be weighing one down like "a millstone around one's neck." (See also Jewels/Jewelry, Ring).

NECKTIE

A loose-fitting necktie around one's neck can be a symbol of "tying up" loose ends in one's business world. If however, the necktie is drawn too tightly, then a condition of entrapment may be causing the dreamer some anxiety. (See also Knot, Noose.)

NEEDLE

If something were "needling" a person, then this dream symbol would be appropriate. A threaded needle can indicate the repairing of, or the sewing up of, unfinished issues in one's personal or business life. If, however, a needle is seen as an instrument of health in the hands of a doctor or a nurse, then health issues may be of concern to the dreamer. (See also Syringe, Vaccination).

NEST

To see a nest or to be building a nest may indicate that a new home is being prepared or built. A strong sense of homemaking, or having the "nesting" instinct, occurs when a woman is pregnant. A desire to go home may be expressed by this dream symbol.

NET

To cast a net as one does when attempting to catch fish or anything of value suggests that one is caught up in a net of intrigue or a complicated life situation.

NEWSPAPER

If there is anxiety felt in a newspaper dream, then reading a newspaper may indicate concern about one's reputation. It may also signify the desire to be recognized and acclaimed.

NIGHT

Dreaming about the darkness of the night often indicates that situations are not clear or need to be put to rest before accurate decisions can be made. If nighttime indicates pleasure to the dreamer, then recreation and entertainment may be in order.

NIGHTMARE

Too much indulgence in the things that cause upset to the mind, the body, or the spirit is indicated by nightmares, indicating it is time to cut back, identify problems, and reorganize one's lifestyle.

NOOSE

A hanging tree with a noose is a symbol of fear and anxiety. If the noose is around the neck of someone, perhaps there is repressed anger and rage at a person or a condition. (See also Necktie).

NORTH

A dream that calls attention to the northerly direction could be saying any number of different things. The north is the direction of cold and frozen wastes. But it also attracts a compass needle, so it provides direction and guidance. The North Pole is where Santa Claus lives, who annually showers the world with gifts.

NOSE

The nose is a source of much energy and wisdom. Having "a nose for the news" or "sticking one's nose into someone else's business" can be important messages for the dreamer to heed. A nosey neighbor or business associate may be sticking their nose into your personal life. Or the dreamer may be "brown nosing" too much at the job or in some other arena of life.

NOTEBOOK

Keeping notes and taking notes indicates that the dreamer is trying to stay on top of things and keep detailed records. Such a dream would be quite appropriate if the dreamer were preparing for an I.R.S. audit.

NUMBERS

Numbers pervade our experience of the world, so they can have a complex range of different meanings. The number one, for example, can represent everything from oneness to aloneness. Two can represent both togetherness and opposition. A dream about numbers that does not emphasize a particular number can be alluding to the meaning of any one of a number of different idioms: "your number is up," "a numbers game," "crunching numbers," or "to have someone's number." (See also Seven, Six, Sixteen).

NUMBNESS

Being unable to relate to feelings in the physical body while dreaming may indicate that the dreamer has been in a state of REM (rapid eye movement) sleep, in which the body is temporarily unable to move. Alternatively, this experience may indicate that the incident being dreamed about was too emotionally numbing for the dreamer to feel.

NUN

Graduates of parochial schools have numerous associations with nuns that go beyond the scope of this book. Otherwise, nuns can represent everything from spirituality to religious authority to sexual repression.

NURSE

Dreaming of a nurse suggests a need to be taken care of and to be healed. It also sometimes indicates a healing is in progress. This dream also implies that strained or unpleasant conditions are being set aright.

NUT

Nuts symbolize the "squirreling away" of ideas or of one's creativity for a more opportune time for receiving recognition and appreciation. They also represent the "kernel" or the "meat" of an idea or situation.

DREAM SYMBOLS

OAK

The sturdy and majestic oak tree represents stability, steadfastness, truth, tolerance, and wisdom. Psychologically, persons who identify with this symbol are seen to embody these qualities in their character. Commercially, the symbol of the oak tree is frequently used as a logo, implying strength and stability in business practices or civic pursuits.

OAR

Oars represent a journey across the surface of the unconscious. They also symbolize masculine power. Oars penetrate the waters of the emotions and the psyche, moving through the issues at hand. Having only one oar and being motionless, or trying to row with only one oar, may depict the need for a partner or mate.

OASIS

An oasis may suggest the need to give oneself a respite from conditions or relationships that may be overwhelming. The water nourishes the soul and the psyche. Emotional needs may be an issue that require immediate attention. Also, this dream symbol sometimes indicates the need for a vacation.

OBESITY

The popular psychological interpretation of obesity is lack of self-esteem and overindulgence in fear and denial; layers of protection to insulate the dreamer from involvement or action; hopelessness and helplessness to express power and authority; fear that rejection will be the only reward for effort. Other possible meanings are the "fat cat" who ate the mouse, being "full of oneself," or fattening up the livestock (for slaughter). (See also Fat).

OBSTACLE

Dreaming about encountering an obstacle can reflect feelings of being blocked in our waking life. Can also involve the ways we block ourselves, or, alternatively, indicate uncertainty and inhibitions.

OCEAN

The meaning of a dream about the sea can vary, depending on whether the ocean is a vast, imposing body of water, or a peaceful sea beside a resort. The sea can have waves as high as a thirty-story building, or be as calm and clear as a piece of glass. Sailing the high seas may give a sense of elation, or lead to a feeling of helplessness, especially if the dreamer is lost at sea. Unless tied to specific experiences near the water, the sea often represents the state of our emotions and/or the unconscious mind.

OCTOPUS

An octopus in a dream may signify that a situation or a personal relationship has completely entangled the dreamer. Alternatively, the dreamer may be too possessive and clinging in a relationship. If the dreamer is leaving home or a job in real life, this dream symbol may indicate the dreamer is clinging to a family member (e.g., the person's mother or spouse) or to the employer or fellow employees. If the dream has a positive emotional tone, it may show someone involved in many different things.

OFFICE

Dreams about one's place of work may simply indicate that one can't leave work at the office, has too much to do, or too much on one's mind. An office is often a symbol of authority and of one's professional esteem and position in the world. Other kinds of meanings are indicated by the nature of a particular office (e.g., the welfare office, a lawyer's office).

OFFICIALS

Officials in a dream may signify high-ranking people in the dreamer's life who may or may not give affirmation to the dreamer. A dream about being a particular type of official (e.g., school teacher or principal, supervisor or boss, police officer or mayor) may show something about one's attitude toward the world.

OGRE

An ogre in a dream may symbolize authority issues related to discipline in one's business or personal life. Alternatively, this symbol may represent being an "ogre" to oneself through constant self-criticism. (See also Monster).

OIL

Oil in a dream may symbolize religious matters, for example, the holy oil used in extreme unction (oil of the sick) or the holy oil used in baptisms, ordinations, and consecrations (oil of catechumens). Oil can also signify an excessively smooth-spoken ("oily-tongued") or unctuous person. Crude oil may represent great wealth from under the ground or riches from one's own inner resources.

OINTMENT

Ointment in a dream may symbolize the need for a salve to soothe or heal a condition in the dreamer's life.

OLD MAN

An old man in a dream usually represents wisdom, and sometimes forgiveness. The old man may be either a specific person or a generic aged one who, regardless of his race or color, is usually adorned with white hair and a full beard. An old man can also stand for a deteriorating person whose only power lies in the memory of a journey that has already taken place. Whether the old man exhibits stamina or lacks physical strength also affects the dream's interpretation.

OLD WOMAN

An old woman is an archetypal symbol whose feminine energy is the power of life and death, having brought forth life as a mother and now ushering in the last phase of life as physical deterioration leads to mortal death.

OLIVE BRANCH

A symbol of peace, the olive branch is associated with the dove bringing God's message of hope for a peaceful new world to Noah. It represents resolution of conflicts and reconciliation, and perhaps the lifting of a burden in the life of the dreamer.

ONIONS

Onions can symbolize many-layered issues, like the many aspects of life to be discovered and revealed. Also, onions, like garlic, are sometimes used as talismans against evil forces.

OPERA

Dreaming about being in an opera, or even just watching an opera, can be about dramatizing our feelings, or dramatizing the roles we feel that we play in life. Alternatively, feeling like one is on stage, or the desire to be on stage (the desire to be noticed).

OPERATION

A medical procedure being performed on the dreamer may signify old issues being "cut out" or patched up. If the dreamer is doing the operating, then deep unconscious issues are being faced, worked on, and healed. The overall implication of this dream depends on one's experiences with medical operations.

ORANGE

The orange is a symbol of physical health and spiritual vitality, evoking comparison with the fruit of knowledge and the luscious indulgences of the body.

ORGY

A dream about an orgy suggests repressed desires of the id, desires for expression of one's sexuality and passion. It indicates the need to be surrounded by the vital forces of life.

ORPHAN

The orphan is a symbol of an unwanted, unloved child, one who is needy, misunderstood, and abused by strict, un-nurturing people who exert merciless control and authority. This symbol may represent childhood memories and fears of being abandoned. The dreamer may be resisting inner needs to be childlike, or be emotionally cold and withdrawn from others who are close to the dreamer.

OSTRICH

The ostrich may indicate that one is ignoring reality to the point of peril, especially if the ostrich has its head buried in the sand. If the ostrich is strutting about with its head held high, the dream may indicate a "know-it-all" smugness.

OVEN

An oven suggests a womb, as in the expression "a bun in the oven," which means to be pregnant. An oven can also represent transformation, as an appliance that transforms food. Ovens are featured in some fairy tales, too, as a means of punishment (Hansel and Gretel throwing the witch into the oven) or as a means of transformation (the Gingerbread Man becoming a real person after being cooked in an oven).

OWL

A symbol of wisdom and virtue, as a night bird the owl is also a natural symbol of the unconscious. Solemn and wide-eyed, the owl may bear a message the dreamer needs to heed.

OX

The ox symbolizes the strength and capacity to endure great hardship and toil. One is "as stubborn as an ox" when one's tenacity is greater than one's reason.

OYSTER

Symbolizing pearls of beauty, wealth, or wisdom, the oyster can also symbolize sexual arousal. In a dream the oyster may represent something of great value to be "shucked" in one's waking hours.

DREAM SYMBOLS

P

PACKING

A dream in which one is packing for a trip or in preparation for moving to a new residence may imply some significant change in the dreamer's life. Perhaps a reorganization is in store or old issues or relationships are being left behind.

PAIN

Experiencing pain in one's dream may be a reflection of real pain that exists somewhere in the dreamer's body. Alternatively, the dreamer may consider someone or something to be a "pain." The suppression of painful memories may also be an issue.

PAINTING

A dream about painting may indicate a cover-up in progress. Alternatively, the dream may mean renewal and restoration of the object receiving the paint. The significance of this symbol lies in the reason for painting. The dreamer may be expressing creativity or artistic talent.

PALM TREE

The palm tree has come to be known as the Christian religious symbol for Christ's victory over death, celebrated as Palm Sunday at the Easter holiday season. It can signify a victory over

adversities and a blessing to the dreamer. It can also represent an oasis or a vacation.

PAN

See Pot.

PAPER

Dreaming about a blank sheet of paper can refer to something that is not expressed, something we have not "put down on paper," which can be an idea or a communication. Wrapping paper can refer to a gift or to the outer impression something conveys. A dream about paper can also be alluding to the meaning of a familiar idiom, such as "paper tiger," "paper over the cracks," a "paper trail," or "not worth the paper it's written on."

PARACHUTE

Parachutes obviously represent a means of escape from a dangerous situation. In a dream, a parachute could refer to our coping mechanisms, or it could refer to bailing out of a difficult predicament. Alternatively, some people sky dive for fun, so parachuting in a dream could refer to thrill-seeking or a sense of total freedom. Also note the idiom "golden parachute."

PARALYSIS

Being unable to move may mean the dreamer feels helpless to control the situation at hand. Alternatively, perhaps the dreamer needs to "freeze" and do nothing about some issue for awhile.

PARASITES

Parasites are straightforward symbols for people who seek nourishment from others but who give nothing in return. Parasites in a dream could refer to others who drain us, or representations of projects and activities that we feel "drain" our time.

PARROT

As beautiful tropical birds, parrots may represent the paradise from which they originate. As trained mimics mechanically repeating words, they may symbolize someone who mechanically repeats the words or actions of someone else ("parrots") without fully understanding them.

PARTY

A dream about a party can be a straightforward representation of social pleasure. If we are the primary guest (e.g., at a birthday party), then it could be reflecting either our experience of receiving recognition or our desire for recognition. The dream might also be drawing on any number of different idiomatic connotations, such as the "life of the party," a "party pooper," or "the party if over."

PASSENGER

A passenger is a passive participant in a vehicle that is moving along. Positively, it could be a sense of going away to a vacation spot. Alternatively, a dream about being a passenger could represent a sense of being borne along by circumstances we do not control. If we are the driver, then perhaps we are taking responsibility for the passengers.

PASSPORT

Dreaming about a passport can be a dream about travel. Alternatively, a passport can represent our identity. Metaphorically, a passport is anything that allows us entry. It used to be said, for example, that a college education was a passport to a good job.

PATH

A quiet, spiritual walk down an unobstructed, open path signifies clarity of thought and peace of mind. A blocked and twisted path, however, means one needs to give serious attention to the direction one is taking in one's business or personal life. The dream may imply the need for a time-out to consider the outcome and the consequences of the issues at hand.

PEACOCK

A beautiful bird of exquisite color and grace that seems to strut with pride and even with arrogance, the peacock may indicate that the dreamer is as "proud as a peacock" about some accomplishment and would like to "show off."

PEARL

The pearl is sometimes associated with the feminine principle, lunar forces, intuition, and water (all of which are identified with the unconscious). Mother of pearl lining the shell of the abalone suggests a fetus emerging to life. Alternatively, pearls in a dream may symbolize "pearls of wisdom" regarding a new idea or venture or a warning not to "cast your pearls before swine" by compromising oneself or one's values.

PEDESTAL

Something on a pedestal is something to be admired, even worshiped. A dream about being on a pedestal can represent either a feeling that someone else admires us or a desire to be admired. We also sometimes talk about "knocking someone off their pedestal."

PEEL

To see peeling skin, or to peel away the outer covering of something may indicate the shedding of old ways or conditions. Alternatively, peeling away outer coverings may indicate the discarding of unneeded exterior pretenses.

PEN/PENCIL

A pen or a pencil can represent male sexuality; it can also represent communication or a desire to communicate. The symbol might also be referring to an idiom, such as "pen pusher," "the pen is mightier than the sword," or to "pencil someone in."

PENGUIN

Dreaming about a penguin or about being a penguin can indicate emotional coldness or a sense of isolation. A penguin, as a bird that can't fly, can also represent someone who seems to be able to function despite lacking something essential. A penguin might also symbolize a recalled image of someone wearing a tuxedo.

PENIS

The universal symbol of the male, the penis represents energy, vital force, sexual power, and fertility. One's sexual energy or matters of orientation may be at issue, depending upon the gender of the dreamer. (See also Genitals).

PEPPER

Pepper can represent spiciness, irritation, or warmth—all of which are metaphors for aspects of human interaction. In a dream, pepper could be representing any one of these qualities.

PET

If we have a pet that we are close to, then a dream about this animal can simply be a reflection of our everyday life experience. Alternatively, a tame animal such as a pet can represent our animal drives, though they tend to represent a domesticated version. This dream could represent a desire to be treated like a pet—to be "petted"—or to have someone else become dependent on us like a pet.

PHOTOGRAPH

Because it is a representation, to dream of a photograph may indicate that a deception of sorts is surrounding the dreamer.

PHYSICIAN

See Doctor.

PIG

Dreaming of a pig may symbolize dirtiness, greediness, or selfishness. For example, someone who overindulges in food is said to eat "like a pig," and a dirty or slovenly person is sometimes disparagingly called a"pig." Alternatively, the pig may represent feasting and opulence, as in banquets where the roasted pig with an apple in its mouth is the adorned centerpiece on the table. In Chinese astrology, the pig is the twelfth sign of the zodiac and symbolizes manly strength.

PILL

If the pill is a vitamin, then swallowing a pill in a dream might reflect a desire to take care of one's health. Taking a pill can be a metaphor for accepting something unpleasant—"swallowing a bitter pill." Pills could be a reference to "The Pill" used in birth control, and sometimes irritating people are referred to as "pills."

PILLOW

Pillows are obvious symbols of sleep and/or of comfort. In a dream, perhaps we are feeling comfortable or, alternatively, we want to feel comfortable. Also note associations with the expression "pillow talk."

PIN

A pin might have several meanings. Pins are small tools that help us sew something together, so perhaps we are dreaming about knitting something together. Pins can also hold a notice to a bulletin board, so perhaps the dream is trying to call our attention to something. We sometimes talk about "pinning blame" or "pinning on hopes" on someone. We can also "pin something down" or "walk on pins and needles."

PINK

The color pink is often associated with baby girls and with feminine matters of the heart. Also, a person in a healthy or happy condition might respond that he or she is "in the pink" if asked how he or she is doing. Good feelings are generally associated with this color.

PIPE

A pipe may indicate a peaceful outcome to a troublesome situation, as in smoking a "peace pipe." A pipe may also represent knowledge or contemplation, as symbolized by the stereotypical professor puffing on his pipe. Alternatively, if the pipe in the dream is a conduit, as in a pipeline, then the interpretation may be of communication—hopefully the pipe is clear of rust and corrosion.

PISTOL

To take aim with a pistol may indicate the dreamer is trying to target a specific goal. Alternatively, if feelings of anger or helplessness and fear play a part in the dream, then the dreamer's sense of self-defense is at stake and the pistol may represent the power the dreamer needs to defend against some anger or aggression in waking life.

PIT

A pit is something we fall into, get stuck in, and have difficulty getting out of, so dreaming about being in a pit could reflect these feelings. We also talk about being in a "bottomless pit" or taking a "pit stop." (See also Cave, Hole).

PLANET

A planet may symbolize the exploration of another "world"—Of new dimensions of thought and creativity—or a new adventure.

PLANK

As a floor plank, this symbol could mean the dream is about physical or moral support. More frequently, we associate this term with the legendary pirate practice of "walking the plank," which was a simple form of execution. Yet another association is describing someone as "dumb as a plank" ("dumb as a post").

PLANTS

For a person devoted to gardening, plants can have a wide range of meanings. More specifically, most of us associate plants with life and especially with growth, so a dream about plants could be drawing on either of those associations. Planting has other associations, such as beginning a new project.

PLATE

A plate contains nourishment, so dreaming about a plate can refer metaphorically to how we nourish our emotional life. An empty plate can thus mean that our needs are not being fulfilled. If the plate is overly full, it could be alluding to the expression about being overly busy, having a "full plate."

PLOUGH

The plough represents the cultivation of new ideas and new projects, tilling the soil for new growth and expansion.

PLUG

Putting a plug into an outlet or a socket may indicate getting an increase in one's energy or knowledge. Could also suggest the dreamer will be getting hooked up with new people or new ideas that will plug her or him into a better social network for business or personal goals.

PLUMBING

A conduit of water or of waste, plumbing symbolizes the flow of emotions. If the plumbing is stopped up, the dreamer may need emotional "release."

POCKET

A pocket can be a symbol of female sexuality. In a dream, a pocket might contain our possessions or, alternatively, things that we hide or keep secret. A dream about pockets might also be alluding to the meaning of certain idioms, such as someone "lining their own pockets," "burning a hole in one's pocket," "deep pockets," or "to be in someone's pocket.".

POINTING

Pointing in a dream may mean the dreamer is trying to determine the best direction for reaching some goal. The dreamer may have reached a fork in the road and can no longer proceed along the same old path.

POISON

Poison in a dream may represent an attempt to get rid of something within oneself that is producing sickness. A violent rejection of a condition or a relationship may be causing the dreamer to suffer.

POLE

A pole can be a symbol of female sexuality. There are a number of idiomatic uses of the term to which a dream might be alluding, as in the expression "poles apart" or "low on the totem pole." The word is also sometimes used to refer to someone who is extremely thin.

POLICE

Authority symbols, police officers enforce the rules in life. Dreaming about police can indicate apprehension over failure to perform or to honor obligations and commitments. It can also be a warning to avoid reckless behavior.

POMEGRANATE

To dream of pomegranates traditionally signifies good health and longevity. Alternatively, they are tied to the myth of Persephone who is said to have become trapped in the underworld (a common symbol of the unconscious) due to her consumption of a pomegranate seed.

POOL

A pool contains water, which can symbolize emotions or the realm of the unconscious mind. Unlike the ocean, however, a pool of water is more manageable, more domesticated, and thus easier to deal with. Dreaming about a pool could be alluding to these meanings, though it could be something simpler, like relaxing around a pool or around a pool table. Yet another meaning of this term is "pooling" resources.

PORPOISE

See Dolphin.

POT

A symbol of female sexuality. We could be dreaming about "cooking up" something, or about examining one's emotions close up. We can create things in a pot, but a "chamber pot" can also receive our waste materials. Pots are used in many idiomatic expressions, and a dream might be drawing on one of these meanings: "pot luck," "pot calling the kettle black," "a watched pot never boils," "doesn't have a pot to piss in," "a melting pot," etc.

POTATO

As a subterranean vegetable, the potato represents a symbol of the unconscious. Socially, it is a symbol of laziness ("the couch potato") or of a person considered to be a "lump" ("potato head").

PRECIPICE

See Cliff.

PREGNANT

It is quite normal for someone who is pregnant, concerned about being pregnant, or wishing she could become pregnant to dream about it. Preg-nancy can also be a metaphor for being "pregnant" with a new idea, and dreaming about being pregnant could symbolize the development of a new aspect of one's personality. (See also Baby, Embryo, Miscarriage).

PREPARATIONS

Preparations suggest getting ready for a new idea or undertaking. The time of year (e.g., income tax season) and other aspects of the dream determine its specific meaning.

PRESIDENT

Dreaming about the chief of the company or the country suggests concerns about the status and security of one's job or perhaps one's opinion about the country's leader.

PRIEST (MINISTER OR RABBI)

A spiritual authority figure may symbolize the dreamer's spiritual needs. In interpreting such a dream, one should note whether the figure was loving and caring, or dictatorial and condemning, as the character of an overbearing parent may be associated with a negative religious figure.

PRINCE/PRINCESS

Dreaming of royalty may indicate bestowal of honors and recognition upon the dreamer for accomplishments in mastering personal or professional obstacles.

PRISON

See Jail/Jailor.

PRIZE

Receiving a prize may indicate that the dreamer thinks an award is merited for some outstanding accomplishment.

PROFESSOR

As a symbol of wisdom and higher learning, a professor may represent preeminence in some field of endeavor. A professor also symbolizes someone who is conspicuously quiet and serious.

PROPHET

A prophet in a dream may indicate that the dreamer is seeking or needs guidance and spiritual advice. The dream itself may provide that assistance, if the dreamer internalizes the inspirational feeling they receive from the dream encounter.

PRUNES

Prunes may symbolize an emotional or creative blockage. They may also represent aging ("wrinkled as a prune").

PULL

Pulling in a dream can be a direct reflection of exerting effort in one's waking life. If we dream about being pulled, it represents our sense of being influenced, of being "pulled" in a certain direction. The dream might also be drawing on a idiomatic sense of pull, as in "pulling strings," to "have pull," to "pull something off," to "pull together," or to "pull rank."

PUMPKIN

Pumpkins might simply represent the fall season and harvest time, especially Halloween.

PUNISHMENT

Punishment in a dream reflects guilt or shame about some actions committed by the dreamer. Even if the punishment is being inflicted upon someone else, the dreamer is most probably "feeling" the punishment as well.

PUPPET

A puppet can be a toy or it can be entertainment. A dream puppet is often a straightforward representation of someone who is being manipulated by someone else. Perhaps we feel powerless, or perhaps we feel like we are a "puppet" of our addictions.

PURPLE

Used by monarchs for centuries, purple is the color of royalty, high rank, and dignity. This highly regarded color has connotations of transformation, particularly personal transformation. Esoterically, it represents the crown chakra, which is the highest center of consciousness in certain metaphysical systems.

PURSE

Carrying a purse in a dream may signify the secret place of important possessions, which are being closely held. Losing the purse might suggest loss of power and control of possessions.

DREAM SYMBOLS

QUACK

A denigrating word for an incompetent doctor, or the sound that a duck makes, especially if the dreamer is looking forward with anticipation to the duck hunting season.

QUAKE

Tumultuous movements or quaking in a dream may indicate inner turmoil and upset in the dreamer's life that needs to be addressed. The dreamer may be repressing anxiety and need to change conditions to alleviate it.

QUARANTINE

A quarantine may indicate the dreamer feels the need to prevent contact with people or situations that might contaminate the dreamer or the dreamer's family.

QUARREL

A quarrel in a dream often suggests an inner conflict over ideas and values. Alternatively, one may feel burdened by a person in authority.

QUARTET

A quartet may indicate that the dreamer requires other persons to create the harmonious situation that the dreamer may be seeking in either business or personal endeavors.

QUEST

A quest indicates an attempt to achieve some kind of goal. The dreamer may have reached a stage in life where the status quo is no longer acceptable and some adventure is beckoning.

QUICKSAND

Quicksand may symbolize losing one's footing and sinking into the quicksand of one's emotions or the unconscious. Dreaming about being in quicksand may reflect circumstances in the business or personal life of the dreamer that are beyond the dreamer's control.

QUILL

As a writing instrument often associated with refinement and gentility, the quill can symbolize superior social status or prestige, sophistication or style, false delicacy or affectation, and belles lettres, among others. In a dream it may provide inspiration to write about thoughts and dreams.

QUILT

A patchwork quilt may indicate the many parts of the dreamer's life that have been pieced together and stitched into a cover or skin to provide protection and warmth for body and soul.

QUININE

Quinine water is the solution that is drunk to relieve the fever of persons suffering from malaria. Perhaps the dreamer thirsts after self expression, and a situation or a condition has them in such an untenable position that they are feverish with frustration.

DREAM SYMBOLS

RABBIT

Rabbits symbolize opulent fertility and spirituality. The Easter Bunny brings rewards of sweetness and gifts to celebrate new life. The magician's hat from which rabbits materialize gives this animal magical associations.

RABBIT HOLE

The hidden furrows that wind underground may represent the cliché "I feel like crawling into a hole," suggesting that embarrassment or guilt causes one to hide from an unpleasant situation or deed.

RACE

Running a race may depict how the dreamer feels about his or her waking life (a hectic "rat race," perhaps?), possibly indicating the dreamer should slow down or change his or her approach to life.

RACIAL

To experience different ethnicities of people in one's dream may be suggesting that the dreamer either needs to—or has successfully accomplished—integrating him- or herself into a better understanding of the humanity of others.

RADAR

If one monitors a radar screen in a dream, it can represent one's sense of intuition; being receptive to the signals other people are giving out.

RAGS

Old, tattered rags may mean the dreamer is cleaning up old problems and issues. Ragged clothes may mean the dreamer is going "from rags to riches" in the world.

RAIN

Rain is a natural element of cleansing. Because it is essential to plant growth, rain is a symbol of fertility. In a dream, rain may indicate a new direction of thought and purpose—washing away the old and fertilizing the new. Alternatively, gray, dismal clouds and rain may indicate desolation or barrenness.

RAINBOW

The rainbow is a very happy and promising sign. Hopes and dreams are denoted by this wonderful symbol. Good luck comes to those who dream rainbow dreams.

RAM

The ram is the symbol of the first sign of the zodiac, Aries. It is characterized by energy, aggression, and impulsiveness. In a dream, a ram may suggest that the dreamer rams headlong into situations that should be approached with more tact and consideration.

RAPE

A dream about rape may symbolize a violent assault on the dreamer's physical environment or a devastating blow to the person's financial security.

RAT

Rats are often associated with the decaying conditions of poverty ("rat trap") or illness. To betray someone is to "rat" on them. Dreams of rats can also indicate a need to take some time out from the "rat race." (See also Mouse, Rodent).

RAVEN

Ravens are symbols of diabolical evil in traditional Christianity. This bird also symbolizes uncleanliness and death because it feeds upon dead and decaying animals. Because it is a sign of transformation, the raven is also associated with magicians and sorcerers.

REBIRTH/RESURRECTION

A dream about being born again or resurrected may indicate that the dreamer needs to deal with issues that have been avoided or, alternatively, is being given another chance to recover what was previously thought to be lost.

RECORD (CD, LP, CASSETTE, ETC.)

A dream that includes some sort of recording can simply be a reflection of our everyday life, particularly if we often listen to music. Alternatively, it can symbolize the impressions other people leave on us or the impressions we would like to leave on them.

RED

A color of vitality and energy, red symbolizes the heart and blood. Red can also represent the emotional state of anger or rage. This color also symbolizes profligacy, raciness, and the immorality of "fallen women" (e.g., Hester Prynne in *The Scarlet Letter*).

REFEREE

Encountering a referee in a dream may suggest an inner battle between one's ideals and the ego requirements imposed by what others value. The dreamer may need help defining the rules needed to settle this conflict.

REFRIGERATOR

A refrigerator can represent a nurturing of the spirit as well as sustenance for the body. Opening the refrigerator door and standing there looking in and seeing the refrigerator amply supplied, without having to partake from it, many times reassures a person that what he or she seeks is really there for the taking.

REFUGEE

A refugee may indicate the dreamer feels like a displaced person, belonging to another place or time.

REFUSE

See Garbage.

REJECTION

Rejection in a dream may suggest that there are feelings or situations the dreamer wants to be rid of.

RELATIONSHIPS

Relationships encountered in a dream involve either real people that are consciously known by the dreamer in their waking-life, or meetings with persons that are unknown to the dreamer. The latter may represent the relationship between different aspects of the dreamer's psyche.

REMOTE

Remote in the sense of a television remote may relate to control issues that suggest the dreamer's "buttons are getting pushed" by a relationship that feels too controlling. If, in terms of the alternative meaning of the term "remote," the dreamer feels distanced by the objects or people in their dream, perhaps they are mirroring the ways in which they distance themselves from people in their environment.

RENOVATE

A dream about renovation may indicate that old ideas or habits are being replaced by new ways of looking at the world and interacting with others.

REPTILE

See Dinosaur, Lizard, Serpent, Snake, or Turtle.

RESCUE

Being rescued from a pursuing animal, a potential drowning, etc. often indicates the dreamer needs to rescue themselves from a disturbing or even a potentially threatening situation that they are experiencing in their business or in their personal life.

RESERVOIR

A dream about a reservoir may indicate that the dreamer has stored up emotional energy, especially if the reservoir is full. If it appears to be empty, the dreamer may have expended all available emotions on others.

RESTRICTION

Any form of restriction in a dream often mirrors some frustration in the dreamer's personal or business life. The dreamer may be imposing restrictions on himself or herself as well as on others.

RETIREMENT

Retirement dreams represent the end of one's contribution and value to the workplace, as well as an end to doing what others dictate and becoming one's own boss.

REVOLT

The person who dreams of revolt may not want to do what they are doing, be with whom they are associated, or go where they are expected to be going. The dreamer may also be revolting against facing issues within themselves.

RHUBARB

The bitter rhubarb plant, which takes on a sweet flavor when cooked with sugar, is a symbol of taking the good (sweet) with the bad (bitter). Because it is often used as a purgative, it can also represent freeing oneself of something unwanted.

RICE

Rice, the main staple of food for many of the peoples of this planet, is a symbol of fertility and good luck, as evidenced by it being thrown over newlyweds at wedding ceremonies.

RIDE

Riding in a dream—be it in a car, train, ship—may indicate that the dreamer is seeking a destination. Alternatively, it may reveal that the dreamer is in a relationship or other situation that he or she feels is going nowhere, and it may require that they "ride it out" for awhile.

RIGHT

In addition to its directional meaning, being on the right can also mean being correct (e.g., to be on the right side of a situation). Being at the right hand of God also says one is in the righteous place of good instead of evil. The right in a dream can also mean to stand up for one's "rights" or "to right" (rectify) a wrong.

RING

To dream of a ring as a piece of jewelry may indicate the expression of commitment to a relationship or to marriage. A ring can also represent the completion and wholeness that the dreamer is experiencing within themselves. In the case of a ringing sound, it may indicate that the dreamer needs to shift his or her attention to some issue or situation in their waking life. (See also Jewels/Jewelry, Necklace).

RITUAL

This dream may represent one's commitment to an ideal or to a relationship. It is symbolic of a ceremony that may be expressing the dreamer's change in attitudes or some other major change in their life.

RIVER

Rivers, like other bodies of water, may represent the dreamer's emotional state. Watching a river roll by may indicate that one is allowing his or her life to float on down the river without any particular direction, perhaps indicating that one should take a more decisive hand in directing one's life. With too little control in one's life, the river may have raging waters that run up over its banks. If the water is peaceful and tranquil, then a restful break to regenerate one's energies might be in order. In some mythologies rivers are symbols of death, which could also be interpreted as the passing from one state of consciousness to another.

ROAD

Dreams about roads often represent one's direction or goal in life. If the road is straight and narrow, what has been planned is being successfully carried out. If the road is winding or bumpy, the dreamer's plans are vague or flexible, or the dreamer is meeting with unexpected change or difficulty. A roadblock may mean the dreamer needs to be more persistent and diligent, or double back and take another route.

ROADBLOCK

See Obstacle.

ROBBERY

Being robbed of one's valuables may indicate that the dreamer is experiencing an identity crisis or a loss in his or her life (e.g., a divorce, serious illness, or some other irretrievable loss). (See also Burglar, Stealing, Thieves/Theft).

ROCK

Rocks usually embody stability and permanence, as signified by the expression "solid as a rock." A large rock or boulder in a dream may indicate the dreamer is making a commitment to a relationship or contemplating some change that will provide a more solid foundation.

ROCKET

A rocket in a dream may symbolize that the dreamer's ideas or plans are about to take off like a rocket, very rapidly achieving orbit and bringing the dreamer the success he or she has been working for.

RODENT

Gophers, rats, mice, and the like are a constant source of irritation and often spread disease, thus requiring extermination. Rodents in a dream may represent issues that are pestering the dreamer and perhaps confounding the dreamer as to how to dispose of them. (See also Mouse, Rat).

ROLLER COASTER

A roller coaster may indicate that the dreamer is experiencing frequent ups and downs, perhaps caused by erratic behavior on the part of the dreamer or an associate.

ROOF

A roof symbolizes a cover for that which needs protecting. It can also indicate a barrier between two states of consciousness. A leaking roof sometimes means that there is new information dripping through.

ROOM

Dreams of rooms have a wide variety of meanings. An appealing and comfortable room may indicate that the dreamer is enjoying opulence and satisfaction in life. A stark and confining room, like a prison cell, may mean the dreamer feels repressed and trapped. Sometimes rooms are simply stages for the dream and harken back to earlier periods of life, for example, childhood or a previous marriage. Dreams about rooms often relate to hidden areas of the unconscious mind.

ROOTS

The significance of roots in a dream lies in the unconscious mind. As a metaphor, roots reaching deep into the earth symbolize delving into the depths of the self, expressing the potentials of the soul. Roots erupting from the earth expose these talents to the world. Roots can also symbolize the concept of origin, as in the expressions "their roots go back quite a ways," "their family has strong roots," and "the root word."

ROPE

If we are tied down, a rope can be what we feel is holding us back. If we dream about tying up someone else, it could represent our efforts to restrain ourselves, perhaps holding back desires. (See also Chains).

ROSE

The rose symbolizes femininity, beauty, love, and romance. Roses also have profound spiritual significance, representing good and evil, life and death. The colors of the petals are also symbolic: white is purity, red is passion, pink is romance, black is death.

RUBBISH

See Garbage.

RUBY

A gemstone that varies from light pink to deep red, the ruby represents passion, the life force, and prosperity. The deeper and more intense the color, the more precious and expensive the stone.

RUNNING/RUNAWAY

Running away or escaping may indicate that the dreamer needs to get away from a person or situation that is overwhelming the dreamer. A slower pace of life may be indicated.

RUST

Anything that develops rust is usually old and no longer in use. In a dream rust may symbolize neglect, lack of care, old age, or a "rusty" skill.

DREAM SYMBOLS

SACK

Dreaming about a large sack, particularly one that a person might fit into, might be a womb symbol. Alternatively, corpses are sometimes placed in sacks, so a sack can suggest death as well. The dream might also be alluding to idioms such as "getting sacked" or "hitting the sack." (See also Bag).

SACRED

A church, temple, synagogue, or any place considered sacred may indicate a renewing of what the dreamer considers to be important or venerable.

SACRIFICE

A dream of sacrifice may indicate that the dreamer feels "martyred" because of the time and energy they have sacrificed for others. The dreamer may need to eliminate certain conditions to allow for more productive and rewarding experiences.

SADDLE

Animals in dreams often represent the animal side of ourselves, particularly aggressive and sexual drives. So a saddle can indicate our efforts to direct and control these drives. It could also symbolize controlling others or being controlled by others. Finally, note that we can be "saddled" with a difficult responsibility.

SAFE

To dream of a safe in which to store valuables may indicate that the dreamer is hiding a sense of self worth and self value. To dream of being in a safe place may also indicate that the dreamer feels safe within themselves.

SAILOR

Dreaming of being a sailor or being with a sailor often reflects a desire to be adventurous. Perhaps the dreamer is ready to explore new areas and venture into deeper waters, particularly in personal relationships.

SAINT

Dreaming of a saint may indicate that a special message is being given to the dreamer from the spiritual realm, and therefore may be an especially significant dream.

SALT

Used as seasoning in food, salt symbolizes flavor or piquancy. As one of the three primary elements of matter in alchemy representing—in contrast to mercury and sulfur—the principle of fixity and solidity, salt symbolizes someone who is steadfast and dependable, "the salt of the earth."

SAND

A dream about sand might relate to pleasant memories of being at the beach. Alternatively, sand can represent time—as in "the sands of time"—or the insecurity of building one's house in the sand. Sand is also associated with deserts and the lack of nourishing water. (See also Beach, Desert).

SAP

The vital juices of plants and animals, sap represents bodily health and vigor (the sap of youth), which is why someone who feels depleted is "all sapped out." Like the sap from the maple tree, someone who is excessively gullible or sentimental is "sappy" (sweet, syrupy).

SAPPHIRE

A precious stone of penetrating cobalt blue, the sapphire is associated with protection (e.g., by the archangel Michael).

SATAN

Dreaming of Satan often indicates that there is some wrongdoing in the dreamer's life or environment. The dream may be the direct result of evil thoughts and deeds, either by the dreamer or by someone with whom the dreamer is involved.

SATELLITE

A dream about a satellite is most likely about communication, particularly at a global level. Alternatively, a satellite is something that is trapped by the gravitational pull of another heavenly body.

SAUSAGE

Could indicate that the dreamer feels stuffed into a situation that confines her or his expression of ideas and potential recognition. May also have sexual connotations.

SAVIOR

Dreaming of a savior may indicate that a spiritual healing is taking place in the dreamer's life or that prayers are being answered.

SCALES (WEIGHTS)

Scales symbolize justice, but also weighing something, which can symbolize making a decision. Scales in a dream can also be drawing on the expression "to tip the scales."

SCHOOL

As a place to learn, to "brush up" on subjects previously studied, or to further one's education, a school in a dream may indicate inadequacy, especially if related to unpleasant early school experiences. If the dreamer is a teacher, the dream may symbolize authority. In some esoteric groups it is said that during sleep the soul attends classes "on the inner planes" (in the spiritual realm), so that dreams about being in a classroom would be interpreted as reflecting this type of "spiritual learning" experience. (See also Class, Seminar).

SCIENTIST

As a learned person who discovers, invents, and develops new ideas, the scientist represents experimentation and invention. In the popular mind, the scientist also symbolizes eccentricity and absentmindedness.

SCISSORS

A dream that emphasizes scissors can have a variety of different meanings. Scissors can be used in construction or in destruction. We could be cutting the umbilical cord (asserting our independence) or cutting ourselves off from someone.

SCREEN

The dreamer may be needing to "screen out" information that she or he may not be able to assimilate.

SCREW

The dreamer may feel as if they are being turned like a screw in a situation where someone is taking advantage of them.

SEA

See Ocean.

SEARCH

Searching for something in a dream often indicates the need to find something that is missing or needed in one's life. Finding it may mean the dreamer will recover something important.

SEDUCTION

Seduction in a dream often is an expression of the dreamer's sexual desires.

SEED

The seed represents reproduction of life—human, animal, or plant. Everything from the knowledge we import ("plant a seed in their memory") to the money we use to finance business ventures (seed money) germinates metaphorically from a "seed." A seed may indicate an idea has been planted in the dreamer's mind and is germinating into new life experiences.

SELF

To encounter one's self in a dream indicates that one has come face to face with issues and needs that can no longer be ignored.

SEMINAR

In a seminar, the dreamer could be the leader dispersing knowledge or the participant receiving information. Does the dreamer feel a need to teach or learn? In some esoteric groups it is said that during sleep the soul attends classes "on the inner planes" (in the spiritual realm), so dreams about being in a classroom could be interpreted as reflecting this type of "spiritual learning" experience. (See also Class, School).

SERPENT

See Snake.

SERVICE

Providing a service in a dream, depending upon how one feels about the service, may indicate something the dreamer wishes to share, or an ability that needs to be expressed. If, however, one is in need of the service—such as automobile service at a gas station, then a stop or respite to replenish or renew oneself may be indicated.

SEVEN

In numerology, seven represents music and psychic abilities. It is also a mystical number; in Hinduism and Christianity it is the number of God.

SEWER

Sewers signify putrid conditions, perhaps the "rotting" remains of old circumstances or relationships. Waste also fertilizes and thus can signify regeneration. Perhaps the dreamer needs to eliminate noxious conditions or ideas before beginning new endeavors.

SEWING

A dream about sewing can be about creating something new or about repairing something than has been torn. We also talk about "sewing something up," meaning to assure the success of something. (See also Knitting).

SEX

Having sexual relations in a dream or seeing others having sex may indicate repressed desires for physical or emotional love, as well as the urge to "bond" and create new life. Sexuality is too complex and confused an area of modern life to capture here its broad range of possible meanings.

SHADOW

A shadow may represent the hidden aspects of the self. The dreamer often does not accept these parts of his or her personality and they are projected upon others until the dreamer can accept them and incorporate them into his or her psyche.

SHAMPOO

A dream about shampooing one's own head can represent a need to clear our thoughts or to clean up something.

SHEEP

Dreaming about sheep may indicate the dreamer feels uncreative and lacks initiative to venture out on his or her own. The dreamer may be just following along, letting others direct his or her life.

SHELL

Shells may represent the womb and the desire to be once again sheltered, nourished, and protected from life's problems.

SHEPHERD

Shepherds may represent the nurturing part of the dreamer's psyche, taking care of the dreamer and guiding him or her in a safe direction. Shepherds

also represent spiritual nurturance and direction, as with a pastor guiding his or her flock.

SHIP

Large bodies of water are natural symbols of both the unconscious and the emotions. Thus, a ship may represent a vessel of the self moving through the dreamer's emotions or unconscious. Many other interpretations are possible, depending on whether the ship is large and secure or small and fragile, whether the body of water is smooth and peaceful or disturbed and dangerous, and so on. Naturally, if the dreamer is a sailor, an engineer, or someone else for whom ships are part of daily life, the ship would probably have a more mundane meaning as simply the stage setting for his or her everyday activities.

SHOE

To dream of shoes may mirror an old cliché, "if the shoe fits, wear it," and may indicate that the dreamer is coming to grips with accepting who and what they are in their expression in the world.

SHOOT/SHOOTING

To shoot in a dream (e.g., a gun or a game of pool) indicates success in the dreamer's endeavors if they hit their target or pocket their ball. Shooting is a central activity in our entertainment media, so a dream about shooting may just be something from a movie we have seen. Alternatively, shooting is an obvious symbol for anger, aggression, and even aggressive male sexuality. Dreams can also be alluding to the meaning of familiar idioms, such as "shoot your mouth off," "shoot yourself in the foot," "shoot someone down," "shoot the messenger," etc.

SHOPPING

All of us shop, so a dream about shopping can simply be a reflection of our everyday lives. It can also mean that we are seeking something, or it might be an allusion to an idiom like "shop talk" or "like a bull in a china shop."

SHORE

The shore is the place where water and land meet. Perhaps the dreamer is experiencing an internal meeting of their emotional needs with their ego and psyche and are integrating these parts of their personality.

SHOULDERS

A dream in which one's shoulders are prominent may mean the dreamer feels that he or she is shouldering too much responsibility and is over-burdened by circumstances in his or her life.

SHOVEL

A dream about shoveling often represents self-reflection and digging into our own past. Alternatively, maybe we want to bury something. (See also Digging).

SHOWER

Dreaming about taking a shower may indicate spiritual or physical renewal or the need to wash a burden out of the dreamer's life. Alternatively, it may suggest rewards being showered upon the dreamer.

SHRINK

If we dream about shrinking, perhaps the dream relates to our childhood. Alternatively, maybe we are "feeling small." When other things shrink, it may be a representation that they are playing a smaller role in our life than formerly. We also sometimes refer to shy people as "shrinking violets," and to psychiatrists as "shrinks." (See also Little, Small).

SICKNESS

See Illness.

SIGNS

A dream about a road sign may be indicating a direction in which the dreamer should go in their journey through life.

SILVER

Silver is a precious metal associated with the emotions, the feminine quality, and the moon.

SINGING

Singing in a dream may signify a happy feeling of freeing up the emotional self from restrictions.

SINKING

A sinking feeling may symbolize the dreamer's waking world if the dreamer is overwhelmed by business and financial responsibilities.

SISTER

To dream of one's sister is complex because of the complex relationship we usually have with a sibling. It may indicate a union of family or the need to relate to one's family. This kind of dream can also acknowledge one's close feelings with others who are like a sister.

SIX

In numerology the number six represents harmony and peacemaking qualities.

SIXTEEN

This number traditionally represents a young girl's debut into womanhood when she celebrated her sweet sixteen birthday, so it could represent a time of maturity. In numerology, the numerals in the number 16 add up to seven, a lucky number.

SKELETON

A dream about a skeleton is often about death or something within us that has died. Like ancient ruins, a skeleton can symbolize the past, too. Also note the familiar idiom about the "skeleton in the closet."

SKULL

Danger and death are symbolized by the skull and crossbones, which is often found on labels that warn of poisonous contents. The skull and crossbones was also adopted by pirate ships and the Hell's Angels. Each Halloween the skull—with or without the crossbones—is still used to warn of danger and death.

SKY

The sky usually signifies peace and freedom of expression when it is clear and blue. If cloudy and overcast, the sky may be forecasting sadness and trouble.

SLAUGHTER/SLAUGHTERHOUSE

Most people become deeply and violently repulsed after visiting a slaughterhouse. In a dream, a slaughterhouse could be a response to a traumatic experience in one's waking life.

SLEEPING

Dreaming of sleeping may indicate that the dreamer's life is peaceful. Alternatively, it may mean the dreamer is not fully aware of conditions and needs to "wake up and smell the coffee."

SLIP/SLIPPERY

Stumbling or slipping in a dream may signify that the dreamer is forcing himself or herself to do things incompatible with the dreamer's nature or destiny.

SLOPE

A slope may indicate the direction one's business or personal life is headed. An obtuse decline indicates a slow descent and a sharp incline suggests the dreamer needs to pay more attention to his or her responsibilities and also to the duties that others are obligated to perform on his or her behalf.

SLOW MOTION

Moving in slow motion is evidenced in many anxiety dreams. The dreamer may be wading through heavy waters, engulfed in mud, or merely running in tortuously slow motion. This type of dream indicates that the dreamer is experiencing great stress in waking life. (See also Swamp).

SMALL

If something looks small and distant in a dream, it may be something related to an experience way back in the dreamer's past. This was an interpretation put forward by Sigmund Freud. (See also Little, Shrink).

SMELL

Experiences from the past play a part in distinguishing what a smell in a dream means to the dreamer. Sometimes we remember people by the odors we identify them with, like grandpa's pipe tobacco. In this example, the significance of the dream would depend on what grandpa meant to the dreamer.

SMOKE

To be surrounded by smoke in a dream indicates that the dreamer is suffering from confusion and anxiety. Often a dreamer will be choked and disoriented suggesting the need to "clear things up."

SNAIL

We often association snails with slowness, and a dream about snails could relate to our sense of something moving as a "snail's pace" or a communication arriving via "snail mail." Alternatively, as an animal with a hard shell, a snail can represent someone's psychological shell.

SNAKE

Serpents are ancient symbols, often associated with goddesses of fertility. Because they live in the ground, serpents may represent the healing, nurturing earth; they can also symbolize knowledge. In some cultures in southern Asia, serpents symbolize primordial spiritual power. Alternatively, they may be emblems of the mysterious dangers of the underworld. The Christian tradition incorporated the latter meaning into its mythology, making snakes an embodiment of evil, particularly the evil of temptation (e.g., the snake in the Garden of Eden). For this reason, in Western cultures especially, snakes are images for people who are sneaky and deceptive. The cliché, "they behave like a snake in the grass," captures this derogatory reference.

SNOW

Because water is a natural symbol of emotional states, snow may indicate chilled and unexpressed emotions, either in the dreamer or in someone else. Naturally, a snowy landscape might simply be a part of the setting for dreamers living in the Snow Belt.

SOAP

A dream about soap is typically a dream about something that needs to be "cleaned up" in some fashion. Perhaps we need to "clean up our act," or just "come clean" about something.

SOARING

Soaring through the air symbolizes freedom from restrictions. The dreamer may have gotten out from under a burdening situation or relationship.

SOLAR PLEXUS

This is the area of the body that is also known as the psychic brain center. Here is the source of all those deep feelings and empathic experiences.

SOLDIERS

In esoteric belief, soldiers symbolize God's army of angels, and signify to the dreamer that divine retribution will expiate the wrongs experienced by the dreamer.

SON

To dream of a "son" could actually signify the son of the dreamer, or it may symbolize something else, such as a creation or an aspect of oneself. If the dreamer is a male this symbol may indicate an internal aspect of his youth.

SPACESHIP

Spaceships in a dream may indicate a spiritual journey into the realms of the mysterious and the unknown. Spaceships (or flying saucers), have become, according to Carl Jung, the technological equivalent of angels in the modern world.

SPECTACLES

See Eyeglasses.

SPEAR

Throwing a spear in a dream represents thrusting one's will and power into the world and is thus a statement of strength and commitment.

SPENDING SPREE

This symbol may refer to the overindulgences in the dreamer's waking life. The dreamer may be concerned about the time they are spending in their work or in relationships, causing their quality of life to be less than desirable. Perhaps the dreamer should consider letting go—a little at a time—of some of the tension and repression they may be harboring.

SPIDER

A common household spider may symbolize the intricate web that the dreamer has woven or a web that has entrapped the dreamer. Alternatively, it may indicate feeling entangled in a sticky, clinging relationship.

SPINNING

Spinning in a dream can be represented by spinning of thread on a spinning wheel to create fabric, or a child spinning a top, or even themselves, in circles. It may be that the dreamer is about to embark on some sort of industrious task. It also suggests conjuring up a story or tale.

SPIRAL

Spiraling, either upward or downward, is often used figuratively to refer to the rapid rise and fall of finances. It may also symbolize flux in weather, health, and employment cycles, to name just a few. It can also simply mean that the dreamer feels things are "spiraling out of control."

SPLINTER

If we get a splinter in a dream, it can represent something that has caused us minor pain or irritation. Splinter is also a slang term relating to male sexuality. Additionally, splinter can embody the sense of separating, as in the expression "splinter group."

SPLIT

To break apart from or be broken apart, perhaps referring to a relationship or a partnership. This may bring relief, or the dreamer may be experiencing separation anxieties.

SPORT

Dreaming of participating in a sport may suggest that the dreamer is in excellent physical condition or needs some exercise or recreation.

SPRING

Spring symbolizes new tasks and creative endeavors.

SPRING CLEANING

As the entry on spring suggests, the dreamer is cleaning out old ideas and may actually be physically preparing themselves for new business, relationships, and new beginnings in their life.

SQUARE

Squares suggest stability, which in a dream may reflect a felt state or indicate a need for more stability. Squares also signify strength and solidity (square jaw or square shoulders).

STAG

The word stag is associated both with the adult male version of the red deer, and with an all male event. The deer can represent either the forces of nature that are hunted down and killed, or masculinity.

STAIRS

Climbing or descending a flight of stairs denotes, respectively, a rise or fall in social or economic status. The same actions may also be interpreted as an increase or decrease in consciousness.

STALLION

This animal represents the embodied power of strength, courage and of independence. To be riding this magnificent animal suggests the dreamer may have attained these virtues.

STAR

Stars are prominent in the mythologies from cultures the world over. In a dream they can symbolize anything from heaven to the mysteries of the universe to luck ("born under a lucky star") to fame and fortune.

STATUE

People that we know who appear in dreams as statues may indicate that relationships are inflexible and that communication has reached a standstill. If the dreamer is a statue it may mean that the true self has become far removed from reality.

STEALING

To steal in a dream could indicate that the dreamer is deprived and the neediness can be fulfilled where the stealing takes place—e.g., at home, the office, or school. (See also Burglar, Robbery, Thieves/Theft).

STEAM

Seeing and hearing steam in a dream may symbolize the dreamer's emotional state about an issue or situation. To have a "head of steam" about something means to be full of resolve and ready to proceed full steam ahead with a great deal of personal power to accomplish whatever is to be done. Alternatively, it may indicate anger about someone or some situation and the need to "let off steam."

STIFFNESS

Stiffness may represent some aspect of the dreamer's personality or disposition, or that of someone else in the dreamer's life.

STOMACH

Dreaming of one's stomach may indicate that the dreamer has lost his or her appetite for ("can no longer stomach") a situation, relationship, or job. The stomach also symbolizes the source of the feelings and the emotional power or capacity to meet or withstand a demand on the feelings ("need a strong stomach" to handle a situation or event).

STORM

Taking shelter from a storm indicates that whatever disturbance is occurring in the dreamer's business or personal life will quickly blow over.

STRAIGHT

For a dream to somehow emphasize straightness (as in a straight road) can indicate that the dreamer intends—or needs to—get things straightened out in her or his life. Perhaps a situation or a business deal was underhanded or "crooked."

STRANGER

From a Freudian perspective, a stranger in a dream may symbolize meeting a part of one's own psyche, or shadow self. According to an ancient Chinese belief, a stranger in one's dream is another soul from the spirit realm.

STRANGLING

A dream about strangling someone or being strangled may indicate that the dreamer is denying a vital aspect of his or her expression, and thus satisfaction, in life.

STRING

Dreaming about string often refers to something that needs to be secured or mended, particularly a relationship or some other situation. There are, however, many idiomatic expressions containing the word "string," and a dream could be alluding to one of these meanings: "purse strings," "to string someone along," "first string," "no strings attached," "pull some strings," etc.

SUBMARINE

A submarine can be a symbol for male sexuality. Alternatively, dreaming about a submarine could represent exploring one's emotions or unconscious mind. Also, to get someone "submarined" is slang for getting someone overly inebriated.

SUBWAY

As a way to travel to one's destination underground, a subway may symbolize the dreamer's reaching a goal through unconscious methods.

SUCK

Sucking is an instinctive act of seeking nurturance. A dream about sucking can relate to childhood feelings of being nurtured or of being dependent. There are also numerous slang usages of this term, including advice to "suck it up" and "sucking up" to someone in authority.

SUFFOCATION

Suffocation in a dream may represent intense anxiety associated with being confined or mean the dreamer feels smothered by some situation or relationship.

SUGAR

Dreaming about sugar could reflect a sense that life is sweet or a wish that life could be sweeter. Sugar is also a symbol of love, as when some refers to their love interest as "Sugar." Sugar can also be slang for everything from a kiss to cocaine.

SUICIDE

A dream about suicide may suggest that conditions in the dreamer's life are so frustrating that the dreamer is no longer willing or able to cope with a business or personal relationship in the same way as in the past.

SUITCASE

A dream about a suitcase can have a surprisingly large number of meanings. Some obvious associations are travel (which could also be a symbol of independence) and a place where we store things (which could represent feelings we have stuffed away).

SUN

The sun shining upon the dreamer indicates good fortune or goodwill. The sun is also energy, especially the life energy that gives one health and makes crops grow. Alternatively, excessive sunlight dries up and kills, as symbolized by animal skulls in the desert.

SUNRISE

A sunrise may indicate that the dreamer is about to embark on a new adventure in the dreamer's work or personal life. This symbol is about new beginnings, renewal of life and energy, and fulfillment of one's purpose in life.

SURGERY

If someone has experienced surgery, a dream about surgery could be putting one back in touch with the emotions one felt around the operation. Alternatively, a dream about surgery could represent a more general concern about one's health. Metaphorically, a dream surgery could reflect a feeling that we are "operating" on our emotions, such as removing our heart (a symbol of affection).

SWAMP

When we dream about being in a swamp, we are often feeling bogged down with something. Water often symbolizes emotion, so it could be our emotional life that is causing us to feel bogged down. (See also Slow Motion).

SWAN

The swan is a traditional symbol of beauty, grace, and dignity. It can also symbolize a farewell appearance or final act, as in "swan song."

SWASTIKA

The swastika is an ancient symbol of creative, life-giving power. The direction that it turns—clockwise being good, counterclockwise being destructive—are important in the religious traditions that utilize the swastika. The phenomenon of Nazism has imbued this symbol with evil associations, no matter which direction it turns.

SWEEP

A dream about sweeping is likely about clearing away something, either feelings or something else in our life we want to "clean up." A dream about sweeping could also be drawing on one of the many expressions that use "sweep" metaphorically, such as "making a clean sweep," "sweeping

something under the carpet," or "sweeping someone off their feet."

SWEETS

Dreaming of sweets may indicate the dreamer's sense of pleasure and enjoyment.

SWIMMING

Bodies of water are natural symbols of both the unconscious and the emotions. Dreaming about swimming can thus be related to the emotions or to an exploration of one's unconscious (a natural dream image for someone undergoing therapy). Also, because we spend the first nine months of our lives in a liquid environment, swimming is also a symbol of birth or rebirth.

SWINGING

To be swinging on a swing or to be dancing the "swing" indicates that the dreamer is expressing a great deal of satisfaction and freedom.

SWORD

Swords can represent a severing of obstacles, as well as matters requiring aggressive and forceful action. The dreamer may need to use a sword, or may be wielding it with authority and commitment.

SYRINGE

A syringe is a fairly obvious symbol of male sexuality. A dream about being injected with a syringe can reflect concerns about one's health, or it can be a more general anxiety dream if we have a particular dislike of shots and of having our blood drawn. It could also represent a feeling that we are being influenced by someone else. (See also Needle, Vaccination).

DREAM SYMBOLS
T

TABLE

Tables usually represent social functions, such as dining together at a table, though tables can also represent work if one has a desk job or a job where one crafts objects on a table, for example. Tables in dreams can draw on meanings associated with the "head of the table," "a bare table," "the tables are turned," being paid "under the table," or "on the table."

TAIL

A tail can refer to excitement, as in a dog that wags its tale, or the opposite, as when a tail is dragged between one's legs. There are numerous idioms involving this word, and dreams in which a tail is featured can be alluding to the meaning of any one of them: "turn tail," "on someone else's coattails," a "tail wagging the dog," or the "tail end" of something.

TANK (MILITARY)

A dream about a military tank can simultaneously represent being defensive and being aggressive.

TANK (WATER)

A water tank can represent a womb, or one's inner feelings.

TARGET

Dreaming about a target often reflects one's aims and goals. Alternatively, perhaps the dreamer feels like she or he is the target of something.

TATTOO

Since a tattoo is originally a sign of initiation, this dream symbol may indicate that the dreamer is entering a new stage in his or her life.

TEACHER

Because we spend so much time in school, teachers in dreams can represent many different aspects of the human experience. In general, teachers represent authority. Perhaps the situation we find ourselves in at the moment is a "learning experience."

TEARS

Tears often represent the waters of cleansing and release, indicating that a healing of some sort is taking place in the dreamer's life.

TEDDY BEAR

A teddy bear was part of many people's childhood experience, so in a dream it could simply be a symbol of some aspect of one's childhood. A teddy bear can also represent comfort and unconditional love, or even a childish relationship. (See also Bear).

TEETH

Something that one can "get one's teeth into" relates to a power or control issue. Losing the teeth may reflect a loss of power as well as a loss of one's grasp of life circumstances. Biting or being bitten suggests struggling for control in an aggressive manner. (See also Bite, Dentures).

TELEPHONE

The telephone is a symbol of communication with multiple meanings. If the dreamer is not available, does not want to answer the ringing telephone, or hangs up it may indicate that communication from the unconscious is being ignored.

TELESCOPE

Dreaming about a telescope can represent the need to take a closer look at something. Alternatively, it could represent exaggerating something, making it bigger than it actually is.

TENT

A tent in a dream could mean protection or it could mean feeling a part of the natural world. Tents can be symbols of nomadic life, of feeling on the move and not being able to put down roots.

THIEVES/THEFT

Witnessing a theft or an attempted theft may indicate that others are stealing time, energy, or ideas. If the dreamer is one of the thieves, the dreamer may be usurping the value of others and needs to avoid overstepping boundaries in regard to time, ideas, or other elements of value. (See also Burglar, Robbery, Stealing).

THORN

Thorns are usually associated with suffering. The dreamer may be "sacrificing" his or her own life for others, thereby becoming a "martyr."

THREAD

Thread sometimes represents the link one has to this world, such as the umbilical cord. Thread also suggest binding together and strengthening. The dreamer may be strengthening commitments or relationships.

THREAT

Someone who dreams of threatening another in a dream may need to assert himself or herself in some area. If, however, the dreamer is being threatened, the dream may mean that some internal fear of inadequacy needs to be addressed.

THRESHOLD

A threshold is a symbol for passing from one state or condition to the next, indicating a transition in some aspect of the dreamer's life.

THROAT

Dreaming about a constriction of the throat or hoarseness may mean the dreamer cannot easily or fully express ideas or feelings.

THUNDER

Thunder may indicate a loud knocking at the door of the dreamer's conscious mind to force the dreamer to pay attention and to learn. If accompanied by lightning bolts, inspiration and enlightenment may be indicated.

TICKET

Having a ticket gives us a right to enter everything from a theater to an airplane. So tickets in a dream could represent a sense of entitlement. A dream could also be drawing on the meaning of a ticket idiom, such as a "meal ticket," a "big ticket" item, or a "one-way ticket."

TIME

An emphasis on time in a dream may indicate a great deal of stress in the dreamer's life, perhaps the feeling that time is running out in either a business or a personal matter.

TOILET

Dreaming about a toilet can relate to any number of different meanings regarding waste products. A toilet dream could reflect something as simple as the feeling that one has unloaded something that was burdening him or her, or even releasing tightly held feelings. The dream might also be drawing on the meaning of such common idioms as "in the toilet" or "down the toilet."

TOOLS

Beyond the phallic connotations, tools in a dream can represent our practical abilities. Different specific tools represent different things, such as "hammering" someone or throwing a "monkey wrench" into something. Also might be alluding to the meaning of certain idioms, such as "tools of the trade." If one works regularly with tools, then tools in a dream could just be a reflection of daily life.

TORNADO

Dreams about tornadoes may indicate issues or conditions that make one feel overwhelmed and out of control. There may well be repressed rage. Tornadoes can also reflect some sort of tremendous upset in the immediate environment.

TOTEM

In American culture, we usually think of animals carved upon a tree trunk by Native Americans in the Pacific Northwest (totems were also found among ancient cultures throughout the world). These carvings of sacred animals would embody their stories and myths. Perhaps the dreamer has a story that needs to be deciphered. The type of animal on the totem pole will indicate the direction of interpretation.

TOWER

A tower may be a symbol of vigilance (a watchtower) or a symbol of punishment and imprisonment (a guard tower). Scholarship and abstract ideas that seem to be isolated from everyday life are sometimes said to be the purview of someone who lives in an "ivory tower." Similarly, the invitation to "come down from your tower" (ivory or otherwise) is an invitation to rejoin life. As in the fairy tale Rapunsel, perhaps the dreamer should "let her hair down" and become more accessible to others.

TOYS

Generally, toys indicate a hearkening back to childhood. The dreamer may be searching for the comfort and security that comes with being a child. Perhaps the dreamer is working too hard and needs to take time out to play.

TRACKS

Train tracks can represent certain commonly accepted attitudes or ways of doing things. A dream about an athletic track often indicates some form of competition. Race tracks, on the other hand, are more about the feeling that one's life is a race (the "rat race"). The meaning of tracks in a dream might also be drawing on familiar idioms, such as "off the beaten track," "on the right track," or "to lose track" of something.

TRAIN

The train as a dream symbol is often linked with the Freudian interpretation of the train (phallus) going through the tunnel (vagina), representing intercourse. Yet even Freud gave trains alternative meanings (e.g., missing a train might represent missed opportunities or even missing one's death (rather than missing intercourse). Being the engineer on a train and traveling smoothly down the track may mean staying "on track" in one's life. As with all such symbols, the dreamer's prior associations with trains determines their meaning in a particular dream.

TRAPPED

A feeling of being trapped may indicate a job-related problem or a stifling personal relationship. Pregnant woman in their last cycle of pregnancy often have a dream of being entrapped in small places.

TRAVEL

There are many possible meanings of travel dreams, including freeing oneself of obstacles and restrictive circumstances. Dreaming about a journey can be about our life journey, so how we feel about our dream journey can reflect how we feel about our lives. A dream journey can also symbolize something less comprehensive, such as some specific move we have made in our lives. (See also Voyage).

TREASURE

Discovering treasure may indicate that the dreamer has some hidden skills or talents that can be unearthed if the dreamer can determine the hidden meaning of the symbol.

TREE

The sobriquet "tree of knowledge" and the proverb "they shall be known by their fruits" reflect the ancient heritage of this archetypal dream symbol. The size and the condition of the tree may indicate how one views one's inner strength and "growth" in the world.

TRIAL

Dreaming of being on trial may indicate that the dreamer needs to be more accepting of himself or herself and less judgmental of others.

TRUNK

The trunk of a tree may represent one's inner sense of well-being and personality. A thick bark over a large, hefty trunk denotes a strong, rugged, and durable person. A thin, narrow, bark-free tree trunk suggests a highly sensitive but wiry individual. If the trunk is the long nose of an elephant, the dreamer may have a strong "nose for the news" and a very good memory. Alternatively an elephant's trunk may have a phallic and sexual meaning. Finally, a trunk in the sense of an old-fashioned storage case may reveal the old memories and secrets to which the dreamer is clinging.

TSUNAMI/TIDAL WAVE

Because water often represents the emotions, a tidal wave may indicate a billowing emotional situation that must be faced and handled.

TUNNEL

A tunnel represents transition from one set of conditions to another. The "light at the end of the tunnel" may represent relief from old conditions. With or without the presence of a train, this symbol can also have the Freudian sexual interpretation of tunnel-as-vagina.

TURQUOISE

A precious stone of blue and green mined by Native Americans throughout the southwestern United States, the turquoise has spiritual significance. It is the sacred stone of the Navajo associated with natural forces and healing.

TURTLE/TORTOISE

We associate turtles and their shells with their reputation for slowness and their protective coverings. So turtles in a dream could represent one's emotional shell or one's need to protect something. Alternatively, they could be representing some experience in which things seem to be going too slowly. But dream turtles could also be alluding to the tortoise who won the race against the hare because caution wins over haste.

TWILIGHT

Twilight is usually thought of as a peaceful and colorful time of day. In a dream it may signify that someone is well along in years or represent an end to old conditions or circumstances.

TWINS

The appearance in a dream of two of a kind (people or animals) may symbolize the union of opposites, or a duality of consciousness, either in harmony with, or in conflict between, ideas and decisions. The dreamer may be demonstrating two distinct personalities.

DREAM SYMBOLS

U

UMBILICAL CORD

An umbilical cord in a dream can represent a source of nourishment, but it often carries less pleasant connotations of dependency, or a crippling emotional tie to one's mother.

UMBRELLA

The open umbrella protects the dreamer from the waters of the emotional unconscious when the unconscious showers its lessons upon the conscious self. If the umbrella is closed and the water freely pours upon the dreamer, it indicates that the dreamer is open to his or her feelings and emotional needs.

UNDER

Anything that is obscured by being underneath something else can represent the contents of one's unconscious mind. Dreaming about seeing something beneath oneself can be about feelings of superiority or feelings of being on top. Alternatively, dreaming about being under someone or something can represent a feeling of being oppressed. Also note the possibility that this dream image might be drawing on a familiar idiom, such as "under the weather," "under someone else's wing," "under someone else's thumb," "under the counter," or "under one's nose."

UNDERGROUND

A dream of being underground may indicate that the dreamer has subconscious issues that have been kept under wraps. Going down under to retrieve them shows a readiness to bring them back up to the surface.

UNICYCLE

If riding high on a large single wheel, the dreamer may be totally in control and exercising authority in both personal and business matters, appearing to be the "big wheel" in these arenas. If, however, the dreamer's ride seems precarious and unstable, going it alone may not be the wisest strategy with respect to some situation.

UNIFORM

Uniformed individuals in dreams can represent authority. Uniforms also symbolize the function of the people who wear them, so that a nurse's uniform would refer to a medical situation. If one has ever worn a uniform, then that particular uniform could have a wide range of different associations.

UNPREPAREDNESS

In Western cultures, this motif often emerges in dreams in which we find ourselves taking an examination for which we are completely unprepared. For example, college students often have anxiety dreams around the end of the term that involve examinations they have not studied adequately for; this occurs regardless of whether or not the student has actually studied enough. The unpreparedness motif can also emerge in other ways, such as when we dream about standing before a crowd on a stage or at a public forum, then realize that we have forgotten what we were going to say, or discovering we were never prepared to say anything in the first place. A dream about being unprepared to take a test or give a speech might reflect anxieties about anything from how we will do on an upcoming job interview to whether we will succeed in a new mar-

riage. The core anxiety concerns doubts about our adequacy.

URINATION

Urination in a dream has several interpretations that range from inhibited sexual desires to the outpouring of emotional feelings that have been repressed.

UTOPIA

A dream about utopia could reflect an individual's ideals. It could also represent impossible ideals and a retreat from life's difficulties.

DREAM SYMBOLS

VACATION

See Holiday.

VACCINATION

Vaccination in a dream can relate to sickness in one's waking life. Perhaps feeling the need to protect oneself from a particular situation or the influence of others. Could also be a sexual symbol. (See also Illness, Needle, Syringe).

VAGRANT

A vagrant in a dream may indicate that the dreamer desires to escape from the confines of social expectations. Likewise, the dreamer could also be worried about becoming a vagrant if they can no longer keep up with their bills.

VALLEY

Dreaming about a valley can represent everything from fertility (a valley is a symbol of female sexuality) to depression and "feeling down."

VALUABLES

Finding something of value may represent discovering one's own value and self-regard. The dreamer may need to reevaluate his or her worth in the world.

VAMPIRE

As important figures in folklore, vampires can simply be representations of our generic fears and anxieties. As creatures of darkness, vampires can particularly represent fears and anxieties arising out of our unconscious. Symbolically, a vampire is someone or something that sucks the life blood out of us. Alternatively, vampires can embody anxieties about our sexuality.

VANISH

Something that vanishes in a dream can represent something—which can be an insight into ourselves—that we forget and lose awareness of. Perhaps it is an unpleasant item of self-knowledge that disappears.

VASE

A cracked or broken vase suggests a crack in the dreamer's life—a broken relationship; a weakening outlook; and, possible sorrows ahead.

VAULT

A vault in a dream is an indication of wealth and success. This could be an indication of prosperity, the fulfillment of one's creative urges, or a future of great happiness.

VEGETABLES

Vegetables may stand for one's dietary needs or, more symbolically, of the need to feed one's spiritual self.

VEHICLES

A vehicle in a dream sometimes represents one's life journey. If the dreamer is driving the vehicle, it may signify that the dreamer is in control of his or her life or exerts power over others ("is in the driver's seat"). (See also specific modes of transportation.)

VELVET

The appearance of this elegant material in a dream may represent the dreamer's emotions—soft, sensuous, and elegant. If the dreamer is wearing velvet, it may indicate that some honor is forthcoming.

VENTRILOQUISM

For the dreamer to throw his or her voice could indicate a part of themselves that they may not be revealing. This dream may also indicate that the dreamer feels beside themselves about a relationship or some other issue.

VESSEL

A vessel in a dream may be the container that holds the dreamer's valuables. The size and the condition of the vessel—e.g., old and tarnished or new and shiny—may indicate if these are established ideals or things newly acquired. Vessels can also be containers of the self.

VICTIM

Being a victim in a dream or seeing another being victimized may denote a condition about which the dreamer feels helpless. Because the victim/rescuer theme is so widespread in life, dreams about victimization can also echo past experiences in which one felt victimized.

VILLAGE

If we were raised in a small town, a dream about a village can relate to our childhood. A village can also symbolize everything from the community we have at our workplace to the global community.

VINE

Dreaming about a growing vine can relate to our fruitfulness as individuals, or to our family lineage. Vines can also be plants that grow up and choke us. The dream might also be alluding to the expression "to whither on the vine."

VIOLENCE

Horrifying scenes of violence and destruction may indicate an overwhelming fear of the loss of one's sense of power and control. Because of this fear, the dreamer may be in rage at others. An upheaval may have taken place in the dreamer's work or personal life prior to such a dream.

VIOLET

A light shade of purple and pink, violet is regarded as a spiritual color by many religions. It symbolizes purification and illumination.

VIRGIN

A virgin can represent innocence and purity. A feeling of being free, unattached, and receptive. Alternatively, a virgin can represent barrenness.

VISION

Vision is a common metaphor for insightfulness, perceptiveness, and point of view. Any of these meanings could be indicated in a dream emphasizing vision. To experience an obstruction to one's vision could indicate that the dreamer is having difficulty perceiving such things as errors in judgment, or how significant and important their role is in the world. The term "vision" can also be used in the sense of an apparition, which in a dream could indicate that a spiritual message is being given to the dreamer.

VISITOR

Dream visitors can represent any number of new conditions, changes, or information. Of particular importance is the manner in which visitors are received: Are they welcomed and greeted, or unexpected and unwelcome?

VITAMIN

If we take vitamins on a daily basis, then a dream about vitamins could simply be a reflection of our daily activity. Or, it could represent a concern about health. Vitamins can symbolize that we need to feed our minds with ideas that are "good for us."

VOICE

A voice in a dream could be another part of ourselves trying to get our attention, either our unconscious or an aspect we have cut ourselves off from. A dream voice could also be drawing on the meaning of expressions like "a voice in the wilderness" or to "speak with one voice."

VOLCANO

A dream about an erupting volcano often represents an emotional eruption that is building up within the dreamer's psyche, and hence is a warning to the individual to let off steam before a blowup.

VOMIT

The retching sensation of vomiting in a dream often indicates that one needs to discard and eject from one's life something that is revolting to the person.

VOYAGE

Dreaming about a voyage could be a dream about changes that are taking place—or that one would like to see take place—in one's life. Perhaps a voyage of discovery into oneself. Dream voyages can also be about new relationships or new projects. (See also Travel).

VULTURE

A vulture is a bird that feeds on carrion (dead animals). Popular culture has further invested them with the associated trait of waiting for something to die. So a dream about a vulture often reflects a situation in our waking life in which we feel that someone else is waiting for us to die, or death in a less literal way, such as waiting for us to fail. A vulture dream can, of course, represent the opposite situation in which we are waiting for someone or something else to die or to fail.

DREAM SYMBOLS

WAIT

Waiting can be a straightforward representation of some situation we are waiting for in our waking life. It also might be an allusion to an idiom, such as "waiting in the wings," "wait and see," or "waiting for the other shoe to drop."

WAITER/WAITRESS

Unless we have actually had a job as a waitperson, dreaming about being a waiter or waitress can be a straightforward representation of the feeling that we are being made to wait on others. If we dream about being in the customer role, maybe we desire to be waited on.

WAKE

Dreaming about waking up (but remaining asleep) can simply be reflecting our anxiety about waking up in time. Awaking is also a common metaphor for realizing something. Also note possible idiomatic meanings, such as a "rude awakening," a "wake up call," or "wake up and smell the coffee."

WALK

Walking in a dream can simply reflect our day-to-day experience of walking. If the act of walking is somehow emphasized in a dream, the dream might be alluding to the meaning of an idiom, such as to "walk out" on some situation, "walk on eggshells," "walk on air," "walk a thin line," "walk all over someone," "walk a tightrope," or "walk and chew gum."

WALL

Dreaming about a wall could be about our defensiveness, or a dream wall could represent a sense of security. The term "wall" is also central to many idioms, and the dream could be drawing on the meaning of one of these, such as: the "writing on the wall," "off the wall," our "back against the wall," "talking to a brick wall," or "hitting one's head against the wall."

WALLET

Like all other dream symbols, the dream setting provides clues for interpreting this symbol. A wallet may indicate financial resources or self-identification (e.g., an I.D. kept in a wallet).

WALLPAPER

A dream that focuses on wallpaper could be calling attention to the surface appearance of something, or our attempts to cover something up.

WALNUT

A walnut has a significant resemblance to the human brain. In a dream a walnut may indicate a great deal of mental activity is being expended or, alternatively, that someone in the dreamer's environment is a "nut." In some cultures, to dream of walnuts is an omen of excessive joys and favors.

WAND

A magic wand can represent a kind of power. It might also represent the male organ. Dreaming about a wand might be an allusion to the familiar expression about how one can't solve a certain problem by "waving a magic wand" over it.

WAR

A common dream experience if one is a military veteran, a dream about war can also represent conditions that call for aggression (war) or for a resolution (peace treaty).

WAREHOUSE

Dreaming about a warehouse might be about past memories or something else in the past. Alternatively, perhaps we have put something in storage, such as artistic ambitions, in order to pursue something else.

WARMTH

Warmth in a dream can be a reflection of warm feelings and comfort. Perhaps cheerfulness or love. We also tend to refer to preliminaries as "warm up exercises."

WARNING

A warning in a dream is often a warning about something in our everyday life, though it could also be an unwarranted feeling of alarm. Alternatively, a dream warning could be a message that something in our life needs attention.

WASHING

Washing oneself may represent cleaning away the dirt and debris of unhappy experiences or emotions in the dreamer's life.

WATCHING

Watching something in a dream could reflect suspicion, though it could also simply be a message from our subconscious that we need to pay more attention to something. A dream about watching could also be alluding to the meaning of a common idiom, such as "watch your back," "a watched pot never boils," "it's like watching grass grow," "watch the clock," etc.

WATER

Water is a very common symbol for the emotions. A large body of water like a sea or a lake is often a symbol for the unconscious. Because sex involves fluids, Freud viewed water in dreams as a sexual symbol.

WAVES

Water is a common symbol for the emotions. Waves, being either smooth or violent, may therefore indicate either emotional calm or emotional turbulence.

WEAPON

Weapons are usually symbols of aggression, either aimed toward, or exhibited by, the dreamer. Weapons may also represent inner struggle and conflict.

WEATHER

The weather in a dream often indicates the emotional undertone of the dreamer or of the matter that is the subject of the dream: storms and winds may represent conflict and aggression; rains or drizzling conditions, depression and sadness; rainbows and sunshine, hope and happiness.

WEB

Dreaming about being caught in a web is likely a straightforward representation of some sticky situation we feel caught in, or that we might get caught in. We also talk about a "web of lies" or "a tangled web." In the contemporary world, dreaming about a spider web might be a symbolic way of referring to the Internet—the "worldwide web."

WEDDING

The joyous celebration of the uniting of two people in a spiritual contract of love, a wedding in a dream sometimes signifies the inner uniting of aspects of one's psyche. Alternatively, to dream of a wedding has traditionally come to symbolize something of a dire portent—either downfall or death.

WEEDS

Weeds could indicate that the dreamer may have to weed out some ideas or negative thoughts from their consciousness. Their appearance could also indicate that some good friendships and/or relationships have gone to seed.

WEIGHT

Being weighed down in a dream may indicate that the dreamer is waiting for someone or something to change before they can feel unburdened in their life. Lightness, alternatively, often represents lighter, or more positive, emotions.

WELL

The depth of emotional and spiritual resources, a well in a dream often represents knowledge and nurturance, a place from which emotions "well up." It can also symbolize good health and physical well-being.

WEST

We associate the westerly direction with where the sun sets, so dreaming about the West could be alluding to the end of something (sunset) or to rest (after the sun goes down). In the United States, the west is traditionally associated with expansion and opportunity.

WHALE

Whales in a dream may represent a relationship or a business project that the dreamer considers too enormous to handle. The dreamer may fear that they will, in effect, be swallowed up. Alternatively, large bodies of water are symbols of the unconscious, so that a whale, as a mammal at home in the water, can also represent a wholesome relationship between one's conscious and unconscious mind.

WHEAT

A symbol of prosperity and nourishment, wheat can also suggest that the dreamer can "separate the wheat from the chaff."

WHEEL

A wheel may indicate completion of a project or the continuation of a familiar situation. A circle is also a spiritual sign of that which has no beginning and no end. Alternatively, the dreamer may be caught in a situation in which he or she feels they are going in a circle.

WHIP

A whip is a symbol of authority and punishment. How it is experienced in the dream determines whether the dreamer is imposing the punishment or receiving it. In either scenario, whips have acquired connotations of abuse, so the punishment represented is often abusive and an occasion for guilt and shame.

WHIRLPOOL

A dream in which a whirlpool poses a threat could indicate that the dreamer is resisting a confrontation with a person or situation that he or she must inevitably confront. A whirlpool can also represent being pulled unwillingly into a confrontation with repressed material in the unconscious mind.

WHIRLWIND

To encounter a whirlwind in a dream may indicate that the dreamer has been on a whirlwind schedule. The force and power of a whirlwind might also indicate that the dreamer is being lifted up and placed on an entirely new life path.

WHITE

In Western culture, white is commonly used to represent cleanliness, purity, and dignity; in Eastern traditions white is associated with mourning and death.

WIDOW/WIDOWER

It has been said that a woman dreaming about being a widow can represent either fear of losing a husband or a desire to be free of one's marriage. The same meaning can be extended to a man dreaming about being a widower.

WIG

A dream about wearing a wig could represent everything from disguising oneself under a new identity to adopting false or unnatural ideas. It has also been said that wearing a wig in a dream could reflect anxiety about losing one's hair.

WIND

Wind in a dream may represent turmoil in the dreamer's emotions. It can also indicate the energy available for launching in new directions in life.

WINDOW

Looking through an open or a closed window may represent something about one's outlook on life. A "window of time" is a time frame in which to do something or to recover from an error. This dream symbol may signify some major insight in the dreamer's life. (See also Glass).

WINE

The fermented juice of the grape, wine has for centuries been romantically considered the "nectar of the gods." It is a symbol for blood and sacrifice in Christian liturgy and may hold transformative significance for the dreamer.

WINTER

A winter dreamscape could indicate the dreamer's favorite time of the year for fun and frolic. However, winter is also a season in which many people experience depression. This dream could indicate an emotional withdrawal from a personal relationship or a withdrawing of one's emotional investment in the workplace.

WISE OLD PERSON

Whether it be a man or a woman, a wise old person is a symbol of deep suitable "authority," in contrast with the sometimes arbitrary authority of some of our social institutions.

WITCH

From a Christian perspective, witches represent evil. From a more "New Age" perspective, the witch is the mother earth goddess. From a Walt Disney perspective, there is an evil witch, a good witch, and the fairy godmother who grants wishes. The meaning of this symbol depends on the tone of the dream as well as how the dreamer relates to a certain kind of witch.

WOLF

The wolf is another symbol that may be regarded as either good or evil. The fairy tale of Little Red Riding Hood represents the onset of sexual maturity in young women, and the wolf represents the seductive "evil" male who tries to eliminate the protection of the wise old woman, Grandma. The honorable "good" male figure of the woodcutter values the feminine principle by protecting Red with his strength. The Native American values the wolf as a serene, majestic teacher, guide, and source of sacred wisdom. Some tribes relate the feminine lunar aspect of life to the wolf, while other tribal groups consider the wolf a strong warrior symbol for the male. Unless other dream elements point to a "big bad wolf" interpretation, this dream symbol may well represent "good medicine."

WOMB

A dream about being in a womb could represent regression—or a desire to regress—to one's childhood. Alternatively, it could reflect the feeling that one is being reborn in some way.

WOOD

Wood is a traditional source of heat and is one of the five elements used in clinical diagnosis in Chinese medicine. Wood also represents life and springtime.

WOOL

As a symbol, wool often represents nurturing warmth. A dream that emphasizes wool could also be alluding to certain common expressions, such as to "pull the wool over someone's eyes" or to be "dyed-in-the-wool."

WORK

As an activity that occupies a large part of our lives, a dream about work can simply be a reflection of our everyday experiences. Perhaps a work dream can be symbolizing other kinds of efforts, such as "working" on one's marriage. The term "work" is also a part of several dozen different idioms, from "dirty work" and a "nasty piece of work" to making "short work" of something and "working one's fingers to the bone."

WORKMAN

To dream of workmen may represent that the dreamer needs to be working on themselves. For example, if the "men working" signs are up while no one is working, laziness and irresponsibility may be at issue. The workmen may be drilling into the earth, which suggests that the dreamer may be embarking on an exploration of the unconscious mind.

WORM

The term worm is used metaphorically in some common English expressions to represent weakness and sneakiness, as in "he wormed his way into the group" or "what a worm he turned out to be." The worm also symbolizes bait and rich, fertile soil.

WORSHIP

A dream about worship can embody a straightforward religious meaning. It could also be a representation of something that we adore, as in the expression "He worships the ground she walks on."

WOUND

The term wound is often used as a metaphor for the impact of negative emotional experiences. The healing of old wounds may thus be indicated by this dream symbol.

WRESTLING

This dream could indicate that the dreamer is grappling with a problem in their personal or professional life. Wrestling might also suggest that the dreamer is wrestling with ideas or habits that may need to be brought into control.

WRITING

To be writing or to observe another person writing in a dream may indicate that the dreamer is trying to communicate with someone. It could also indicate that the dreamer himself is trying to communicate with his own conscious self. The term worm is used metaphorically in some common English expressions to represent weakness and sneakiness, as in "he wormed his way into the group" or "what a worm he turned out to be." The worm also symbolizes bait and rich, fertile soil.

DREAM SYMBOLS

X

X in a dream can refer to the Roman numeral for ten, for "X marks the spot" in a map, the cross, an error, or "X-rated."

XEROX

Xerox may be a trade name for photocopying but it has also become synonymous with the activity of paper copying. Therefore, this term can be simply represent copying at your office, thus referring to a familiar activity. It can suggest wanting to repeat, or re-do, an action of some kind that one is either dissatisfied with or wishes to repeat.

X-RAY

Being X-rayed in a dream may signal wanting to see through a situation or the intentions of someone who is emotionally significant in one's life.

XYLOPHONE

If one is not a xylophone player thinking about his or her music, the dream might concern awkwardly trying to hit the keys with two small wooden mallets. This might symbolize a hit-or-miss situation in one's life, or it might represent being off key in an emotional relationship.

DREAM SYMBOLS

YAM

Yams are usually associated with the holiday season. The dreamer's associations with this symbol may be rooted in memories of family celebrations. As a plant that grows under the ground, the yam is also a natural symbol of something deeply rooted in the unconscious mind.

YARD

As the place to play in and around one's home, the yard may symbolize recreation or the carefree days of youth. As a metaphor for a unit of measure, the yard may signify a great length or quantity (yards and yards of material).

YARN

To see yarn tangled and knotted up in a dream may indicate something about one's emotions or about the condition of the dreamer's personal life. To be untangling a ball of yarn may suggest that the dreamer is slowly but surely clearing things up.

YAWN

Yawning in a dream can represent the things we typically association with yawning, such as boredom or tiredness. It can also refer to our attempt to say something.

YELL

To yell out, or to scream in fright, anger, or surprise, is a definite indication of suppressed agitation and frustration in waking life. It could also be a forewarning of a catastrophic event that is forthcoming and perhaps avoidable.

YELLOW

Yellow usually represents energy, vigor, and enthusiasm. This color also has a negative connotation, indicating cowardice.

YOKE

A cumbersome wooden collar worn about the neck and closed with a lock and key, in earlier times the yoke was associated with farm animals and with punishment and slavery. The yoke can also have spiritual fulfillment, as when Jesus said, "My yoke is easy and my burden is light."

YOUTH

The vision of youth in a dream may represent the younger aspect of the dreamer. To dream of one's original innocence stimulates and invigorates the self and the psyche.

YO-YO

It may be fun to be playing with a yo-yo in a dream, but it also may indicate that someone in one's life has been behaving like a yo-yo and needs to be reeled in with communication skills and precise direction.

DREAM SYMBOLS

Z

ZENITH

May indicate aspiration and culmination of achievement in the world.

ZERO

The zero carries the same connotations as the circle. It suggests infinity and the eternal unknown, as well as life's ultimate mysteries. It also suggests completeness—the dreamer may have come to a spiritual wholeness within.

ZODIAC

This spherical symbol of the astrological signs that bear the names of the constellations could be an indication that one's subconscious is guiding one to investigate astrology, or to have a chart cast by an astrologer—especially if this dream occurs around one's birthday. Alternatively, it could also represent a sense of feeling fated or even fatalistic.

ZOMBIE

A person in a dream who acts like a zombie could indicate one or more "emotionally dead" persons in one's life, people who have a devitalizing influence on one's vitality and enthusiasm.

ZONE

To experience being in a zone may relate to a war zone or a demilitarized zone. A place or an area with designated boundaries and points of protection. This dream could indicate one is involved in too much daily activity and needs to find a neutral place to recover a sense of physical or emotional equilibrium.

ZOO

"This place is a zoo!" is a common description of chaos and confusion. Dreaming of a zoo may indicate that the dreamer needs to tidy up some situation.

RESEARCH SOURCES

ACHEBE, CHINUA. *The World of the Ogbanje.* Enugu, Nigeria: Fourth Dimension Publishing, 1986.

ACKROYD, ERIC. *A Dictionary of Dream Symbols.* London: Blandford, 1992.

ALMEDER, ROBERT. *Beyond Death: Evidence for Life after Death.* Springfield, IL: Charles C Thomas, 1987.

ANCH, A. MICHAEL, CARL P. BROWMAN, MERRILL M. MITLER, AND JAMES K. WALSH. *Sleep: A Scientific Perspective.* Englewood Cliffs, NJ: Prentice-Hall, 1988.

ARTEMIDORUS. *The Interpretation of Dreams (Oneirocritica),* translated by Robert J. White. 2nd ed. Torrance, CA: Original Books, 1990.

ARTHOS, JOHN. *Shakespeare's Use of Dream and Vision.* London: Bowes & Bowes, 1977.

BADHAM, PAUL, and LINDA BADHAM, eds. *Death and Immortality in the Religions of the World.* New York: Paragon House, 1987.

BASKIN, WADE. *Dictionary of Satanism.* New York: Philosophical Library, 1962.

BASSO, ELLEN B. *The Kalapalo Indians of Central Brazil.* New York: Holt, Rinehart & Winston, 1973.

BENEDICT, RUTH FULTON. "The Vision in Plains Culture." *American Anthropologist 24,* no. 1 (January–March 1922): 1–23.

BENSON, CARMEN. *Supernatural Dreams and Visions: Bible Prophecy for the Future Revealed.* Plainfield, NJ: Logos International, 1970.

BERGSON, HENRI. *The World of Dreams.* New York: Philosophical Library, 1958.

BETHARDS, BETTY. *The Dream Book: Symbols for Self-Understanding.* Petaluma, CA: Inner Light Foundation, 1983.

BLACK, JEREMY, and ANTHONY GREEN. *Gods, Demons and Symbols of Ancient Mesopotamia: An Illustrated Dictionary.* Austin: University of Texas Press, 1992.

BLETZER, JUNE G. *The Donning International Encyclopedic Psychic Dictionary.* Norfolk, VA: Donning, 1986.

BORDWELL, DAVID. *Making Meaning: Inference and Rhetoric in the Interpretation of Cinema.* Cambridge, MA: Harvard University Press, 1989.

BOURGUIGNON, ERIKA. *Religion, Altered States of Consciousness, and Social Change.* Columbus: Ohio State University Press, 1973.

BRANDY, LEO. *The World in a Frame: What We See in Films.* Garden City, NY: Anchor Press/Doubleday, 1976.

BRO, HARMON H. *Edgar Cayce on Dreams.* New York: Warner Paperback Library, 1968.

BROOKE, NOEL MOORE. *The Philosophical Possibilities beyond Death.* Springfield, IL: Charles C Thomas, 1981.

BROWN, MICHAEL F. "Individual Experience, Dreams and the Identification of Magical Stones in an Amazonian Society." In J.W.D. Dougherty, ed., *Directions in Cognitive Anthropology.* Urbana: University of Illinois Press, 1985.

BULKELEY, KELLY. *The Wilderness of Dreams: Exploring the Religious Meanings of Dreams in Modern Western Culture.* Albany: SUNY Press, 1994.

————. *An Introduction to the Psychology of Dreaming.* London: Praeger, 1997.

CAMPBELL, HORACE. *Rasta and Resistance: From Marcus Gorier to Walter Rodney.* Trenton, NJ: Africa World Press, 1987.

CAMPBELL, JOSEPH. *The Hero with a Thousand Faces.* Princeton, NJ: Princeton University Press, 1949.

CAMPBELL, JOSEPH, with BILL MOYERS. *The Power of Myth.* New York: Doubleday, 1988.

CARSKADON, MARY A., ed. *Encyclopedia of Sleep and Dreaming.* New York: MacMillan, 1993.

CHAPLIN, J.P. *Dictionary of Psychology.* 2nd ed. New York: Dell, 1975.

CLARK, JEROME. *The UFO Encyclopedia: The Phenomenon from the Beginning.* 2nd ed. Detroit: Omnigraphics, 1998.

COXHEAD, DAVID, and SUSAN HILLER. *Dreams: Visions of the Night.* New York: Thames & Hudson, 1976.

CRAPANZANO, VINCENT. "Saints, Jnun, and Dreams: An Essay in Moroccan Ethnopsychology." *Psychiatry 38* (1975): 145–159.

CRIM, KEITH, ed. *The Perennial Dictionary of World Religions.* San Francisco: HarperCollins, 1981.

CUMBERLAND, CLARK. *Shakespeare and the Supernatural.* New York: Haskell House Publishers, 1931.

CUNNINGHAM, SCOTT. *Sacred Sleep: Dreams and the Divine.* Freedom, CA: Crossing Press, 1992.

D'ANDRADE, R.G. "Anthropological Studies of Dreams." In *Psychological Anthropology: Approaches to Culture and Personality,* edited by R K. Hsu. Chicago: Dorsey Press, 1961.

DAVIS, WADE. *The Serpent and the Rainbow.* New York: Warner Books, 1985.

D'AZEVEDO, W.L., ed. *The Traditional Artist in African Societies.* Bloomington: Indiana University Press, 1973.

DE BECKER, RAYMOND. *The Understanding of Dreams; or, The Machinations of the Night,* translated by Michael Heron. London: Allen & Unwin, 1968.

DE GEORGE, RICHARD T., and M. FERNANDE. *The Structuralists: From Marx to Levi-Strauss.* Garden City, NY: Anchor/Doubleday, 1972.

DEN BLANKEN, C.M., and E.J.G. MEIJER. "An Historical View of 'Dreams and the Ways to Direct Them; Practical Observations' by Marie-Jean-Léon LeCoq, le Marquis d'Hervey-Saint-Denys." *Lucidity Letter,* Vol. 7, no. 2 (December 1988), pp. 67–78.

DENNING, MELITA, and OSBORNE PHILLIPS. *Voudou Fire: The Living Reality of Mystical Religion.* St. Paul, MN: Llewellyn Publishing, 1979.

DESCARTES, RENE. *Discourse on Method.* Translated by Arthur Wollaston. Chicago: Penguin, 1962.

DEVEREUX, GEORGE. *Dreams and Greek Tragedy.* Oxford, England: Basil Blackwell, 1977.

DILLEY, ROY M. "Dreams, Inspiration and Craftwork among Tukolor Weavers." In *Dreaming, Religion and Society in Africa,* edited by M.C. Jedrej and R. Shaw. Leiden, Netherlands: E.J. Brill, 1992.

DODDS, E.R. *The Greeks and the Irrational.* Berkeley: University of California Press, 1951.

DOMHOFF, G. WILLIAM. *The Mystique of Dreams: A Search for Utopia through Senoi Dream Theory.* Berkeley: University of California Press, 1985.

Dreams and Dreaming. Alexandria, VA: Time-Life Books, 1990.

EDEL, ABRAHAM. *Aristotle and His Philosophy.* Chapel Hill: University of North Carolina Press, 1982.

EDWARDS, PAUL, ed. *The Encyclopedia of Philosophy.* New York: Macmillan & The Free Press, 1967.

EDWARDS, ROBERT R. *The Dream of Chaucer: Representation and Reflection in the Early, Narratives.* Durham, NC: Duke University Press, 1989.

EGGAN, DOROTHY. "Hopi Dreams in Cultural Perspective." In G. E. Von Grunebaum and Caillois, Roger, eds., *The Dream and Human Societies.* Berkeley: University of California Press, 1966.

ELIADE, MIRCEA. *Shamanism: Archaic Techniques of Ecstasy.* 1951. Reprint. Princeton, NJ: Princeton University Press, 1964.

———. *Myths, Dreams, and Mysteries: The Encounter between Contemporary Faiths and Archaic Realities.* 1957. Reprint. New York: Harper Colophon, 1975.

———. *Rites and Symbols of Initiation: The Mysteries of Birth and Rebirth.* 1958. Reprint. New York: Harper Colophon, 1975.

———, ed. *Encyclopedia of Religion.* New York: Macmillan, 1987.

ELKIN, A.P. *The Australian Aborigines: How to Understand Them.* Sydney, Australia: Angus & Robertson, 1954.

EMPSON, JACOB. *Sleeping and Dreaming.* London: Faber & Faber, 1989.

FADIPE, N.A. *The Sociology of the Yoruba.* Ibadan, Nigeria: Ibadan University Press, 1970.

FARADAY, ANN. *The Dream Game.* 1974. Reprint. New York: Perennial Library, 1976.

FEUERSTEIN, GEORG. *Encyclopedia Dictionary of Yoga.* New York: Paragon House, 1990.

FIELD, M.J. *Search for Security: An Ethno-Psychiatric Study of Rural Ghana.* London: Faber, 1960.

FIRTH, RAYMOND. *History and Traditions of Tikopia.* Wellington, Zealand: The Polynesian Society. 1961.

FONTANA, DAVID. *The Secret Language of Dreams.* San Francisco: Chronicle Books, 1994.

FOUCAULT, MICHEL. "Dream, Imagination, and Existence." *Review of Existential Psychology & Psychiatry 19,* no. 1 (1984–85): 31–78.

FRAIBERG, SELMA. "Kafka and the Dream." *Partisan Review 23,* no. 1 (winter 1956): 47–69.

FREUD, SIGMUND. *On Dreams.* Translated by James Strachey. New York: W.W. Norton, 1952. (1st German edition originally published 1901.)

FREUD, SIGMUND. *The Interpretation of Dreams.* Translated by James Strachey. New York: Avon, 1965.

FRY, PETER. *Spirits of Protest: Spirit-Medians and the Articulation of Consensus among the Zezuru of Southern Rhodesia (Zimbabwe).* Cambridge: Cambridge University Press, 1976.

GARBER, MARJORIE B. *Dream in Shakespeare: From Metaphor to Metamorphosis.* New Haven, CT: Yale University Press, 1974.

GARFIELD, PATRICIA. *The Healing Power of Dreams.* New York: Fireside, 1991.

Gestalt Therapy Verbatim. Moab, UT: Real People Press, 1969.

GIFFORD, DOUGLAS, and PAULINE HOGGART. *Carnival and Coca Leaf.* New York: St. Martin's, 1976.

GILLESPIE, GEORGE. "Lucid Dreams in Tibetan Buddhism." In Jayne Gackenbach and Stephen LaBerge, eds., *Conscious Mind, Sleeping Brain.* New York: Plenum, 1988.

GLASSE, CYRIL. *The Concise Encyclopia of Islam.* San Francisco: HarperCollins. 1989.

GNUSE, ROBERT KARL. *The Dream Theophany of Samuel: Its Structure in Relation to Ancient Near Eastern Dreams and Its Theological Significance.* Lanham, MD: University Press of America, 1984.

GOODWIN, JAMES. *Akira Kurosawa and Intertextual Cinema.* Baltimore, MD: The Johns Hopkins University Press, 1994.

GRIM, JOHN A. *The Shaman: Patterns of Siberian and Ojibway Healing.* Norman: University of Oklahoma Press, 1983.

GUILEY, ROSEMARY ELLEN. *The Encyclopedia of Ghost and Spirits.* New York: Facts on File, 1992.

———. *The Encyclopedia of Witches and Witchcraft.* New York: Facts on File, 1989.

———. *The Encyclopedia of Dreams.* New York: Crossroad, 1993.

HALL, CALVIN S. *The Meaning of Dreams.* 1953. Reprint. New York: McGraw-Hill, 1966.

———, and Vernon J. Nordby. *The Individual and His Dreams.* New York: New American Library, 1972.

———. *A Primer on Jungian Psychology.* New York: New American Library, 1973.

HALL, JAMES A. *Jungian Dream Interpretation.* Toronto: Inner City Books, 1983.

HANDY, E.S. CRAIGHILL. *Polynesian Religion.* 1927. Reprint. Millwood, NY: Kraus, 1985.

HARTMANN, ERNEST. *Dreams and Nightmares.* Cambridge, MA: Perseus Publishing, 1998.

HASTINGS, JAMES, ed. *Encyclopedia of Religion and Ethics.* Edinburgh: T. & T. Clark, 1980.

HEAD, JOSEPH, and S.L. CRANSTON. *Reincarnation: The Phoenix Fire Mystery.* New York: Julian Press/Crown, 1977.

HERDT, GILBERT H. "Sambia Nose-Bleeding Rites and Male Proximity to Women." *Ethos 10* (1982): 189–231.

HERVEY DE SAINT-DENYS. *Dreams and How to Guide Them,* translated by N. Fry, edited by Morton Schatzman. London: Gerald Duckworth, 1982.

HEXHAM, IRVING. *Texts on Zulu Religion: Traditional Zulu Ideas about God.* Lewiston, NY: Edwin Mellen Press, 1987.

HIEATT, CONSTANCE B. *The Realism of Dream Visions: The Poetic Exploitation of the Dream-Experience in Chaucer and His Contemporaries.* The Hague, Netherlands: Mouton & Co., 1967.

HILLMAN, JAMES. *The Dream and the Underworld.* New York: Harper & Row, 1979.

HIRSCHFELDER, ARLENE, and PAULETTE MOLIN. *The Encyclopedia of Native American Religions.* New York: Facts on File, 1993.

HOBBES, THOMAS. *Leviathan; or, The Matter, Form and Power of a Commonwealth, Ecclesiasticall and Civil.* Cambridge: Cambridge University Press, 1935.

HOBSON, J. ALLAN. *The Dreaming Brain.* NewYork: Basic Books, Inc., 1988.

HOLY, LADISLAV. *Religion and Custom in a Muslim Society: The Berti of Sudan.* Cambridge: Cambridge University Press, 1991.

HOWITT, A.W. *The Native Tribes of South-East Australia.* London: Macmillan, 1904.

HULTKRANTZ, AKE. *Conceptions of the Soul among North American Indians.* Stockholm: Ethnographic Museum of Sweden, 1953.

HULTKRANTZ, AKE. "A Definition of Shamanism." *Temenos 9* (1973).

HUNT, HARRY T. *Multiplicity of Dreams: Memory, Imagination and Consciousness.* New Haven, CT: Yale University Press, 1989.

JAYNE, WALTER ADDISON. *The Healing Gods of Ancient Civilizations.* 1925. Reprint. New Hyde Park, NY: University Books, 1962.

JEDREJ, M.C. "The Social Organisation of the Ingessana." *Sudan Notes & Records 56* (1975).

——, and Rosalind Shaw, eds. *Dreaming, Religion and Society in Africa.* Leiden, Netherlands: E.J. Brill, 1992.

JONES, ERNEST. *Nightmares, Witches, and Devils.* New York: W.W. Norton, 1931.

JUNG, C.G. *Memories, Dreams, Reflections.* New York: Vintage Books, 1965.

——. *The Archetypes and the Collective Unconscious.* 2nd ed. Bollingen Series 20. Princeton. NJ: Princeton University Press, 1968.

KAFKA, FRANZ. *The Penal Colony: Stories and Short Pieces.* New York: Shocken Books, 1948.

KALWEIT, HOLGER. *Dreamtime & Inner Space: The World of the Shaman.* Boston: Shambhala, 1988.

KENTON, EDNA. *The Indians of North America.* 2 vols. New York: Harcourt Brace, 1929.

KESEY, MORTON. *Dreams: The Dark Speech of the Spirit.* New York: Doubleday, 1968.

KESSELS, A.H.M. *Studies on the Dream in Greek Literature.* Utrecht, Netherlands: HES Publishers, 1978.

KILBORNE, BENJAMIN. "Moroccan Dream Interpretation and Culturally Constituted Defense Mechanisms." *Ethos 9* (1981): 294–312.

KRACKE, WAND H. "Dreaming in Kagwahiv: Dream Beliefs and Their Psychic Uses in an Amazonian Indian Culture." *Psychoanalytic Study of Society 8* (1979): 119–171.

KRAKOW, BARRY, and JOSEPH NEIDHARDT. *Conquering Bad Dreams and Nightmares.* New York: Berkley Books, 1992.

KRAMER, KENNETH PAUL. *Death Dreams: Unveiling Mysteries of the Unconscious Mind.* New York: Paulist Press, 1993.

KRIPPNER, STANELY, FARIBA BOGZARAN, and ANDRE PERCIA CARVALHO. *Extraordinary Dreams and How to Work with Them.* New York: SUNY Press, 2002.

LAME DEER, JOHN, and RICHARD ERODES. *Lame Deer, Seeker of Visions: The Life of a Sioux Medicine Man.* New York: Touchstone, 1972.

LEADBEATER, C.W. *Dreams.* Adyar, India: Theosophical Publishing House. 1984. (Originally published 1898.)

LEE, S.G. "Social Influences in Zulu Dreaming." *Journal of Social Psychology 47* (1958).

LEVINE, ROBERT A. *Dreams and Deeds: Achievement Motivation in Nigeria.* Chicago: University of Chicago Press, 1966.

LEVY-BRUHL, L. *Primitive Mentality.* 1922. Reprint. Boston: Beacon Press, 1966.

LEWIS, JAMES R. *The Astrology Encyclopedia.* Detroit: Gale Research, 1994.

————. *Encyclopedia of Afterlife Beliefs and Phenomena.* Detroit: Gale Research, 1994.

————. *The Gods Have Landed: New Religions from Other Worlds.* Albany, NY: SUNY Press, 1995.

————. *UFOs and Popular Culture: An Encyclopedia of Contemporary Myth.* Santa Barbara, CA: ABC-Clio, 2000.

————, and J. Gordon Melton, eds. *Perspectives on the New Age.* Albany: State University of New York Press, 1992.

LINCOLN, JACKSON STEWARD. *The Dream in Primitive Cultures.* New York: Johnson Reprint Corporation, 1970.

LITTLEJOHN, J. "Temne Space." *Anthropological Quarterly 36* (1963).

MacGregor, Trish and Rob. *The Everything Dreams Book*. Avon, MA: Adams Media Corporation, 1998.

Mack, John E. *Nightmares and Human Conflict*. Boston: Little, Brown, 1970.

———. "New Facts about Nightmares." In Ralph L. Woods and Herbert B. Greenhouse, eds., *The New World of Dreams*. New York: Macmillan, 1974.

Mackenzie, Norman. *Dreams and Dreaming*. New York: The Vanguard Press. 1965.

Masello, Robert. *Fallen Angels … and Spirits of the Dark*. New York: Perigee, 1994.

McCall, Henrietta. *Mesopotamian Myths*. Austin: University of Texas Press, 1990.

McKenzie, P.R. "Dreams and Visions in Nineteenth Century Yoruba Religion." In *Dreaming, Religion and Society in Africa,* edited by M.C. Jedrej and R. Shaw. Leiden, Netherlands: E.J. Brill, 1992.

"The Meaning of Dreams in Tikopia." In E.E. Evans-Pritchard, R. Firth, B. Malinowski, and L. Schapera, eds., *Essays Presented to C.G. Seligman*. London: Kegan Paul, 1934.

Meggit, Mervyn J. "Dream Interpretation among the Mae Enga of New Guinea." *Southwestern Journal of Anthropology 18* (1962): 216–220.

Melton, J. Gordon. "The Revival of Astrology in the United States." In Rodney Stark, ed., *Religion Movements: Genesis, Exodus, and Numbers*. New York: Paragon, 1985.

———. *The Vampire Book: The Encyclopedia of the Undead*. Detroit: Gale Research, 1994.

———, Jerome Clark, and Aidan A. Kelly. *New Age Encyclopedia*. Detroit: Gale Research, 1990.

Memories, Dreams, Reflections. New York: Vintage Books, 1965.

Messer, W.S. *The Dream in Homer and Greek Tragedy*. New York: Columbia University Press, 1918.

Moffitt, Alan, Milton Kramer, and Robert Hoffmann, eds. *The Functions of Dreaming*. Albany: SUNY Press, 1993.

Monroe, Robert A. *Journeys Out of the Body*. Garden City, NY: Anchor Press, 1977.

Moody, Raymond A. *Life after Life*. New York: Bantam, 1976.

———. *Reunions*. New York: Villard Books, 1993.

Morgan, William. "Navaho Dreams." *American Anthropologist 34* (1932): 390–405.

Morris, Ivor. *Obeah, Christ and Rastaman Jamaica and Its Religion*. Cambridge: James Clark, 1982.

MULDOON, SYLVAN J., and HEREWARD CARRINGTON. *The Phenomena of Astral Projection*. London: Rider & Company, 1969.

NEEDHAM, RODNEY. *Primordial Characters*. Charlottesville, VA: University Press of Virginia, 1978.

NEPPE, VERNON M. *The Psychology of Déjà Vu*. Johannesburg, South Africa: Witwatersrand University Press, 1983.

NIELSEN, NIELS C., JR., et al. *Religions of the World*. New York: St. Martin's Press, 1983.

O'FLAHERTY, WENDY DONIGER. *The Rig Veda*. New York: Penguin, 1981.

———. *Dreams, Illusions, and Other Realities*. Chicago: University of Chicago Press, 1984.

OPPENHEIMER, PAUL. *Evil and the Demonic*. New York: New York University Press, 1996.

PACE-SCHOTT, EDWARD F., MARK SOLMS, MARK BLAGROVE, and STEVAN HARNAD, eds. *Sleep and Dreaming: Scientific Advances and Reconsiderations*. Cambridge: Cambridge University Press, 2003.

PACKER, SHARON. *Dreams in Myth, Medicine, and Movies*. London: Praeger, 2002.

PASCAL, BLAISE. *Thoughts on Religion and Philosophy*. London: Simpkin, Marshall, Hamilton, Adams, & Co., 1894.

———. *Pensées*. New York: E.P. Dutton, 1958.

PASSIN, HERBERT. "The Place of Kinship in Tarahumara Social Organization." *Acta Americana 34* (1943): 360–83, 471–95.

PENNINGTON, CAMPBELL W. *The Tarahumara of Mexico: Their Environment and Material Culture*. Salt Lake City: University of Utah Press, 1963.

PERLS, FRITZ. "Four Lectures." In *Gestalt Therapy Now*. Palo Alto, CA: Science and Behavior Books, 1970.

PETERS, RODERICK. *Living with Dreams*. London: Rider, 1990.

PLATO. *The Last Days of Socrates*. London: Penguin Classics, 1969.

PROPHET, ELIZABETH CLARE. *Forbidden Mysteries of Enoch: Fallen Angels and the Origins of Evil*. Livingston, MT: Summit University Press, 1983.

The Projection of the Astral Body. New York: Samuel Weiser, 1970.

RATTRAY, R.S. *Ashanti*. Oxford: Clarendon Press, 1923.

RAY, BENJAMIN C. *African Religions: Symbol, Ritual, and Community.* Englewood Cliffs, NJ: Prentice-Hall, 1976.

REICHARD, GLADYS A. Navajo *Medicine Man: Sandpaintings.* New York: Dover Publications, 1977.

REYNOLDS, PAMELA. "Dreams and the Constitution of Self among the Zezuru." In *Dreaming, Religion and Society in Africa,* edited by M.C. Jedrej and R. Shaw. Leiden, Netherlands: E.J. Brill, 1992.

RICHMAN, JOHN, ed. *A General Selection from the Works of Sigmund Freud.* Garden City, NY: Doubleday, 1957.

ROSS, W.D. *Aristotle: A Complete Exposition of His Works & Thought.* New York: Meridian Books, 1960.

RUSSELL, J. STEPHEN. *The English Dream Vision: Anatomy of a Form.* Columbus: Ohio State University Press, 1988.

SAMUELS, ANDREW, BARN SHORTER, and FRED PLANT. *A Critical Dictionary of Jungian Analysis.* London: Routledge & Kegan Paul, 1986.

SANDARS, N.K., trans. *The Epic of Gilgamesh.* 1960. Rev. ed. New York: Penguin, 1972.

SANFORD, JOHN A. *Dreams: God's Forgotten Language.* Philadelphia: J.B. Lippincott. 1968.

SANGREE, W.H. *Age, Prayer and Politics in Tiriki, Kenya.* London: Oxford University Press, 1966.

SCHROETTER, K. "Experimental Dreams." In *Organization and Pathology of Thought,* edited by D. Rapaport. New York: Columbia University Press, 1951.

SHAW, R. "An-bere: A Traditional Form of Temne Divination." *Africana Research Bulletin 9* (1978).

SHEPARD, LESLIE A., ed. *Encyclopedia of Occultism & Parapsychology.* Detroit: Gale Research, 1991.

SHULMAN, DAVID, and GUY G. STROUMSA. *Dream Cultures.* New York: Oxford University Press, 1999.

SHWEDER, R. "On Savages and Other Children: A Review of *The Foundations of Primitive Thought,* by C.R. Hallpike." *American Anthropologist 84* (1982).

SHWEDER, R., and R.A. LeVINE, "Dream Concepts of Hausa Children: A Critique of the 'Doctrine of Invariant Sequence' in Cognitive Development." *Ethos 3,* no. 2 (summer 1975).

SMITH, MAXWELL A., ed. *Blaise Pascal.* Boston: Twayne Publishers, 1983.

SPEARING, A.C. *Medieval Dream-Poetry.* Cambridge: Cambridge University Press, 1976.

STATES, BERT O. *Dreaming and Storytelling.* Ithaca, NY: Cornell University Press, 1993.

STEVENS, ANTHONY. *Private Myths.* Cambridge MA: Harvard University Press, 1995.

STEWART, KILTON. "Dream Theory in Malaya." In *Altered States of Consciousness,* edited by Charles T. Tart, New York: John Wiley & Sons, 1969.

TANNER, ADRIAN. *Bringing Home Animals.* New York: St. Martin's Press, 1979.

TEDLOCK, BARBARA. "Quiche Maya Dream Interpretation." *Ethos 9* (1981).

TEDLOCK, BARBARA, ed. *Dreaming: Anthropological and Psychological Interpretations.* Santa Fe, NM: School of American Research Press, 1992.

TEDLOCK, DENNIS. "In Search of the Miraculous at Zuni." In *The Realm of the Extra-Human: Ideas and Actions,* edited by Agehananda Bharati. World Anthropology Series. The Hague: Mouton, 1976.

THOMPSON, KEITH. "Portrait of a Sorcerer: An Interview with Carlos Castaneda." *New Age Journal* (April 1994): 60–71, 152–156.

TUFUO, J.W., and C.E. DONKOR. *Ashantis of Ghana People with a Soul.* Accra, Ghana: Anowuo Educational Publications, 1969.

TWAIN, MARK. *The Adventures of Tom Sawyer.* London: Dent, 1943. (Originally published 1876).

TYLER, PARKER. *Magic and Myth of the Movies.* New York: Henry Holt, 1947.

TYLOR, E.B. *Primitive Culture.* New York: Gordon Press, 1974.

ULLMAN, M., S. KRIPPNER, and A. VAUGHN. *Dream Telepathy: Experiments in Nocturnal ESP.* Jefferson, NC: McFarland, 1989.

VAN DE CASTLE, ROBERT L. *Our Dreaming Mind.* New York: Ballantine, 1994.

VAN DER LEEUW, G. *Religion in Essence and Manifestation,* Vol. 1. Gloucester, MA: Peter Smith. 1967. (Translation of first German edition, 1933.)

VAN LIESHOUT, R.G.A. *Greeks on Dreams.* Utrecht, Netherlands: HES Publishers, 1980.

VON GRUNEBAUM, G.E., and ROGER CAILLOIS, eds. *The Dream and Human Societies.* Berkeley: University of California Press, 1966.

WAGNER, G. *The Bantu of North Kavirondo,* Vol. 1. London: Oxford University Press, 1949.

WALLACE. ANTHONY F.C. "Dreams and the Wishes of the Soul: A Type of Psychoanalytic Theory among the Seventeenth Century Iroquois." *American Anthropologist 60* (1958): 234–248.

———. *The Death and Rebirth of the Seneca.* 1969. Reprint. New York: Vintage, 1972.

WAYMAN, ALEX. "Significance of Dreams in India and Tibet." *History of Religions* (1967): 1–12.

WEDIN, MICHAEL V. *Mind and Imagination in Aristotle.* New Haven, CT: Yale University Press, 1988.

WIJSENBEEK-WIJLER, H. *Aristotle's Concept of Soul, Sleep and Dreams.* Amsterdam, Netherlands: Adolf M. Hakkert, 1978.

WOLMAN, BENJAMIN B., ed. *International Encyclopedia of Psychiatry, Psychology, Psychoanalysis, & Neurology.* New York: Aesculapius Publishers, 1977.

———, ed. *Handbook of Parapsychology.* New York: Van Nostrand Reinhold, 1977.

ZIMMER, HEINRICH. *Myths and Symbols in Indian Art and Civilization.* Princeton, NJ: Princeton University Press, 1946.

———. *Philosophies of India.* New York: Bollingen, 1951.

INDEX

Notes: **boldface** entry indicates main entry; (ill.) indicates photos and illustrations.

E

Hopkins, Budd, 7, 9
horama, 94, 106
Hormakhu, 77
Horney, Karen, 102, 107–8
horns, 292
horse, 292
horseshoe, 292
hose, 292
hospital, 292
hostility, 269
hot, 292
hotel, 293
hourglass, 293
house, 213, 293, 309
housework, 293
hugging, 312
human nature, 88
humanity, 329
Humbaba, 92
humility, 283, 300
humor, 246, 266, 309
hun, 43
hunger, 272, 293
hunting
    deer, 270
    dog, 273
    as dream symbol, 293
    falcon, 279
    Native Americans, 153
    quack, 327
    stag, 342
hurt, 250
Husserl, Edmund, 31–32, 86
hypermnesic dreams, 55
hypnagogic experiences, 51, 100, 108, 143, 174, 198
hypnopompic experiences, 108
Hypnos, 230
hypnosis, 7–9, 109, 109 (ill.), 219

I

Ibn al-`Arabi, 111–12
ice, 295
ice cream, 295
iceberg, 219
id, 76, 88, 112, 174, 205
ideals, 330, 354
ideas
    air/atmosphere, 244
    awakening, 248

    cafeteria, 259
    garbage, 285
    library, 303
    morning, 309
    paper, 319
    quarrel, 327
    seed, 337
identification, 295
identity, 320, 362
identity crisis, 332
Igbo, 112–13
igloo, 295
ignobility, 290
Igrath, 59
ikenga, 112
Iliad (Homer), 106–7
illness, 295, 330
illumination, 247, 269, 281, 286, 356
illusory body, 213
imagination, 18, 86, 105
immobility, 295
immortality, 277
impotence, 261
impressions, 330
imprisonment, 349
improvement, 264
impulsiveness, 330
imspiration, 247
inadequacy, 285, 301, 336, 348
inauspicious dream, 133, 225
incentive, 299
incest, 295
incompatibility, 340
incompetence, 291
incubation, 77
incubi and succubi, 81, 113 (ill.), 113–15, 142, 145, 192
indecision, 262, 289, 309
independence, 261, 271, 292, 343, 344
India, 115–16, 183, 222–23
indigestion, 296, 297
individual dreaming, 153
individuation process, 6, 128, 130, 142
indulgence, 262, 271, 275, 282, 313
industriousness, 252, 291, 342
inebriation, 344
infantile desires, 254
infection, 296
inferential dreams, 154–55

infidelity, 296
infinity, 369
inflexibility, 295, 343
influence, 282, 325, 345
information, 337
Ingessana, 116–17
inhibitions, 315
initiation, 117, 226, 272, 282, 296, 347
initiative, 291, 338
initiatory dreams, 197–98
injection, 296
"inner balls," 263
inner child, 40, 276
inner desires, 293
inner emotional feelings, 309
inner feelings, 347
inner guidance, 287
inner resources, 309
inner self, 305
inner soul, 201–2
inner state, 273
inner struggle, 360
inner tensions, 280
inner value, 304
inner wealth, 297
inner wisdom, 309
innocence, 255, 269, 356, 367
Innocent, Pope, 114
inoculation, 296
insects, 296
insecurity, 108, 336
insight, 252–53, 256, 306
insightfulness, 356
insomnium, 20, 142
inspiration, 217, 348
integration, 308
integrity, 272
intelligence, 271
Intendant Sensho (movie), 148
internal chaos, 273
internal consistency, 206
internal imbalances, 130
Internet, 361
interpretation of dreams, 117–19
The Interpretation of Dreams (Freud), 89
interviews, 296
intimacy, 291
intimidation, 285
intolerance, 253
intrigue, 312

mundane needs, 275
murder, 309
Murup tribe, 25
muscle spasms, 124
museum, 309
mushrooms, 309
music, 309, 337
Muslims, 120–22
Mwari, 237
myclonic jerk, 124
Myers, Frederick, 108
mysteries, 263, 292, 341, 369
mystical powers, 297
mysticism, 149–50
mythology and dreams, 150
 Campbell, Joseph, 35–36
 Judaism, 128
 Navajo, 155
 Ojibwa, 162
 totem, 349
 trickster archetype, 215

N

Naamah, 59
nail, 311
nakedness, dreams of, 151–52, 152
 (ill.), 311
names, 311
Naropa, 213
Narrang-ga tribe, 25
narrow, 311
Native Americans, 152–53, 153
 (ill.), 311. *See also* individual tribes
natural, 266
natural disaster dreams, 153–55,
 154 (ill.)
natural world, 311, 348
nature, 281, 311
Nature (goddess), 39
nausea, 311
Nausicaa, 106
Navaho, 152–53, 155
navel, 312
Nazism, 345
near, 312
near-death experiences and dreams,
 155–56
Nebuchadnezzar, 53–54, 128
neck, 312
necklace, 19 (ill.), 312

necktie, 312
neediness, 343
needle, 312
needs, 337
negativity, 296, 361
neglect, 256, 333
nengk, 117
Nephilim, 113
Neptune, 337
nest, 312
net, 312
New Age, 156–57
new attitude, 283
new beginnings, 245, 309, 342,
 344–45
new birth, 276
new business, 342
new circumstances, 285
new condition, 283
new direction, 311, 362
new home, 312
new idea, 253, 323, 324
new life, 261, 302
New Mexico, 239
new possibilities, 249
new projects, 357
new relationships, 357
new religions (dream revelations),
 157
new stage of life, 277
new tasks, 342
New Testament, 30–31
New Thought churches, 50
newspaper, 312
Ngarigo tribe, 25
Nicomachus, 16
nicotine patches, 72–73
Niger Republic, 101
Nigeria, 101, 112, 235
night, 312
Night Journey, 121, 148, 157
night terrors, 157–58
Night Visions (journal), 158
nightmares, 158–60, 159 (ill.)
 Artemidorus, 21
 Bes, 77
 cancer, 36
 chase dreams, 38
 children, 40–42, 41 (ill.)
 control of, 49 (ill.), 49–50
 demons, 59, 81
 dream control, 64

 as dream symbol, 313
 drugs, 72
 fires, 215–16
 Goya, Francisco, 93–94
 guilt, 97
 Hartmann, Ernest, 100–101
 Hawaii, 101
 jackal, 297
 Johnson, Lyndon B., 125
 knife, 86
 Lilith, 137
 lucid dreaming, 137, 189–90
 Mack, John E., 141
 Macrobius, 142
 metaphors, 144
 night terrors, 157
 Ovid, 164
 post-traumatic stress disorder, 172
 pregnancy, 172–74, 173 (ill.)
 spicy food, 62, 86
 Stevenson, Robert Louis, 202–3
 Tikopia, 214
 tsunamis, 215–16
 Zuni, 240
Ninsun, 92
nobility, 275, 292
nocturnal penile tumescence (NPT),
 167
nomadic life, 348
non-rapid eye movement (REM)
 sleep, 158
non-Shona, 237
nondeficiency explanations of
 dreams, 56
nondreamers, 85, 143, 160
noose, 313
Nordby, Vernon, 206
north, 313
nose, 313
notebook, 313
nourishment
 bag, 249
 bread, 255
 corn, 266
 cow, 266
 crab, 267
 eating, 275
 excrement, 278
 farm/farmer, 280
 fish/fishing, 282
 food, 282
 fountain, 283